Pity, Power, and Tolkien's Ring

Pity, Power, and Tolkien's Ring

To Rule the Fate of Many

Thomas P. Hillman

The Kent State University Press

Kent, Ohio

© 2023 by The Kent State University Press, Kent, Ohio 44242
All rights reserved
ISBN 978-1-60635-471-1
Published in the United States of America

No part of this book may be used or reproduced, in any manner whatsoever, without written permission from the Publisher, except in the case of short quotations in critical reviews or articles.

Cataloging information for this title is available at the Library of Congress.

27 26 25 24   5 4 3 2

Richard Charles Hillman

1947–2008

manibus fratris

sacrum

Per tai difetti, non per altro rio,

semo perduti, e sol di tanto offesi,

sanza speme vivemo in disio.

—*Inferno* IV.40–42

Contents

Acknowledgments ix

List of Abbreviations xi

Introduction 1

1 Bilbo's Lie and the Ring 16

2 Bilbo's Pity and the Ring 37

3 The 1951 *Hobbit* and "The Shadow of the Past" 57

4 From Bag End to Rivendell 75

5 From Rivendell to Amon Hen 96

6 From the Emyn Muil to the Dead Marshes 112

7 From the Black Gate to Ithilien 130

8 From Ithilien to Cirith Ungol 154

9 Hobbits in Darkness 170

10 From the Black Land to the Undying Lands 206

11 Pity and Power in Time 233

Notes 268

Works Cited 289

Index 299

Acknowledgments

First and last, I thank Laura Lee Smith, whose indispensable kindness, wit, and love outmatch my greatest challenges. Verlyn Flieger comes next in thanks, no friend more gracious, no scholar more generous. Among many other Tolkien scholars, I name S. J. Cook, J. Garth, J. Hoffman, S. Marchese, C. Olsen, R. Rohlin, A. Sisto, and J. Tauber. The friends of my green youth beside the Great Sea, Don, Roger, Lorna, and Brooks walk with me on every page. A few live only in my past, remembered still with love: CAC, MLM, SDQ.

The staff of the Kent State University Press, and their outside readers, I must thank and thank again for their skill, professionalism, and tireless dedication.

Abbreviations

TOLKIEN

Arthur	*The Fall of Arthur.* Edited by Christopher Tolkien, Houghton Mifflin, 2013.
B&C	*Beowulf and the Critics.* Edited by Michael D. C. Drout, 2nd ed., ACMRS, 2011.
Beowulf T&C	*Beowulf: Translation and Commentary: Together with Sellic Spell [and the Lay of Beowulf].* Edited by Christopher Tolkien, Houghton Mifflin, 2014.
Children	*Narn i Chîn Húrin: The Tale of the Children of Húrin.* Edited by Christopher Tolkien, Houghton Mifflin, 2007.
FR	*The Fellowship of the Ring,* in *The Lord of the Rings.* 50th anniversary 1 vol. ed., Houghton Mifflin, 2005.
H	*The Annotated Hobbit: The Hobbit, or, There and Back Again.* Edited by Douglas A. Anderson, Houghton Mifflin, 2002.
Kullervo	*The Story of Kullervo.* Edited by Verlyn Flieger, Harper Collins, 2015.
Lays	*The Lays of Beleriand. The Lays of Beleriand,* vol. 3 of *The History of Middle-earth.* Edited by Christopher Tolkien, Houghton Mifflin, 1985.
Letters	*The Letters of J. R. R. Tolkien.* Edited by Humphrey Carpenter with Christopher Tolkien, Houghton Mifflin, 1981.
Lost	*The Lost Road and Other Writings: Language and Legend before* The Lord of the Rings, vol. 5 of *The History of Middle-earth.* Edited by Christopher Tolkien, Houghton Mifflin, 1987.

LT 1	*The Book of Lost Tales, Part 1*, vol. 1 of *The History of Middle-earth*. Edited by Christopher Tolkien, Houghton Mifflin, 1984.
LT 2	*The Book of Lost Tales, Part 2*, vol. 2 of *The History of Middle-earth*. Edited by Christopher Tolkien, Houghton Mifflin, 1984.
M&B	*The Battle of Maldon together with The Homecoming of Beorhtnoth and "The Tradition of Versification in Old English."* Edited by Peter Grybauskas, HarperCollins, 2023.
M&C	*The Monsters and the Critics and Other Essays*. Edited by Christopher Tolkien, HarperCollins, 2006.
Morgoth	*Morgoth's Ring: The Later Silmarillion, Part 1, the Legends of Aman*, vol. 10 of *The History of Middle-earth*. Edited by Christopher Tolkien, Houghton Mifflin, 1993.
Nature	*The Nature of Middle-earth: Late Writings on the Lands, Inhabitants, and Metaphysics of Middle-earth*. Edited by Carl F. Hostetter, Houghton Mifflin, 2021.
OFS	*Tolkien on Fairy-Stories*. Edited by Verlyn Flieger and Douglas A. Anderson 2008, HarperCollins, 2014.
Peoples	*The Peoples of Middle-earth*, vol. 12 of *The History of Middle-earth*. Edited by Christopher Tolkien, Houghton Mifflin, 1996.
RK	*The Return of the King*, in *The Lord of the Rings*. 50th anniversary 1 vol. ed., Houghton Mifflin, 2005.
Sauron	*Sauron Defeated: The End of the Third Age*, vol. 9 of *The History of Middle-earth*. Edited by Christopher Tolkien, Houghton Mifflin, 1992.
Shadow	*The Return of the Shadow*. vol. 6 of *The History of Middle-earth*. Edited by Christopher Tolkien, Houghton Mifflin, 1988.
Shaping	*The Shaping of Middle-earth: The Quenta, the Ambarkanta, and the Annals, Together with the Earliest* Silmarillion *and the First Map*, vol. 4 of *The History of Middle-earth*. Edited by Christopher Tolkien, Houghton Mifflin, 1986.
S	*The Silmarillion*. 1977. Edited by Christopher Tolkien, 2nd ed., Houghton Mifflin, 2001.
Treason	*The Treason of Isengard*, vol. 7 of *The History of Middle-earth*. Edited by Christopher Tolkien, Houghton Mifflin, 1989.

TT   *The Two Towers* in *The Lord of the Rings*. 50th anniversary 1 vol. ed., Houghton Mifflin, 2005.
UT   *Unfinished Tales of Númenor and Middle-earth*. Edited by Christopher Tolkien, Houghton Mifflin, 1980.
WJ   *The War of the Jewels: The Later Silmarillion, Part Two, the Legends of Beleriand*. vol. 11 of *The History of Middle-earth*. Edited by Christopher Tolkien, Houghton Mifflin, 1994.
WR   *The War of the Ring*, vol. 8 of *The History of Middle-earth*. Edited by Christopher Tolkien, Houghton Mifflin, 1990.

REFERENCE WORKS

C&G   Scull, Christina, and Wayne G. Hammond. *The J. R. R. Tolkien Companion and Guide*. 2nd ed. 3 vols. HarperCollins, 2017.
RC   Hammond, Wayne, and Christina Scull. The Lord of the Rings: *A Reader's Companion*. 2005. Harper Collins, 2014.

Introduction

THE BURDEN ON FRODO AND THE STORY

"Tolkien was his own best critic," writes Anna Vaninskaya (156). Not only did revising his works release a torrent of new ideas, as C. S. Lewis pointed out, but reading and thinking about them revealed depths he had not fathomed before.[1] We can see this in his letters as well as in every phase of the creation of his legendarium, so masterfully laid out by his son and editor, Christopher, in *The History of Middle-earth*. An essential part of being his own best critic was being his own best reader. We can see Tolkien the reader, the critic, and the writer, coming together in his response to the request of his publisher, Allen & Unwin, for a sequel to *The Hobbit*. In a 1964 letter to Christopher Bretherton he recalled: "They wanted a sequel. But I wanted heroic legends and high romance. The result was *The Lord of the Rings*. . . . The magic ring was the one obvious thing in *The Hobbit* that could be connected with my mythology. To be the burden of a large story it had to be of supreme importance" (*Letters* no. 257, p. 346).

To call the Ring "the burden of a large story" is to perceive that it is as much the burden the story has to bear as it is the burden Frodo has to bear. It is at once supremely important in and to the story. Similarly, in *The Lord of the Rings* Tolkien saw the blending of the Elvish perspective found in the "high Legends of the beginning" with the "human point of view," which first arose in *The Hobbit* (*Letters* no. 131, p. 145). At the same time he knew, more abstractly, that the tales of his mythology "must, as all art, reflect and contain in solution elements of moral and religious truth (or error)" (*Letters* no. 131,

p. 144). What is reflected is seen indirectly, if not darkly; what is in solution is seen barely, if at all.

The Lord of the Rings embodies the synthesis of each of these three theses—the burden of the story and the burden of Frodo, the perspectives of Elves and Men, and the reflection and solution in a Secondary World of truths fundamental to the Primary World—not just individually but into a greater whole, which, presented mythically and realized artistically, creates and shares the significance of these truths, perspectives, and burdens metaphorically. "Tolkien is thinking in story," Simon Cook tells us in *The Apprenticeship of J. R. R. Tolkien,* in which he argues forcefully that the "allegory of the tower" which Tolkien told as a means to understand *Beowulf* is also of vital importance for understanding Tolkien's own writing (13). In employing this allegory Tolkien "is exploring a metaphor and making meaning, yet we remain on the surface and have not the key to his intentions" (13).

A work "so multifarious and so true" as *The Lord of the Rings* will contain many essential elements besides those introduced above (Lewis, *Letters* 383). Some of these Tolkien employed consciously, but there were others the extent of whose presence he recognized only subsequently. The notion that authors do not understand their own works as much as they might be expected to do is at least as old as Plato's *Apology of Socrates* (22b–c), though then as now authors and their fans are not always candid enough to allow that their works are often something other than the sum of their intentions. Whether Tolkien first learned this lesson (which should be a given of poetics) when reading Plato as a schoolboy, he knew it well. The exemplary candor and open-mindedness of his responses to his readers in these letters of 1956 and 1958 make this clear.

> Of course my story is not an allegory of Atomic power, but of Power (exerted for domination).... I do not think that even Power or Domination is the real centre of my story. It provides the theme of a War, about something dark and threatening enough to seem at that time of supreme importance, but that is mainly "a setting" for characters to show themselves. The real theme for me is about something much more permanent and difficult: Death and Immortality: the mystery of the love of the world in the hearts of a race "doomed" to leave and seemingly lose it; the anguish in the hearts of a race "doomed" not to leave it, until its whole evil-aroused story is complete.
> (*Letters* no. 186, p. 246)

As for "message": I have none really, if by that is meant the conscious purpose in writing *The Lord of the Rings*, of preaching, or of delivering myself of a vision of truth specially revealed to me! I was primarily writing an exciting story in an atmosphere and background such as I find personally attractive. But in such a process inevitably one's own taste, ideas, and beliefs get taken up. Though it is only in reading the work myself (with criticisms in mind) that I become aware of the dominance of the theme of Death.
(*Letters* no. 208, p. 267)

In his essay "*Beowulf*: The Monsters and the Critics," Tolkien talks about the *Beowulf*-poet writing his poem without full awareness or understanding of the theme he had set himself, and this, Tolkien asserts, was a good thing: "Had the matter been so explicit to him, his poem would certainly have been worse" (*M&C* 18). This remark follows from his earlier comment that myth "is at its best when it is presented by a poet who feels rather than makes explicit what his theme portends; who presents it incarnate in the world of history and geography, as our poet has done" (16). Whether the *Beowulf*-poet ever looked back and saw more clearly what he had felt when composing the poem, no one can say. But Tolkien did. By far the greater part of his fascinating, insightful, and expansive commentary on *The Lord of the Rings* comes from the letters he wrote in the years after he had finished and then published it. To be sure, his published letters are only a selection, but the principle of that selection was to make available the material that would be of the greatest interest to readers of *The Lord of the Rings* and his other published works (*Letters* 1).[2] It is reasonable then to see the letters we get before and after Tolkien declared the work finished as generally representative of his chief concerns in each period.

The ever-cited Letter 131 to Milton Waldman in late 1951 marks a terminus before which Tolkien's comments to his correspondents almost invariably addressed the practical challenges of finishing the work, and after which theological, philosophical, and thematic reflections, often in response to questions or criticisms of readers and critics alike, became increasingly common (167). Wishing to see *The Lord of the Rings* and *The Silmarillion* published together, a desire Allen & Unwin seemed reluctant to gratify, Tolkien set out to persuade Milton Waldman of Collins to take on both works. To accomplish this, he had to step back and think through his legendarium as a whole just as he had done with *Beowulf* in his 1936 lecture and as he had done with Faërie in *On Fairy-stories* in 1939.[3] So many of the larger questions he weighs in his later correspondence find their first expression in this letter, which stands in the same relationship to his legendarium as "*Beowulf:* The Monsters and the Critics" stands to *Beowulf,* and *On Fairy-stories* stands to fairy stories.

Clearly *The Lord of the Rings* reflects its author's mind and meditations from beginning to end. Such themes as Death and Immortality, Power realized in Art versus Power realized in Domination, the role small hands play while the eyes of the great are elsewhere, and the essential relationship between high and low, great and small, which gives meaning to the lives and efforts of both, are present throughout, but in telling his story the elements of the metaphor remained largely in solution. With the Waldman letter, he begins to precipitate those long-meditated elements out of solution.

Indeed, important texts he composed in the 1950s, such as "Laws and Customs among the Eldar" and the "Athrabeth Finrod ah Andreth," both published in *Morgoth's Ring,* certainly seem to owe their existence to the shift away from narrative to the philosophical and theological concerns that we first see manifested in Letter 131. Commenting on "Notes on Motives in *The Silmarillion,*" another text of the 1950s also included in *Morgoth's Ring,* Christopher Tolkien remarked that the letters his father exchanged with readers figured prominently in shaping his thinking on the legendarium (*Morgoth* 406). "The association between the letters and Tolkien's focus on metaphysical and philosophical issues during that period is evident," writes Elizabeth A. Whittingham (168). "Dealing with matters of Mortality and Immortality, the fall, Death, and the afterlife," she goes on to say, "required him to be a philosopher and theologian."

The much-lamented failure to complete the tale "Of Tuor and His Coming to Gondolin" at all or *The Silmarillion* to his satisfaction probably finds some of its explanation here, alongside the profound disappointment inflicted by Collins's unwillingness to publish *The Silmarillion,* which was so severe that for some time he stopped working on it entirely (*C&G* 1.405–06). Much as C. S. Lewis might have predicted, Tolkien explored so many thoughts in the process of reviewing his entire legendarium that it led him to produce new works and to reexamine and reformulate the metaphysical foundations of his world more directly.

One important element we do not find reflected upon in Letter 131, or anywhere before Letter 153 of 1954 in fact, is pity. A part of Gandalf's exchange with Frodo on pity is present from the very first draft of *The Lord of the Rings.* Crucially, however, the effect of Bilbo's pity in that draft is solely to save him from becoming another Gollum, or worse: "He would not have had the ring, the ring would have had him at once. He might have become a wraith on the spot" (*Shadow* 81). There is not the least hint that "the pity of Bilbo may rule the fate of many" (*FR* 1.ii.59) as in the published text, or, as in Letter 153, that "it is the Pity of Bilbo and later Frodo that ultimately allows the Quest to be achieved" (*Letters* 191). Consider, too, Letter 181 of 1956 in which Tolkien states that "the 'salvation' of the world and Frodo's own 'salvation' is achieved by his previous *pity* and forgiveness of injury" (*Letters* 234). Letters 191 and 192, both of 1956, also emphasize the importance of pity, mercy, and forgiveness in this context, and in letter 246 of 1963 Tolkien again calls out "that strange element in the World that we call Pity and Mercy" (*Letters* 251–53, 326).

Before we go any farther, however, let us take a moment to clarify what Tolkien means when he speaks of this "strange element" on which the fate of the world and Frodo so emphatically depends. To many, pity savors of condescension and even contempt, as if those who feel "pity" for the suffering of others feel themselves not only circumstantially better off than those suffering but morally better as well. To be sure, we may detect some of this kind of pity in Sam's early observations of Gollum's misery and wretchedness (*TT* 4.ii.614, iii.623, 624, 631), and such an understanding of pity seems to lie behind Éowyn's disdain for what she mistakenly suspects Faramir is offering her (*RK* 6.v.964).

Gandalf's pity is clearly not of this kind. We would do well to parse the pity he shows and which he urges Frodo to adopt in "The Shadow of the Past" in terms of the "cognitive, affective and volitional features" of pity that Brian Carr describes (411). That is, Gandalf recognizes Gollum's suffering, feels pity—or what we might better call "compassion"—for him, and wishes to help him or see him helped if possible. In this third element, Gandalf far outstrips the pity Bilbo had felt for Gollum long ago, a pity that has since been consumed entirely by the Ring even as it slowly devours Bilbo. Tolkien, however, will likely have known of this aptly described "volitional" element from the *Summa* of Thomas Aquinas or from Saint Augustine's *City of God* (ix.5), which Aquinas himself quotes in part, but which we should see in full: "What is Mercy [misericordia] but a certain compassion felt in our own heart for the misery of another, by which we are compelled to come to the aid of the other if we can? This emotion, moreover, acts in the service of reason when it is shown in such a way that justice is preserved, whether our compassion is shown when alms is bestowed upon the poor or when forgiveness is granted to the penitent"(*De Civitate Dei* ix.5). And upon this, Aquinas comments: "dicitur enim misericordia ex eo quod aliquis habet miserum cor super miseria alterius": "for it is called mercy [misericordia] from the fact that one has a heart [cor] which is miserable [miserum] over the misery of another" (*Summa Theologiae* II.II *q.* 30 *a.* 1).

Since the "pity" or "mercy" or "compassion" of which Aquinas and Augustine speak is also "proper to God," we can begin to see why Tolkien uses the word *strange* to describe it (*Summa Theologiae* II.II. *q.* 30 *a* 2, 4). For what is proper to God is not of this world. We must recall here the point I made above, that the Pity of which Gandalf speaks not only suspends the justice Gollum deserves in favor of mercy and the possibility of healing, but it is also Providential, moved by the same power that led Bilbo to the Ring. So, while Gandalf would certainly agree that pity is the "social virtue" of which Carr speaks, he knows that Pity is much more than that (425–29). So, too, would Tolkien, as a man must who believed that the merciful will be shown mercy in their turn (*KJV,* Matt., 5:7), though not, as the Beatitudes imply, by their fellow humans.

The transcendent nature of Pity is essential for another very important reason. For within Arda, at the end of the Third Age, whatever effect pity might have as a "social virtue" or, in C. Fred Alford's formulation, as a "civilizing passion" that might countervail the "uncivilized passions, such as naked ambition, lust for power, greed, envy, and unbridled sexual desire" found within a normal human society, it will nevertheless fail utterly against the Ring and Sauron most of whose native strength dwells within the Ring (260). For Middle-earth is not a normal human society. Sauron is a being of angelic stature and Satanic power who has made himself incarnate in order to dominate all other creatures. The pity of this world cannot prevail against him. Exposed to the power of the Ring, even such pity as Gandalf possesses becomes dangerous. And so Gandalf refuses the Ring. The Pity of Bilbo, however, is written in the "strange" hand of Providence.

A word on the distinction between *pity* and *Pity* in *The Lord of the Rings* and elsewhere in Tolkien also seems in order. Regardless of capitalization, the word describes—and I am going to stick with Tolkien's word rather than imposing another—a deep, benevolent compassion such as one person might feel for the suffering of another, whether that suffering seems deserved or not. Importantly, *pity* is limited in its efficacy and exists on a strictly mundane or earthly level. Yet *Pity* either originates on the level of the supernatural or divine or somehow attains that level even if only for a moment. Capitalized, *Pity* occurs just eight times in *The Lord of the Rings* and only ever in the mouth of Gandalf speaking to Frodo at Bag End—four times in "The Shadow of the Past" and four times in Frodo's recollection of this conversation in "The Taming of Sméagol" (FR 1.i.59, TT 4.i.615)—and it is of course in this same conversation that Gandalf suggests that Bilbo's discovery of the Ring was Providential and that his pity for Gollum may prove to be all important in deciding the fate of the world (FR 1.i.55–56).[4] *Mercy,* as we just saw in Letter 246, can also share that initial capitalization, as it does when Gandalf pairs it with *Pity* in talking to Frodo. As we shall see, the inner revelation of *Pity* and its outward manifestation in *Mercy* together bring on the eucatastrophe of Mount Doom.

Parallel with the limited scope of pity in the first draft of *The Lord of the Rings* is the limited conception of the power of the Ring. It is not yet the One Ruling Ring. Until Bilbo's magic ring becomes the One, Bilbo's pity cannot play the role Gandalf suggests it may well do in the fate of the world. Indeed, it has no need to do so. Once the conception of the Ring changes, the two are woven together, with each other and with the themes of Death and Immortality. For the power of the Ring confers on mortals a semblance of Immortality, and on immortals the notion that they can preserve the world from the fading that is a part of its nature, and their own. Yet mortals with Rings of Power like the Nazgûl end up undead; immortals like the Elves embalm what they would save.[5] Against the Ring, pity offers the only real defense, but in the end the pity of this world cannot withstand the enticements of such power. Frodo will fail. (On the nature of the Ring, see further on pages 19–23.)

Pity thus plays an essential and paradoxical role in the lives of the characters and in the fate of all Middle-earth and is a key to understanding *The Lord of the Rings* and seeing more deeply into Tolkien's legendarium as a whole. If pity does not rule the fate of many, the Ring of Power will. For that is what Sauron made it to do. I shall trace the long arc of pity and the Ring from the moment Bilbo stood poised in the darkness behind Gollum until Frodo, hurt beyond worldly healing by the burden of the Ring, gazed on Saruman's corpse in the morning of the Shire and watched his fallen spirit scattered on the wind, both of them unable to return home.

PITY OR THE RING

If the "real theme" of *The Lord of the Rings* is Death and Immortality, and if the power of the Ring seems to offer Men and Elves the means to challenge these dooms of their nature and, much more obviously, to dominate their world, we must also address the nature of the Ring. How we answer will affect our understanding both of the temptations offered by the power of the Ring, and of the interplay of pity and the Ring.[6] The psychological, moral, and spiritual complexity of the struggle between the Ring as burden and the Ring as possession poses a challenge for both the reader and the Ring-bearer. No less complex and important is Frodo's transition, first insisting that Gollum justly deserves death, not pity; then discovering that he has come to pity him regardless of justice; and at last becoming someone who looks on Gollum without pity because he has gone beyond its reach himself. Sam, just coming to pity on the slopes of Mount Doom, naturally describes this phase of Frodo's development. For Frodo has now lost himself to the Ring, even if he has not yet taken the now imminent final step of claiming it as his own. Frodo's failure at Mount Doom, moreover, precipitates his final transition, in which he forgives Gollum and pities Saruman, hoping the fallen wizard might somehow find healing just as Gandalf had hoped for Gollum.

At Mount Doom, Gandalf's paradoxical and prophetic claim about Bilbo's pity proves true (FR 1.ii.59). It is paradoxical not just because it is the little noticed and less regarded hobbits who bear it and thus turn the wheels of the world, but also because it is precisely the fate of the world that Sauron created the Ring to rule. Like his master before him, Sauron wished to be master of Arda. Further, Gandalf's assertion is prophetic not solely because it comes to pass but because it does so uncannily, in a reversal in which Gollum's "final evil deed was the most beneficial thing" (*Letters* no. 181, p. 234). Pity thus usurps the fatal role Sauron meant the Ring to play, and in doing so pity sets free the many rather than subjugating them. It is this release from bondage, but not without cost, that puts Frodo and Sam in the same tale as Beren and Lúthien and suggests that such a release through joy and sorrow has been—and perhaps always will be—part of the story of the Children of Ilúvatar from the First Music of the Ainur to the Second (*S* 15–16).

Within the tale, uncertainty about the Ring is an essential part of the way the characters confront the evil possibilities of power used for domination. Not only does it make for a better story if Frodo is not merely a puppet controlled by an evil and conscious Ring or even a victim enticed and seduced by a Ring that whispers his name as in Peter Jackson's films; it also prevents *The Lord of the Rings* from becoming the black-and-white morality play some have accused it of being. The uncertainty of how much is Frodo and how much is the Ring is analogous to the uncertainty of how much of the tragedy of Oedipus arises from the mistakes of Oedipus and how much from the prophecy of Apollo. Who Oedipus is propels his destiny as much as Apollo does.

The lack of an easy or simple answer about the nature of the Ring, however, is as much a part of the realism of Frodo's journey whether we are speaking of the temptations and treachery of the Ring or the unforgiving cruelty and ill will of Caradhras. Hammond and Scull are correct to point out in their assessment of the ambiguities in "The Ring Goes South" that "here as elsewhere in *The Lord of the Rings* the work is improved by the reader experiencing the same uncertainty and suspense as the characters" (RC 270).[7]

A fascinating point to recall in considering this shared experience is that Frodo is purportedly the narrator of most of the book as well as the character bearing the burden, whether we mean the story or the Ring. That Frodo wrote most, if not quite all, of the story of *The Lord of the Rings* the text asserts in "The Grey Havens" when he turns the book he has been writing—aptly titled "The Downfall of the Lord of the Rings and the Return of the King" and explicitly described as his and Bilbo's memoirs—over to Sam and tells him that the last pages are for him to write (RK 6.ix.1027). That the reader may not perceive this until that moment does not alter the fact that Tolkien meant it to be understood to be so in the end. To what extent the text we have is, or is not, or is meant to be the text Frodo handed to Sam is uncertain.[8] Yet it is also true that the runes and Tengwar on the title page of *The Lord of the Rings* proclaim it to be "translated from the Red Book of Westmarch by John Ronald Reuel Tolkien." So again, what the reader may not perceive or understand about the claims this book is making for itself does not alter or affect the claims themselves. All of this is of course a fictional conceit, indeed layer upon layer of it.

In a tale, however, in which the revelation of a lie told by the narrator of the preceding tale plays so very consequential a part in creating the story and in demonstrating the burden of the great tale and its power, we cannot disregard the assertion of the tale itself that Frodo, who bears that burden, is both narrator and character. We must also not ignore one of the very first lessons we learn about the darker side of the Ring's power. To borrow the *Beowulf*-poet's phrase, the Ring is *iumnona gold galdre bewunden*, "gold of the ancients bound in enchantment," and one of the first fruits of that enchantment is deception of self and others (3052). The Ring at once became Gollum's birthday present, Bilbo's prize, Isildur's weregild (FR 1.ii.56, 1.ii.48, 2.ii.245). So, whether Frodo is the narrator of the text we have or only of the text he gave to Sam in "The Grey Havens" is quite relevant to this study. We may question or challenge the notion that he is, but unless and until we have disproved the assertion of the text by extensive study of the question by means of the text, we should not ignore or dismiss it.[9]

Whatever position we take on this question, however, it remains true that the narrator leaves unsettled some of the things Frodo was uncertain about. That Frodo's identity and memory faded under the power of the Ring may well mean that even as narrator Frodo would have no clearer understanding of certain things than he had as a character. We hear never a word about the return of his memory. Rather we hear of memories of burden, fear, and darkness (RK 6.vi.974, 975, vii.989). The narrator never allows the reader as clear a look at the temptations Frodo experienced as he does at those of Galadriel, Boromir, and Sam, for example. The deceptions of self and others that surround possession of the Ring affect Frodo as much as anyone else who bears or wishes to bear it, and the periodic reappearance of his fixation on it after its destruction suggests that the Ring remained a focus of his life.

We may, however, find gleanings of the temptations Frodo endured as he drew closer to the Cracks of Doom and the moment in which his will, its last strength spent, succumbed to his desire. Exploration of these gleanings is essential. For it is in the moment he submits that the interwoven arcs of pity and the Ring transform his failure through eucatastrophe, no other instance of which in the legendarium owns so strong a claim to the glimpse of the transcendent such a reversal affords, as Tolkien argues in *On Fairy-stories* (¶ 99, p. 75). Since for him it is through eucatastrophe that we are catching "the far-off gleam or echo of *evangelium* in the real world," the issues of Death and Immortality in *The Lord of the Rings* provide an analogy for the issues of Death and Immortality in the Gospels (¶ 103, p. 77). Thus, the tale of pity and the Ring, while neither allegory nor apologetic, has its mythopoeic roots in, and for Tolkien draws much of its power from, its author's Roman Catholic worldview. When Tolkien says *The Lord of the Rings* is "a fundamentally religious and Catholic work," we must take the etymology of *fundamentally* as seriously as a philologist like Tolkien properly would (*Letters* no. 142, p. 172). Deriving from the Latin *fundamentum—foundation—fundamentally* means "at its foundation" ("Fundamentally, adv.").

In *The Nature of Middle-earth* Carl F. Hostetter points out that many have failed to take sufficient account of Tolkien's use of "fundamentally" here; it is to be taken "quite literally, and not merely as a throwaway rhetorical intensifier; that is, I take it, that Tolkien is saying that The Lord of the Rings and, by extension, his larger legendarium... is at its core and foundation, or as one might say in its essential nature, based on religious, and specifically Catholic, beliefs and thought." (401-02) He further notes, again rightly, that the Catholic faith "in addition to a set of dogmas and religious rites entails a worldview encompassing *inter alia* a distinctive theology, metaphysics, cosmogony, and anthropology" (402). All of these elements lie at the foundations of *The Lord of the Rings* and the legendarium but especially the elements composing the worldview.

Like elements held in solution, foundations often go unseen even as they determine the strength and character of all that rests on them. Frodo's tale and the larger tale in which he and Sam find themselves are not revelation but a mythic analogy of it. For in the writing of such a tale, Tolkien says, "inevitably one's own taste, ideas, and beliefs get taken up" (*Letters* no. 208, p. 267) and become, as it were, incarnate in the telling (*M&C* 15). For the teller of tales, whether the *Beowulf*-poet or Tolkien, it is more a matter of feeling than analysis, of minstrelsy than history. As Malcolm Guite tells us, "the poetic imagination can complement...knowledge, can offer us some apprehensions that begin just where comprehension has found its limit" (33).

Together Pity and the Ring are key to unlocking not just Tolkien's intentions, which never suffice for the composition or interpretation of a great work, but also his not always conscious understanding of what the story he was writing was about. Together they will allow us to peer beneath the surface of story and metaphor (to adapt Simon Cook's phrasing) to see the meaning Tolkien found in the Dooms of Elves and Men and by analogy in our own.

FRODO'S JOURNEY AND OURS

Tolkien read *Beowulf*, Tom Shippey tells us, "not like a literary critic, but like a philologist. His insights tended to be drawn from tiny details, often very technical ones" ("*Beowulf*-poet" 13). He created his legendarium in much the same way, through the accumulation of tiny, often technical, details of language and story that allowed insight not only to his later readers (himself included), but also to himself as he wrote. Since Tolkien's and Frodo's understandings of many of the elements I have sketched in the previous sections walk in parallel along the road to Mordor and back again, so must ours. Close reading of the text is as indispensable for explicating the nature and role of pity and the Ring as it is for perceiving the details which enable us to describe them. I shall thus proceed through the hobbits' journey with the Ring from Bilbo's discovery of it to the departure of Frodo and Bilbo across the Sea, before considering the wider implications of the elements of pity and power as exemplified in the Ring for the legendarium overall.

Chapter 1 establishes the crucial part played in the transformation of Bilbo's magic ring into the One Ring by the lies he told about how he came by it, signaling that the Ring's power affects the character of its bearer immediately and that deception of self and others is a key element of that power. The evidence for questioning the assumed consciousness of the Ring leads to a more complex moral portrayal of both Bilbo and Frodo. The paradox presented by pity weighs against the ambiguity surrounding the nature of the Ring.

In chapter 2, the histories of Sauron and Gollum and Frodo's reaction to them reveal more clearly the deceit at the heart of the Ring's power, but the pity Bilbo showed Gollum also reveals a path to resist that power. The portrayal of Gollum underlines the difficulties of pity, especially for one like Frodo, who has only stories to go by, even as Gandalf situates pity and Gollum in confrontation with Frodo's denial that he and Bilbo could be anything like Gollum.

Chapter 3 examines in depth how Tolkien's falsification of Bilbo's original story in "Riddles in the Dark" recontextualizes *The Hobbit* and makes it essential to the interpretation of *The Lord of the Rings*. For Bilbo's moment of horror and pity allows him to see Gollum as an individual. It thus averts tragedy by turning him away from murder toward mercy and establishes a landmark by which the text navigates through the story of Frodo and Sam and Gollum. Careful excavation of the layers of development of that encounter shows how Tolkien leveraged his own drafting and revising process to create profound uncertainties about the truth of the matter. Gandalf's efforts to awaken pity in Frodo serve instead to awaken fear; and truth, which could lead Frodo to pity and so offer him a measure of protection, is the first victim of the Ring.

In chapter 4, we follow Frodo as he leaves behind the perquisites of being "*the* Mr. Baggins of Bag End," who found the Ring of use for ducking his relatives, but with every step he takes along the road to Rivendell new physical and spiritual challenges arise—Black Riders first and last, Old Man Willow, Tom Bombadil, and the Barrow-wight—and his encounters with these characters reveal how complicated and often murky his relationship with the Ring can be (FR 1.ii.43). While his courage and vision grow as a result, his foolhardy attempt to command the Black Riders at the ford betrays the influence of the Ring drawing him across the line that separates defiance from domination.

In chapter 5, I shall focus on three particular moments to illuminate how Frodo is simultaneously coming closer to pity and feeling the pull of the Ring's power more keenly. At Rivendell, while Gandalf tends to think Frodo will not come to evil in the end, the vehemence of Frodo's reaction when Bilbo reaches for the Ring shows that the ending Gandalf hopes for is by no means certain. In Lothlórien, Frodo asks Galadriel about using the Ring himself, a troubling reaction to her dramatic demonstration of why she must reject the Ring. At Amon Hen, the horror Frodo feels at seeing the Ring's effect on Boromir, followed by his own momentary captivity by the Ring and narrow escape from the Eye, prepares him to pity Gollum at last.

Chapter 6's scrutiny of Frodo's Ring-forged master-servant relationship with Gollum attests the truth of Gandalf's fear that pity not only offered no defense against the Ring but could even make a Ring-bearer more susceptible to the temptation to use its power. Frodo's use of the Ring to dominate Gollum—essentially to compel him to assist in a hopeless Quest—only hastens the erosion of Frodo's own will to resist the Ring. It increases the burden Frodo feels and his awareness of the malice of Sauron's mind, while dooming any attempt to help Gollum find Sméagol again.

In chapter 7, as the Ring-shattered state of Gollum's identity reveals itself to Sam through the competing intentions of the Sméagol-will and Gollum-will—both of which lust for the Ring—we also see fractures beginning to manifest in Frodo's identity. Frodo becomes cruel to Gollum at times, threatening him with the Ring and taunting that he will never get it back. Neither Sam nor Gollum yet grasps the transformation Frodo is undergoing, since he is still enough himself to rebound to kindness after cruelty and to play the role of Gandalf in urging Faramir not to put Gollum to death as he deserves.

In chapter 8, Faramir's outright rejection of the power no mortal can resist and Gollum's wavering momentarily between villainy and repentance highlight questions of identity and self-deception as the gap narrows between Frodo's acceptance of the Ring as his burden and his desire to use it. The seeming wisdom of his realization that he cannot yet challenge the Witch-king is vitiated by the self-deception on which that realization rests, namely, that he will soon be able to do so, a delusion that adumbrates the direct challenge to Sauron implicit in his claiming the Ring as his own. For the moment, Frodo's deteriorating identity can still be called back by memories of the Shire and the light in Galadriel's phial. The scene of Gollum's near repentance underscores that love, like pity, can counteract the Ring's effects, if only for a time, depending on the rootedness of the love and one's capacity for unflinching self-knowledge. Gollum fails in this regard, but Sam will succeed when his moment comes.

In chapter 9, the all-consuming darkness of Shelob, in which even the Ring is forgotten, strips away all but will and desire, allowing the reader to see the essential importance of these factors in Sam's choices first to take the Ring and then return it to Frodo, and Frodo's struggle between the will to carry his burden to the fire and the desire to claim it. Sam's choices are filtered through the Great Tales, and a series of unspoken lies underpin his momentary illusions about the Ring; yet he chooses rightly, at first by heeding reason and then by recklessly following his heart. His humility and love for Frodo enable him to give up the Ring, but already subtleties of language demonstrate that Sam would not have been able to do so for long. In the final approach to Mount Doom, Sam's resilience contrasts with Frodo's descent into hopelessness and the death of memory. Inevitably, the long erosion of Frodo's identity is complete as the distinction between the Ring as his burden and the Ring as his own collapses. Sam's choices and Frodo's struggle both reveal the limits of human pity and set the stage for the eucatastrophe at Mount Doom.

Chapter 10 follows the paths of joy and sorrow opened by the destruction of the Ring. While a broken Frodo begins to fade along with much in the world for which the Rings of Power were made, Arwen's pity makes his healing beyond the Sea possible; and while Saruman dies outwardly scorning the mercy Frodo offers him in the hope that he might find healing, Frodo's pity for him allows the Shire to be healed. Healing made possible through pity and mercy brings the tale told within *The Lord of the Rings* proper to an ending full of both sorrow and hope.

In chapter 11, other works—"*Beowulf*: The Monsters and the Critics," *On Fairy-Stories*, "The Tale of Aragorn and Arwen," the "Athrabeth Finrod ah Andreth"—deepen our understanding of the prevalent themes observed in *The Lord of the Rings* and how they come to bind together the whole of Tolkien's mythology. For the power used to dominate other beings and other things exemplified by the Rings of Power challenges the parameters of Arda set by Eru Ilúvatar for his Children. It is the Doom of Men that they must live, die, and leave the world and the Doom of the Elves that they must live on, fading in a fading world, until all that remains is memory and the world itself ends. With power such as the Ring offers. Men gain not immortality but undeath, and Elves do not heal or preserve Arda but embalm it. Since the desires of Men to live on in the world they love and of Elves to heal its hurts are natural, their attempts to resist a physically incarnate evil they cannot hope to defeat without becoming it are as spiritually perilous as they are materially hopeless. Through writing *The Lord of the Rings,* Tolkien discovered the sole answer to this power in pity and thus provided the pagan world of his legendarium with a "fundamentally religious and Catholic" substance, a foundation set in the evangelium for the *eald enta geweorc,* or "ancient works of giants," with which his mythology presents us (*Letters* no. 142, p. 172). Pity establishes a continuum of sorrow and beauty that extends from the Music of the Ainur before Time began, through the eucatastrophe of Mount Doom, to the entry of Ilúvatar into his creation to recreate and heal it as prophesied by Finrod in the "Athrabeth."

All translations are mine unless indicated. All italics in quoted passages are original unless indicated.

CHAPTER ONE

Bilbo's Lie and the Ring

TWO STORIES AND ONE BILBO

In the spring of 1944, as Tolkien blazed through book 4 of *The Lord of the Rings*, taking Frodo, Sam, and Gollum from the Emyn Muil to Shelob's Lair, he made the crucial decision to rewrite "Riddles in the Dark," the chapter in *The Hobbit* in which Bilbo obtains the Ring from Gollum.[1] His choice here has more than one consequence. It transforms the tale told in the 1937 *Hobbit*, in which cleverness and luck win him the ring, into a lie told in self-justification and self-aggrandizement. Thus, *a* ring proves to be *the* Ring, the gravity of whose power is at work even from the first moment of possession.

Now, to be sure, Tolkien had already decided that the Ring was far more important and pernicious than it had seemed in *The Hobbit*, and from early on he had made it central to *The Lord of the Rings*. That much is certain. But giving Bilbo the lie, as it were, elevates the Ring and the story by establishing a starting point for every lie, temptation, and delusion that follows, from the darkness beneath the Misty Mountains to the fires of the Sammath Naur. It is a dark, downward road that Bilbo steps into here, so far from his front door, and it will very nearly sweep him away before he relinquishes (if he does) both the lie and the Ring: "'Well, if you want my ring yourself, say so!' cried Bilbo. 'But you won't get it. I won't give my precious away, I tell you.' His hand strayed to the hilt of his small sword" (FR 1.i.34). And this road *will* sweep Frodo away on the slopes of Mount Doom. What begins with Bilbo's lie ends with Frodo's delusion that the Ring is his. The lie is the final step in the transformation of the Ring.

Yet, paired with the moral failure of Bilbo's lie is an astonishing and even more important instant of humanity, likely prompted by grace in which Bilbo's native morality reasserts itself and he unexpectedly glimpses the horror of Gollum's life. That Bilbo *can* reassert his morality—beginning with his recognition that it was unfair to kill Gollum out of hand—indicates that his lie is his choice, even if influenced by the Ring. Poised there, soul in the balance and sword in hand, despite the terror he feels of this murderous, cannibalistic creature, Bilbo discovers pity and shows mercy. Though he had begun his adventure with an equally unexpected wish to wear a sword instead of carrying a walking stick (H 45), he did not stab Gollum in the back "when he had a chance" as Frodo later wishes he had (FR 1.ii.59). In the moral balance between the lie and the pity, and in the practical movement from the lie to the delusion, the power of the One Ring reveals itself.

In the chapters that follow, I shall explore these connections within *The Lord of the Rings* primarily, but also, essentially, in the profound intertextuality of its story and the chapter "Riddles in the Dark" of *The Hobbit*. As Tolkien tells it, the Doom of the world of Middle-earth rested on the power of the One Ring and what was done with it and about it, a matter of such importance that Providence itself (whether the Valar or The One) took a hand. So, this study shall focus on the dynamics and meaning of that power through a close and detailed reading of the text. Since both God and the Devil are in the details, we might expect much to be found there in a writer so fundamentally Christian as Tolkien.

Inseparable from our understanding of the power of the Ring is an understanding of pity as the necessary quality that will nevertheless not save the Ring-bearer from the Ring. Making the morally correct choice is of course always of the greatest moral value in Tolkien, but it is also usually effectual even when no one expects it to be (Dickerson 95–107). That is fundamental to the larger spiritual context of his vision. That a character like Gandalf, who kindles hope in others and hopes for the cure of one as nearly lost as Gollum, recommends a seemingly hopeless virtue should give us pause, especially since failure for the Ring-bearer means a far worse outcome than failure would have done for Aragorn, Legolas, and Gimli in their pursuit of the orcs, for example. For Gandalf, the failure of pity to defend against the Ring would have meant that he became another—and a worse—Dark Lord (see below on pages 110–11); for Frodo, it would have meant at best the living death of a wraith.

Here we discover another dimension of pity, in which we make the moral choice knowing it will not avail and in which we find no refutation of the worth of that choice in our personal and inevitable defeat. Yet, Bilbo's Pity plays precisely the role Gandalf had foreseen even as the Ring's power overwhelms Frodo's hard-earned pity for Gollum. Once he becomes "untouchable... by pity," Frodo succumbs to the lie of the Ring (RK 6.iii.944). Their individual experiences of pity differ, as do their fates, but in making the moral choice, late or soon, each of them unwittingly becomes the instrument of the Power by which they were intended to have the Ring. The one suffers unbearable sorrows, and the other mostly "live[s] happily ever afterwards to the end of his days" (2.ii.269). *The Hobbit* and *The Lord of the Rings*, "being the memoirs of Bilbo and Frodo of the Shire," together weave that sorrow and joy into a tale whose beauty only gains from their blending, thereby echoing the Third Theme (RK 6.ix.1027; S 16–17). From the deeps beneath the Misty Mountains, Pity thus reaches beyond the Circles of the World, and together with the Ring raises questions of Power and Choice (Free Will), Death and Immortality.

Each of the first two chapters of *The Lord of the Rings* invokes the memory of Bilbo's meeting with Gollum in *The Hobbit*. On a simple level, this invocation links the two works and identifies the Ring as central to the plot of "the new Hobbit" (*Letters* no. 98, p. 112). There are, however, far more significant aspects of this invocation. First, *The Lord of the Rings* presents the reader with many scenes that replay or reflect the moment of decision in which Bilbo chose to spare Gollum's life out of pity. Second, Gandalf foresees for that pity a decisive role in the world, for Frodo and everyone else. Third, though Gandalf urges Frodo to pity Gollum, his portrayal of Gollum to Frodo scarcely inspires it, nor does the narrator's portrayal of Gollum throughout the book. This is as true in the chapters where others speak of him, or in which he lurks offstage, stalking the action, as it is after he enters the story in "The Taming of Sméagol." The groundwork for the meeting with Gollum in the Emyn Muil is long and carefully prepared, and Frodo's own journey with the Ring has made him ready for it. It is not only pity that Frodo embraces when Gollum is at his mercy. Finally, in rejecting the Ring when Frodo offers it to him, Gandalf leaves no doubt that pity offers no final defense against the Ring, and yet it is the best way forward. Indeed, no other way offers the least hope.

So, "A Long-expected Party" and "The Shadow of the Past" not only establish Bilbo's ring as the One Ring that Sauron lost long ago, but, more importantly, they also establish that it is the character of the Ring-bearer—any Ring-bearer—

on which the massive gravity of the Ring's power exerts its pull. That Tolkien from first to last describes the grave burden of the Ring in terms of its perceived weight is a brilliant metaphor for its effect on the Ring-bearer and others. It pulls them down, but inwardly. On the slopes of Mount Doom, Frodo is so overcome by the weight of the Ring that he cannot stand, yet Sam picks him up, feeling none of the burden himself, though he had expected he would, given his own recent experience. And on those same slopes three thousand years ago, Isildur claimed the Ring that his father, Elendil, his brother, Anarion, and Gil-galad had died to destroy, and he later dies using the Ring in an attempt to save himself while his men perish.[2] Compared to this, the physical effects on a mortal of bearing and using a Ring of Power—an existence attenuated, quite literally, to the vanishing point—are but the suits of woe. How does the Ring have this effect? How does it pull down Isildur and Boromir, and Sméagol, Bilbo and Frodo? How is its attraction for Gandalf and Galadriel so much more powerful and dangerous than it is for Frodo?

To speak of its "gravity," its "pull," and its "weight" is to indulge in metaphor, but is there anything more literal that we can actually say? As C. S. Lewis pointed out, to refer to "the law of gravity" is to use a metaphor (*Discarded* 92–94). It is no more "a law," he argues, and no less a metaphor than when philosophers of Medieval and Ancient times held that objects, being made of elemental "earth," fell to earth because of their "desire" to return there. Consider the words of Lady Philosophy to Boethius in *The Consolation of Philosophy [De Consolatione Philosophiae]*: "Even those things which are believed to be inanimate each in a sense desire what is their own, do they not? Why does the lightness of flame carry it upwards, why does the weight of earth press it downwards, except that these places and movements are proper to each of them?" (3.P11.71–76). The desire that one would seek to gratify through the Ring—whether it is Gandalf's "desire of strength to do good," Galadriel's and Boromir's desire to defeat evil and to rule, or even Frodo's to destroy the Ring itself and save the Shire—is the substance, the mass, as it were, on which the Ring exerts its pull (FR 1.ii.61). And spanning the ever-closing distance between the desire and the Ring are the lies, temptations, and delusions.

What more can one say? To understand what the Ring is, whether it is conscious and self-aware, what it does and how it does it, is a matter as important as it is difficult. To understand what, if anything, it properly stands for or represents is impossible otherwise. Yet we would be unwise to expect any explanation to answer every question we might raise. As Tolkien wrote,

"You cannot press the One Ring too hard, for it is of course a mythical feature" (*Letters* no. 211, p. 279). Let's begin with the words inscribed on the Ring itself: "One Ring to rule them all, one Ring to find them / One Ring to bring them all, and in the darkness bind them." These verses are the testimony of Sauron himself. These are the words he inscribed on the Ring and spoke as a spell to imbue it with his power—to rule, to find, to bring, to bind—and the words that as he spoke them revealed his treachery to the Elves (FR 2.ii.254). The verbs are all about discovery and control. In a word, power. The structure of the verses, too, reinforces this: each line begins with *one,* while *them all* ends the first half of each line, and *them* ends the second. The rhythm beats like hammer blows. Everything about these lines speaks of power, "ominous and sinister" power (*Letters* no. 131, p. 152).

As Gandalf tells Frodo, "[Sauron] let a great part of his own former power pass into it, so that he could rule all the others" (FR 1.ii.51). A key feature of this is discovery or finding. With the Ring on Sauron's hand, the other rings, the deeds done with them, and even the minds of those who wield them will be revealed to him, as both Gandalf and Galadriel tell Frodo (1.ii.52, 2.vii.365). As long as Sauron does not have the Ring, Galadriel can know his mind but remain unknown herself. The importance of discovery as a means to power had long been clear to Sauron, who defeated Finrod, Galadriel's brother, in a duel of enchantments, in the First Age: "He chanted a song of wizardry, / Of piercing, opening, of treachery, / revealing, uncovering, betraying" (S 171).[3] We also learn, from Frodo's conversation with Galadriel in "The Mirror of Galadriel," that one who wields the Ring can also read the thoughts and dominate the wills of others (FR 2.vii.634). With power of this kind inherent in the Ring, is it any wonder that Sméagol, who was so fascinated by uncovering secrets, fell a prey to the Ring the instant he saw it? Is it any wonder that Saruman, who by the power of his voice could persuade his peers and daunt the rest, strayed from the path of wisdom?

This brings us to what Tolkien called "the Ring's power of lust," whose working I likened above to the pull of gravity: "Anyone who used it became mastered by it; it was beyond the strength of any will (even his own) to injure it, cast it away, or neglect it" (*Letters* no. 131, p. 154). Note that not even the will of Sauron himself is sufficient to act against the Ring, a chilling indication of just how much of his own strength he must have put into it. No wonder then that he could not guess that anyone would want to destroy it or why its destruction would forever reduce him to impotence (FR 2.ii.269; RK 5.ix.879).

That much power spurs an overmastering desire, especially in those already mighty enough "to wield [it] at will" (FR 2.ii.267).

Has all of this power infused into the Ring made it to some degree conscious? It is certainly hard to get past what Gandalf says to Frodo: "A Ring of Power looks after itself" and "It was not Gollum but the Ring itself that decided things. The Ring left *him*" (FR 1.ii.55). However, if we look at other objects in the legendarium that are or may be sentient, we find both the ridiculous and the tragic. The troll's purse in *The Hobbit* is amusing but seems little more than a magical burglar alarm (73). The Two Watchers at the fortress in Mordor are "aware," "a spirit of evil vigilance abode in them," and Sam feels their hostility as he forces his way past them, causing them also to cry out in alarm (RK 6.i.902–03). We know from the case of the Barrow-wights, moreover, that sorcery can summon into lifeless things evil spirits with no prior connection to them (RK App. A 1041; UT 348). Yet it is wildly implausible that Sauron would have allowed even a spirit to "possess" the Ring and the greater part of his strength.

And it is always Sauron's strength or power he is said to put into the Ring, never his "self," his "mind," or his "spirit" (FR 1.ii.51; 2.ii.254; RK 5.ix.878; S 287, 295, 302; *Letters* no. 131, p. 153). The same was true of Morgoth, who in the First Age dispersed much of his power into the substance of Arda so he might have more control over it. He diminished his power in doing so but remained himself. So, too, the substance of Arda may have been marred, tainted by Morgoth, but it did not become Morgoth. It matters little whether the power was dispersed into many places as Morgoth did, or concentrated into one as Sauron did, once transferred it may not be regained (*Morgoth* 133, 394–401). By contrast, we may see that Sauron can not only use his mind to dominate others and "steer" them like vehicles of his malice, but he can withdraw his thought and leave them "steerless." He objectifies them and uses them as tools, but it is his "mind and purpose" he communicates for a time, not himself that he permanently transfers in whole or in part (RK 6.iii.946).

Not to be forgotten in this context is the famous black sword of Túrin, son of Húrin, which speaks and displays a surprising sense of loyalty, justice, and mercy: "Yea, I will drink thy blood gladly, that so I may forget the blood of Beleg my master, and the blood of Brandir slain unjustly. I will slay thee swiftly" (S 225). We should, however, overlook neither the overall mythic nature of Túrin's story nor the contradiction arising within it at this particular moment. Not only was no one present to witness Túrin's exchange with his sword, but the words it says to him seem to refute the warning of the normally Cassandra-like Melian that "there is malice in this sword. The dark heart of the smith still dwells in it. It will not love the hand it serves; neither will it abide with you long" (202). Yet, a possessor's malice may leave its mark upon an object without bestowing consciousness on it, as was the case with Smaug and his gold (*H* 323); and indeed, we can see from the words of the sword that the sword feels tainted by Túrin and his deeds. Prophecies, moreover, seldom refer to what they seem to refer to at first. It is not Beleg's hand the sword will not love, but Túrin's. The smith, Eöl, Beleg, and Túrin, all seem to have made imprints on the blade, but it does not follow that whatever consciousness the sword possesses comes from any of them.

Elsewhere we shall see Tolkien employ to great effect scenes the narrator cannot have witnessed, such as Gollum's near repentance (below on pages 168–69) and the sunrise on Tol Eressëa (below on page 232). In each case the scenes point to something mythically larger than their narrative content, the first inspiring the reader to pity unforeseen, the second to joy unguessed. So, too, here. What comes between Melian's prophecy and the sword's refutation of it is Beleg's love of Túrin, which costs him everything, and because of which we might allow that the darkness in Eöl no longer inhabits the sword (*S* 200, 204, 208). While the mythic truth imagined here resolves the contradiction within its own tale, it offers no answers about the Ring.

Yet perhaps the most telling point of all comes in "Of Aulë and Yavanna." There Aulë, a Vala and far greater than Sauron, could indeed make the fathers of the Dwarves, but he could not give them independent life and consciousness: only Ilúvatar could do so (*S* 43–44).[4] Similarly, we learn later in this same story that the parts Manwë and Yavanna sang in the Music contained pre-echoes of the Eagles and the Ents, but it was again by the will of Ilúvatar that they received spirits and therefore became conscious beings (45–46). This is consonant with the opinion voiced most famously in *The Lord of the Rings* by Frodo: "The Shadow that bred [orcs] can only mock, it cannot make: not real living things of its own" (*RK* 6.i.913), a position Treebeard also took when speaking to Merry and Pippin of Orcs and Trolls (*TT* 3.iv.485).

Finally, consider Tolkien's statement in Letter 131, in which he distinguishes between the power Sauron vested in the Ring, Sauron's being, and Sauron himself: "If the One Ring was actually *unmade,* annihilated, then its power would be dissolved, Sauron's own being would be vastly diminished, and he would be reduced to a shadow, a mere memory of malicious will" (153). Gandalf says much the same in "The Last Debate": the destruction of the Ring would forever strip Sauron of "the best part of the strength that was native to him in the beginning" and reduce him to inanition (*RK* 5.ix.878). His spirit, however, is indestructible, though he will never again be able to take on physical form.[5] Read in the context of these other quotes, Tolkien's description of the Ring as "one of the various mythical treatments of the placing of one's life, or power, in some external object" points to life and power as distinct alternatives, of which the One Ring is unquestionably an example of the second (*Letters* no. 211, p. 279).

So, it does not seem that Sauron could or would endow the Ring with a life and consciousness of its own. The distinction between his power and his being, which is implicit in *The Lord of the Rings* and explicit in Letter 131, further argues against any notion that he had somehow transferred a part of his own consciousness into the Ring. Eöl may have tainted the black sword with his malice, but the sword was not a version of Eöl because of that, not even in a mythic tale where a sword may speak. Morgoth may have corrupted the substance of Arda by disseminating his power into it, but Arda thus became "Morgoth's Ring," connected to him in being, but it did not become Morgoth himself (*Morgoth* 400). Sauron's Ring is not Sauron, nor a piece of him, despite the "rapport," to use Tolkien's word, that existed between them.[6]

Does the Ring then possess a consciousness and agency of its own? Scholars and fans alike commonly speak as if it does.[7] Gandalf does so himself when he tells Frodo the Ring left Gollum, a statement that gives by far the strongest evidence for consciousness and agency, but only if Gandalf means what he says to be taken as completely literal rather than as a metaphor, a convenient shorthand of the sort people have long used. That Frodo mocks Gandalf's assertion, I would argue, leaves room for us to doubt that he means what he says literally, especially since Gandalf does not reply with a reaffirmation that the Ring indeed made a conscious decision to leave Gollum and acted on it, a point not to be neglected or passed over if true, but hammered home. Who would need to understand this more than Frodo?

Gandalf, however, does pass over it, moving immediately on to another point that he considers more important and which he admits he cannot state "more plainly," that Bilbo was "*meant* to have the Ring and *not* by its maker" (*FR* 1.ii.55). Any agency the Ring might have seems downplayed here in the grand scheme of things. Gandalf, moreover, has used metaphor earlier in this conversation to describe the Ring *devouring* its possessor (1.ii.47, 55, 57). He has even employed outright deception, withholding as long as he can the truth that the hobbit Sméagol is in fact the creature Gollum, because he believes it of the utmost importance to the world that Frodo, who is also "*meant* to have the Ring," pity Gollum as Bilbo had done.

This combination of reticence, deception, and metaphor warns against making any easy judgement about the Ring and its effect on its possessor. While Frodo reasonably and rightly scoffs at Gandalf's assertions about the Ring's consciousness and agency, he is nevertheless rarely sure whether the urge to put on the Ring comes from the Ring, from within himself, or from elsewhere. Such uncertainty makes it inherently difficult to discern where the possibilities integral to the power of the Ring begin and where the desires of those who possess or might possess it leave off. It is akin to the ambiguous intertwining of Fate and Free Will that Gandalf hints at when he speaks of the Ring and the importance of pity.

Middle-earth is a world that is alive in a mythic sense. Foxes think. The trees of the Old Forest are aware. The stones of Hollin remember. Caradhras is cruel. Birds and beasts have languages that a wizard or a Ranger might know. And Goldberry, the daughter of the river, can rise from her bed to take a husband. Some, but not all, of these may be metaphors. In a world so imagined, in which there is more to be perceived than mortal minds can dream of, realms both seen and unseen (Hillman, "Not the Elves" 114–40), a world that exists only in a mythical past (Rateliff, "All the Days" 67–100), it should not be unexpected that we cannot say for sure whether "the Ring left" Gollum means what it literally says, or whether it is a metaphor to describe how it inexplicably fell out of his pocket.

The approach to myth Tolkien takes in the *Beowulf* essay is instructive for thinking about the Ring and the power of its effects (*M&C* 15). If we probe myth too far and too analytically, like a scientist rather than a poet, we shall miss something critical that must instead be felt and spoken of in metaphors (even if they are scientific metaphors). We shall kill the myth by "vivisection," a brutal image that evokes a murderous and controversial practice and demonstrates Tolkien's attitude about the care one must take in speaking about and understanding myth and which we hear echoed in Gandalf's words to Saruman about the folly of breaking something in order to understand it. On this showing, Tolkien seems unlikely to have undertaken so detailed an analysis of the properties of the Ring. The truth of the Ring needed magic and myth, parable and metaphor, not an exacting inquiry into the arts of the Enemy. Such an analysis would lessen the Ring, just as Saruman's coat of many colors lessens him, gaining nothing but Gandalf's mockery.

Thus, we shall best learn about the Ring and its effects gradually, through the slow unfolding of the portraits of Frodo and Gollum in particular, both before and after they meet. Their roads to each other are as important as their road with each other, and we shall learn as much about them along the way as we do about the Ring. For it reveals their character just as much as its character is revealed by them. And together the Ring's great power and the small hands that would bear or wield it change everything, as Elrond gnomically observes (FR 2.ii.269). Yet it is with Bilbo's lie, and with the revelation of that lie, that this road begins.

Whether as readers we first encountered Bilbo in "An Unexpected Party" or "A Long-expected Party," the portrayal of him we meet in the first chapter of *The Lord of the Rings* has to stand on its own merits. Not all readers come to *The Lord of the Rings* through *The Hobbit*. Many, like me, read the later work first, and, having experienced its more mature subject and high-romantic storytelling, we find ourselves in that moment too old—I'm younger than that now—to appreciate this story, written by Tolkien for his children, for what it is. Even with "Riddles in the Dark" rewritten to reflect the transformation of the ring found by Bilbo into something darker, *The Hobbit* remains a children's book, however excellent. Its importance within the legendarium is as a significant precursor to *The Lord of the Rings*. For, although Tolkien could have easily left *The Hobbit* as it was in 1937 and still represented the story Bilbo told as a lie, he did not. This decision bespeaks more than a donnish cleverness that he and the other Inklings would have laughed about in Lewis's rooms of a Thursday evening. Rather, by rewriting the earlier work to match the later one he indicated which he considered the primary text and evinced his desire for a more meaningful intertextuality. For these reasons we will take the Bilbo of "A Long-expected Party" first and leave aside the Bilbo of *The Hobbit*.

Indeed, it is remarkable how quickly the Ring makes its presence felt. By the fourth sentence of the first paragraph, we can see that more is peculiar about Mr. Bilbo Baggins of Bag End than remarkable adventures and legendary wealth. "Time wore on"—six decades in fact—but Bilbo looked "*unchanged*" (FR 1.i.21). Of course, neither the hobbits nor the reader know about the Ring or about its effect on the lifespan of mortals just yet.

Yet, while the hobbits are disquieted by his ageless longevity, Bilbo's generosity, kindness, and possession of a proper condescension win him respect and indulgence. Such forgiveness, reinforced by Gaffer Gamgee's stout but humorous defense of him against allegations of queerness, primes the reader to forget the uncanny amid the charm and fun of the leadup to the party, just as the hobbits seem to do. Gandalf's arrival, the delighted hobbit children, the promise of fireworks, the prospect of a practical joke, the splendid invitations, the stupendous orders for food and drink, the toys from Dale, the music and dancing, even the lovely weather—all of these—are quite diverting. Even Bilbo's after-dinner speech meets with tolerance, and seems perfectly normal, until he vanishes in plain sight by means of the Ring, which he had been playing with in his pocket all the while. Though his guests are outraged at his absurdity and bad taste, just as before there's no queerness that further generous helpings of food and drink won't cure. Even the shrewd and sober Rory Brandybuck, who suspects there's something more to it, concludes that, since "he hasn't taken the vittles with him," things can't be all that bad (FR 1.i.31). The party goes on.

The two outward signs of the Ring's power seen thus far seem to have done Bilbo no harm. Invisibility will be familiar to any reader of *The Hobbit* as a useful effect that saved Bilbo's life more than once and enabled him to perform heroic deeds. It also comes in handy for a joke. Worth noting here are the echoes of an understanding of the Ring abandoned after an early draft. There Bingo (as Frodo was called in earlier drafts) recounts advice Gandalf had given Bilbo about the Ring, that he should "only use it for proper purposes. I mean, do not use it except for jest or for escaping from danger and annoyance" (*Shadow* 73–74).[8] That Tolkien so quickly eschewed the idea that some uses of the Ring did little or no harm but kept the actions themselves is the first hint that if the Ring is the means it will corrupt the ends or the agent or both.

Bilbo's enduring youthfulness, however, is a new feature, whose connection to the Ring is not yet openly expressed but easily inferred. Having drawn this inference, we may well recall the hobbits' expectations of trouble, and wonder whether Rory Brandybuck's sanguine conclusion that all was well if there were still vittles is as right as it is funny. The immediate turn from him to a more melancholy Frodo prepares us to find out the truth. Though Bilbo's joke amused him, he was troubled by the contrast between the scandal it has caused and his own love for Bilbo whom he knows to be leaving. The strength of their bond is plain. For him, the party is over.

As the guests eat and drink themselves into a more forgiving mood and Frodo looks silently on, a very different scene begins to unfold at Bag End, where Bilbo is quickly completing the last of his preparations for departure. Unlike his adventure sixty years before, he already has a hood of his own, together with a sword and walking stick. However well-preserved, he is not what he was. All is going according to a well-made plan, until he comes to what Gandalf shall presently call "the only point I ever saw in the whole affair" (FR 1.i.35).

Bilbo had meant both to use the Ring to vanish and then to pass it on to Frodo, but his first attempt to leave he Ring behind ends with him putting it back in his pocket (FR 1.i.32). Impulse overcomes intent the instant he tries to let it go, a foreshadow of the difficulty of relinquishing the Ring willingly. This shadow becomes all the more troubling when, asked by Gandalf where the Ring is, Bilbo first claims that it is on the mantelpiece but then appears surprised to discover it in his pocket as if by accident—"Isn't that odd now?" (1.i.32). While he doesn't seem to be lying, he also has no recollection of taking back the Ring. Given that he has also just been honest enough to acknowledge that his legendary youthfulness is in fact an uncomfortable illusion, and he has declared his need of a permanent holiday where he can find rest, Bilbo's unconsciousness of taking an action directly contrary to his intentions suggests the strength of the Ring's pull on both thought and action, body and spirit. Note also that once he realizes he still has the Ring, he does scarcely more than note the discrepancy and begins at once to rationalize keeping it, despite what he had meant to do only a few moments ago.

After the generally lighthearted and humorous tone of the story's first dozen pages, in which even the menace of the darker elements is easily missed, the scene between Gandalf and Bilbo that follows quickly becomes shockingly tense, rising from discomfort to anger to accusations to the threat of violence. His face flushed and hard looking, his eyes alight with anger, his voice loud, his tone obstinate, one hand clutching the Ring, the other the hilt of his sword. To lay one's hand on a weapon in the midst of a heated argument is a threat. This is not the kindly and generous, clever and funny old hobbit we saw before. When? Before Gandalf pressed him about the Ring, yes, but also before Bilbo used the Ring at the party only a few minutes ago. That Bilbo has disappeared, for now. In his place we have someone prepared to draw his sword on a friend. That he does not do so must not obscure the fact that he has nevertheless come to this point. Sixty years earlier he had been on the verge of killing Gollum with this same sword, but Gollum posed an actual threat to his life and Bilbo had been quite reasonably terrified. Here the threat he perceives is only to his possession of the Ring and the desire to keep it, which is of course precisely why Gollum had wished to kill him at that moment. So much for the safety of using the Ring for a joke.

Can this dark turn be wholly unconnected to Bilbo's use of the Ring only minutes earlier? That does not seem likely. Even if the Ring is not the immediate cause, however, the juxtaposition of Bilbo's use of the Ring with his behavior when asked to give it up as promised marks a connection between the two. Bilbo's behavior where the Ring is concerned, moreover, is the very thing that prompts Gandalf to make the comparison between Bilbo and Gollum to which Bilbo responds so fiercely:

> "If I am [angry] it is your fault," said Bilbo. "It is mine, I tell you. My own. My precious. Yes, my precious."
>
> The wizard's face remained grave and attentive, and only a flicker in his deep eyes showed that he was startled and indeed alarmed. "It has been called that before," he said, "but not by you."
>
> "But I say it now. And why not? Even if Gollum said the same once. It's not his now, but mine. And I shall keep it, I say."
>
> (FR 1.i.33)

The old hobbit's reaction is rather telling and disturbing. Bilbo does not, as we might expect, deny the applicability of the comparison. Far from it. He flatly denies its relevance.

"So what?" is the essence of Bilbo's reply. He simultaneously accepts the accuracy of Gandalf's statement and rejects its significance out of hand. None of this, of course, escapes the wizard, whose manner now becomes stern and whose warnings now characterize Bilbo as a fool and a slave of the Ring if he is determined to keep it. When the hobbit responds by proclaiming his freedom to choose and to act as he wishes, Gandalf stresses the obligations of their long friendship and demands that Bilbo keep the promise he had made to give it up. Again, as with the comparison to Gollum, Bilbo's response is not what the earlier scenes of this chapter, or earlier moments of this scene, lead us to expect. From obstinacy Bilbo passes into paranoia, accusing his old friend and threatening him with his sword.

Gandalf's response here is also significant. What exactly is he doing? Is it merely physical intimidation and moral authority, or is there more to it than that? There may be a clue in the words "Gandalf's eyes remained bent on the hobbit," which find a parallel in "The Mirror of Galadriel" when Galadriel holds each of the Company with her eyes and seems to test them mind to mind (FR 1.i.34, 2.vii.357). Here we see an example of what she later describes as using the will to dominate others (2.vii.366). That, I argue, is what Gandalf is doing here, not to force Bilbo to give up the Ring but to compel him to back down from the savage pitch he has reached, so that long trust and friendship may reach him. If so, we see the difficulty of reaching someone in the Ring's power, even someone who has not used it for evil.

Even after Gandalf daunts him into backing down, Bilbo still speaks at first as if he were the wronged party, full of the same attempts at justification as he was before. Yet, that Gollum would have killed him if he had not kept the Ring is the hollowest excuse of all. For however true it may be, it reduces his claim to the Ring to one of expediency, and Bilbo is making the claim to someone he has just threatened with a sword himself. This threat of murder vitiates the pretext he offers about the threat he had felt then: both center on keeping the Ring. But Gandalf lets this pass, and Bilbo's wrath fades. The hobbit returns to himself, not quite knowing what had come over him—just as he had not recalled taking the Ring back out of the envelope—but aware that the Ring had something to do with it.

We can see much here about Bilbo, or, if one prefers to speak more cautiously, about the Ring's effect on Bilbo. The use of the Ring, and indeed the mere possession of it (as Bilbo's remarks after his threat demonstrate), subverts the mind and the will. Even the fabulous birthday party and his soon-to-be-legendary practical joke were made possible, and indeed necessary, by the Ring. Bilbo says that they were his vain attempt to cozen himself into giving it away painlessly by giving away everything else along with it. So, the prospect of life without it is painful enough that he must trick himself into letting it go.

As Bilbo's wrath runs off, his sense of humor returns, but what was so wry before has now become rueful. And still the Ring remains in his pocket even after he again agrees to give it up. Another nudge from Gandalf, another twitch of reluctance, another flash of anger, and the Ring is finally delivered up—and with it, Bilbo himself. Only then comes the laughter of heart's ease. And off Bilbo goes on a new adventure with dwarves, trying perhaps to return to who he was before the Ring. His feet are now "eager" for the road (FR 1.i.35). As if to confirm his recovery and essential goodness, the letters and gifts Bilbo leaves behind for his friends and relations remind us of the generosity and wit he displayed before putting on the Ring at his party (1.i.37). "He felt better at once," Gandalf later tells Frodo (1.ii.48).

Bilbo's struggle to relinquish the Ring begins the illumination of its power, and no study of that could be complete without a detailed examination of this scene. Indeed, were it practical, I would quote the scene in its entirety. The gravity of the Ring is so strong that it can pull the Ring-bearer out of himself, as it were, so that he takes an action he does not remember, or one he cannot comprehend his motivations for. It undermines the will and the character even as it prolongs life and the appearance of youth. The bonds of friendship and trust and the need to keep promises diminish under its influence. The Ring-bearer becomes "thin and stretched" morally and physically (FR 1.ii.47). When he feels his possession of it threatened, as Bilbo does, he turns into someone who resembles Gollum.

Bilbo thus also serves as the reader's first introduction to Gollum in *The Lord of the Rings*. So, if we are to believe Gandalf, which it seems we are, since Bilbo doesn't dispute the accuracy of the comparison, what does this passage tell us of Gollum? Explicitly? That he called the Ring "My Precious," that he would have killed Bilbo if he could, and that he called Bilbo a thief. Implicitly? The words that prompt Gandalf to see the likeness between Bilbo and Gollum reveal someone who dotes on the Ring with a most jealous gaze, a vigilant eye of resentment, solicitude and suspicion. And even if Bilbo has become such a person only for this instant, it is still enough to tell us of Gollum and to suggest why he might have wished to kill Bilbo, called him thief, and declared his hatred forever.

As he will remain for most of *The Lord of the Rings*, the Gollum we glimpse here is a shadow cast from offstage, a murderous, resentful ghost from the past, summoned into the present by Bilbo's words and deeds on the night of the party. He may also be seen as a harbinger of what Bilbo might permanently become if he does not let go of the Ring and become free. But we see him only through Bilbo, who is also the source of all Gandalf's current knowledge, and there is at this point no hint that he will ever enter this Tale—nor would we want him to. We begin with a negative image, however darkly reflected through Bilbo.

A related question arises, if we are considering the effects of the Ring. Bilbo feels better the moment he no longer has it. What about Gollum? Keep in mind that so far readers know nothing more about him than *The Hobbit* told them, or than "A Long-expected Party" suggests. But is recovery of some kind possible for him? Bilbo's experience allows us to suspect that it might be. We shall return to this question more than once as we consider the influence of the Ring. For now, we don't even know if Gollum still lives.

In the end, however, Bilbo chooses to trust in Gandalf and let go of the Ring, to "stop possessing it," which has two ironic consequences (FR 1.i.34). First, it makes him more like the Gollum of the 1937 *Hobbit*, the Gollum of the lie, who was going to give Bilbo the Ring as a gift for winning the riddle game, than the Gollum of the 1951 *Hobbit*, the true Gollum, savage and murderous. Second, it means that Frodo actually receives the Ring as a birthday present, the very thing Gollum falsely claimed the Ring was to him. So, the Ring passes on to Frodo, who arrives from the party not long after Bilbo has departed. Discovering that Bilbo has left him the Ring, Frodo is surprised, but not displeased: "Still, it may be useful" (1.i.36).

Gandalf does not overlook Frodo's remark about the Ring's utility, and neither should we. This is especially so, since the very next morning, during the uncomfortable visit by the Sackville-Bagginses, he is already contemplating the usefulness of the Ring he had inherited the night before: "I longed to disappear" (FR 1.i.38, 40).

TWO FRODOS AND ONE RING

In his commentary on *Beowulf*, Tolkien states, "Heathobard tradition must nevertheless have contained at least two Fródas: one the historical father of their last king Ingeld, and one the remoter (perhaps mythical) ancestor: the Fróda of the Great Peace" (*Beowulf T&C* 331). The historical Fróda died in battle against Hrothgar, who then sought to make peace by marrying his daughter to Fróda's son, Ingeld, but Ingeld broke faith and attacked Heorot, burning it down and dying in the process; the mythical Fróda lived in the days of Augustus and Christ, and during his halcyon reign a gold ring could lie beside the highway without a thief to pick it up. That last detail should certainly sound familiar, since Faramir, speaking of the Ring, says to Frodo that he "would not take this thing if it lay by the highway" (TT 4.v.671, 681). Readers of Appendix F, moreover, will know that if the form of Frodo's name were true to the native language of the Hobbits, he would actually be Fróda (RK App. F 1135).

In *The Lord of the Rings*, we may also glimpse two Frodos, so to speak: the one who claims the Ring for his own on Mount Doom and the other whom Gandalf and Sam both see shining with an inner light, that is, the Frodo who takes the Ring as his burden (FR 2.i.223; RK 4.iv.652). In these their most extreme forms, we recognize a likeness to the divided self of Sméagol and Gollum, or Slinker and Stinker, as Sam calls them. We may also reflect on how Bilbo can do things under the Ring's influence that he doesn't remember or doesn't understand. Frodo's flaws and virtues, however, are fully integrated, woven together to make a single person.

Then, too, his flaws are small in comparison to those of others as well as to his own virtues, so much so that Bilbo and Gandalf can consider him the best hobbit in the Shire (FR 1.viii.140). The problem with Frodo is that he undertakes so much and suffers so much, with such courage and nobility, that it is easy to miss his flaws, which are important even if small. We can thus overlook how the pull of the Ring corrupts us through both our virtues and vices by seeming to offer the power to do good or evil. This is what Gandalf and Galadriel fear in the Ring (1.ii.61, 2.vii.365-66). This is what Boromir doesn't understand (2.ii.267, 2.x.397-400). This is what Sam sees—and sees through—in Mordor (RK 6.i.900-01).

These scenes—in which the virtuous and the honorable face temptations of their own making, conjured in their hearts by the meeting of the Ring's power and their own good intentions—are among the most dramatic and moving in *The Lord of the Rings*. Each plays off Frodo's own continuing experience with the Ring, which is framed very differently from theirs. For the others a time comes when they see quite vividly what they would do with the Ring, but there is little trace of such a moment for Frodo. If Frodo is in fact the narrator of *The Lord of the Rings*, as he certainly was of the book he handed to Sam, then his silence becomes especially intriguing (RK 6.ix.1026-27). It is also true that of the others only Sam ever does more than briefly touch the Ring. He wears it and soon finds himself tempted, through his desire to do good. Frodo, too, will have been tempted in this way, by means of his desire to save the Shire (FR 1.ii.60-62). We needn't imagine that Frodo is thinking of the good of the Shire in the instant he claims the Ring to recognize that the temptation to take advantage of its usefulness would start here. Such a justification would not have been far from his thoughts. As the Ring-bearer he will have been subject to the pull of the Ring for years in ways unguessed and unnoticed until, like Bilbo discovering the Ring unexpectedly back in his pocket, "he found that," while meaning to destroy it, he had claimed it instead (1.ii.60).

So, we cannot dismiss scenes like those I drew attention to above, where Frodo declares that the Ring could be useful or where he toys anxiously with it in his pocket during the Sackville-Bagginses' visit. It is the very usefulness of the Ring that makes it so tempting. Frodo's offhand, bemused, remark sums it up nicely. Frodo will try to use its power for more than invisibility. If we overlook his faults and mistakes, we will not fully appreciate his character, and, since he is our main example of the effects of the Ring, we will misunderstand the Ring. A brief example will suffice to illustrate the interplay between the two.

Early in "The Shadow of the Past" we learn that once Frodo grew accustomed to "being his own master and *the* Mr. Baggins of Bag End," he rather enjoyed it (FR 1.ii.43). In a society like the Shire, where class matters, such a statement carries a great deal of weight. Like Bilbo before him, Frodo is a "gentlehobbit," to use the Gaffer's phrase; his closest friends, Meriadoc Brandybuck and Peregrin Took, are heirs to the Shire's most important and illustrious families (1.i.22).[9] As *the* Mr. Baggins, Frodo can expect a certain deference from others, like the Gamgees and the other hobbits featured in the pub scenes in both of the first two chapters (at least when face to face). Indeed, working for Mr. Bilbo Baggins confers a status and authority that the Gaffer would not otherwise possess (1.i.22). We may thus suspect a bit of snobbery in Frodo's pleasure in being the master of Bag End, and we can find some confirmation of this in his statement that at times he has "thought the inhabitants [of the Shire] too stupid and dull for words, and ha[s] felt that an earthquake or an invasion of dragons might be good for them" (1.ii.62). As we shall discover later, at this point he felt much the same about Big People (2.i.220-21). His attitude here toward his fellow hobbits, however, is that of someone who at least sometimes believes not only that he knows better than others—which to a degree he does—but also that he knows what's best for them.

What has any of this to do with the Ring? It is precisely his position as *the* Mr. Baggins of Bag End that the decidedly snobbish Sackville-Bagginses come to contest, precisely Frodo's membership in the family that motivates Lobelia's sneer at the Brandybucks, and precisely the unpleasantness of this encounter that first tempts him to use the Ring, even though Gandalf had warned him against it only the night before (FR 1.i.36, 38-39). It is also the threat to the Shire posed by the Ring which begins to shake Frodo out of his parochial snobbishness and moves him (since destroying the Ring in his parlor isn't an option) to volunteer to save the Shire by going into "exile, a flight from danger into danger, drawing it after me" (1.ii.62).[10]

Where the Ring is concerned, then, every facet of the human character is involved. Consequently, if we limit our inquiry only to Frodo's many good points, our understanding of Frodo and of the Ring will suffer. This, I think, is a problem faced often but by no means exclusively by scholars who examine *The Lord of the Rings* from a Christian perspective, not always successfully.[11] By focusing too narrowly on how Frodo suffers and sacrifices to save the Shire and destroy the Ring, we can develop a simple image of him as saintly or even messianic. Yet, the longer Frodo has the Ring and the closer he comes to the source of its power, the more both darkness and light grow within him and advance his weary feet. Without the chiaroscuro the shadow of his faults brings to his nobility, our understanding can only be incomplete.

If anything, Frodo is not a messianic figure because he fails the final test, as every human would.[12] Human strength even at its limit cannot prevail against the Ring and Sauron. The best it can accomplish is to come to the brink of victory, where an ineffable Providence, by bringing Bilbo first to the Ring and then to pity, takes a hand. Both Frodo's virtues and his flaws bring him to the Cracks of Doom, but they cannot bring him further. Nevertheless, his failures may yet be held to prefigure the victory of Christ in a battle that is greater still, in which he triumphs, as only he could—because only he is fully human and fully divine. Again, the religion is certainly there, not obviously but fundamentally so, just as Tolkien said it was.[13]

A perfect illustration of the importance of Christianity to Tolkien's work and of the subtlety with which he handles it is the date of Sauron's downfall, 25 March. In the Christian calendar, that is the date of the Annunciation, as is fairly well known among Christians. Less well known is that in Early Medieval England it was also held to be the date on which Adam and Eve fell and Christ was crucified. The Fall, the Annunciation, and the Crucifixion all on the same date certainly demonstrate the significance of the Ring's destruction and Sauron's downfall. Or they would do if Tom Shippey had not had to point them out to us (*Author* 208). Likewise, the Company departed Rivendell on 25 December, so that, as Shippey says, "the main action of *The Lord of the Rings* takes place, then, in the mythic space between Christmas, Christ's birth, and the Crucifixion, Christ's death" (208–09).[14] Yet, to know this date requires reading "The Tale of Years" in Appendix B. So again, Christianity is fundamental but not obvious. If it were, Stratford Caldecott, writing on Tolkien from a Christian perspective, could not have said that "the majority of his readers [were] not aware" that he was "a devout Roman Catholic" (1); nor could Ronald Hutton, who argues for a more pagan Tolkien, have said that *The Hobbit* and *The Lord of the* Rings "are enjoyed by huge numbers of readers who lack any sense that these books are specifically Christian works" (91). Jonathan S. McIntosh has recently put it nicely: "Yet an important distinction needs to be made (and which not all Tolkien's readers have succeeded in making) between Eru's unquestionable, palpable presence in Tolkien's fictional world at the metaphysical level, that is to say, at the level of the world's being and existence, and Eru's comparative absence at the narrative or historical level" (59). The point here is not to single out for criticism or refutation the Christian scholars who have made valuable contributions to the evolution of our understanding of *The Lord of the Rings* in particular and of the legendarium in general.[15] Rather, it is to suggest that *any* scholarly approach to this subject must examine every aspect of the Ring and those who interact with it. Even without Tolkien's express statements on the inherence of Christianity in his work, its importance cannot be denied or ignored. It can, however, be overemphasized, and the theological, metaphysical, and philosophical cornerstones that lie at the foundation of his legendarium and *The Lord of the Rings* can be improperly thrust into the foreground. As scholars have recently begun to see, Tolkien, like the *Beowulf*-poet before him, composed a work at the border of two worlds, the pagan and Christian, and draws from them both.[16]

Another perspective we must consider, if we mean to assess the Ring and its effects on those around it, is Tom Shippey's explanation of the Ring as "addictive," which was classic and persuasive even before Andy Serkis and Elijah Wood adopted it in their performances in Peter Jackson's films (*Road* 139–40). No opinion of Shippey's on Tolkien is without weight, nor am I rejecting this valuable approach (see on pages 163–64). Yet, I would argue that the power of the Ring has an inevitable effect that ultimately cannot be resisted even by those who have not previously tasted of its power as the addict has tasted of the drug. "Were it buried beneath the roots of Mindolluin, still it would burn your mind away," says Gandalf to Denethor (*RK* 5.iv.814). Its allure is beyond mere temptation. If it is there, whether used or unused, it will corrupt in the end. In this way, its power is far more like gravity, whose effect is proportional to mass and distance. The great feel the pull of the Ring more profoundly than the small; the near feel it more than the far. No rejection of the Ring is final, not even Faramir's.

TRUTH, LIES, PITY, THE RING

At the beginning of this chapter, I hinted at a paradox. Gandalf feels certain that in the end the "Pity of Bilbo will rule the fate of many," Frodo included, yet he also indicates that pity offers no defense against the Ring. Bilbo's pity is for the unpitiable, which Gandalf urges on Frodo against all the claims of justice. Gandalf knows the truth about Gollum, as he knows the truth about himself: the Ring would devour him, too, and turn him into a far more frightful monster. Jane Chance hits the nail on the head when she says that the "hero must realize that he can become a monster"—or in this case, *the* monster—a statement that neatly summarizes the reality Gandalf is trying to get across to Frodo (*Mythology* 147). Bilbo saw the truth about Gollum for himself, on the day he first found the Ring and as he was desperately trying to escape with his life. Seeing the truth of Gollum's life, he found pity, though Gollum was howling out hatred.

Just as truth lies at the heart of pity, so lies lurk at the heart of the Ring. From the instant he let Gollum try to answer his impossible and unfair question about the contents of his pocket, Bilbo was playing false. And if this deceit is justifiable under the circumstances, the lie he tells everyone for the next half century is not. As a result, the second lie makes the first a part of its own story. It may be a less sickening lie than the one Gollum tells about his birthday present, but it has proved so only because seeing the truth about Gollum led Bilbo to pity from murder.

Between the lie and the pity the struggle of the Ring-bearers reveals not only their humanity but also the nature and effects of the Ring. Gollum's journey and near repentance, Frodo's journey and his failure, and Sam's own slow, punctuated education in pity, are the most proximate to the Ring, but the temptations of Boromir and Galadriel, for example, and Bombadil and Faramir's apparent indifference to the Ring intersect with these in significant ways. So, too, do the increasingly close encounters of Frodo with evil in the form of Black Riders and the Eye of Sauron. By examining these and other moments in detail, we will come closer to understanding the tale of power Tolkien is telling and how he may reconcile the paradox of the necessity of pity that does not defend us.

CHAPTER TWO

Bilbo's Pity and the Ring

THE UNCHANGING MR. BAGGINS

Just as the first two chapters of *The Lord of the* Rings both invoke the memory of "Riddles in the Dark," each also starts with an emphasis on time. In "A Long-expected Party," the passage of the years without apparent effect on Bilbo hints at trouble to come, which the party festivities allay, but only in public. Privately it is clear, as Gandalf says to Bilbo even before their conversation grows ugly, that he has "had [the Ring] quite long enough" (FR 1.i.33). And Bilbo concedes—before discovering the Ring in his pocket—"it's time that [Frodo] was his own master now," a part of which includes leaving him the Ring with everything else (1.i.33).

Even the title of the first chapter invites us to think of time: long-expected by whom? Certainly not by the hobbits who learn of the party just a few short weeks before it takes place. It must refer to Bilbo, just as "An Unexpected Party," the first chapter of *The Hobbit*, does. This question leads to the next: how long had Bilbo been expecting it? The text offers two clues, both related to the Ring, one directly, the other indirectly. Twelve years earlier, when he was ninety-nine, Bilbo had become indignantly aware of how "*well-preserved*" other hobbits said he was (FR 1.i.21, 32). The gossipy notice taken of his age may not be unconnected to his adoption of Frodo that same year, thus making him his heir, a point the chapter revisits several times (1.i.21, 31–33, 36, 39). Is this how long he's been waiting for this party, so he can leave and find the rest he says he needs, and write the happy ending he has thought of for his book? To be sure, Bilbo avers his mind was long since made up to go, but he also later concedes that he has actually been unable to do so (FR 1.i.25, 34). In conjunction with Frodo's adoption, with the remarks of his fellow hobbits, with the joint birthday parties he throws for himself and Frodo every year, this indecision suggests that Bilbo has wanted to have *this party* for a very long time. It is the end of a long process.

Significantly connected with Bilbo's desire for rest, and preliminary to it to judge by his phrasing, is another desire: "I want to see mountains again, Gandalf, *mountains,* and then find somewhere where I can *rest....* I might find somewhere where I can finish my book. I have thought of a nice ending for it: *and he lived happily ever after to the end of his days*" (FR 1.i.32). The emphasis in these sentences is original, and so it represents the character's idea of the importance of these three elements, the second and third of which we have already noted. The first, moreover, he repeats and expands on a moment later, qualifying his desire with "before I die" (1.i.33). Thus, the pressure of time is relevant here, too, as Bilbo seems to be seeking to recover a vision of the world he has lost because of the Ring, which has increasingly become the central object of his attention and anxiety, even as it feels "like an eye looking at me" and he is left wishing he could just put it on and disappear.

Two opposite progressions are at work here, and not for the last time. The pull of the Ring commands Bilbo's focus more and more as time goes on, denying him rest and occluding his sight of other things. By contrast, seeing the mountains once more before death seems to promise to lead to rest and happiness until death. As Bilbo's words suggest, the Ring has denied him the fairy-tale ending he longs for, and his one hope of attaining it is to renew his vision of the world. But first, he must renounce the Ring.

It is noteworthy that Bilbo's notion of what he needs so resembles the elements of escape, recovery, and consolation that Tolkien was enumerating at just this time in another text he was writing, his essay "On Fairy-stories." More revealing for our immediate purposes, however, is that not only does possession of the Ring deny the Ring-bearer a fairy-tale ending, it also threatens to strip away the gentler aspects of his humanity. We have seen how quickly kindness can yield to anger, paranoia, and violence. Here we see a restlessness and unhappiness and a loss of the power and meaning of home, which was so essential to the Bilbo of *The Hobbit* even as he grew and changed.[1] The homecoming for which he longed has been cheated of its final significance. With the Ring, there will be no happily ever after, and Bilbo's days shall prove interminably long. Without it, however, he is free to begin moving toward both.

"The Shadow of the Past" also begins with attention to the passage of time, now for Frodo in the years after Bilbo's departure, who seems to harmlessly embrace the eccentricity that was as much Bilbo's legacy as the Ring was, continuing to hold joint birthday parties and lead hobbit walking parties but also being seen out at night alone nowhere near Bag End, perhaps visiting the Elves. Yet this eccentricity is only the beginning of the likeness. Frodo shares the same signs of preservation that had disquieted those who knew Bilbo and no doubt with all the expectation of trouble to come that such queerness entails. He believes the age of fifty portentous, since Bilbo had been that old when he first bade Gandalf good morning. Like the older Bilbo, however, he is already without rest and eager for a sight of a world different from the one he has known, that same world Bilbo thought might give him the fairy-tale ending he had been unable to find in the Shire in possession of the Ring. Also like the older Bilbo, he is of two minds. He cannot bring himself to go.

Frodo's regret about not following his beloved uncle is understandable but also curious, since it grows on him as the effect of the Ring does. The oddness here is that it suggests a part of Frodo already wishes he had never received his legacy, a desire that will become more prominent once he begins to learn the truth about the Ring. For had he left with Bilbo, he never would have received the Ring. A part of Bilbo did not want to give it up, and yet he had also told Frodo the true story of the Ring, as if he did not wish to make Frodo an heir to the lie he had "told the Dwarves and put in his book" (FR 1.i.40). Even so, when Bilbo told Frodo the truth, he ended by emphasizing that the Ring "is mine anyway." Again, Bilbo concedes the truth, yet denies its relevance.

For all that this chapter begins with its focus on Frodo in the years after Bilbo's departure, the perspective deepens quite soon. It reaches back across thousands of years to the forging of the One Ring before returning to Frodo's present, but always with a view to the future. And with that deepening comes a broadening. Not just Frodo's future is in peril, as was the case with Bilbo, but the Shire's and all of Middle-earth's. The background of this perspective first comes into view in the dire news of the world outside reaching the Shire. Until now, this part of the story of the Ring had been as blank as the white spaces that surround the Shire on hobbit maps. No overt connection is made at first, but we may suspect it in the conversation at The Green Dragon, with its unequal blend of sympathy and denial at the troublous news of the world outside. How different this conversation is from that at The Ivy Bush in "A Long-expected Party," where local gossip was all they knew or cared about. As we have seen, however, that local gossip was not wholly off the mark, and even many years later Frodo could feel the sting of it in Farmer Maggot's shrewd connection of the Black Riders to Bilbo's old adventures

(FR 1.iv.94–95). The story of the Ring will affect these folk, too, now and not just through the outrageous pranks of a Baggins.

With Gandalf's return after a long absence, his first words to Frodo tie this moment to his conversation with Bilbo: "All well eh? ... You look the same as ever, Frodo" (FR 1.ii.46). We know, however, that the state of his preservation is an illusion, a lie that conceals the truth that within he does not feel the same, but restless and on his way to feeling as Bilbo had (1.i.32). Similarly, the usefulness of the invisibility conferred by the Ring is a lie. Bilbo used this power as soon as he found it, and we saw Frodo contemplate doing so the moment he received it. We never learn how often Frodo may have used the Ring over the years, yet, given the hints we saw in "A Long-expected Party" and a statement Galadriel makes later—"Only thrice have you set the Ring upon your finger since you knew what you possessed" (2.vii.366)—we can conclude that he probably did so more than once in the seventeen years between "A Long-expected Party" and "The Shadow of the Past." But the invisibility Bilbo found so useful in *The Hobbit* became in the end a desire simply to disappear. Not only is deception in the form of lies and illusions an effect of the Ring's power, but the advantages it confers prove disadvantages, too, as will soon be brought home to Frodo.

Gandalf wastes little time filling Frodo in about the true nature of the Ring in his pocket and connecting it to the world that lies in those blank spaces beyond the borders of the Shire. "Something dark and deadly was at work" in Bilbo on the night of his party, he says, something he has since been on a Quest of his own to fathom (FR 1.ii.48). The danger of this Ring lies in its irresistible power, which will ultimately possess its possessor:

> A mortal, Frodo, who keeps one of the Great Rings, does not die, but he does not grow or obtain more life, he merely continues, until at last every minute is a weariness. And if he often uses the Ring to make himself invisible, he fades: he becomes in the end invisible permanently, and walks in the twilight under the eye of the Dark Power that rules the Rings. Yes, sooner or later—later, if he is strong or well-meaning to begin with, but neither strength nor good purpose will last—sooner or later the Dark Power will devour him.
> (1.ii.47)

All is revealed here. The preservation, the changeless youth, the useful invisibility are deceptions. Yet let us be clear. The deception is not one of false pretenses—the only sign of intent here is in the one wielding the Ring—but of the false appearances that are an effect of its power and that encourage the bearer to lie to himself as he is drawn into the darkness. Strength and character, traits one might imagine could defend against the Ring, are also finally irrelevant. They, too, are deceptions, as "The Shadow of the Past" demonstrates.

As Frodo confronts the fuller implications of Bilbo's legacy, he asks how long Gandalf has known, and how much Bilbo had known of, questions that suggest he is wondering if they both had lied to him, just as Bilbo had lied to everyone else. Though Gandalf allays Frodo's fears about Bilbo, assuring him that Bilbo would never have knowingly imperiled him, the Ring's power to threaten the bonds of love and friendship reappears.

When Frodo continues to press Gandalf about his knowledge, the wizard responds by talking about his suspicions of Bilbo's account of how he came by the Ring. Clearly, Gandalf knew a fairy tale when he heard one. Yet it took him quite some time, perhaps as many as fifty years, to discover the truth: "that [Bilbo] had been trying to put his claim to the ring beyond doubt. Much like Gollum with his 'birthday present.' The lies were too much alike for my comfort" (FR 1.ii.48).[2] Again, we see a lie bound to a keeper coming into possession of the Ring, even though Gandalf does not yet disclose why he believes Gollum was lying.

We also see Bilbo more openly likened to Gollum than we have before, and the points that Gandalf goes on to make underline what we saw in "A Long-expected Party." Now it is not the parochial Shire-folk commenting on Bilbo's preservation and expecting trouble to come of it, but one of the Wise of Middle-earth, who has a much better idea of the peril a Great Ring might pose. We learn that Bilbo had a history of resentment and anger when pressed about the Ring and that his outburst the night he left Bag End was new only in its extremity. "Clearly the ring had an unwholesome power that set to work on its keeper at once," that is to say, in the very moment that both Bilbo and Gollum sought to cover with a lie (FR 1.ii.48).

To Frodo's credit, his concern now shifts to Bilbo's well-being, Gandalf's response to which is revealing. Just as the corrupting effect of the Ring begins immediately, so, too, does recovery once the Ring is relinquished. Gandalf even echoes his own words when he says that Bilbo "felt better *at once*" (FR 1.ii.48, emphasis mine). Two points are worth noting here. First, the pull of the Ring diminishes slowly, especially on one who possessed it for a long time, as Bilbo did. Second, how one comes to be no longer in possession of the Ring is important. Bilbo gave it up voluntarily, even if he needed considerable nudging. He would have been harmed mentally had Gandalf forced him to give it up (1.ii.49; see also 1.ii.60). While we could not say that Bilbo took the Ring from Gollum by force, Gollum certainly did not surrender it willingly—as he seemed prepared to do in Bilbo's lie about the Riddle Game—but regarded Bilbo as a thief. He also bore the Ring far longer than Bilbo did, and thus the link established between them suggests that the loss of the Ring will affect him quite differently.

But of course, the link between Bilbo and Gollum is not the only, or even the most important, one. The Ring connects Frodo to Sauron and the Shire to Mordor, as Gandalf now makes explicit. His list of Hobbit names recalls the one Bilbo recited at his party. Yet how different the context is. Bilbo wished to know and like them better; Sauron will as gladly enslave them out of "malice and revenge" (FR 1.ii.49). When a mystified Frodo asks, "Revenge for what?" Gandalf's reply is so indirect as to seem no answer at all. He begins by proving the ring to be the One Ring by tossing it into the fireplace—to Frodo's considerable dismay—and then recounts how Sauron had it taken from him in The War of the Last Alliance. He remarks how the Ring was lost in the river Anduin "and passed out of knowledge and legend" (1.ii.52).

It is perfectly fitting then that the tale as he now continues to tell it takes on, at least at first, a fairy-tale air. "Long after, but still very long ago, there lived by the banks of the Great River on the edge of Wilderland a clever-handed and quiet-footed little people. I guess they were of hobbit-kind." (FR 1.ii.52). It sounds like a passage early in *The Hobbit* that conjures in much the same way: "By some curious chance one morning long ago in the quiet of the world, when there was less noise and more green, and the hobbits were still numerous and prosperous" (H 31). Even the names, Sméagol and Déagol, have the ring of the rhyming sets of dwarves who knock on Bilbo's door in the first chapter of *The Hobbit*. Yet fairy-tale beginnings are as inimical to the Ring as fairy-tale endings. With the discovery of the Ring, the tale turns swiftly. The comedy of Déagol being pulled under by the fish becomes the horror of Sméagol calling him "my love" three times before murdering him for his birthday present (FR 1.ii.53).

The absurd lie—as Gandalf calls it—that Gollum's grandmother gave him the Ring for his birthday seeks to conceal the dread lie of "my love" (FR 1.ii.56). Hammond and Scull rightly identify Gollum's use of this phrase as "a form of address to a friend or companion" (RC 87). Yet, its reiteration over Déagol's shoulder as his death draws steadily closer is scarcely trivial. The colloquialism here bears a nightmarish weight of irony, which warns more vividly than Bilbo's threat in "A Long-expected Party" that the pull of the Ring breaks every bond. Together these lies hint at Sméagol's potential depravity from the beginning. Despite being intelligent and of a good family, he seems to have always been strangely different: "The most inquisitive and curious-minded of that family was called Sméagol. He was interested in roots and beginnings; he dived into deep pools; he burrowed under trees and growing plants; he tunnelled into green mounds; and he ceased to look up at the hill-tops, or the leaves on the trees, or the flowers opening in the air: his head and his eyes were downward" (FR 1.ii.52–53).

The substance and movement of this description is revealing. Sméagol is always seeking but never finding. He dives, burrows, tunnels, ignoring what is green and alive around him. This is quite unlike the others of his kind we meet, who may dwell in holes in the ground but cherish the natural world in which they live. Their attitude is part of the very bones of the story, from Bilbo's famous conversation outside his front door with Gandalf, on a morning when "the sun was shining, and the grass was very green," to the evocative descriptions of the lands through which they travel in *The Lord of the Rings* (H 33).

Note also how each clause of the expanding structure of the second sentence in the paragraph just quoted includes a new element, until the clause after the last semicolon ("and he ceased") where the use of *or* begins to exclude the life and beauties of the world above, and this leads to the final full colon and the verdict: "his head and his eyes were downward." Like Melkor long before him, he has turned himself away and lost all love, and can look upon others only with envy and malice (S 65–66). Despite his intelligence and his sweet addresses to Déagol, he has no love in him.

Unlike Saint Peter, however, no cock crows to announce the dawn and pierce Sméagol's heart with repentance. For him only more darkness will come. Soon, the invisibility conferred by the Ring allows him to learn "secrets, and he put his knowledge to crooked and malicious uses. He became sharp-eyed and keen-eared for all that was hurtful. The ring had given him power according to his stature" (FR 1.ii.53). Like the description of his downward looking nature, this, too, ends in a verdict. The malice of Gollum (the name he has now earned from his revolted family) will play a role as important in the end as the Pity of Bilbo. It also links him from the first to Sauron, to whom Gandalf has already attributed malice as a motive (1.ii.49).

Gollum's family now "shunned" and "kicked him" because of what he had become. Finally, his sneaking and spying and thieving caused such strife that "his grandmother, desiring peace, expelled him from the family and turned him out of her hole" (FR 1.ii.53–54). *His own grandmother disowned him.* Again, we have something that passes for a judgement—if being cast out by your own grandmother out is not damning, what is? Alone with the Ring, he becomes more animal-like, catching fish by hand rather than a hook; he resents the Sun which, he believes, is watching him and whose light and heat pain him. He still looks for secrets and beginnings, though, and in doing so he becomes the greatest secret of the mountain darkness in which he hides.

The three judgements offered here bring together several noteworthy points. The first and the last not only further establish the portrait of Gollum as repulsive, vicious, and dangerous even to his friends and loved ones, but they also demonstrate how quickly and powerfully the Ring can affect those nearby. This is especially the case when the person nearby is open to the temptations that such power can bring, as Sméagol appears to have been. At the same time, the way one comes into possession of the Ring matters. The murder of Déagol to gain the Ring plunges Sméagol headlong down his dark path, which mirrors how swiftly Bilbo's recovery began once he surrendered, a reflection made all the more telling by Bilbo's own near violence when he supposed Gandalf wanted the Ring. Yet Gandalf is no weak, unsuspecting prey like Déagol, and the wizard's ability to daunt Bilbo into backing away from violence is essential to the old hobbit's healing.

The most fascinating of these three verdicts, however, is the second: "The ring had given [Gollum] power according to his stature," which, despite the humor latent in such a remark about someone probably about three and a half feet tall, is finally no joke at all. For, as Gandalf has already told us, possession and use of the Ring inevitably result in the keeper's destruction. Yet what precisely Tolkien means here by *stature* is not at first apparent, since it does not match well any of the meanings the OED gives the word. We find some help in the statement Galadriel makes when she warns Frodo for his own safety not to try to use the Ring to dominate others: "Did not Gandalf tell you that the rings give power according to the measure of each possessor?" (FR 2.viii.366). *Stature* then stands metaphorically for a condition of mind or spirit in which one person can be larger than another.

Still, I suggest that there's more to stature here than the notion that Gollum received the power he did because he was mean in spirit. While this statement is true, further investigation of Tolkien's use of *stature* will repay our scrutiny. We can begin by noting that every use of it in *The Lord of the Rings* but one employs the most basic meaning of the word, that is, height or size

(FR 1.ii.53; 2.i.226; TT 3.i.415, ii.431, 433, vi.522; 4.iv.657; RK 5.1.749, ii.777, iii.803; 6.vi.975; App. A 1060). The exception is found in "The Tale of Aragorn and Arwen" in Appendix A: "But Aragorn was grown to full stature of body and mind" (RK 1.v.1060). Here, too, we see the word in a nonphysical sense. This use of the word and indeed almost this very phrase appears in "The Akallabêth" to describe the effect living in Númenor had upon the Dúnedain, who "dwelt under the protection of the Valar and in the friendship of the Eldar, and they increased in stature both of mind and body" (S 261-62).

Their stature increases because of their association with others *of greater stature*, because that is what the Valar and the Eldar of the Undying Lands are. This suggests that *stature* refers at least in part to the capacity of those to whom the word is applied, which harmonizes with Galadriel's use of *measure* when speaking to Frodo. Tolkien in fact elsewhere uses *stature* to denote differences of degree among the Children of Ilúvatar. In Letter 200 he refers to Men and Elves as "of less 'stature' [than the Ainur], and yet of the same order," and again in Letter 156 as "having a relation to the Creator equal to [the Ainur], if of different stature" (260, 203). In both of these letters, moreover, the point is made that it is wrong for those of greater stature to dominate those of lesser stature by force or intimidation, which is, of course, the whole purpose of the Ring. Letter 246 presents one of Tolkien's most intriguing and touching readings of his own text, discussing how things might have gone differently at The Cracks of Doom, had Gollum repented on the stairs of Cirith Ungol (329-30). While speculative and written a decade after he had completed *The Lord of the Rings*, this discussion employs *stature* in the same way, tying it in to the present and potential stature of Gollum and Frodo and the power for domination the Ring affords.

Stature is thus innate and hierarchical among the Children of Ilúvatar, but it is not wholly fixed or limited. The Valar and Maiar—the "offspring of his thought"—are greater in stature than the Eldar, the Eldar greater than the Dúnedain, both of whom surpass their kindred who remained in Middle-earth (S 15). From the references to Hobbits, it seems that the other sentient peoples also fit in here, though it remains impossible to be specific about their place or capacity. Still, this explains why Gandalf can speak only of mortals when he tells Frodo how a mortal with a Ring of Power will fade into a wraith. Immortals would not disappear or become wraiths; Elrond, Galadriel, and Gandalf have long worn and wielded such rings without suffering this fate, and even the One Ring cannot make Tom Bombadil invisible—quite the contrary, in fact. The ineffable Bombadil aside, however, the Ring is even more perilous for those whose stature is more commensurate with its power. On them, its pull would be all the greater.

Taking the three judgements together once more and applying them to Gollum, we see that not only can one's stature become greater, as it did for the Dúnedain under the influence of the Valar and the Eldar, but it can also grow less. Before he feels the Ring's pull, he is a strange and perhaps misguided hobbit; afterward all his flaws are intensified and warped into a sneaking paranoia that would strike the sun for watching him too closely. And the verdict on the Ring's power and Gollum's stature holds the balance between his old and his new lives: the first power the Ring gives him is the will to murder a friend even as he professes his love for him. As the Ring empowers him, it demeans him, confounding love and malice. Expelled from home and family, treated like an animal and biting like one, catching fish with his hands and eating them raw, Sméagol becomes less human, becomes Gollum, a thing aware of his fall but not comprehending it because of the lie:

> "Gollum," cried Frodo. "Gollum? Do you mean that this is the very Gollum-creature that Bilbo met? How loathsome!"
>
> "I think it is a sad story," said the wizard, "and it might have happened to others, even to some hobbits that I have known."
>
> "I can't believe that Gollum was connected with hobbits, however distantly," said Frodo with some heat. "What an abominable notion!"
>
> (FR 1.ii.54)

Frodo's initial reaction here is natural. When another human commits some atrocious act, we protect ourselves by imposing distance. We dehumanize them; we call them monsters or animals; we reduce them to creatures and things because we like to tell ourselves the lie that no one like us could do such a thing. Yet, within, we know that describing them so is a metaphor born of horror.[3] In response to Gandalf's reminder about hobbits, however, Frodo goes further. He declares himself unable to believe not that Gollum *was* a hobbit but that he was *connected* to Hobbits at any remove.[4] His passion borders on anger, and he dismisses the very idea with disgust. That's a lot of denial for one sentence.

It's also the second time in as many chapters that the temper of a hobbit and a Ring-bearer has flared when Gandalf suggests a connection to Gollum. Bilbo, having seen Gollum, did not deny the similarity. He denied its relevance, however, and went on to say and do things that frightened Gandalf for his friend's sake and made him fear for Frodo until this morning. It was the events of that night that led to Gandalf's having the story of Gollum to tell at all, a story that took him seventeen years to get to the bottom of. Frodo denies the possibility of a connection and even the humanity of Gollum. In doing so he inherits the lie, not the lie Gollum told or Bilbo told, but the lie of the Ring itself, whose power warps even our most natural responses and desires, just as gravity warps space, creating a well with an increasingly precipitous and irresistibly downward slope.

THE SHAPE OF LIES

In each case, the lie takes its shape from the desire of the Ring-bearer, or would-be Ring-bearer, to gain, keep, or use the Ring. Nor need that desire be evil in its beginning to prove so in its ending. Sméagol's first request for the Ring may well have been selfish and greedy, but did the desire become irresistibly murderous before Déagol's second refusal? When Bilbo allows his absentminded question about the object in his pocket to stand as his riddle, he *is* being tricksy and false, as Gollum might have put it, and when he deceives the dwarves to establish his place among them and his claim to the Ring, he is not being the honest burglar whose worth the Elven King later honors (H 125–26, 331). Yet, though born of fear for his life and insecurity about his claims to position and possession, these deceits lead to his threatening Gandalf sixty years later.

What of Frodo, then? His thought that the Ring might prove useful and his desire to use it to hide from the Sackville-Bagginses are innocent enough, but his heated denial of Gollum seeks to put distance between them, just as much as Gollum's insistence that the Ring was a birthday present from his grandmother seeks to distance him from Déagol's murder. And Frodo also pointedly fails to respond to Gandalf's suggestion that Bilbo could have turned into a Gollum himself, had things gone differently, which is as much an evasion as Bilbo's declaring any resemblance to Gollum irrelevant. Anything that might have happened to Bilbo because of the Ring may yet happen to Frodo.

Yet another seeming evasion or denial on Frodo's part may be seen in his failure to respond when Gandalf says Sméagol demanded the Ring from Déagol *as his birthday present*. Now Frodo knows both versions of Bilbo's tale, in which the birthday present is a constant. If that knowledge alone were not enough to prompt his memory, Gandalf has just mentioned it to him this very morning (FR 1.ii.48). How does Frodo not make the connection until Gandalf explicitly identifies Sméagol as Gollum? To be sure, Frodo is becoming increasingly terrified as Gandalf spells out the connections between the hand of Sauron and his own. Gandalf has implied that the Ring will in the end devour him, as it does everyone in time, and has said that Sauron will visit his malice and revenge on all the silly hobbits of the Shire (1.ii.49). But the text gives no hint that Frodo is not listening or is lost in thought. Even earlier, in the long silence after Gandalf's account of what Rings of Power do to mortals, he is clearly thinking about what Gandalf has told him (1.ii.47). And his outburst—"Do you mean..."—and the passion with which he speaks show he has been listening and rejecting what Gandalf has been saying and the implications of it for all hobbits, Bilbo, and himself.

A crucial and intimately related question we must also ask in this connection is why Gandalf does not openly say from the first that Sméagol and Gollum are one? But Gandalf is up to more than merely narrating the history of the Ring and trying to save the world. As we all know, one of the most important and often quoted sentences in *The Lord of the Rings* is Gandalf's assertion that Gollum "has some part to play yet, for good or for ill, before the end; and when that comes, the pity of Bilbo may rule the fate of many—yours not least" (FR 1.ii.59). How often we overlook those last three words! How often we scant them in our discussions of the role of Pity. We focus on the tides of fate, on seeming chance on the Rings of Power, and Towers White and Dark, and the Dooms of Elves and Men, Dwarves and Hobbits; and on the Pity that saves the world from a darkness deeper than any since Morgoth (1.vii.126, 1.ii.51). And it's easy to do so because Pity accomplishes precisely that. Those last three words seem almost an afterthought.

But Gandalf is a wizard and therefore subtle. As his words suggest when taken together, he gives thought to the fate of Middle-earth, the Shire, and Frodo, too. His pity reaches still farther, however, into the future and to all those in darkness (RK 5.iv.813–14). Indeed, Tolkien regarded pity as so essential a characteristic of Gandalf that when he subsequently wrote him into the legendarium, he made sure to point it out twice in as many paragraphs of "The Valaquenta." Pity seems to be fundamental to Gandalf's wisdom and ability to inspire and awaken hope in others and to be the chief lesson he learned from the Vala Nienna (S 30–31, 28). A contrast will make this still clearer. Tolkien revised the history and character of Galadriel over and over again from the moment she stepped fully formed into the woods of Lothlórien until the very end of his life.[5] Gandalf's pity from its inception in "The Shadow of the Past" is as constant as the Northern Star.

It is precisely because Gandalf is trying to elicit Frodo's pity that he suppresses the identity of Sméagol. He does so—and given Frodo's reaction, he is entirely correct in this—in the hopes of saving Frodo along with Middle-earth, but not even Gollum is absent from his thoughts. For, moved by pity and a desire to do an undeniable good, Gandalf deceives Frodo. He lies. We have seen how firmly embedded among the other hobbits of the Shire Bilbo was, and yet, the Ring also isolated him from them. So, too, Frodo. And Gollum nevertheless sought to return to his hobbit family despite the murder of Déagol, but that deed in the service of his lust for the Ring took him far beyond any eccentricity or queerness Bilbo and Frodo exhibited. It cut him off and made him a creature, a thing, as lonely and isolated as Grendel on his misty moors. From past anxieties about Bilbo to present worries about Frodo and pity for Gollum now that he has met him, Gandalf pursues a direct line of pity or compassion interlaced with concerns for the fate of Middle-earth as a whole. From this perspective, which perceives the connections between the great and the small, Gandalf sees the necessity to try to drive home the fact that Gollum is a hobbit and is to be pitied and that such compassion is of both personal and global importance. Thus, he lies.

Yet his attempt to cozen Frodo into pity fails, largely because Frodo is trammeled in his own self-protective lie—that Gollum could not conceivably be a Hobbit. Undeterred, Gandalf insists on it, averring that he knows more about the history of Hobbits than hobbits do and that Bilbo and Gollum understood each other as only two hobbits could (FR 1.ii.54). When Frodo again rejects this claim, Gandalf uses the assertion that Gollum is a hobbit to introduce his strongest plea for pitying Gollum on his own merits. He intimates that it was the Hobbit toughness in Gollum that kept him from being "wholly ruined" and left "not no hope" of a cure for the evil in him (1.ii.55). Nor is this suggestion a mere sop to Hobbit vanity. Even when deceiving Frodo, Gandalf was sincere in his intention to foster pity in him. He offers the notion that Gollum seldom wore the Ring as another part of the reason a cure is not out of the question. It was nevertheless "eating up his mind" (1.ii.55). The hope of a cure for Sméagol, the hobbit within Gollum, the creature, and the inevitability of his final corruption without some change, are both there by implication for Bilbo and Frodo. Bilbo began to recover at once. Why not Frodo? Gandalf tries to stir Frodo's memory of Bilbo's pity for Gollum, and more than that, he suggests that in meeting Bilbo Gollum had a moment in which he recalled and relished "a light out of the past.... memories of wind, and trees, and sun on the grass, and such forgotten things" (1.ii.54-55).

It all starts off with such promise. After hearing of the murderous, malicious, sneaking Gollum whose offenses were so rank that his own grandmother cast him out, who shook his fist at the sun, and who "wormed his way like a maggot into the heart of the hills," we are afforded a glimpse of the last remnant of Sméagol the hobbit, whom Bilbo the hobbit had touched (FR 1.ii.54). It's a rare moment of pure pity for Gollum, the last for a very long time, but also the first hint of the two Gollums Sam overhears in "The Passage of the Marshes" (TT 4.ii.632-34).

Yet Gandalf's pity is not blind. As the contrast he draws between the different aspects of Gollum illustrate, he sees that the largest part of his mind is evil. He does not ignore or conceal his repulsive deeds of ancient days when he still might have been called Sméagol, or suppress the "rumour of him" now current among the birds, beasts, and men of Mirkwood, of "a ghost that drank blood" robbing dens, nests, and cradles to satisfy its thirst (FR 1.ii.58). Gandalf has no illusions about the monster that has emerged from beneath the mountains to hunt Bilbo.

And Gollum's wickedness has attracted him ineluctably to Mordor, as if by some gravitational property inherent in the evil, and from there he has lately returned, so Gandalf thought, "on some errand of mischief" (FR 1.ii.58, 59).[6] Given the Ring, given the malice that moves both Gollum and Sauron, it seems inevitable that they meet and at least appear to be in league.[7] From murderer of poor Déagol to vampire-like cannibal of children in their cradles, from outcast consumed with self-pity after being justly cast out for his misdeeds to vengeful ally of Sauron, Gollum may stir Gandalf's fathomless pity, but that does not alter the truths of his character that the wizard so clearly sees. The Ring has devoured so much of him that only a bit remains, the very last of Sméagol, for whose cure Gandalf nevertheless holds out an unlikely hope (1.ii.55). Yet even so, he cannot deny that Frodo is right when he declares that Gollum deserves death. Here is a lie he cannot tell. All he can do is urge him to pity, and explain that life is often more complicated than verdicts of death would have them be. Let us turn back again to the passage with which we began when we asked why Gandalf did not identify Sméagol:

> "Deserves [death]! I daresay he does. Many that live deserve death. And some that die deserve life. Can you give it to them? Then do not be too eager to deal

out death in judgement. For even the very wise cannot see all ends. I have not much hope that Gollum can be cured before he dies, but there is a chance of it. And he is bound up with the fate of the Ring. My heart tells me that he has some part to play yet, for good or for ill, before the end; and when that comes, the pity of Bilbo may rule the fate of many—yours not least." (1.ii.59)

That Gollum deserves death is a large part of the reason why Gandalf fails and why he suppressed the identity of Sméagol in the first place. He hoped to win Frodo to pity before he knew the truth and to suggest through the fact that Sméagol was a hobbit that the same could have happened to Bilbo and still might. But Gandalf cannot make an argument strong enough, or present a portrait of Gollum pitiable enough, to overcome Frodo's fear of Sauron and loathing of Gollum, passions that play the same role here as Bilbo's anger and jealousy of the Ring did the night he left. Every time Gandalf appeals to pity, Frodo rejects him. He does not care that his friend has seen Gollum, and he doesn't want to see him for himself. Frodo will remain untouched by pity until experience of evil and suffering teach him otherwise.

Nor is it accidental that Gandalf never refers to Gollum as Sméagol anywhere but in this conversation. This isn't just cleverness, as it might at first seem. It also confirms something for us: that for Gandalf Sméagol is a remote figure gone so far away that there is little or no real hope that he can ever return, even if not all hope is gone in truth. For Gollum, too, Sméagol is a sad distant figure, gone since he lost the Ring, if not before (TT 4.i.616). And Frodo fiercely resists Gandalf's attempts to get Frodo to look at Gollum more closely, a resistance that continues until the subject of Gollum is dropped (FR 1.ii.54). Even then, Frodo's last words on Gollum in "The Shadow of the Past"— "All the same... even if Bilbo could not kill Gollum"—are words of unwilling concession and chilling disappointment (1.ii.60). Though hardly to his credit, they illumine the depths of his fear, loathing, and failure to comprehend so much of what Gandalf has been trying to make clear. It is only when Frodo sees and pities Gollum that he will use the name (TT 4.i.615–16).

In "A Long-expected Party," we learned about Gollum only what we might glean from Bilbo's words and deeds. "The Shadow of the Past" lends him a substance beyond hints and inferences. Gollum is the murderer of a friend, a cannibal who preys on the young and weak; he is vengeful, resentful, full of justifications and self-pity; he is a sneak, a spy, a liar, a spirit of malice; at best he is a tool of Sauron, at worst a servant. He hates even that which he holds most precious. The Ring and the Dark Power that rules it have devoured him almost completely.

THE PARADOX OF PITY

Thus far the portrayal of Gollum. Given all that Gandalf has said, and all that Frodo learned from Bilbo, Frodo's loathing of Gollum is entirely justified. It is also clear that there was a darkness in Gollum before he ever touched the Ring, a darkness that responded to its call. The Ring may begin to corrupt its bearer immediately, but it makes a difference who that keeper is. The touch of the Ring alone is not enough to work the instantaneous corruption of its keeper. It does not have this effect on Bilbo or Frodo, who each possess the Ring for many years, or on Gandalf, who handles it (1.ii.49–50). Moreover, the wizard's description of what the Ring would do to him if he took it harmonizes with this assessment (1.ii.61). And when Frodo says that he will keep the Ring to guard it, Gandalf replies, "Whatever it may do [to you], it will be slow, slow to evil, if you keep it with that purpose" (1.ii.62). This statement can only remind us of almost the last thing Gandalf says about Bilbo and the Ring:

> "What a pity that Bilbo did not stab that vile creature, when he had a chance!" [cried Frodo.]
> "Pity? It was Pity that stayed his hand. Pity, and Mercy: not to strike without need. And he has been well rewarded, Frodo. Be sure that he took so little hurt from the evil, and escaped in the end, because he began his ownership of the Ring so. With Pity."
> (1.ii.59)

Gandalf's Pity is high and pure. It is written out, along with Mercy, in Mythic Capitals. It knows well the crimes or sins of its object and does not excuse them. It can even agree that those crimes may merit death. It proceeds, as Saint Augustine would put it, "with a love of men and a hatred of their sins" ("*cum dilectione hominum et odio vitiorum*," Letter no. 211.11). When embodied in Mercy, which does not "strike without need" and which spares those who in fact deserve punishment, it comes near to Grace.[8] It cannot lie about the justice Gollum merits, even if it would spare him the sentence. Unlike Gollum, Bilbo, and Frodo, Gandalf is not deceived by the lie he tells for pity's sake. The distinction between *pity* and *Pity*, and *mercy* and *Mercy* is that the first is strictly human and bounded by the Circles of the World, and the second partakes of the divine, which looks beyond justice to healing (*Morgoth* 239–41).

Such Pity is impossible for Frodo to comprehend. Even when he reluctantly concedes the wisdom of Gandalf and Bilbo's pity for Gollum, he does not understand them (FR 1.ii.60). He is too afraid, too filled with loathing, and too inexperienced. The crimes and character of Gollum are too undeniably dark for that and have been portrayed as such at such great length that it is quite difficult for the reader, who experiences Middle-earth through the eyes of Frodo (and the other hobbits), to see Gollum except as he does here. The effects of this will be long-lasting. Moreover, even when Frodo finally comes to pity Gollum, his need to use the Ring to control him eats away at the protection his pity and mercy for Gollum have conferred. Bilbo needed only find a moment of pity. Frodo's road is longer.

Yet while pity imposes a limit of truth on Gandalf, it is also his greatest weakness. Terrified by all he has heard, Frodo offers Gandalf the Ring because he is "wise and powerful" (FR 1.ii.61). Now it is Gandalf's turn to reply with some heat, and he twice enjoins Frodo not to tempt him (1.ii.61). How different this is from the moment in "A Long-expected Party" when Bilbo wished to give Gandalf the Ring to hold until Frodo came home. Then he simply told Bilbo to put it on the mantelpiece, where it would be safe. When Bilbo drops the envelope containing the Ring, Gandalf scoops it up and deposits it on that same mantelpiece. It also differs from the moment earlier in this chapter when Gandalf asks Frodo to give him the Ring so he can test it in the fire on the hearth. Clearly while Gandalf does not want to handle it, he can do so briefly. In Rivendell, too, someone must have handled the Ring to place it on its new chain (2.i.232). Frodo, however, is offering to relinquish the Ring to him, which is very, very different.

What a remarkable moment this is for Frodo, for Gandalf, and for our understanding of the Ring. Frodo, having just been told that he has not been chosen because he is more deserving than others, offers to surrender freely the Ring that Sméagol had killed to possess, that Bilbo had twice contemplated violence to keep, and that Gandalf is afraid to take. In an instant, he belies Gandalf's statement of his unremarkable merit and unconsciously surpasses Bilbo, who "alone in history" passed a Ring of Power on to another (FR 1.ii.55). It is true, of course, that Bilbo needed all Gandalf's help to do so and true again that Frodo is possessed by a terror, which, notwithstanding his lack of pity, embitters his tongue when he reproves Bilbo, Gandalf, and the Elves for allowing Gollum to live after all his crimes (1.ii.59). That Frodo would challenge the judgement of those he respects most gives the measure of his fear.

There is so much else here besides pity, however, that Frodo fails to grasp. He has not understood Gandalf's hint that "there was more than one power at work" (FR 1.ii.55-56). He has not understood the Ring's grip on Gollum or Bilbo, and so, most importantly, he does not understand his own attachment to the Ring (1.ii.55). Consequently, he can ask, "Why did you let me keep it? Why didn't you make me throw it away, or, or destroy it?" Note how he stumbles over his words when he tries even to suggest destroying the Ring, anticipating his inability to throw the Ring into a hearth that he knows will not even heat it (1.ii.60-61, 49-50). He then puts the Ring back in his pocket, just as Bilbo had done (1.i.31-32, 34-35, ii.60).

Seeing Gandalf's fear of what would happen if he accepted the Ring breaches the wall of Frodo's self-deception and terror and allows him to emerge from this moment accepting the burden of the Ring: to keep it and guard it in order to save the Shire. As wise and as powerful as Frodo believes him to be, Gandalf leaps to his feet and twice cries out, "Do not tempt me" (FR 1.ii.61). Ironically, it is the wizard's humility here—his knowing the limits of his strength and wisdom—that helps Frodo move forward, just as it was Bilbo's testing the limits of Gandalf's pride and temper by accusing him of wanting the Ring for himself that enabled Bilbo to relinquish the Ring to Frodo (1.i.34-35). Yet even so, Frodo has not had some serene awakening. He still feels no pity for Gollum and will not until he sees him.

For Gandalf it is a very different moment. The offer of the Ring frightens him because the Power it would confer on him according to his stature is vast. That is, in fact, the problem. As his stature is greater, so is his temptation. "Do not tempt me! For I do not wish to become like the Dark Lord. *Yet the way of the Ring to my heart is by pity, pity for weakness and the desire of strength to do good.* Do not tempt me!" (FR 1.ii.61, emphasis mine). The prohibitions against temptation neatly bookend his explanation of its allure, and so, like bookends, support his explanation. The seed of the lie Gandalf would tell himself, were he to accept Frodo's offer, is already present in his good intentions. Recall how he lied to Frodo in his attempt to elicit pity. Recall also how he lied when he claimed Bilbo was a burglar. And we may measure the strength of the temptation he feels now by his commanding Frodo twice not to tempt him. *Yet*, for all that he would not want the Ring for domination, malice, and revenge, as the Dark Lord does, he recognizes that in the end his better motives would avail him nothing against the pull of the Ring's power.

Pity offers no defense—quite the opposite in fact, where Gandalf is concerned. The Ring will still devour him. Indeed, Gandalf seems convinced that the Ring would devour him more quickly than it would Frodo, as Frodo's lesser stature makes his good intentions more potent in resisting the Ring (1.ii.61). Like the power conferred by the Ring, the temptations arising within us in response to that power are proportional to our stature.

In view of the final inefficacy of pity against the corruption of the Ring, it remains quite remarkable that Gandalf should try as hard as he does to get Frodo to pity Gollum. Yet as with his refusal to accept that deserving death is a sufficient reason for execution, Gandalf is thinking on a very different level, one we will do well to attend to since people today often see *pity* as condescending, another word that has lost any positive meaning. What does *pity* mean when Tolkien puts it into Gandalf's mouth? In discussing the question of Frodo's pity for Gollum, Tolkien writes in his *Letters* that for "'pity' to be a true virtue [it] must be directed to the good of its object. It is empty if it is exercised *only* to keep oneself 'clean,' free from hate or the actual doing of injustice, though this is also a good motive" (no. 246, p. 330). Given Gandalf's hope, however small, that Gollum might one day be cured, his pity is clearly of this kind. His remark that Bilbo "took so little hurt from the evil [of the Ring]" because of his pity for Gollum suggests that his concern here is as much for Frodo as for Gollum (FR 1.ii.59). If Frodo pities Gollum for Gollum's sake, he may benefit himself and Gollum. One might call pity twice blest.

So in the heart of this crucial moment for Middle-earth as a whole, Gandalf not only gives thought to the well-being of Bilbo and Frodo, but he also never stops hoping for the redemption of the monstrous Gollum. He does so knowing that whatever other good pity might do them, it will not save them from the Ring. Yet, the healing of spirit that pity may bring is as at least as important as saving the world from oppression by Sauron. It seems a spiritual truth that Gandalf can see because he sees the truth about himself and is therefore not easily deceived by the lie of the Ring. Similarly, knowing the depths to which such irresistible power could bring him allows him to fathom the darkness in which Gollum languishes. Thus, as Bilbo once did, Gandalf sees the waste of Gollum's spirit as a story both abhorrent and sad.

In examining passages such as these we may see an example of what Tolkien meant when he said that "*The Lord of the Rings* is of course a fundamentally religious and Catholic work" but that "the religious element is absorbed into the story and the symbolism" (*Letters* no. 142, p. 172). He means "fundamentally" quite literally, and he means "absorbed" as literally as only a philologist could mean a metaphor. So thorough is this absorption that in *The Lord of the Rings* he rarely uses the word "spirit," as I have just done above, and "soul" appears but once, to mean "a living person."[9] In a place, moreover, where *spirit* would have suited perfectly (and likely gone unnoticed), namely, the Witch-king's threat to Éowyn, he uses *mind* (RK 5.vi.841). He does, however, use *ghost* to describe those who are in some unnatural state that is truly neither death nor life. The Oathbreakers from the Paths of the Dead are called ghosts, for example (5.ii.786, 789). They are disembodied spirits still bound to this world by their oath. Most significantly, however, Faramir says of the men who became the Ringwraiths that "to them the Enemy had given rings of power, and he had devoured them: living ghosts they were become, terrible and evil" (TT 4.vi.692). Their unseen bodies still walk and move and speak, and have "flesh" and "sinew" against which weapons can avail (RK 5.vi.844).

Coming to the end of "The Shadow of the Past," it seems quite clear that the final destination of a mortal who possesses a Ring of Power is to be a "living ghost" bound in "undead flesh." Preferring to skirt openly religious and Catholic matters, Tolkien avoids using the words *soul* and *spirit* in the context of the effect of a Ring of Power on its bearer, where it might provoke theological questions. Yet, all other things being equal, *soul* and *spirit* would be the ideal words to describe the noncorporeal site of the Ring's corruption. This is why longeval beings like Elves and Istari must also fear the Ring and why the morality of a Ring-bearer's initial intentions and actions can affect the speed with which the Ring devours its bearer.

The portrayal of Gollum, much more direct and explicit in this chapter, goes far beyond the inferences we had to draw about him in "A Long-expected Party." Gandalf's account of how Sméagol the hobbit became the creature Gollum withholds no detail of his depravity and crimes but also shows the horror that his life has become owing to the Ring. He withholds only his present name, concealing a lesser truth in the hope that the greater truth of suffering will move Frodo to pity. It does not. For Frodo cannot yet accept a truth so threatening, and we will be left with this picture of Gollum the loathsome creature and a pitiless Frodo for quite some time. For the moment, Frodo is able to pity only those he can admit are like him, the other hobbits of the Shire. That pity of Bilbo's, moreover, which Gandalf claims is so important as he urges it on Frodo, seems both ineffectual and essential. It points to a truth beyond itself.

CHAPTER THREE

The 1951 *Hobbit* and "The Shadow of the Past"

THE HOBBIT'S NEW CONTEXT

When the story Bilbo told the dwarves and Gandalf became a lie, *The Hobbit* retroactively became a much more serious book. It had long been heading in that direction. Since Tolkien composed it when the tide of the Silmarillion was at its flood, we shouldn't be surprised to find that Beren and Lúthien were originally mentioned, as was their foe the Necromancer; that there was an Elrond who was not quite Elrond; and that the Elven King and his halls recalled Thingol and the Thousand Caves (Rateliff in Tolkien, *History of the Hobbit* 81–84, 121–23, 324–25). It's visible, too, in the plain shift it makes from fairy-tale beginnings to the prose epic we meet face to face in Smaug's attack on Lake Town, where we hear "a whisper from the narrator who speaks in full voice in *The Lord of the Rings*" (Thomas 179). Tolkien later declared that the Silmarillion drew *The Hobbit* toward itself (*Letters* no. 257, p. 346). Such attraction is clear now even if it was not so in 1937.

We should not, however, regard *The Hobbit* as merely a prelude to *The Lord of the Rings*. For the lie, in a sense, created two separate works. The original recounts Bilbo's adventure there and back again and answers the question of "whether he gained anything in the end" (*H* 30). For the answer is not that he gained the Ring, but it is in fact the way Bilbo began his possession of the Ring that makes the first version possible. A Bilbo who stabs Gollum in the back when he has the chance does not become the Bilbo who saves Dwarves, Elves, and Men from themselves and owns the courage to face the dragon alone. A Bilbo who stabs Gollum does not use the Ring to rescue his endangered comrades. A Bilbo who stabs Gollum becomes Gollum (see page 62).

The first version thus becomes the model for the adventures that Frodo, Sam, Merry, and Pippin *wish* to have befall them.[1] That is more than any prelude.

The lie reveals a second version, a true one, that recontextualizes not just the events of "Riddles in the Dark" but also many of the moments that reveal Bilbo's character both before and after chapter 5. It could hardly be otherwise. For the lie demands a hindsight we cannot possess if we cast our eye only on Bilbo and Gollum alone in the darkness as if that were the whole story. As we have seen, Gandalf emphasizes to Frodo the saving benefit Bilbo gained from beginning his possession of the Ring with an act of pity. He thus invites Frodo to look back on Bilbo's actions and regard them as an essential guide to his own, precisely as he is about to embark upon an adventure of his own with the Ring. Frodo, however, scorns pity and quickly forecasts that his adventure will be nothing like Bilbo's (FR 1.ii.62, iii.66). Given this new context, how do we see Bilbo both before and after "Riddles in the Dark," what do we make of Bilbo's example, and what does Frodo's rejection of Bilbo's pity augur for him on his Quest?

When we look back at Bilbo, as Gandalf urges Frodo to do, after he and the narrator have done so much over the first two chapters to underscore the peril to the Ring-bearer of possessing and using the Ring, the impact of the recontextualization of all of *The Hobbit* quickly becomes evident and quite likely surprising. For Bilbo repeatedly uses the Ring to do good. He drives off the spiders and saves the dwarves. He rescues Thorin and Company from the dungeons of the Elven King. He employs the Ring to smuggle the Arkenstone out of Erebor in an attempt to resolve the siege peacefully. Not even counting the many names he gave himself when riddling with Smaug, for the good he does Thorin calls him "Child of the kindly West," and the Elven King names him "elf-friend" and "Bilbo the Magnificent" (H 279, 348, 353).

For all the good we see Bilbo accomplish using the Ring, we must acknowledge that he also took and concealed from Thorin and the Dwarves the Arkenstone which he was aware they were looking for even before he found it (H 292–93).[2] This magnificent jewel was bewitching enough in itself, judging by the way Thorin and Company speak of it, and even without considering the "dragon-sickness" produced by Smaug's brooding upon it for a hundred and seventy years (287, 323; RK App. B 1088–89). This may seem sufficient to explain Bilbo's theft of the stone. Yet it would be foolish to think that the power the Ring conferred on Bilbo to get away with the theft had no effect. The rationalization that he could claim it as his promised share is unconvincing even to himself from the start and bears no little resemblance to the lies he and Gollum told themselves about how they came by the Ring (H 293, 295).

Now, unless we are to imagine that more than Bilbo's tale of how he came by the Ring was a lie, we must take his subsequent words as true. The contrast with Sméagol is of course stark. He begins his possession of the Ring by murdering Déagol, who had found it by chance, and returning home suspiciously without him he acts so abominably that his own grandmother casts him out of the family and community. He loses even his name, becoming Gollum, a creature so called because of a swallowing noise he makes in his throat, who bites those who kick him, dines on goblin when he can get it, and hungers for the daintier meats he finds in nests and cradles, as if his appetite were fed by that which fed on him.

To argue that Bilbo's courage and generous heart come from the Ring would be a post hoc fallacy, but who Sméagol was before the Ring is not irrelevant to who he becomes afterward. Tolkien later said that Sméagol already had a "mean soul" and had already "become a mean sort of thief" before the Ring (*Letters* no. 181, p. 234). That is one of the lessons of Gandalf's story about finding the Ring, and the same lesson is implicit in the grounds of Gandalf's own refusal of the Ring. Galadriel, too, allows as much when she tells Sam that she would begin her possession of the Ring by dispensing justice, though it wouldn't end there (*FR* 2.vii.366). Yet Sam is here the best parallel, since like Bilbo he actually uses the Ring to do good deeds, and who he is before he takes the Ring protects him while he rescues Frodo: "In that hour of trial it was the love of his master that helped most to hold him firm; but also deep down in him lived still unconquered his plain hobbit-sense" (*RK* 6.i.901). The Ring thus no more gave Bilbo his courage than it gave Sam his love of Frodo, but Bilbo's pity rooted him and so allowed his courage to flower. As I remarked above, the Bilbo who stabs Gollum in the back does none of these things. It is both of these possible Bilbos of whom Gandalf wants Frodo to think when he invites him to reflect on the story of the hobbit who murdered Déagol to get the Ring and thus became Gollum and on the story of Bilbo who pitied that murderer and would not commit murder to keep the Ring. In Gandalf's mind these tales are not merely lessons in history with a practical aim but moral exempla meant to reveal to Frodo the consequences of character and moral choice in obtaining, possessing, and using the Ring. For in ascertaining the identity of Bilbo's ring, Gandalf has discovered dimensions to its power that he barely suspected the night of Bilbo's party; and there is no single person in Middle-earth to whom these concerns are more relevant than the Ring-bearer.

But there are none so blind as those who will not see. Frodo will, therefore, begin his Quest "to lose [a treasure], and not return, as far as [he] can see" without the benefit of any of the lessons that Gandalf has tried to inculcate

(FR 1.iii.66). Is Frodo's resistance to Gandalf's advice, like Bilbo's in "A Long-expected Party," another sign of the hold that the Ring *already* has on him? When Frodo tried to cast the Ring into the fireplace but could only put it back in his pocket, Gandalf laughed and compared him to Bilbo: "*Already* you too, Frodo, cannot easily let it go" (1.ii.60, emphasis mine). Thus, Frodo is at even more risk as he sets out without Gandalf than he seems at first glance. Besides all the other perils, a greater danger he does not suspect lies within him: his own response to the Ring's power.

A GLIMMER IN THE DARK

We began this study by examining the portrayal of Gollum we find in the first two chapters of *The Lord of the Rings* only. The reasons for doing so were quite simple. First, there can be no certainty that first-time readers of *The Lord of the Rings* will have already read *The Hobbit* or even the prologue, nor indeed that they ever will read them. Second, Tolkien rewrote *The Hobbit* to suit the darker and more tormented creature into which Gollum had evolved in *The Lord of the Rings*, but he did not do so until Gollum had already entered the tale in "The Taming of Sméagol." Thus, the portrayal of Gollum in *The Lord of the Rings* must be sufficient, per se. Yet Bilbo's lie links the story of *The Hobbit* more closely to *The Lord of the Rings* than it would have been otherwise, and Gandalf's conversation with Frodo in "The Shadow of the Past" directs our attention back to it. The prologue to *The Lord of the Rings*, moreover, very openly addresses both versions of "Riddles in the Dark" and expects most readers to be familiar with one version but not both (FR Pr. iv.11–14). Indeed, the prologue declares that Bilbo never changed the original version of his story even after publicly admitting it was a lie (Pr. iv.12). What is a straightforward narrative of how Bilbo came by the Ring in each edition of *The Hobbit* now becomes a complex tale of open lies and silent dishonesty, theft and hatred, near murder and sudden pity, which reveals more about the corruption worked by the Ring than either edition does if taken alone. We have also already seen how the recontextualization of *The Hobbit* shifts the perspective on Bilbo's actions after he escapes from Gollum with the Ring. Let us look more closely now at the 1937 and 1951 versions of "Riddles in the Dark."

In 1947, when Tolkien submitted his proposed revisions to *The Hobbit* to Allen and Unwin, he added a handwritten note to the typescript, which said that "if The Hobbit ran so the Sequel would be a little easier to <conduct> as a narrative (in Ch. II [i.e., "The Shadow of the Past"]), though not necessarily 'truer'" (quoted in J. R. R. Tolkien, *History of the Hobbit* 732). Those last few words make a fascinating comment in their suggestion that some doubt may attach even to the second version. It brings to mind how Bilbo is still attempting to justify how he got the Ring many years after the wizard had harassed him into telling the truth; and Gandalf emphasized the disturbing similarity of the lies Bilbo and Gollum each told about how they came by the Ring (*FR* 1.i.33, ii.48). If, as Gandalf also says, "Gollum is a liar, and you have to sift his words," what does that mean for Bilbo, whom we also know to be a liar? It is quite possible that Bilbo never told the whole truth until the Council of Elrond, years after he had let the Ring pass to Frodo, but only the morning after he had been bitterly confronted with the spiritual and moral effect his legacy was having on his heir (1.ii.56). For only then can he say that he "understand[s] now" and ask forgiveness for his lies (2.i.232, ii.249).

One might object that the simultaneous existence of two versions—the one a lie, the other not necessarily truer—was an accident owing to a misunderstanding by Allen & Unwin (Rateliff in Tolkien, *History of the Hobbit* 760).[3] Tolkien never heard back from his publisher about his proposed changes until the proofs of the second edition arrived in 1950, with his suggestions already incorporated into the text. As Hammond and Scull put it, "Tolkien seems to have forgotten about the revision" in the long silence between 1947 and 1950 (*RC* 39). Yet, if so, it is a felix culpa. Tolkien quickly embraced the situation: "The story as a whole must take into account the existence of two versions and use it" (*Letters* no. 129, 130, p. 142). He expanded the prologue and revised the main text to accomplish just that.

Until now, "A Long-expected Party" contained no dangerous quarrel between Bilbo and Gandalf about letting the Ring go and no mention of different versions of Bilbo's story (*Treason* 18–21; *FR* 1.i.40). "The Shadow of the Past" also lacks any trace of the two stories, though the murder of Déagol and the birthday present lie had made their appearance, a necessary precursor to the crucial moment in the revised "Riddles in the Dark" (*Treason* 23, 27–28). In "The Council of Elrond," Bilbo's story is unremarkable, since here the known facts are indeed the facts: Bilbo prefaces his tale with no apology to those he had previously deceived, such as Glóin, no confession of a new understanding, before telling his story again and yielding the floor to Aragorn (111). Tolkien had spoken true when in 1950 he told Sir Stanley Unwin that until then his tale had been based on the first version (*Letters* no. 128, p. 141).

Another essential change is the increased emphasis on the importance of pity. In the early versions of Frodo's conversation with Gandalf, the wizard responds very differently to his host's wish that Gollum had perished at Bilbo's hands: "'What nonsense you do talk sometimes, [Frodo],' said Gandalf. Pity! It was pity that prevented him. And he could not do so without doing wrong. It was against the rules. If he had done so he would not have had the ring; the ring would have had him at once. He might have become a wraith on the spot" (*Shadow* 81). This is a far cry from the published text we saw above (page 52). There not only do we find *pity* four times rather than twice, but it is attached importantly to the exercise of mercy. More than that, we see Gandalf assuring Frodo of the positive effects—the reward in fact—of pity rather than positing a contrafactual assertion of what would have happened had Bilbo committed murder in defiance of all that was right and legitimate. Finally, Gandalf does not claim that "the pity of Bilbo will rule the fate of many" before the final text of "The Shadow of the Past" took shape and took "into account the existence of the two versions and use[d] it" (*Letters* no. 129, p. 142). With the introduction of the second version of "Riddles in the Dark," Tolkien brings both lies and pity to the fore in *The Lord of the Rings*. So, how do these two texts, read together, allow us to construe Gollum and Bilbo?

Until recently, interpreting this was a more difficult task, since the first edition of *The Hobbit* had long been out of print. We were not without resources, however. John Rateliff's edited volume of Tolkien's *The History of the Hobbit* and Douglas A. Anderson's edited volume *The Annotated Hobbit* are works of the first importance. Still of great worth is Bonniejean Christensen's "Gollum's Character Transformation in *The Hobbit*," the first work to study both texts. With the publication of the facsimile of the first edition, however, an invaluable tool for comparing the two editions became available.

The 1937 and the 1951 texts of "Riddles in the Dark" are virtually identical for about the first 3,500 words. The differences in the first part of the chapter, moreover, are quite telling, since they are further revisions Tolkien introduced after 1951 to correct oversights in the changes to this edition, sentences that still needed rewriting to bring them into harmony with the "true" story (*H* 122n17, 125n20). The last moment of the first section is also quite significant. For it brings the tale to the point where Gollum shrieks his last wrong answer and Bilbo, sword in hand, puts his back to the wall (126). The similarity to the moment in "A Long-expected Party" when Bilbo backs up against the wall and lays his hand on the hilt of this same sword is uncanny if not intentional. Since the conceit of *The Hobbit* and *The Lord of the Rings* is that Bilbo is the ultimate source of both versions of this chapter, we can only conclude that he chose this particular moment, when he had a perfectly legitimate reason to fear Gollum, to be the point at which to begin the lie. Why this is so is not irrelevant to our concerns here. So before examining the differences between the two accounts, which quite naturally have garnered the most scholarly attention, let us look at the words that are the same. In both cases, the chapter up to this point establishes a foundation for the rest of the action.

"Riddles in the Dark" has scarcely begun when Bilbo finds the Ring in the darkness (H 114). It seemed inconsequential to him at the time, because he is too given over to the "complete miserableness" of being lost and cut off from his friends. Yet the narrator makes sure we know the importance of the discovery. "It was a turning point in his career, but he didn't know it. He put the ring in his pocket almost without thinking. It did not seem of any particular use at the moment" (115). As Paul Edmund Thomas has noted, this sentence in *The Hobbit* "show[s] the narrator as a guide who wants the reader to comprehend the story in a particular way" (163). With the revision of "Riddles in the Dark," this truth becomes even more significant.

Bilbo's mind, however, turns to the idea of frying bacon and eggs at home, a comforting thought if his hunger had not made his misery even worse. Next, the hope of homely solace that his pipe promises is "shattered" by a lack of matches, leaving him "crushed" (H 116). So, though his thought seeks back beyond the moment for comfort, it fails to find any in the usual places. Yet his search is not wholly vain, for he finds his sword from the storied elven city of Gondolin, so small that he had forgotten he had it, but its legendary connections and his sudden grasp of its usefulness against goblins comfort him (116). They enable him to go on. In the sword, Bilbo "comes upon" another ancient artifact, endowed with a certain power, which he has discovered only belatedly and which he had forgotten he possessed, and it helps him to continue on his journey. The same will be true of the Ring. Most importantly at this moment, however, is that Bilbo has reached beyond the normal hobbitish comforts of food and pipe-weed to take hold of a wider and deeper world, one in which he "explore[s] . . . caves, and wear[s] a sword instead of a walking-stick" just as he had fancied he might do while still in Bag End (45; Olsen, *Exploring* 85–87, 109). "Go forward? Only thing to do. On we go" (H 116). And now that Bilbo has recovered from his initial desperation and by means of the sword and its associations found the courage to move forward, his native hobbit talents—resilience, stealth, a sense of direction underground—and his native Hobbit fund of "wisdom and wise sayings" come to the fore (116–17). A turning point indeed.

Advancing through the darkness steadily, though not without fear of "goblins or half-imagined *things*," Bilbo is brought to a halt by a lake that blocks his path. We are told that the water may be home to "nasty, slimy *things* with big bulging eyes . . . *strange things*" and "*other things* more slimy than fish" and in the tunnels are still "*other things*," which had been there before the goblins and still lived in "odd corners, slinking and nosing about" (*H* 117–18, emphasis mine). By this lake beneath the mountains, in this darkness full of *things,* lives Gollum, "darker than the darkness." His origins are a mystery, and even the goblins keep away from his lake, "for they had a feeling that *something* unpleasant was lurking down there" (119, emphasis mine).

Thus, as we see later in *The Lord of the Rings,* the reader is prepared for Gollum's entrance. For he is both like and unlike those *things* in the lake and the tunnels; he preys on the blind fish that he can see with his no longer human eyes; and though he does not seem to be one of the original residents of the tunnels, he, too, lurks about the odd corners of the darkness. But he also practices something that is not quite cannibalism, but also not quite not, on the goblins whom he "throttles from behind," which should remind us of the murder of Déagol. Mysterious, monstrous, and murderous describe, but don't disclose just what he is.

Yet we also may see similarities to Bilbo: in the darkness of the tunnels Gollum retains his sense of direction, and he can move stealthily. As with Bilbo, his eating habits and opinions on food also receive emphasis. These similarities furnish a common stage upon which the riddles and the well-known, supposedly inviolable, rules of the ancient Riddle Game play themselves out. Together with the memories of sunlight on daisies and of his grandmother when they lived "in a hole in a bank by a river"—which suggest that Gollum was not always so monstrous and a devourer of squeaking baby goblins—these similarities establish a link not just between Gollum and Bilbo, but between Gollum and humanity, and in retrospect Hobbits (*H* 122, 120–21, 128). Gollum may be depraved and monstrous, but he is not a monster per se, a creature of a different order like trolls or goblins, Mirkwood spiders or dragons. For him, too, there must have been a turning point. He was not born this way.

Nor do the similarities and links end here. Gollum invites Bilbo to sit and chat and enjoy a homely game of riddles in the darkness, just as Bilbo had invited Gandalf to sit and enjoy a pipe in the morning sun. Since Bilbo too is familiar with the Riddle Game, there is a cultural affinity of some kind between who Bilbo is and who Gollum was. Whatever Tolkien may have envisioned Gollum to be when first writing the story, he also comes of a people who dwelt in holes. More than that, as Bilbo and Gollum both play for time, the close verbal and structural parallelism of the sentences that describe their thinking reinforces how alike they are: "[Gollum] was anxious to appear friendly, at any rate for the moment, and until he found out more about the sword and the hobbit, whether he was quite alone really, whether he was good to eat, and whether Gollum was really hungry," and "Bilbo ... was anxious to agree, until he found out more about the creature, whether he was quite alone, whether he was fierce or hungry, and whether he was a friend of the goblins" (H 120, 121).

Yet, these similarities open a dangerous door, as the most chilling difference between them turns their conversation into a contest for Bilbo's life. And that brings us to the first divergence in the texts, which begins directly after "If it asks us, and we doesn't answer": "We gives it a present, gollum" (1937, 85) or "then we does what it wants, eh? We shows it the way out, yes!" (1951). In both of these statements there is a severe dissonance between the two parts of the wager: Bilbo is supper, or gets a present; Bilbo is supper, or gets shown out. Having introduced us to Gollum by first indicating his strangeness and monstrosity and by then seeming to temper that impression through the suggestion that he and Bilbo are not so different after all, Tolkien now brings that strangeness and monstrosity rushing back again with the shockingly unequal terms of the contest. For, while being eaten is not a good result for Bilbo, not getting to eat him is scarcely an equivalent evil for Gollum.

Then, too, there is the absurdity of his sincere offer of a present and, though Bilbo wins the contest in a questionable fashion, of Gollum's distress at being unable to find it and his many apologies as he shows Bilbo the way out instead. As John Rateliff has pointed out, in the 1937 *Hobbit* Gollum is more honorable than Bilbo (Tolkien, *History of the Hobbit* 166–67). And Bilbo obviously believed that even a ghastly creature like Gollum would abide by the rules, or else he would not have begun "to wonder what Gollum's present would be like" when it appeared he was about to lose (1937, 86). Not until Gollum begins to paw at him and Bilbo asks his unexpected and unfair final question does Bilbo become unsure of how it would all end, whoever won the contest (89–90). And even then, with his back to the wall and his sword out, Bilbo insists on asking about his present, which he had won "pretty fairly" and had a right to by the time-honored children's law of "finding's keeping" (91, 92). Yet the narrator dismisses Bilbo's fears and asserts that even for creatures like Gollum the rules of the Riddle Game are inviolable.

As frightening and dangerous as Gollum is in the 1937 *Hobbit*, his firmly abiding by the rules of the game which he initiated (no doubt thinking he would win) renders him harmless in this instance and almost admirable (but not quite entirely so, since he considers cheating). Indeed, Bilbo, having realized that he already possessed the present Gollum had meant to give him, prevaricates and manipulates his dismayed competitor:

> "The ring would have been mine now, if you had found it; so you would have lost it anyway. And I will let you off on one condition."
> "Yes, what iss it? What does it wish us to do, my precious?"
> "Help me get out of these places."
> Now Gollum had to agree to this, if he was not to cheat. He still very much wanted just to try what the stranger tasted like; but now he had to give up all idea of it. Still, there was the little sword; and the stranger was wide awake and on the look out, not unsuspecting as Gollum liked to have things which he attacked. So perhaps it was best after all. (1937, 93)

Now we should not be too hard on Bilbo here. That would be missing the point about both Gollum and Bilbo. For using cunning and lies to escape from a dangerous creature is as old as heroic tales themselves. It is a mark of the hero's intellectual prowess. We need only cite the story of Odysseus and Polyphemus, the cyclops, in book 9 of *The Odyssey*. There Odysseus is trapped underground with a cannibalistic adversary, as remarkable for his one eye as Gollum is for his two. Odysseus uses his wits to save himself and many of his men, though he also commits the nearly disastrous mistake of telling the creature his true name.[3] Bilbo is clever enough to use the rules of the game against Gollum, so Gollum thinks he has no choice but to keep his promise. To be sure, he remains aware of Bilbo's sword, but that seems more to confirm him in his decision than to decide him.

Still the last we see of Gollum, and the last any public reader ever expected to see before he returned in *The Fellowship of the Ring* in 1954, is him fulfilling the obligation imposed on him by the terms of the contest he had proposed. So, he is a strange creature, frightening, dangerous, capable of monstrous acts to satisfy his hunger, but not so different from Hobbits that he can't be dealt with. Unlike the Gollum we meet in *The Lord of the Rings*, who haunts Frodo's tracks from Moria onward and who cannot be gotten rid of, this Gollum goes away once he has lived up to his promise. To have met him makes for a good story, which is precisely what Bilbo does.

The 1951 version, with which we are all familiar, tells another story. How different from the positive, near sprightly "We gives it a present!" is the concessive, almost disappointed "then we does what it wants, eh? We shows it the way out, yes!" Not very convincing. Every reference to the present disappears.

The 1937 Bilbo's curiosity about what kind of present it would be becomes in 1951 a "hope that the wretch would not be able to answer" (*H* 122). When Gollum seems about to be stumped by the egg riddle, Bilbo pushes him about his guess instead of his present. And when Gollum finally loses the match, Bilbo is much more interested in what he has won, and more pushy about getting it, whereas in 1937 it had been more a matter of principle: "'What about the present?' asked Bilbo, not that he cared very much, still he felt that he had won it, pretty fairly, and in very difficult circumstances too" (1937, 91), compared with "'Well?' he said. 'What about your promise? I want to go. You must show me the way'" (1951, 127).

When the Ring is no longer a gift, one of the most touching links between Bilbo and Gollum in the 1937 *Hobbit*, this connection vanishes without a trace: that Gollum had received *as a birthday present* the very ring he meant to give Bilbo a for winning their contest; and Gollum, dismayed that he cannot find it, splutters profuse apologies. There's a charm in this, that he was going to pass on the present that he had received. Nor does the 1937 text cast the least doubt cast on Gollum's claim that it was his birthday present.

But from Gandalf we know that Gollum's story was a lie, even if he had all but convinced himself of its truth—he was still telling the tale over seventy-five years later—and only he could have told Bilbo (*FR* 1.ii.48, 56). So, the birthday present part of the story is no invention of Bilbo's. What is more, in the 1951 version the introduction of the Ring as belonging to Gollum, and his assertion that it was his birthday present darkens the narrative. Whereas in the 1937 version Gollum went to fetch his birthday present to give it to Bilbo, in the 1951 work he goes off to get it so he can kill and eat Bilbo. That is what his birthday present is good for—just ask the orc child he had dined on earlier that day—and that is his sole motive for fetching it. So, what had supplied a charming touch in the first edition is turned on its head in the second to illustrate Gollum's treachery and ghoulish appetites. The transformation is so complete that we might well wonder whether Tolkien had this partly in mind when he said the second version was not necessarily truer.

Indeed, the whole new section introduced in the 1951 text—from Bilbo's demand that Gollum fulfill his promise to Gollum's discovery that his Ring was lost—does not just explain Gollum's motives and provide details about his use of the Ring and its effects on him. It also contains information that Bilbo could not have known at the time (what Gollum was thinking), or at any time before Gandalf learned it from Gollum decades later (how Gollum handled the Ring), or, finally, before Gandalf had disclosed to him that this Ring was connected to Sauron. Just as Gandalf had detected the falsity of Bilbo's initial story, so we, too, may come to believe that Bilbo's new version is too much like the version Gandalf tells Frodo decades later. It is also true, however, that the claim that Gollum meant to cheat all along seems to have existed before Gandalf spoke to Frodo about it, since Frodo himself advances it (FR 1.ii.54).

This argues the existence of three and perhaps four versions of the story: the first coming down to us in the 1937, which represents what Bilbo "told the dwarves and put in his book"; the second being that which he told Gandalf and then Frodo; the third being the tale as he told it at the Council of Elrond when he had come to a better understanding; and the fourth—which may or may not be the same as the third—coming down to us in the 1951 text, and which was preserved in the Red Book as "the true account (as an alternative), derived no doubt from notes by Frodo and Samwise, both of whom learned the truth" (FR 1.i.40, 2.ii.249, Pr. 13). In this context, which Tolkien's own assertion that the later version was "not necessarily 'truer'" has provided us, it will be interesting to note that while Bilbo says that the tale he tells at the Council of Elrond is the truth, Gandalf says only that Bilbo's and Gollum's versions agree (2.ii.254). Consider also the implications of the statement about true story's preservation in the Red Book of Westmarch. Whatever Bilbo told Frodo, Gandalf, and the Council, he never changed his memoir. The lie persisted as the effect of the Ring.

What we should take away here is not that none of these accounts are reliable but that anyone who possesses the Ring, even briefly, is susceptible to its dire influence. Viewed together from the perspective of *The Lord of the Rings*, both the 1937 and the 1951 versions show this influence. In the first tale, Bilbo substantially whitewashes Gollum's character to support the story of how Ring was a present for winning the riddle game; in the second, he blackens Gollum's name by adding grisly emphasis to his cannibalism and by portraying him as intending to break his promise the moment he had the opportunity to do so.[4] The falsehoods Bilbo told to justify himself and his possession of the Ring in the 1937 version have their analog in the falseness of Gollum in the 1951 work. Confronted in the page proofs of the 1951 text with revisions to the story he had wished for but not planned on, Tolkien used both versions to create a layered intertextuality that tells a richer, more complex, and more complete tale about Bilbo, Gollum, and the Ring than either could have done alone. With the lie given and the truth introduced, the power of the Ring to warp and of pity to defend come together in a hostile counterpoint not unlike that which we encounter in the interplay of the Third Theme of Ilúvatar and the discord of Melkor in "The Ainulindalë" (S 16–17). For the former was full of sorrow, and the latter sought to dominate all else. This echo of a larger world and a more fundamental struggle will have escaped Frodo, who knows too little to grasp even Gandalf's hints of Providence, but the lessons of the lies and truth, of the power and pity contained in the wizard's tale of the Ring and of how Gollum and Bilbo came by it should not have eluded Frodo, were he only willing to look (FR 1.ii.56). Seeing, moreover, is essential to what comes next.

For with the revelation that Gollum was not a funny little creature of gruesome appetites who nevertheless kept his promises, a new door opens. Not a drop of the "bless us and splash us" Gollum survives. He is shrewd, horrid, and terrifying, relishing the squeak of the goblin child he had devoured earlier that day and seething with a rage at the loss of his Precious, which boils over when he realizes what Bilbo has in his pocket. Bilbo, a bit highhanded in demanding the fulfillment of Gollum's promise, now runs for his life, and now it is a murderous creature with glowing eyes that pursues him through the darkness.

At this instant, Gollum becomes for the reader what we have seen him portrayed to be in the first two chapters of *The Lord of the Rings*. At this instant Bilbo, with rage and murder at his heels, discovers the power of the Ring and the tables turn. He becomes the pursuer, and invisibility gives power to his fear and desperation, the power of murder with impunity, just as it had to Gollum. But Bilbo, unseen, glimpses what was invisible to him before.

> Bilbo almost stopped breathing, and went stiff himself. He was desperate. He must get away, out of this horrible darkness, while he had any strength left. He must fight. He must stab the foul thing, put its eyes out, kill it. It meant to kill him. No, not a fair fight. He was invisible now. Gollum had no sword. Gollum had not actually threatened to kill him, or tried to yet. And he was miserable, alone, lost. A sudden understanding, a pity mixed with horror, welled up in Bilbo's heart: a glimpse of endless unmarked days without light or hope of betterment, hard stone, cold fish, sneaking and whispering. All these thoughts passed in a flash of a second. He trembled. And then quite suddenly in another flash, as if lifted by a new strength and resolve, he leaped.
> (H 133)

The first thing to note here is how Bilbo's terror of this dehumanized creature shifts from homicidal desperation to attempted justification. Something in his character feels it necessary to take this step, and he tries to plead self-defense, with the added rationalization that he, a person, would be acting against a "thing" and an "it." Yet, his sense of fairness stops him here, as it did not in the somewhat dodgily won riddle game. His justifications now run the other way, toward mercy, since Gollum has not forced his hand. He rejects the power to kill with impunity and looks instead for reasons to show mercy.

Focused on the second half of this paragraph, however, we tend to minimize the importance of the first half. It is Bilbo's turn away from murder toward mercy that allows him to see Gollum as a person, despicable, to be sure, but a person and not a thing. With that, the consequential force of the words *and he* with which the second half begins becomes clear. Like Bilbo, he is miserable. Like Bilbo, he is alone. Like Bilbo, he is lost, though in a different sense of the word. Yet it is a sword's thrust of difference. Without consciously recognizing what he is seeing, Bilbo identifies the ways they are most alike in this moment. From the start, Bilbo has thought of, longed for, and reveled in the thought of good food, sunlight, and companionship and in dreams of home, the very things which he sees the Riddle Game recall for Gollum (H 64–66, 69, 72–73, 82, 87–88, 101, 107, 113, 115–16, 120–23).[5]

For Gollum, who has murdered from behind for and with the Ring, such memories make him angry, a reaction which arose from "the evil part of him," the part that the Ring was devouring and that was itself consumed by hunger (FR 1.ii.55). As we also see here in *The Hobbit*, with the anger came hunger and more challenging riddles (H 122). The memory of such things, however, lost to him for the moment only, allows Bilbo to glimpse the horror of a life lost forever, and with the identification of horror comes pity. What he sees quite literally shakes him. Pity enters through the door the Ring has opened.

As Gandalf says to Frodo years later, more than one power was at work in Bilbo's finding the Ring (FR 1.ii.56). Even without this hint, however, it is hard to avoid seeing some measure of the same in Bilbo's back-to-back flashes of insight and inspiration and harder still not to think of the phrase *a leap of faith* when reading the final sentence of this paragraph. Not that Bilbo has undergone some kind of religious conversion here or that Tolkien means to suggest that he has, but he has changed; and by calling this notion to our minds Tolkien suggests a larger spiritual context of which Bilbo, like Frodo later, is unaware. It is also true, however, that the things Bilbo holds dear, as simple as they are, have prepared him for this moment as nothing else could have. Here and now he is no mere puppet either of the Ring or the unseen hand that guided him, "the most unlikely person imaginable," to the Ring (1.ii.56).

And this is of course the third major change in the 1951 text. First we saw the increased savagery and treachery of Gollum in company with the elimination of his present to Bilbo. Then the ring became the One Ring. Now, on the precipice of murder, Bilbo finds insight and pity, and "a new strength and resolve." This leads directly—as it was meant to do, since we must recall that the role of pity was not nearly as significant before Tolkien revised *The Lord of the Rings* to match the revisions of *The Hobbit*—to Gandalf's attempts to elicit Frodo's pity for Gollum and to his flat assertion of the importance of Bilbo's pity.

Here we always think first of Frodo and then of the fact that the Ring is destroyed because Bilbo showed pity and mercy to Gollum. But we should also remember that Gollum is one of those many to whose fate Gandalf refers. For in the midst of all his concerns about Sauron and the Ring, Gandalf has not forgotten him. Gandalf's "And he is bound up with the fate of the Ring" balances Bilbo's "And he was miserable, alone, lost." We should also note here that Gandalf's statement begins and ends with his care and hope for the future of individuals, with Pity and the Ring between them, as if at the fulcrum of their fates. Bilbo's pity is as central to the fate of the world as it is to the structure of these corresponding statements, the second of which points Frodo and the reader back to the first. And central to Bilbo's pity and subsequent experience of the Ring is his identity as a "child of the kindly West" (H 348). However petty Bilbo's longing for good food and cheer may have seemed, his values were correct, and the exaggerated sense of misery he felt without his precious bacon and eggs allowed him, from the vantage point the Ring conferred, to glimpse the truth of a profound misery. Decades later, Frodo is willing to undertake his adventure out of love for the Shire and the desire to save it, but as Gandalf's confession of the insufficiency of his own pity and good intentions illustrates, nobility of spirit will not prevail. Without Bilbo's experience, without his hobbit sense, Frodo cannot make the leap Bilbo made. This will leave him in much greater peril from the Ring.

From this point in *The Hobbit*, the tale moves so swiftly onward, without the least backward glance at Gollum, and so powerfully negative has his characterization been that it is not easy to see even the potential for another view. Nor, moreover, does the least hint of that view become detectable until Gandalf's conversation with Frodo in *The Lord of the Rings*. Even then, Frodo's reaction to the suggestion that Gollum was a hobbit, was to be pitied, and might be better cured than killed is as fierce as only denial can be. Here, too, the story moves swiftly on, and every mention of Gollum until he appears in "The Taming of Sméagol" emphasizes the danger he poses. Even the prologue, written with an air of historiographical detachment, speaks of him with undisguised revulsion (11–12).

In the end, Gandalf's hope that Gollum might be cured proves vain, but the failure of that hope should neither obscure nor invalidate the text's suggestion that by guiding Bilbo's hand to the Ring that day beneath the Misty Mountains the other power at work made redemption something possible to hope for (a fundamentally important point for a Christian like Tolkien). It was a very near run thing, that moment on the stairs of Cirith Ungol when Gollum nearly repented and which Tolkien later called "perhaps the most tragic moment of the Tale" (TT 4.viii.714–15; Letters no. 246, p. 330).

THE HORROR AND THE PITY

Tragedies seldom begin with one feckless friend murdering another over a birthday present fished comically out of a river, but just as the hint at a leap of faith at the paragraph's end suggests a larger spiritual context, one characterized by the intentions of an invisible power, so, too, the echo of Tragedy we hear in Bilbo's moment of horror and pity suggests Tolkien's understanding that elements of Tragedy, like *peripeteia* ("reversal of action"), *anagnorisis* ("discovery"), and *metabole* ("reversal of fortune") are also well suited to a context in which evil is used against itself to create a greater good and beauty (S 17). For the horror and pity Bilbo feels as he sees the truth about Gollum loudly echo the fear and pity Aristotle says Tragedy aims to excite; and hints that chance may not be chance after all goes hand in hand with *The Poetics*' "of wondrous things that seem to happen by chance the most wondrous are those which are revealed to have happened by design" (1452a). Moral choice, which Aristotle calls *prohairesis,* also plays a central role in Tolkien in manifesting character and determining action.

While Tolkien was hardly sitting down with Aristotle's *Poetics* open before him as a primer, he was of course no stranger to that work or to the plays of Aeschylus, Sophocles, and Euripides. Not only would he have read many of these works in his early career at Oxford, but he likely availed himself of the opportunity to attend the lectures of scholars such as Gilbert Murray and L. R. Farnell on Tragedy (C&G 1.34, 39–40, 54). The influence of the *Oedipus Tyrannos,* with its riddles of fate and free will, can also be seen in *Kullervo* and its literary descendant *The Children of Húrin* whose heroes also struggle against their fates as much as against their own headstrong natures (*Kullervo* xv–xvii; Fimi, "Wildman" 43–56). We saw (on page 66) that Tolkien could also profitably recall Homer. Elsewhere he reconstructs the philosophical myth of Atlantis found in the *Timaeus* of Plato into the philological myth of Númenor, or Atalantë, "the Downfallen."[6] So Tolkien's disaffection with the classics is as exaggerated as his dislike for Shakespeare.[7]

In the introduction to their *Tolkien on Fairy-stories* Verlyn Flieger and Douglas A. Anderson do well to recall to the reader's mind that Tolkien's essay is part of a long tradition of works on poetics going back to Aristotle (19–20).[8] We can see this in Tolkien's assertion that *eucatastrophe* is "the true form of fairy-tale, and its highest function" in just the same way as Tragedy is Drama's (*OFS* ¶ 98, p. 75). This places the effects of the Fairy-story, that is, Escape, Recovery, and above all "the Consolation of the Happy Ending" in parallel with the *katharsis* (κάθαρσις) arising through Tragedy.[9] Since, as Flieger and Anderson tell us, *On Fairy-stories* "must be seen as both prologue and guide" to *The Lord of the Rings*, and retrospectively to the new context created by the revisions to *The Hobbit*, the equivalency in poetics Tolkien establishes between Tragedy and fairy stories will offer insights that are not to be ignored (15). Tragedy and fairy stories both touch on the universals best glimpsed through myth, both pagan myth and what Tolkien would have thought of as "true myth."

Yet *The Hobbit* is not the Tale of Túrin, nor is this scene in "Riddles in the Dark" about Sméagol and Déagol and their tragedy (if it is one) but about Bilbo and Gollum and the tragedy that does not happen. Bilbo, as the author of his story twice-over, is his own protagonist, and when he unexpectedly discovers Gollum's lost humanity in himself, the horror and the pity it evokes is a reversal for him. He does not make the mistake (*hamartia*/ἁμαρτία) he was about to make, the one his fear was pushing him toward and his decency was resisting. It would have been just the sort of "mistake" one who "was superior neither in virtue nor justice" might make out of fear (*Poet*. 1453a). He is spared the fall into ill fortune (*dystychia*/δυστυχία) and suffering (*pathos*/πάθος) that Gollum experienced.

We may also mark a striking and meaningful difference between the pity that Tragedy evokes according to Aristotle and the pity we find in this scene (and elsewhere) in Tolkien. For Bilbo pities Gollum even though he does not deserve it, whereas in Aristotle one feels pity because the person suffering ill fortune does not deserve it. In *The Poetics*, Aristotle tells us that "pity concerns the man suffering ill fortune who does not deserve it, and fear concerns the [suffering of the man] like ourselves" ("ὁ μὲν [ἔλεος] γὰρ περὶ τὸν ἀνάξιόν ἐστιν δυστυχοῦντα, ὁ δὲ [φόβος] περὶ τὸν ὅμοιον," 1453a). We must also, however, weigh here Frodo's response to Gandalf in "The Shadow of the Past," when the wizard recalls Bilbo's pity in a failed attempt to elicit the same from Frodo (FR 1.ii.59). Frodo's denial of pity proceeds from his conviction that Gollum deserves death, not pity, and from his heated refusal to see him as anything like Bilbo or any other hobbit. Before he will begin to be able to glimpse what Gandalf was trying to make him see in "The Shadow of the Past," Frodo must first look at Bilbo and see Gollum. Unlike in a Tragedy which we watch as spectators, avoiding the mistake, the *hamartia*, that makes a Tragedy of the story we are within first requires us to recognize that the Gollum before us is to be pitied and spared regardless of his deserts. What is tragic and what is to be pitied thus have a wider compass in Tolkien because his poetics take in both Tragedy and eucatastrophe, both The Tale of the Children of Húrin and The Lay of Leithian, *Beowulf* and the *evangelium*, Gollum and Bilbo.

The invitation to pity is an invitation to judge oneself. Bilbo saw the tragedy of Bilbo Baggins, murderer, played out in the life of Gollum. Gandalf, offered the Ring by Frodo, envisioned his own tragedy as a new Dark Lord. Invited to consider these things for his own good no less than the good of others, Frodo is too afraid to do other than pass a judgement of death on Gollum. He will not see the likeness between Gollum and Bilbo and, therefore, as a hobbit and a Ring-bearer, between Gollum and himself. He cannot back away from the fear, as Bilbo did, and perceive the sad truth of Gollum's story. All he sees is the threat of Sauron, brought closer by Gollum, the both of them moved by lust for the Ring, malice, and a desire for revenge. Granted that Frodo's desire to save the Shire and to follow in Bilbo's footsteps counters the terror he feels, neither of these desires addresses the hold the Ring already has on him, which his fascination with the beauty of the "altogether precious" Ring and his inability to throw it into the hearth amply demonstrate. The truth, which could lead him to pity and so offer him a measure of protection, is the first victim of the Ring. Gandalf knows this, but it is a truth Frodo must learn by suffering, as Aeschylus might have said.

CHAPTER FOUR

From Bag End to Rivendell

DANGER BEHIND, DANGER AHEAD

In "The Mirror of Galadriel," Galadriel notes that Frodo has put on the Ring three times since learning its identity (FR 2.vii.366). She is referring to his use of it in the house of Tom Bombadil, at the Prancing Pony, and on Weathertop. Her remarks respond to Frodo's question about using the Ring to "see all the others and know the thoughts of those that wear them," a conversation we shall discuss in chapter 5. For now, let it suffice that such a question marks a significant change in Frodo's attitude from "The Shadow of the Past," where he told Gandalf that he "would keep it and guard it, at least for the present, whatever it may do to me," an attitude Gandalf assured him would help defend him against the corruption it worked (1.ii.62). None of the three occasions Galadriel has in mind match Frodo's declared intent too well, and so we may conclude that his desire to use the Ring on others also signals that the Ring's effect has not been as slow as Gandalf had hoped.

There are times, too, when Frodo does not put on the Ring despite the temptation to do so. One of these, when he is trapped in the barrow, is an exceptionally precarious moment where Frodo and all else might have been lost. Gandalf calls it "touch and go" and "perhaps the most dangerous moment of all" (FR 2.i.219). Why this is so for the barrow and not so for Weathertop or the ford of Bruinen will reveal much about the power of the Ring. For, as terrible as the Black Riders who hunt him may be, he brings his peril with him, on a chain in his pocket. Yet we must come to that crossroads as Frodo does, while bearing in mind what we have already seen of the Ring. First we need to grasp the dynamics of the changes he undergoes between Bag End and Rivendell, where in the space of a single day Gandalf can see him sleeping and reflect that "he may become like a glass filled with a clear light for eyes to see that can," and Frodo can see Bilbo through a "shadow" as a Gollum-like creature "groping" for his Ring and wish to "strike him" (FR 2.i.223, 232). While Gandalf may not be quite certain of how it will all end for Frodo, Bilbo looks into Frodo's face and understands at last the burden that is his legacy to his nephew. *Burden,* moreover, is precisely the word Gandalf uses to describe the Ring only a moment after refusing Frodo's offer to give it to him (1.ii.61).

In this notion, we may descry the sharp and often noted distinction between Bilbo and Frodo right at the beginning of Frodo's journey. When the elder Baggins left Bag End for the last time, having let go of the Ring, he laughed for heart's ease and sang a version of "The Road Goes Ever On" in which he declared his feet were "eager" for the road (FR 1.i.35). The day after the younger Baggins departs Bag End for the last time *as he supposes,* he, too, sings this song, unconsciously changing a single word, replacing *eager* with *weary* (1.iii.73). We may also see this distinction in their different reactions to leaving the Shire. Bilbo, yearning to see mountains one last time, quits the Shire the instant he lets the Ring go. Frodo, wishing to preserve the Shire by destroying the Ring, can scarcely bring himself to leave and dallies so long that he comes within seconds of being caught by a Ringwraith at his front door.

The mountains Bilbo so much wants to see again before his death represent freedom and adventure, reclaiming a life without the Ring (FR 1.i.32). The mountains that haunt Frodo's dreams make him uneasy, as if he is perhaps having premonitions of other mountains than Bilbo's. A part of him wants to follow Bilbo—indeed the desire to rush off to seek him twice rises up within him—but he does nothing (1.ii.62, iii.66). Yet his doing nothing is itself nothing new. For years before Gandalf returned with the truth about the Ring, Frodo had felt the same "restlessness" that Bilbo did: "He began to say to himself: 'Perhaps I shall cross the River myself one day.' To which the other half of his mind always replied: 'Not yet'" (1.ii.43, 47, 43). Given that Frodo's parents drowned in that same river and that crossing the river on a ferryboat is reminiscent, for the reader if not for Frodo, of Death, two things bear noting here: the night Frodo crosses the Brandywine, he dreams that he hears the sound of the Sea, which "had often troubled his dreams"; and for Hobbits of the Shire the Sea was "a word of fear . . . and a token of death" (1.v.108, Pr. 7).[1] The night before Frodo dreams this dream Gildor, who does not know Frodo has the Ring, had seen clearly that he was at a loss and deeply troubled (see below on page 82). It is of course also true—and a simple, eminently plausible psychological motivation for Frodo's discomfort—that his parents both drowned while boating on the Brandywine (1.i.22-23).

Frodo brings this burden and fear, this weariness and inkling of death with him out of the Shire, and it allows us to make some interesting observations. If, as Gandalf says, restlessness is a sign that the Ring is getting control, that control does not extend to pushing the Ring bearer into leaving the Shire, which we might expect it to do if it were actually as consciously determined to return to the hand of Sauron as it is often imagined to be (FR 1.ii.47). This in turn makes Gandalf's assertion about Gollum and the Ring's choosing to leave Gollum seem far more metaphorical (1.ii.55; see above on page 23). However, it is also possible to see Frodo's reluctance to embark on a journey whose goal is to destroy the Ring as a sign of the control the Ring already has over him, just as when he could not cast it into his hearth to destroy it or when he could not tell if it were he or the Ring which were "reluctant for to Gandalf touch it" (1.ii.49). This inability to distinguish between himself and the Ring bears noting.

At the same time, Frodo desires to save the Shire so much that he will undertake a Quest "to lose [a treasure], and," as he gloomily predicts, "not return" (FR 1.iii.66). This fits with his intimations of death, which Tolkien exhibits both cleverly and subtly in his references to the river and the Sea. For even if crossing a river on a ferryboat is not an image of death for the characters, it is for the readers, and this substitutes nicely for the allusion to the Sea, which only those who have read the prologue can detect. We can likewise find a similar connection in Bilbo's plan to give up the Ring and go see mountains again before he dies. This all makes sense, for the Ring confers a kind of immortality, however ghastly in the end. That is one of its greatest lies, with which it ensnares mortals even if they did not seek it for that reason. The intention to give up the Ring, then, approaches an acceptance of death, whether that will come in nature's course, as it does for Bilbo, or as the consequence of a Quest to destroy what he treasures in order to save what he loves, as for Frodo.

We can begin to see here how Frodo can by quick turns be both one whom Gandalf hopes will prove a beacon of light for others and the jealous possessor of the Ring who would strike even his beloved Bilbo for daring to try to touch *his* Ring. Both possibilities are within him from the start. The desire to save the Shire is side by side with the lust for the Ring. Neither Gandalf nor Elrond can be sure how Frodo's road will end, but they can hope that a fall into evil will not be his final destination (FR 2.i.223). Small wonder that the Ring is such a burden for Frodo, who from the start toils between these conflicting and irreconcilable desires. In fighting the Ring's pull, he is fighting himself, his own attraction to it. Small wonder, too, that Gollum, as he teetered between the healing that Gandalf so wished for him and the dark well of the Ring's power, proved to be two persons, overlapping, divided in purpose and passion, but as one in their lust for the Ring (TT 4.ii.632–34). In a similar way, Bilbo had found himself caught—if only for a moment—between choices. His embrace of pity gave him a way forward that insulated him, for a time, from the effect of the Ring while allowing him to do good using it. Without this protection, Frodo's journey becomes more perilous, within and without.

Even in his first encounter with the Ringwraiths, when Frodo merely overhears Gaffer Gamgee giving one of them a "good night" far more effective than Bilbo's "good morning" to Gandalf, we may see the hint of conflicting feelings in his mind: "Footsteps went away down the Hill. Frodo wondered vaguely why the fact that they did not come on up the Hill seemed a great relief" (FR 1.iii.69). Though resenting the idea that someone was prying into his affairs, a curiosity that these queer, well-preserved Bagginses have both ducked and faced before now, he resists the urge to inquire. His ambivalence, however, may be seen in the wordplay Frodo engages in when (parenthetically) describing his decision not to go: "he thought better (or worse) of it" (1.iii.69–70).[2]

While Frodo avoids danger here, his behavior becomes riskier in the next encounter. Until now, Frodo has expected no danger before leaving the Shire, and his walk through the countryside has been a hobbit's idyll of food, rest, and song (FR 1.iii.72). Yet, as Aragorn will later explain about the Black Riders, "the Ring draws them," and so one appears behind the hobbits on a little-used road (1.xi.189). Thus, Frodo's comment about drawing danger after him is more true than he ever guessed. At first, he still assumes that the rider overtaking them is only a local for whom his affairs would be fodder for gossip at the pub. Owing to "curiosity or some other feeling [that] was struggling with his desire to hide," he hides only at the last instant and watches from concealment (1.iii.74). The game changes when the rider stops directly in front of him, as if he perceives that someone or something may be near.

> A sudden unreasoning fear of discovery laid hold of Frodo, and he thought of his Ring. He hardly dared to breathe, and yet the desire to get it out of his pocket became so strong that he began slowly to move his hand. He felt that he had only to slip it on, and then he would be safe. The advice of Gandalf seemed absurd. Bilbo had used the Ring. "And I am still in the Shire," he thought, as his

hand touched the chain on which it hung. At that moment the rider sat up, and shook the reins. The horse stepped forward, walking slowly at first, and then breaking into a quick trot.
(1.iii.75)

Unreasoning is a revealing word here. It appears nowhere else in *The Lord of the Rings, The Hobbit,* or *The Silmarillion,* for example. We do find it in the *Letters,* however, where Tolkien uses precisely these words—*unreasoning fear*—to describe the Ringwraiths' effect (no. 210, p. 272). Here it is not just fear, but fear of discovery. Revealing, too, is its suddenness: gone at once is any thought of prying neighbors. Frodo's first *thought* is of the Ring. The unreasoning fear is met with the standard Baggins response of finding safety through the Ring, the use of which here he proceeds to rationalize absurdly, much as Bilbo and Gollum had done before him. Fear and desire subvert and enslave his reason.

How close a call this is becomes clear as soon as the Black Rider departs. Frodo's hand was reaching the Ring, as he told himself that he need not heed Gandalf's warning. With the final bit of his self-deception—that being in the Shire made all the difference—his hand moved even closer to the Ring. He touched not the Ring itself but the chain he kept it on. His next action would have been fatal. The Rider's decision saved Frodo from himself.

Close attention to the sequence of events here allows us to make several observations. While the Black Rider senses something, he obviously does not perceive the Ring or the hobbits with sufficient precision to be able to locate it or them without the Ring-bearer betraying himself by putting on the Ring. While it would be easy to guess that the Ring is moving Frodo to put it on, that is not what the text indicates. Frodo's fear is a sufficient and an explicit motive. The Ring thus seems unable to meaningfully signal its presence even to those most sensitive to that presence. Else it would have done so. The same holds true for the conversation Frodo overhears outside Bag End. In both of these near misses, the wraith stalking the hobbits is Khamûl, described in "The Hunt for the Ring" as second only to the Witch-King in sensing the Ring, but also as the wraith most weakened by the sun (UT 352–53). Yet in neither incident, one by dark and one by day, can he locate the Ring when it is only a few meters away.

With Frodo's reaction to this "very queer, and indeed disturbing" incident, we can see some interesting shifts in his behavior (FR 1.iii.75). Now a Baggins, whom the Shirefolk had long thought queer, along with his uncle—never mind their foreign visitors—uses the word *queer* in connection with another being associated with the Ring. Indeed, Bilbo had used the term of his own worst experience with the Ring, and Gandalf later echoes Bilbo's words to Frodo (1.i.34, ii.47). The very queerness of this moment in the heart of the Shire brings home a danger he thought far across the river in the blank spaces beyond the Shire map's borders.

Now, too, he behaves toward Sam and Pippin as Bilbo had toward his dwarf companions, telling them not quite the whole truth. "I felt certain that I did not want him to discover me" is a very smooth and deceptive gloss on the paralysis of his reason by dread, and his failure to mention his desire to put on the Ring and disappear is of special note (FR 1.iii.75). Vanishing then would have been abandoning his friends to the Black Rider. To be sure, Frodo's wish for invisibility here is not cynical—but he doesn't give his friends the least thought—nor is he aware of the effect putting on the Ring would actually have, namely that the wraith would have seen him and seized him, also without a thought for his friends.

As so often, it is Sam who brings Frodo down to earth. His revelation that just such a rider had questioned the Gaffer the night they left Bag End, a conversation Frodo had only overheard, shakes his complacency about the safety of the Shire. Sam's connection of this Black Rider with the one at Bag End turns the world upside down and adds an extra measure of fear (FR 1.iii.75). It earns him a rebuke, unjustly—"*The Gaffer* can't be blamed anyway" (emphasis mine)—and it doesn't make Frodo any more open about what he has just experienced. Yet the recognition that the Gaffer was not just talking to a nosy hobbit makes him leave the road as a precaution. Given the general feeling of cheerful adventure in the songs and remarks about the road in "Three Is Company," Frodo's decision to leave it signals a further darkening of the grim road that he believes he must walk, wearily, isolated and alone, expecting no return. Now the Ring comes between him and his friends, just as before it had set him and Bilbo apart from the Shirefolk in general. This action, in turn, sets up the next encounter.

Still, Hobbits being Hobbits, to walk unmolested through the shadow-dappled wood till sunset, to rest and sup, and to sing another song about the road and adventure are not without effect. Their spirits revive, and evening finds them braving the road once more, though not the main one and not without anxiety. Then, just as Pippin sings the final verse about coming home to bed at the end of their road, the sound of a horseman behind them stills their attempt to whistle past the graveyard. As before, Sam and Pippin hide, but Frodo, now moved by curiosity, imperils them all even more than before by moving back toward the road.

The Black Rider, too, differs from their encounter by daylight. In the darkness, his power and his ability to perceive the Ring appear greater. This time, he has a bearing on the direction in which the Ring lies, as he crawls straight at Frodo. That he does not know precisely where it is argues that his awareness of its presence nearby depends on some kind of resonance between the effect of the Ring on him and on Frodo. He also seems to be exerting his own will in an attempt to dominate Frodo's, so he will put on the Ring and reveal himself completely. Fear is never mentioned here as it was before, nor is thought—only a desire to put on the Ring "stronger than before. So strong that almost before he realized what he was doing, his hand was groping in his pocket" (FR 1.iii.78). The absence of fear and the double emphasis on the overwhelming power of the desire points to the Black Rider's will, not Frodo's. The Rider is of course one who has wielded a Ring of Power himself, and having a mind trained to the domination of other wills is necessary to deploying such power.[3]

The range of such domination can be vast. We have seen it already in a small way when Gandalf intimidated Bilbo into backing down from the savage pitch he reached the night he left Bag End. We saw it when the Black Riders frightened some in Bree into doing their will, and we shall see Frodo attempt to control Gollum and consider attempting to confront the Witch-king. Galadriel will allude to it in describing her contest of spirit with the mind of Sauron and will vainly warn Frodo against trying to use the Ring thus. And Aragorn's power to command the Dead Men of Dunharrow prompts Legolas to consider "how great and terrible a Lord he might have become ... had he taken the Ring to himself" (RK 5.ix.874–76). But greater by far and more terrifying is Sauron's ability to fill entire armies with rage against his enemies by the force of his will, *even when he does not possess the Ring,* so much so that when he falls his armies are left "steerless," "witless," "purposeless," and "mindless" (6.iii.946, iv.949).

There can be little doubt that the Black Rider was on the verge of seizing Frodo and none whatsoever if he yielded to the desire to put on the Ring. The difference between Frodo's wish to vanish in the first encounter, as Bilbo did, and the overpowering desire to put on the Ring in the second is quite literally night and day. In the light of day, Frodo's will is comparatively stronger; by dark of night, the Black Rider's almost preempts his will completely. Relying still on his (already shaken) confidence that the Shire provides safety and that invisibility will protect him, he risks everything to satisfy his curiosity. Unlike Bilbo, who in *The Hobbit* used the Ring to rescue his friends, Frodo imperils his and then wishes to use the Ring to escape, apparently without a thought for his friends' welfare, until he is caught by the searching will of the Black Rider and nearly loses his power of choice. Given pity's concern for the well-being of others, his refusal to pity Gollum and his thoughtlessness correlate.

Frodo's thoughtlessness discloses no want of affection for his friends, of course. Rather, his vision has not yet grown to take account of others in times of immediate peril: he still attends only to his own fear and danger, just as Bilbo had done before his moment of pity for Gollum. In fact, Frodo means to go alone because he does not wish to endanger his friends (FR 1.v.104). Gildor, whose arrival with his fellow elves drove off the Black Rider, seems to sense that Frodo means to go alone, since, when pressed by Frodo for advice, he counsels him not to do so, but to take with him "such friends as are trusty and willing" (1.iii.84). He also sees his fear and that Frodo is "astray bearing a great burden without guidance" (1.xii.210).

Gildor's assessment here deftly sums up how lost Frodo is. *Astray* here— "wandering," "off course"—is not so much a physical description, since Frodo and the others won't get lost until the next day, as it is moral or mental. Even in the early fifteenth century, *stray* and *astray* possessed figurative connotations, "morally astray, away from a moral direction, into error": "Fleschely wille is fendes knaue, / Out of reson, out of stray."[4] Desire (wille), lacking reason and needing guidance, is the servant of the enemy, that is, Satan. Now Frodo's *wille* is surely not *fleschely* in the carnal sense, but if we regard his irrational fear, his lack of guidance, and his desire to put on the Ring to escape, these verses are remarkably apt. His wish to escape by disappearing is but the first of his desires. Soon he will come to desire to defy and then to dominate his enemies. Since, moreover, *wille* means "will, intention, purpose," and "desire," the path he chooses to walk to destroy the Ring is scarcely distinguishable from the path of desire, increasingly so the further he goes and the more the strength of his will is all that remains. The difficulty in distinguishing whether *will* conveys moral choice and purpose or expresses simple desire is immanent in the English language and that ambiguity is as important a problem for Frodo as it is for the narrator and the reader.

The Ring sets the Ring-bearer apart to begin with, as we have seen. Now the threat to himself, to the Shire, and most of all to his possession of the Ring—which has proven to be his business that the Black Riders are prying into—isolates him even more. His desire to escape and the Ringwraiths' desire to capture him both drive him closer to the Ring.

THE BURDEN OF MASTERY

Ever since the thinking fox saw the hobbits asleep in the wood, they have been slowly and steadily moving into a world larger than their mundane perceptions have known so far. It is no accident that this fox encounters them just beyond the limits of Sam's geographical knowledge or that the next day Sam looks on woods he has never before seen and asks if Elves live there. Pippin's main concerns are food and rest; he has no knowledge of and less interest in whether the woods are inhabited. Frodo is preoccupied with the journey from which he expects not to return. Sam, however, has been open to Faërie from childhood, and coming of age did not change that. He may not have seen the fox, but once he has gone beyond what he knows, he *expects* Elves. Thus, he knows that his old life is being left behind as he crosses the Brandywine; thus, he is the least taken in by Old Man Willow's singing; and thus, he alone sleeps peacefully in the house of Tom Bombadil.

This transition from a narrow mentality is essential for all the hobbits, but especially for Frodo, whose perspective has been challenged from the moment Gandalf informed him of the true identity of Bilbo's ring. We have already seen him reject one part of that challenge, that is, pity, but in crossing into Tom's country he will meet the most difficult character to construe in all of Middle-earth and undergo the most unusual of all his experiences with the Ring. As a result, he will take a step forward, but even a positive goal or emotion like Gandalf's pity will be subverted by the pull of the Ring's power. So, the gain Frodo makes will come with its own temptations. That is, of course, part of his journey.

Bombadil has perplexed readers of *The Lord of the Rings* from the beginning, and the Ring's lack of power over him is a remarkable piece of common knowledge among them all. Now, who and what Tom Bombadil is will likely remain an unsolved puzzle. Tolkien never bothered to fit him into the legendarium or the present tale in any way we can ever easily parse. Given his tendency to establish links even to things far outside the legendarium proper, his failure to do so for a character within it is quite curious (*Arthur* 125–68). Just as he did not know of the Entwives' end, he did not want to know the answer to Old Tom's beginnings. He wondered early in the writing of *The Lord of the Rings* if Tom might become "the hero of a story" but decided that the best he could be was "enlarged" (*Letters* no. 19, p. 26).

And enlarged he was, into "an enigma (intentionally)," into a character whose role or function in the story mattered more than he did as a person within it:

> Tom Bombadil is not an important person—to the narrative. I suppose he has some importance as a "comment" ... and he represents something that I feel important, though I would not be prepared to analyze the feeling precisely. I would not, however, have left him in, if he did not have some kind of function. I might put it this way. The story is cast in terms of a good side, and a bad side, beauty against ruthless ugliness, tyranny against kingship, moderated freedom with consent against compulsion that has long lost any object save mere power, and so on; but both sides in some degree, conservative or destructive, want a measure of control. but if you have ... renounced control, and take your delight in things for themselves without reference to yourself, watching, observing, and to some extent knowing, then the question of the rights and wrongs of power and control might become utterly meaningless to you, and the means of power quite valueless.
> (*Letters* no. 144, pp. 174, 178–79)

In a work so devoted to exploring the perils of power to good and evil alike, surely a character who is good but untrammeled by the desire to dominate or possess will have some effect on a character who carries a burden like Frodo's. As with the Ring and *Beowulf* (above on page 24), Tolkien again found himself resistant to the idea of vivisection by scientific analysis and more inclined to feel his way to the truth of a myth he had neither the words nor the desire to explain, if it could be explained. Hence, the enigma that has defied the analysis of scholars, fans, and filmmakers for seventy-five years. We must wait, it would seem, for someone to write *Bombadil: The Master and the Critics* for Old Tom, as Tolkien did for *Beowulf* (M&C 18). Yet, we can make a start by seeing that what is essential about myths like *Beowulf* and mythic figures like Tom Bombadil is not the particular but the universal. "What and who is Tom?" is the wrong question. "Is he the oldest of all living things, or is Treebeard?" is the wrong question. We might do better to let Tom ask the questions. Tolkien's commentary in the letter quoted above and in *Beowulf: The Monster and the Critics* shows that he understood this.

The hobbits' experience of Faërie in Tom's country is mythic and profound and allows them to see into the depths of time and space under his and Goldberry's guidance.[5] Like the star of Eärendil that Sam glimpses above Mordor, everything the hobbits see, hear, and experience in the House of Bombadil speaks of a joy and a beauty beyond any momentary evil, or fear, or burden (FR 1.viii.146). This we can see in the progression of Frodo's dreams, which move from the nightmares he has in Crickhollow and the next night, his first under Bombadil's roof, to the transcendent dream—or is it a vision?—he has of the Undying Lands right before he wakes on the morning he leaves (1.v.108, vii.127, viii.134).

Crucial to this awakening to a larger world is the scene with Bombadil and the Ring. It comes after a day passed with Tom telling many tales, a day whose duration stretched beyond Frodo's ken, and an evening spent in the singing of many songs by Goldberry, songs whose effect was even more remarkable, giving the hobbits the feeling that they were seeing the world from outside the very vault of the heavens (FR 1.vii.131, 132). Like Ariel's song to Ferdinand in *The Tempest,* Goldberry's enchantment allows the hobbits to peer "into something rich and strange" they could never have guessed at before (1.2.377–410). Unlike Ariel's enchantment, however, Goldberry's song contains no deceit. Rather than telling a lie about a particular death as Ariel does, Goldberry offers a vast perspective on the universe in which the Sea seems to merge with the sky and the stars shine like "jewels in their depths" (FR 1.vii.132). In this vision, even the Sea, that Hobbit "token of death," proves to be part of a high and transcendent beauty without fear or hint of evil (Pr. 7).

With this timeless, cosmic Faërian perspective in the background, Tom suddenly begins to ask the hobbits questions which reveal that, unlike them, he knows a surprising amount about what goes on outside his borders and who lives there, including details about their families. Through knowledge and expert questioning he elicits Frodo's "hopes and fears" for his journey, even those he had never before spoken aloud (FR 1.vii.132).

This instant is fascinating and telling in two ways. First, the narrator never reveals what those hopes and fears were, even though the emphasis on the effect of Bombadil's questioning suggests that such a revelation might be coming. Since Frodo wrote his account after the Ring had been destroyed—which, we know, he regrets—against his will, we might reasonably ask whether he withheld the details on purpose.[6] The case for such suppression seems more persuasive when we recall that though many characters provide an account of what they think would happen if they had the Ring, Frodo is not one of them. What tempts Gandalf, Saruman, Boromir, Galadriel, Gollum and even Sam is on record. Yet here silence prevails, despite the best opportunity to tell of Frodo's hopes and fears and despite the text's implication that Frodo told Bombadil more than the narrator tells the reader. We should also recall Bilbo, who admitted several times, once publicly with an apology to Glóin, that his original account of how he came by the Ring was a lie, but he could never bring himself to change it in his book (FR Pr. 13). We can certainly infer Frodo's hopes and fears in part from his desire to save the Shire, but the deception that surrounds the Ring should give us pause when the narrator suggests but then withholds information of this kind.

The second is that Tom is not the dancing fool he seems. Joined to the surprising fact that he knows as much as he does is the even more unexpected description of his questioning as "cunning," not a word the tale has prepared us for (FR 1.vii.132). He nods, apparently in understanding, as Frodo tells the story of his journey thus far, but shifts unexpectedly from questions to something resembling a command as Frodo reaches the Black Riders. "Show me the precious Ring," says Tom (1.vii.132). And, without any reluctance, Frodo hands it over. His amazement at his readiness to do so, and the utter lack of any hint that he is being compelled, as the Black Rider had tried to do back in the Shire, suggest something is at work here other than the power to dominate the wills of others (1.iii.78).

Then, too, after Bombadil has mocked the Ring's most obvious, and for hobbits most useful, power, making it disappear while remaining visible himself, Frodo thinks he must use the Ring to prove that the one Tom gives him back is truly the One. Though he demonstrates this at once, Bombadil sees through the Ring's power as easily as he saw through the Ring. Where Frodo was headed as he made for the outside door is a good question, and Tom answers this by saying he "must teach the right road, and keep your feet from wandering" (FR 1.vii.133). To be sure, he is referring in part to the necessary journey across the Barrow-downs, but his words equally clearly contain a larger message about how he expects Frodo to go astray with the Ring. Wherever Frodo was heading, he was on the wrong road.

Later, in Rivendell, Gandalf will state that it is truer to say of Bombadil that "the Ring has no power over him. He is his own master" (FR 2.ii.265). Here we see two ideas held in balance by a link that English obscures, though it cannot be doubted that Tolkien was well aware of it. As we know, the Ring enables its wielder to dominate others. *Dominate* and *domination* derive from the Latin verb *dominari*—to have mastery over, as a master does over his slaves—and this verb in turn comes from the noun *dominus*, meaning "master." Because he is his own master, the Ring has no power over Tom; and he is his own master because the desire to dominate or possess is not in him. Conversely, as *Letters*, no. 144 suggests, this also explains why the Ring's pull on the good is so strong, because they, too, want "some measure of control," whether to preserve a great realm or a humble shire. Thus, the precise temptations the characters experience arise from within themselves, even if it is the pull of the Ring's seeming power to realize their desires that draws them forth.

"Such things have no hold on his mind," Gandalf says of him at the Council of Elrond, by which I would argue he means domination, possession, and control, not Rings of Power per se (FR 2.ii.265). Consider how Goldberry answers Frodo when he concludes "then all this strange land belongs to him" from her statement that Tom is the Master: "'No indeed!' she answered, and her smile faded. 'That would indeed be a burden,' she added in a low voice, as if to herself. 'The trees and the grasses and all things growing or living in the land belong each to themselves. Tom Bombadil is the Master. . . . He has no fear'" (1.vii.124). She marks out mastery in the sense Frodo means it as a burden, as if she finds the very notion of it oppressive and a source of fear. Of course, fear and a burden are what Frodo feels precisely because he possesses the Ring. Such things do have a hold on Frodo's mind. Tom's mastery, however, is paradoxically and unquestionably a domination without possession, just as Goldberry's words imply.[7]

The next day Frodo persists in his inquiry, asking Bombadil himself who he is. Tom replies, "Don't you know my name yet? That's the only answer. Tell me, who are you, yourself, alone and nameless?" (FR 1.vii.131). Frodo left his own name behind when he took up the fear and burden of the Ring. Here in Tom's country, he is Frodo Baggins, but not beyond it. There he is Mr. Underhill, a name with links both to the address of "Bag End, Under-Hill" and to Gollum, who left his name behind when he took up the Ring and who dwelt in the darkness under the Misty Mountains (H 45–46, 360; FR 1.ii.55). Gollum was also solitary and nameless, as Bilbo descried the instant before he learned pity (H 133).[8] Long before bearing his burden stripped Frodo's memories from him and left him "naked in the dark" with only the Ring, Tom Bombadil and Goldberry showed him a larger world, one full of timeless beauty and fearless memory, and asked him to consider who *he* was, a question not without relevance to the pity Gandalf urged on him (RK 6.iii.937–38). For Bilbo spared Gollum because of who he himself was, just as Gollum murdered Déagol because of who he himself was.

Though Frodo does not know it yet, two roads will soon diverge before him, just as they had for Sméagol and Bilbo in the moments before they acted. Whether he will choose the path that Bombadil means to teach him or another, darker one has been a concern of his since Gandalf first told him the truth of the Ring. He already assumes he will not return from this Quest, and his dreams at Crickhollow and the first night in Bombadil's house reflect (inter alia) his fear of death and his uncertainties about his exile from all but danger. What hope these dreams might offer is nothing he can see. Yet Bombadil's "true road" may manifest itself in Frodo's dream of the "straight road," in which the symbol of death becomes a prelude to a new beginning, first beyond the Sea and then beyond the Circles of the World.

The perception of a broader reality Frodo gains while in Tom's country may not endure in his conscious mind, but we may see its mark on him. It first becomes visible when he is a prisoner in the barrow. He doesn't panic as he did when Old Man Willow seized Merry and Pippin, and he doesn't fail to think of his friends at all as he did twice with the Black Rider in the Shire. The next time Frodo sees Gandalf, the wizard will tell him that the barrow was "touch and go. It was perhaps the most dangerous moment of all" (FR 2.i.219). But as the wording suggests, the danger lay in more than just the risk to the lives of Frodo and his friends. More was at stake than that when Frodo woke to find a naked sword across the throats of Sam, Merry, and Pippin: "At first Frodo felt as if he had indeed been turned into stone by the incantation. Then a wild thought of escape came to him. He wondered if he put on the Ring, whether the Barrow-wight would miss him, and he might find some way out. He thought of himself running free over the grass, grieving for Merry, and Sam, and Pippin, but free and alive himself. Gandalf would admit that there had been nothing else he could do" (1.viii.141). What should strike us immediately here is how Frodo now faces a peril like that which Bilbo faced, not so much to his life but to who he is. A Frodo who uses the Ring to escape and leaves his friends to die falls, just as Sméagol did and just as Bilbo did not. A lie is already forming in his mind to cover his abandonment of his friends—the opposite of what Bilbo did repeatedly for his friends: Gollum had his birthday present, Bilbo his victory in the Riddle Game, Frodo the need to protect himself and the Ring. The lies are too much alike.

That Bilbo went on to save his friends repeatedly after he spared Gollum would only make Frodo's choice to leave his friends behind to die more bitter. Nor could Gandalf's assertion that "the murder of Déagol haunted Gollum" have gone unremarked by Frodo (FR 1.ii.56). Isildur, too, as portrayed in *The*

Lord of the Rings, died trying to save himself while abandoning his men to their destruction.[9] Betrayal lurks at the heart of the Ring; faithlessness is its maker's mark (RK 5.x.891). For the forging of the One Ring was itself an act of betrayal (FR 2.i.242, 254). Frodo's entirely natural fear makes him want to escape, just as it had done in the Shire. The differences between these scenes are significant, however. While Frodo considers the danger to his friends, whom he had not thought of at all when the Black Rider drew near, his awareness of them here is double-edged and treacherous because of the power of escape the Ring seems to offer him. To abandon his friends may not be as savage a betrayal as Sméagol murdering Déagol, but Merry, Pippin, and Sam would be just as dead; and this, Gandalf suggests, would have been enough. At some level Frodo seems aware of this, since he is particularly keen to justify himself to Gandalf, who found Bilbo and Gollum's lies absurd and who had also heard Bilbo attempting to explain his need to keep the Ring as a matter of self-defense against an enraged Gollum who wished to kill him.

It is, however, by thinking of the example of Bilbo and his adventures—so many of which told of the courage that awoke in Bilbo when his friends needed rescue—that his own courage awakens in the barrow (FR 1.viii.140). Though unable so far to profit by the example of Bilbo's pity, the lesson Frodo draws here resonates with the one he is not yet ready to learn, because in the barrow there *is* a need to strike, and so he does. As Bilbo was rewarded, so will Frodo be. For it seems unlikely that even if a spiritually compromised Frodo had somehow managed to meet Strider, he could have withstood the wound he suffers at Weathertop.

PALE KINGS AND HALFLINGS

At Rivendell, Gandalf immediately juxtaposes Frodo's failure at Weathertop with his success in the barrow, thus signaling a continuity between them (FR 2.i.219). One temptation resisted is not the end of temptation. One good deed may confer initial resistance but not final immunity. We saw this much with Bilbo. Gandalf foresaw far worse for himself when Frodo offered him the Ring. This continuity is part of Frodo's journey into a larger world. For the very night he leaves Tom's country, a new phase begins, in which he will learn more about the Black Riders and their world than he ever wished to know, much as Gildor suggested he would (1.iii.84). He will also learn to fear them more, as Aragorn predicts (1.x.165). The first part ends in the barrow, with his refusal to flee and save himself alone, the second at the ford with defiance and an attempt to command the Riders.

Yet the larger world he learns of now is not that of odd, wild animals with whom Tom is on visiting terms or of the most ancient times before fear ruled the night, nor is it even the wild and natural world of the Old Forest's primeval trees, spitefully mindful of their lost lordship (FR 1.vii.130). No, rather, it is akin to what the Barrow-wight tries to conjure in his spell, a place without light or life or warmth (1.viii.141). Even the substance of memory withers here, that vision with which our hearts see the past in our mind's eye. Frodo will not forget the location of Bag End, the position of being Mr. Baggins, or even the name of the Gaffer, but the sensuous emotional connection that gives these things meaning and makes home home (RK 6.iii.939–40). If the Ringwraiths "do not see the world of light as we do, but our shapes cast shadows in their minds," they are only further down the road on which Frodo is journeying (FR 1.xi.189). Being consumed by their own Rings of Power, they have had the horizon of their perceptions shifted entirely out of alignment with those of other mortals, even those like the hobbits in Tom's country or Lothlórien who have entered Faërie because they were enchanted (OFS ¶ 10, p. 32). The wraith world is no different world but, like Faërie, a perceptual aspect of our world that lies beyond our everyday senses.

A ring of power does not confer more life, so Gandalf tells us, but merely stretches the life a mortal already possesses. As a Ring-bearer's existence becomes more attenuated, he fades and becomes invisible to those who can perceive only the world of the five senses. But, as the blindness of the wraiths, and the growing blindness of Frodo's mind's eye shows, the Ring-bearer ends with an attenuated perception of the normal world. Frodo's enchanted wound accelerates this process. While a dark mist at times seems to come between him and the world of his friends, he can perceive the light within Glorfindel from the first and see the true appearance of the Black Riders without wearing the Ring (FR 1.xii.213).

In *On Fairy-stories* Tolkien spoke of the power of language to shape our perceptions of reality and to enable us to subcreate a new one through the thinking and telling of tales. "The mind that thought of *light, heavy, grey, yellow, still, swift,* also conceived of magic that would make heavy things light and able to fly, turn grey lead into yellow gold, and the still rock into a swift water" (¶ 27, p. 41). Such enchantment can also strip those colors and qualities from our sight and even our memory. The Ring strips all this from its bearer. It takes "green from grass, blue from heaven, and red from blood" and replaces them with nothing because the power of the Ring, of Sauron, is not about creation or subcreation, but domination (¶ 27, p. 41). It leaves the Ringwraiths blind and Frodo and Gollum unable to remember the green grass of home or sunlight on daisies. Frodo's loss of the ability to recall these things even when prompted shows he will in some ways go beyond the point Gollum had reached by the time he met Bilbo. For Gollum can be reminded of them. To fall under the domination of the Ring is to become "naked in the dark" (RK 6.iii.940). In this mythical grammar, adjectives are few.

Frodo will enter this world for the first time when he dons the Ring at Weathertop. Let's briefly review his previous uses of the Ring. He put it on without hesitation in the house of Bombadil when he feared Tom had tricked him, and he was both happy and disquieted to learn he had his own Ring back (FR 1.vii.133). Clearly this was his choice. At The Prancing Pony things are a bit murkier. The urge to put on the Ring "seemed" to Frodo to come "from someone or something in the room," and afterward "for a moment he wondered if the Ring itself had not played him a trick" (1.ix.157, 160). Yet using the Ring to avoid embarrassing social situations was very much the Baggins way even when the wearer was not anxious and afraid and hunted by mysterious enemies. We have also seen in the argument between Bilbo and Gandalf how distorted a sense of reality a Ring-bearer may suffer when he believes his possession of the Ring is threatened, as Frodo must here, since his entire ill-advised performance arises from a desire to shut Pippin up before he gives away his identity. Then, too, in his first encounter with a Black Rider, his motive for wanting to put on the Ring seems to him strictly an internal one: fear.

Yet we must question Frodo's perceptions when it comes to the Ring. Under its influence he will see Bilbo as a Gollum-like creature and Sam as an orc; he will threaten Sam with his sword just as Bilbo had threatened Gandalf, and for the same reason (FR 2.i.232; RK 6.i.911–12, 6.iii.937). He will feel the burden of the Ring as a weight around his neck—as will Sam when he wears it—but Sam's experience when he carries Frodo in Mordor proves the total subjectivity of the Ring-bearer's perceptions (TT 4.ii.630, 6.i.898; RK 6.iii.941).[10]

By contrast, when the Black Riders nearly catch Frodo at night in the Shire and then at Weathertop, the text leaves little doubt they are commanding him to put on the Ring. In the Shire, his hand was reaching for the Ring without his volition before he even knew it. At Weathertop, he is able at first to resist the temptation or compulsion to put on the Ring but soon succumbs (FR 1.xi.195).

The next morning Frodo "bitterly regretted his foolishness, and reproached himself for weakness of will; for he now perceived that in putting on the Ring he obeyed not his own desire but the commanding wish of his enemies" (1.xii.199).

Two points are noteworthy here. First, we are seeing precisely the sort of domination of the wills of others that all the Rings of Power except for the three Elven Rings were made for. Second, Frodo's resistance does not end when the compulsion overwhelms him. As terrified as he was to begin with, and seeing the true appearance of the Black Riders, even now he does not freeze or fall as the other hobbits have already done. He draws the barrow sword Tom gave him, cries the name of Elbereth, whom Gildor's elves had also invoked, and desperately hurls himself at the Witch-king (FR 1.xi.195–96). The effect of his attack is not as important as the defiance he musters, so different from the first time he felt the external compulsion.

In Rivendell Gandalf will wish Frodo had resisted as successfully at Weathertop as he had in the barrow (FR 2.i.219). There he withstood his fear and a desire to escape by means of the Ring, even if escape would cost his friends their lives. No external will was affecting his in the barrow as at Weathertop. That Frodo might have chosen to betray his friends' love for him and abandon them makes the barrow more perilous than Weathertop. But if the moment in the barrow was the "most dangerous," other dangers abound (2.i.219). Frodo's brave defiance of the Witch-king at Weathertop encourages him to attempt not only to defy but to dominate his will in their next meeting. This is consonant with the bitter regret he feels when he recognizes that it was "not his own desire" he obeyed at Weathertop, as if it were better to put on the Ring willingly and knowing what it is (1.xii.199). Again, that is the significance of his choice in the barrow. There he sees through the lie. Here he does not.

In this context, turning back to compare the moments when the Ring-bearer does or does not put on the Ring in previous drafts of book 1 of *The Lord of the Rings* will prove illuminating. In the first phase it is plain that before Weathertop, Bingo (as Frodo was then called) puts on the Ring of his own choice (*Shadow* 47, 49, 58, 94, 123, 139, 185, 224). He dons it four times before they even cross the Brandywine, twice in close calls with the Black Riders and twice as a prank. There is no hint of fear or any other influence. Even in The Prancing Pony, the agency is clearly and entirely his own (139). In the second phase, Bingo does not put on the Ring when the Black Riders draw near, but he feels an urge to do so, and, it would appear, either experiences or comes closer to experiencing the same "unreasoning fear" we find in the published text (FR 1.iii.75).

For the first encounter with the Black Riders, we must infer this from a combination of the words "curiosity or some other impulse was struggling with his desire to hide" in the text of this phase and Tolkien's statement written between the first and second phases that "Bingo must NOT put on his Ring when Black Riders go by—in view of later developments. He must *think* of doing so but somehow be prevented. Each time the temptation must grow stronger" (*Shadow* 278, 224). As Christopher Tolkien explains, "later developments" refers to the newly conceived power of the Ringwraiths to see the bearer if he was wearing the Ring and to "communicate their command to the Ring-bearer and make it appear to him that it was his own urgent desire." The silent orders issued to Bingo at Weathertop in the first phase necessitated these changes in the second (199). By the third, Frodo no more knows how he came to have the Ring on than he does in "At the Sign of the Prancing Pony"; here, too, he wonders if the Ring had played a trick on him, presumably by slipping onto his finger "to reveal itself in response to some wish or command felt in the room" (FR 1.ix.160; *Shadow* 334–36).

This moment invites comparison with Bilbo in several ways. In "Riddles in the Dark," he speculated that the Ring might have played a trick on its new owner when it slipped off his finger as he was trying to escape from Gollum; and in "A Long-expected Party" he had also held the Ring in his pocket while performing in public and then vanishing in the midst of a crowd (*H* 135; *FR* 1.i.28). The differences, however, are not to be ignored. In the first place, the Ring slipped off Bilbo's finger, not on.[11] In the second, what was a poor joke in "A Long-expected Party"—and the sole remaining use of the Ring for a prank in the finished story—is an almost catastrophically bad ending in "At the Sign of the Prancing Pony." Finally, Bilbo certainly meant to put on the Ring and vanish. From the first appearance of his disappearance at the party, the agency is his (*Shadow* 237). We observed above that how the Ring ended up on Frodo's finger in Bree was rather murky. It is even more so when compared to Bilbo's story.

At the heart of this darkness, however, which Frodo will not penetrate until the morning after Weathertop, are the Ringwraiths, silently bidding him to put on the Ring, so that their suspicions may be confirmed and its presence revealed. Importantly, we may see that the narrative's trend through the first three phases is to shift the source of the Ring-bearer's desire or urge or temptation to don the Ring from his own wishes to those of the Black Riders. By the Third Phase only Bilbo uses the Ring lightly, as still he does in "A Long-expected Party" or to avoid the Sackville-Bagginses; Frodo certainly knows the desire to vanish as well as Bilbo does, but he seems a more serious guardian of the Ring once he learns what it is (FR 1.iv.104, 2.vii.365).

Once this shift is made, the source of his urge to use it becomes more obscure *to him*. Since it is not his decision plain and simple, as it was at first, and since he does not yet know that the Riders possess this power, he can hardly do other than speculate about the Ring. In "At the Sign of the Prancing Pony," he begins to guess that it comes from another source, but his notion that the command originates within the room is his misinterpretation. No one in the common room of the inn—not Bill Ferny, not Harry Goatleaf, not anyone else—had such power, but in "The Flight to the Ford," Frodo is able to perceive the Ringwraiths commanding him to stop from about a half mile away (FR 1.xii.211–12). As we know from Merry's account, at least one of them was just across the road from the inn (1.x.172–73).

Frodo thus does not understand the urge to put the Ring on at The Prancing Pony any more than he could fathom the paralytic fear and desire to use the Ring he had felt in proximity to the Black Riders in the Shire. If we consider the moments in the house of Tom Bombadil and in the barrow, where his rational choices are each his own and equally a product of who he is and what his relationship is to the power of the Ring, we may see the contrast these afford to his encounters with the Ringwraiths, where fear strips away his ability to think effectively. By leaving these moments essentially untouched from the beginning, Tolkien creates another contrast, which, together with the persistence of Bilbo's lighthearted use of the Ring at his party, subtly illuminates the complex situation Frodo finds himself in.

All of this emerges as the conception of the Ring evolves through the manuscript's first phases. It is not to begin with the One Ruling Ring, the idea of which did not yet exist, as Christopher Tolkien makes clear, but a "highly convenient magical device," though not without "a dark origin and strange properties" (*Shadow* 70). Christopher Tolkien speculates that the unexpected entry into the text of the Black Riders was in fact "the impulse of the new conceptions" (70). It took until Weathertop for the "nature of the Ring in its effect on the bearer" to be "fully conceived" and until Rivendell for Bilbo's magic ring to become the Ruling Ring (*Shadow* 189, 226–27). Even more remarkably, as the Ring grows more powerful and more sinister, the impetus for putting it on comes not from the Ring but from the bearer, as in the house of Tom Bombadil and the barrow, or from the Black Riders, as in the Shire and on Weathertop. Both may in fact come into play in "At the Sign of Prancing Pony" when Frodo's desire to vanish and the Ringwraiths' desire for him to be revealed converge.

When Frodo meets the Black Riders at the Ford, he will learn he does not have the strength for that contest of wills. He will command them to return to Mordor; they will laugh at him. He will lift his sword in defiance. The Witch-king will lift his hand, shatter Frodo's sword and stun him into silence. In these gestures, we may recall that Bombadil raised his hand when he broke the Barrow-wight's spell over Sam, Merry, and Pippin (FR 1.viii.143). The narrator recalls this, too, though Frodo may not perhaps have had it in mind at the moment. Without Tom's power, however, the gesture is empty (1.xii.214). Fearing the Black Riders, and likely deluded by the always improbable lie that he had the strength necessary to command them, he forgets that Bombadil claimed he was not their master (1.viii.147).

In addition to his fear, Frodo's defiance of the Ringwraiths is motivated by hatred of their attempts to dominate his will. Twice in the final race to the Ford of Bruinen, "hatred ... stirred in him" when he feels them trying to control him psychically (FR 1.xii.213, 214). Since this seems so natural a response, we can easily not give it a second thought. Yet, it is a remarkable reply. For Frodo almost alone of the good characters in *The Lord of the Rings* is explicitly said to act out of hate. Gollum, Sauron, Saruman, the Ringwraiths, and various orcs all do so, however.[12] Neither this motivation nor the company it puts him in bode well. Not only does his hatred spur him to try what is beyond his strength, but it may also undermine his invocation of Elbereth and Lúthien. At Weathertop, calling on Elbereth had power, but here it has none. The Witch-king silences and disarms him with a wave of his hand. Will Elbereth not be invoked in hatred or by one trying to wield the Ring?[13] For all the courage of his defiance, to act out of hatred is to stray from the true path and be drawn closer to the Ring. It is playing the Dark Lord's game, and a sign that the sorcery of the Morgul blade has almost overcome him.

CHAPTER FIVE

From Rivendell to Amon Hen

WHITHER FRODO?

When Frodo wakes in the House of Elrond on 24 October at ten o'clock in the morning, he wakes to a different world. His wound has healed, the shard of the Morgul blade is gone, but a scar remains. Only yesterday, the sorcerous wound had been still dragging him into the world of the Ringwraiths, first entered the first time he put on the Ring but first perceived only at Weathertop, when he put on the Ring in the presence of those who dwelt there. In the days since, even without wearing the Ring, Frodo's vision of his own world becomes shrouded; the faces of his friends grow more obscure and those of the wraiths easier to make out. It is, however, the effect of his struggle *against* his wound that is both subtle and striking.

> [Frodo] was smiling, and there seemed to be little wrong with him. But to the wizard's eye there was a faint change, just a hint as it were of transparency, about him, and especially about the left hand that lay outside upon the coverlet.
> "Still that must be expected," said Gandalf to himself. "He is not half through yet, and to what he will come in the end not even Elrond can foretell. Not to evil, I think. He may become like a glass filled with a clear light for eyes to see that can."
> "You look splendid," he said aloud.
> (FR 2.i.223)

We need to weigh these words carefully. It's all too easy to ignore the uncertainty of Gandalf (and perhaps Elrond) about where Frodo is heading and focus instead on the brighter of the two futures that may lie at the end of his journey. The contrasts here between Frodo's outward happiness and Gandalf's silent concern, between how Frodo seems and what the wizard's keen eye detects, and between what Gandalf thinks and what he says, warn us not to do so. His incipient transparency may just as well be the first sign of his actually fading like every mortal Ring-bearer, as it is of his metaphorically becoming "a glass filled with a clear light." Gandalf's special notice of the greater transparency of the hand that suffered most from the Morgul wound indicates we should not be too quick to settle on the brighter possibility.

Gandalf's hope, however, is more obvious and of course more persuasive. The bright October morning of Rivendell after the cleansing victory at the ford is attractive in itself, and Frodo *has* resisted and proven braver than their enemies expected. Gandalf's hope seems obvious, just as it seems obvious that Frodo has "little wrong with him." Yet, while the seed of Frodo's hobbit courage quickened in the barrow, such bravery is a treacherous asset for a Ring-bearer, especially one moved by hatred and fear. And the wider world he has come to know in his journey with the Ring has terrors and temptations to match the wonders and dream-visions that combat them. Frodo's road—"the hateful road" as it looked from Weathertop—continually forks before him (FR 1.xi.188). As Gildor saw, Frodo was lost before he left the Shire.

This is not to dismiss Gandalf's hope but to allow it the same uncertainty he does by giving equal weight to the possible end he fears. His cautious words—"I think" and "He may become"—sway uncertainly against each other in the balance. His certain knowledge of what Rings of Power do to their bearers prevents any easy confidence in the outcome of what he will concede is "a fool's hope" (RK 5.iv.815). Had Frodo successfully resisted the will of the Ringwraiths at Weathertop, this defiance in combination with his behavior in the barrow would have been more encouraging. That he did not is obviously disappointing, even if Gandalf points out how well Frodo has done to reach Rivendell alive and in possession of the Ring.

Nothing during Frodo's stay better demonstrates the peril he faces than a moment with Bilbo that very evening. After his many wonderful meetings in this chapter culminate in a reunion with Bilbo, things briefly take a dark and ugly turn. When Bilbo asks Frodo for a look at the Ring, he complies only reluctantly until the old hobbit suddenly reaches for it: "To his distress and amazement he found that he was no longer looking at Bilbo; a shadow seemed to have fallen between them, and through it he found himself eyeing a little wrinkled creature with a hungry face and bony groping hands. He felt a desire to strike him" (FR 2.i.232). There is so much to see here. Frodo's urge to violence when he feels his possession of the Ring menaced recalls not only his drawing his sword against the Ringwraiths but also Bilbo's hand on his sword hilt when he felt similarly threatened in "A Long-expected Party." Frodo sees a Gollum-like creature instead of Bilbo, and for an instant the murderous cannibal and the dear uncle whose pity has been held out to him as an all-important example become one thing in his sight: a monster grasping at *his* Ring. The "shadow [that] seemed to have fallen between" the two hobbits conjures up the similar "shadow" Frodo had perceived "between him and the faces of his friends" while he was suffering under the sorcery of the Morgul blade (*FR* 1.xii.210). That so dark an evening follows so soon upon so bright a morning underlines the uncertainty of Frodo's fate and the foolishness of Gandalf's hope.

It is, moreover, ironic and sad that a story which began again with Bilbo gaining a "sudden understanding" of Gollum's plight and the pity he showed him because of it has come around to his doing the same again, but now for himself and Frodo (*H* 133). Whatever Bilbo sees when he looks at Frodo now no doubt grieves and teaches him. "Bilbo looked quickly at Frodo's face and passed his hand across his eyes. 'I understand now,' he said. 'Put it away! I am sorry; sorry you have come in for this burden; sorry about everything. Don't adventures ever have an end? I suppose not'" (*FR* 2.i.232). He sees now, however, as he did not on the night he left Bag End, that the Ring is a burden that skews the vision of its bearer and makes monstrous enemies out of the most beloved friends. In Bag End seventeen years earlier, Bilbo did not know what had come over him, but now he does precisely because he looks upon a Ring-bearer, once again from the outside, and with pity. Both Frodo and Bilbo look at each other and, as it were, see Gollum. Yet Bilbo does not recognize that the burden he bequeathed to Frodo does not land him in an adventure like his own, but in a Great Tale, on a Quest like that of Beren and Lúthien, "a very long road, into darkness" (as Sam has already called it; see 1.iii.87). Now in Rivendell, he passes his hand in front of his eyes just as he had that last night at Bag End, as if to wipe from his sight a vision. Or is it a shadow such as Frodo has seen? And a shadow of what? Does he also see himself looking madly at Gandalf, while threatening him with his sword? However that may be, he turns to levity, to talk of the difficulties of finishing his book now that his adventure has passed on to Frodo. His humor here, in a serious situation, is the common Hobbit fallback when they don't know what to say and fear to say too much. We have already seen Bilbo use it in connection with the Ring. Likening himself to butter scraped over too much bread is quite literally the prime example of it (Hillman, "Not Where He Eats" 141).

Bilbo's understanding of Frodo's burden, which manifested itself in his reaching for the Ring and in Frodo's reaction, complements Gandalf's uncertain hopes. If by bearing this burden Frodo "may become" like a vessel of light, bearing it may also deliver him into evil (FR 2.i.232). Even amid all the splendors of Rivendell and the glory of its persons, the memories of Elder Days and the enchantments of elvish minstrelsy, the end of Frodo's journey remains in doubt.

GALADRIEL'S SUDDEN LAUGHTER

At the end of "The Mirror of Galadriel," after she has refused Frodo's offer of the Ring, he asks her a very telling question.

> "I would ask one thing before I go," said Frodo, "a thing which I often meant to ask Gandalf in Rivendell. I am permitted to wear the One Ring: why cannot I see all the others and know the thoughts of those that wear them?"
> "You have not tried," she said. "Only thrice have you set the Ring upon your finger since you knew what you possessed. Do not try. It would destroy you. Did not Gandalf tell you that the rings give power according to the measure of each possessor? Before you could use that power you would need to become far stronger, and to train your will to the domination of others."
> (FR 2.vii.366)

More dramatic scenes usually grab our attention in this chapter: Galadriel's trial of the hearts of the Fellowship at their first meeting, the sights Sam and Frodo see in her mirror, and her eloquent rejection of the Ring just a moment before this. That's all quite understandable, but I'm not sure any of these events could be more revealing than this one: Frodo asks someone who doubtless could use the Ring to devastating effect about using the Ring himself.

Is Frodo's question merely an innocent one? Can any such question about the Ring be innocent? The remark he had "often meant to ask Gandalf at Rivendell" seems almost disingenuous or—what is perhaps more likely—self-deceptive, another instance of the lies the pull of the Ring inspires as the bearer seeks justification for its possession and use. For Gandalf had been telling him since the night Bilbo left the Shire seventeen years earlier that he should not use the Ring, and he pointed out the harmful effects of doing so (FR 1.i.36, 40 [three times]; ii.48–49, 53–54; iii.67, 75; x.170); much of the point of the Council of Elrond was that the Ring could not be used (2.ii.67); and Frodo had also spent over two months in Rivendell with Gandalf. If he failed to ask, it was surely not because an opportunity to do so was wanting. Given the opposition of Gandalf and Elrond to using the Ring, Frodo seems to be overstating the case when he claims that he is permitted to wear it. I can find no passage in The Lord of the Rings to support Frodo's claim. Even if he should view it as implicit in his position as Ring-bearer that he may use the Ring, permissibility and advisability are two different things, and Gandalf and Elrond have made the case against the latter abundantly clear. Not only that, but Galadriel has just pointed out that even Elrond did not have leave to speak of the whereabouts of the Ring Frodo has spotted on Galadriel's finger (2.vii.365). For that matter, he was not permitted to speak openly of his own (2.ii.268). We must cast a wary eye on Frodo's claim here.

Frodo, moreover, phrases the question as if he sought mere awareness (to see the holders of the other Rings) and information (to know their thoughts), but Galadriel understands the matter very differently. It is plainly a question of power and domination, the prerequisite means for using the Ring to the end Frodo mentions. Consider also Galadriel's words about her own experience with Sauron, who "gropes ever *to see me and my thought*. But the door is still closed," (FR 2.vii.365, emphasis mine). She, it seems, can remain unseen and keep her thoughts unknown only because she has her ring and Sauron lacks his. But if he were to regain the One, all will be lost. For "then we are laid bare to the Enemy" (2.vii.365).

That Galadriel has the ability to know Frodo's thoughts here closes the circle opened at their very first meeting early in this chapter. For then she touches his mind and those of the rest of the company with her own and "tests" them by asking them some question like "What do you want?" and a suggestion that their desires were within their reach if they gave up their Quest (FR 2.vii.358). As she "holds" them with her eyes, almost none of them can "long endure" her gaze; and it is she who "at length . . . release[s] them from her eyes" (2.vii.357).

Galadriel here demonstrates the very dominance she later tells Frodo he would need to develop to use the Ring as he wishes. We might also glimpse her abilities elsewhere. Unlike Celeborn, she has no doubt that Gandalf set out with the Company (FR 2.vii.355); she knows Gandalf told Frodo about how the Ring confers power proportionally on its users (1.ii.53); and she knows precisely how many times Frodo has used the Ring since learning the truth about it, which seems an odd detail for Elrond to include in a report, even if entrusted to his redoubtable sons (2.iii.274). Rather, she learned these facts directly from Frodo's thoughts. If we compare this scene to *The Return of the King*, where the keepers of the Three and Celeborn converse with each other telepathically by mutual consent (6.vii.985), it will be evident that Galadriel's practice here and Frodo's desire later are not about consensual perception and knowledge.

Her warning to Frodo in answer to his question at the end of the chapter must be read in the context of her general warning in their first meeting. The narrator here notes that Galadriel is looking at Frodo twice explicitly (FR 2.vii.354–55, 356–57), once implicitly (2.vii.357 ["looked searchingly at each of them"]), and Boromir later stresses how long she looked at Frodo (2.vii.358). Since he points this out in the Company's discussion of her testing them all with her gaze, it seems reasonable her eyes were on Frodo when she warns them: "Your Quest stands upon the edge of a knife.... Yet hope remains while all the Company is true" (2.vii.357).

In hindsight, we most often think of Boromir alone in this context. His eagerness to publicly disdain the temptations he claimed Galadriel had been holding out to him draws our attention uncomfortably to him. In fact, both Sam and Faramir saw his meeting Galadriel as a decisive moment in his misfortunes (TT 4.v.667, 680). The pressure he then puts on Frodo, while addressing him ominously as Ring-bearer, to reveal what he himself would not, pushes us past discomfort toward suspicion, but it also confirms the hints already given in the text that Galadriel's psychic test of Frodo, the most important member of the Company, was of noticeable length—at least it seemed so to the two companions who likely spent the most time thinking about the Ring. Just as the narrator never explicitly tells us what Frodo's specific temptations were (above, page 10), here, too, the narrator tells us nothing of the interaction between Frodo and Galadriel to which he nevertheless draws our attention.

As it is, however, Frodo's experience here will have left him in no doubt of how useful such power might be to a Ring-bearer, especially one as battered and overmatched as he has been. If we look back on Boromir in this passage and spy clues to his later actions, we may surely do the same for Frodo and link his testing and questioning by Galadriel here with his testing and questioning of her later in the chapter. Just as Boromir's experience of Galadriel stirred something in him, so it may have done for Frodo.

So when Galadriel utters her warning, Boromir hardly seems the only one on her mind. Frodo is far more directly and intimately exposed to temptation than any of them. His peril is always the greatest, and our sympathy for him should not blind us to that. His inability to throw the Ring into the fire at Bag End predicts that the lonely road he is traveling ends with the words "the Ring is mine" (FR 1.ii.61; RK 6.iii.945). No matter how much he grows on his journey, he is as powerless to throw the Ring into the fire at the end as at the beginning—more powerless in fact, given the greater pull of the Ring on the powerful. His becoming like a glass filled with light and his slouching toward the evil that awaits all Ring-bearers proceed apace. To attempt to use the Ring destroys the weak, and even to want it "corrupts the heart[s]" of the powerful (FR 2.ii.267). This is fact.

But isn't it only natural that, after all he has been through, Frodo would feel the need for power? After all, he's been hunted by Black Riders, orcs, and Gollum, speared in Moria, stabbed by an enchanted blade on Amon Sûl and nearly turned into a wraith himself, attacked by a blackhearted willow, taken prisoner by the undead, and stunned to witness the death of the most powerful person he knows at the hands of an ancient demon. And, perhaps most pertinently here, when he defied the Nazgûl they laughed at him and would have captured him and the Ring if not for the intervention of others more powerful than they (FR 1.xii.214–15).

Frodo also knows full well how useful it can be to be able to look into the minds of others or to reach out to them from a distance. The Nazgûl had affected him more than once by communicating directly with his mind. Their silent bidding to don the Ring or to stop and wait for them had nearly cost him far more than his life. Even while Frodo lay unconscious in Rivendell and nearly beyond reach because of his wound, Gandalf learned much from Frodo that he had never told anyone. He gleaned enough to think, to hope, that Frodo would not fall into evil, even if he could not be sure of it. Now, after Galadriel's more open, direct, and powerful testing, Frodo has three clear examples of the usefulness of such power.

So, yes, of course, nothing could be more natural under these circumstances than for Frodo to wish for the power to use the Ring, if only to protect himself and his friends, to save the Shire and fulfill his Quest. In the same way, however, Gandalf might desire the strength to do good out of pity, and Boromir the might to defend Minas Tirith, and Galadriel the power to preserve Lórien (FR 1.ii.61, 2.ii.67, x.397–99, vii.366). "That is how it would begin" for all of them. Seen in this way, her words are as much a warning to Frodo not to try to use the Ring as they are an explanation to Sam of why she must not take it.

Here we see quite nicely the gray and subtle dangers of the Ring. In one moment, Frodo is humble and noble enough to offer Galadriel the Ring of his own free will; in the next, he shades the truth and asks her how to use the

Ring to dominate others. Frodo's shift here parallels what Galadriel says her own path with the Ring would be. This scene neatly concludes the testing of hearts, first of the Company together, then of Frodo and Sam apart—as if she knew both would be Ring-bearers—and finally of Galadriel herself, as Frodo gently offers her vast dominion. Yet his test will never end while he carries the One. His emphasis on himself in asking is as telling as the question: "Why cannot *I* see all the others and know the thoughts of those that wear them?" We have not seen the last of the will to dominate shown in these words.[1]

The timing of Frodo's question is also of interest, since his vision in the mirror has just afforded him an even greater proof of the power and the horror of such vision and such direct mind to mind communication. All the mysterious glimpses of disparate parts of stories whose import he does not understand and whose place in time past, present, or future he cannot guess vanish before the coming of the Eye of Sauron. What he sees terrifies him from the first. When he perceives that the Eye desires to find him, he becomes captive to that desire even though he knows the Eye does not see him, "not yet," and he gravitates toward it even though his own will seems opposed (FR 2.vii.364). Only Galadriel's intervention saves him.

Given the terror of the relentless, searching Eye and Galadriel's ability to help him resist the draw of its desire and will, it is no surprise that Frodo offers her the Ring. As at Weathertop and the Ford against the will and mental force of a lesser foe, he fails here, too, against a far more potent mind that does not even know he is there.[2] What is a wonder is that having glimpsed and nearly succumbed to such a horror, Frodo asks about using such power himself. Whether this is brave, foolhardy, or both, the desire to use rather than shun such power further exposes him to the Ring's corrupting influence and to detection by Sauron. The question Frodo began with a lie ends in silence, as he has no response to her warnings about attempting to use the Ring to this end. The last word is Galadriel's, as she points out that despite the best of intentions, she, too, would end badly if she used the Ring.

Finally, Galadriel's words before and after Frodo's question are also important: "In the morning you must depart, for now we have chosen, and the tides of fate are flowing" and "We will speak no more of it. Let us go!" (FR 2.vii.366). *We* have chosen? Let *us* go? Galadriel pairs herself with Frodo. They have something essential in common: both have chosen to reject the Ring—she by refusing Frodo's offer of it and he by making the offer. Both have also been tested, though the form of Frodo's test is less certain. His vision in the mirror and his offering the Ring to her—"It is too great a matter for me"—suggest that he now sees that "the ruin of all" of which Galadriel speaks may prove to be "the fate of many," which Gandalf feared and which he encouraged Frodo to adopt Bilbo's pity to avoid. On one level, he wants to be rid of it and on another, he wishes to use it, just like Bilbo and just like Gollum. Galadriel finds a similar conflict within herself, as the words with which she echoes the Company's perception of her test of them show: "I do not deny that my heart has greatly desired to ask what you offer" (2.vii.365; see also 2.vii.58). She does not confess or admit the desire of her heart. The best she can do is assert that she does not deny it. Galadriel herself is a mirror.

So they will speak no more of it, not because choosing has delivered them from temptation but because there is nothing more to say. The test is never over while the Ring lasts. Thus, *they* must go on. That is all they can do. The tides of fate are flowing.

THE MADNESS OF BOROMIR

So much of what Boromir says in the scene where he tries to take the Ring from Frodo plays off earlier scenes involving the Ring. When Boromir claims it was only luck that gave Frodo the Ring and that it should have been his, his words recall the justifications of Bilbo and Gollum (FR 1.i.33, ii.53, 56–57, 2.x.399). His statement that the Ring is "a gift" to be used as a weapon against Sauron turns on its head Gandalf's assertion that Bilbo and Frodo had been meant to find and have the Ring so that they might destroy it (1.ii.55–56, 2.x.398). When he imagines what he might accomplish with the Ring and avers that ruthlessness—that is, the want of pity—is essential to victory, Boromir follows in the footsteps of Gandalf and Galadriel, who also imagined what they might do with the Ring, but he falls into the trap that they avoided (1.ii.61, 2.vii.365–66, x.398). When he claims that the Ring belonged by right to the men of Númenor, he reasons as Frodo did when he concluded that Aragorn, as the heir of Isildur, should have it, but Aragorn rejects all claims of ownership (2.ii.246–47, x.399). When Boromir threatens to take the Ring from Frodo with his greater strength, he echoes Bilbo's paranoid fear that Gandalf wished to do the same, only now Frodo is not deceived by the Ring as Bilbo was (1.i.34, 2.x.399). And when Boromir's face changes "hideously" and "a raging fire" appears in his eyes, it echoes Frodo's vision of Bilbo as Gollum at Rivendell, but here the change is real, not imaginary (2.i.232, x.399). It is also recalls the fiery Eye of Sauron in Galadriel's mirror (2.vii.364). But the fire in Boromir's eyes is no vision, rather a present threat.

Finally, Boromir's attempt to take the Ring plays off the three scenes in which Frodo has freely attempted to give it away—to Gandalf, Aragorn, and Galadriel (FR 1.ii.61, 2.ii.246-47, vii.365-66), all of whom refused to take it. After Frodo's confrontation with Boromir, however, he never again makes this offer. He has seen for himself, unquestionably, how terrifying the evil that the Ring works can be. He has seen this evil befall a comrade, whom he had so far known to be brave, self-sacrificing, and honorable. This personal experience of the evil of the Ring with Boromir goes far beyond what Frodo saw when Galadriel showed him what she would become with the One Ring in her grasp. The vision and the experience together teach him lessons about himself and the Ring that he did not understand when Gandalf refused the Ring and tried to win his pity for Gollum or when Aragorn refused the legacy Isildur had meant the Ring to be for his descendants (2.ii.243, 252). Deceived, Boromir embraces the legacy Aragorn had rejected (FR 2.x.399; see also TT 4.v.670).

Like Galadriel, Boromir wants more than anything else to preserve a world on the verge of disappearing. Like Galadriel, Boromir envisions himself as a monarch defeating an otherwise unconquerable foe (TT 4.v.672). Unlike Galadriel, however, Boromir lacks the wisdom to see that no matter how just and wise a king he might start out to be, all would end in darkness and despair. Unlike Galadriel, Boromir does not reject his fantasy of the Ring with self-knowledge and denial but stretches out his hand to take it. Only by the most fortunate of actual falls does he avoid a worse fate (RK 5.iv.813). No doubt Boromir found Galadriel's testing of his heart so unnerving because what he saw reflected in her gaze was a desire like his own. No doubt understanding her own temptation helped her to grasp the peril he was in. Perhaps when Galadriel showed him that peril when they first met she allowed him to recognize the madness of his behavior at Parth Galen before it was too late.

Yet, Frodo does not witness Boromir's moment of recognition and repentance. Shaken by "terror and grief," Frodo has put on the Ring and fled (FR 2.x.400). Frodo may not be moved here by horror and pity as Bilbo was (H 133), but he has now come closer to those feelings than ever before. Seeing the effects of the Ring on a comrade and a friend (TT 4.v.664)—and as we know, Frodo has long feared for those whom he calls his friends on this adventure of his—he now grieves for one whom he believes has "fallen into evil" (FR 2.x.401). His terror is natural, just as it was in the barrow, but the grief he feels here is as important as the courage he found there and as important for him as the pity Bilbo felt for Gollum was for Bilbo. For the pity and the grief transcend the horror and the terror. Frodo grieves for someone whom he has run away from in fear of his life. Here is a Frodo very different from the one who sat in Bag End judging Gollum worthy of death, reproving Gandalf because he and the elves of Mirkwood had unaccountably let him live, and yielding the point with only a poor grace. Now, in terror of a present and immediate threat, he shows how he has grown beyond the hobbit who pronounced summary judgements on a potential threat he had never seen.

Just as in *The Hobbit* Bilbo's pity helped defend him against the pull of the Ring's power, with the result that he was able to help his friends, so here Frodo's grief for Boromir leads him to act on behalf of his friends who, even as he climbs the slopes of Amon Hen, are discussing how to help him with what Aragorn repeatedly calls "the Burden," as if that had become a proper euphemism for the Ring within the Company (FR 2.x.402, 404). Yet first Frodo's perspective on that same Burden will broaden and deepen in ways that Bilbo could not have imagined. For he sits atop the Hill of the Eye of the Men of Númenor, wearing the Ring, and the power of the two together shows him all the kingdoms of the earth. After the testing—or tempting—of the Company in "The Mirror of Galadriel," after the testing of Galadriel herself and after Boromir's apparent fall because of the temptation of the Ring's power, the sight of such power at work tempts Frodo to despair because the might of evil seems unconquerable (2.vii.358). As one who began his journey overwhelmed with the fear of Sauron and expecting to die, Frodo is nearly swept away.

His temptation to despair begins the moment he sits down atop Amon Hen. The mists that at first obscure his sight recall his perceptions of the world while he suffered from the wound inflicted by the Morgul blade (FR 1.xii.204, 206, 211–13). They also recall Aragorn's statement about the apparent blindness of the Ringwraiths, that they do not sense the world of light as we do (1.xi.189). Here, this effect is attributed to the Ring, but oddly so: "The Ring was upon him" (2.ix.400). This odd phrase is parallel to "he was sitting upon the Seat of Seeing" several lines later. Together they connote more than position, suggesting a link between the Ring and the Seat and Frodo's vision. An earlier version of this scene reveals more open emphasis on the power of Amon Hen and less on the role of the Ring: "At first he could see little: he seemed to be in a world of mist in which there were only shadows. The Ring was on him. [Then the virtue (written above: power) of Amon Hen worked on him.] Then here and there the mists gave way" (*Treason* 373).

"The Ring was upon him" of the final text is far more forceful and hostile, asserting a sudden influence over him that the words we find in the draft fail to express so clearly ("Upon, prep."). We may see the same or quite similar uses elsewhere in *The Lord of the Rings*, in passages that stress the effect of the White Rider, the armies marching into Mordor, and the King of the Dead, *upon* others whom they come *upon* by surprise (TT 3.vii.542; 4.iii.645; RK 5.ix.875). Although there is no actual movement in the scene on Amon Hen, clearly a shift has taken place due to the power of the Ring. In a passage, moreover, that already seems to echo the Bible, we might suspect that *upon* also echoes the usage in biblical passages such as "The hand of the LORD was upon me, and carried me out in the spirit of the LORD, and set me down in the midst of the valley which was full of bones," and "And, behold, there was a man in Jerusalem, whose name was Simeon; and the same man was just and devout, waiting for the consolation of Israel: and the Holy Ghost was upon him" (KJV, Ezek. 37:1; Luke 2:25).[3]

By subtly suggesting the role of the Seat of Seeing, and by making the Ring's influence more explicit, Tolkien allows the two powers here to combine to support the grand and horrifying vision that opens before Frodo's eyes, which inevitably come to rest upon Barad-dûr.

> And suddenly he felt the Eye. There was an eye in the Dark Tower that did not sleep. He knew that it had become aware of his gaze. A fierce eager will was there. It leaped towards him; almost like a finger he felt it, searching for him. Very soon it would nail him down, know just exactly where he was. . . .
>
> He heard himself crying out: Never, never! Or was it: Verily I come, I come to you? He could not tell. Then as a flash from some other point of power there came to his mind another thought: Take it off! Take it off! Fool, take it off! Take off the Ring!
>
> (FR 2.x.401)

Frodo's vision has already received emphasis in the succession of dreams he had in the early chapters of the book, which the images he sees in Galadriel's mirror recall. His suffering of the wound from the Morgul blade has allowed him to see things that others could not, and the very fact that he is a Ring-bearer sharpens his vision. Not only did he perceive the thoughts of Galadriel more than many of those thought wise, but he could see and recognize the ring, Nenya, upon her finger, while Sam, standing right beside them and privy to their conversation, could not. Even the fact that in Galadriel's mirror he saw the Eye of Sauron contributes to the increasing penetration of his vision. Yet with such sight comes a danger, that he will look too far and his gaze will be detected and he himself will be seen. Not possessing her innate power, he and his thought cannot but be revealed to the Eye, if it finds him (2.vii.364–65).

On Amon Hen that danger rushes toward him like an oncoming storm, far worse than any peril he feared at Boromir's hands. With the power of the Ring upon him, Frodo loses his identity for a moment. He cannot tell whether he welcomes or defies the swift approach of the "fierce eager will" that is searching for him, and he becomes a battleground for the Eye of Sauron and the Voice of Gandalf: "The two powers strove in him" (FR 1.x.401). In the torment of these other wills, "suddenly he was aware of himself again, Frodo, neither the Voice nor the Eye: free to choose." Note his name, emphatically placed like a fulcrum between himself and the others. With his identity, his free will also returns. The immediate effect of the Ring ceases, though that does not mean its pull no longer influences him. For one who has expressed an interest in using it, the demonstration of its power through a vision experienced directly and without the mediation of Elvish enchantment can only be dangerous.

The important link made between Frodo's recovery of his identity and his ability to choose brings to mind two passages we have already discussed. In "The Mirror of Galadriel," choice was central to the tests the members of the Company faced near the beginning of the chapter and Galadriel and Frodo at the end. Indeed, Galadriel takes her own and Frodo's choices (Sam's, too) as signs that it is time for the Company to leave Lothlórien. Here we see choices again pressed on Frodo by the Ring. Then, too, his namelessness and isolation when the Ring is "upon him" raises again the question Tom Bombadil asks: "Who are you, alone, yourself and nameless?" (FR 1.vii.131). The power to choose for himself he gains when he remembers his name recalls the power the Ring does not have over Bombadil. In this instant, when Frodo is, like Tom, his own master, he is for almost the last time free of the Ring, and he sees more clearly than he had only a little while ago.

Where previously Frodo had been afraid to go to Mordor, as Sam correctly told the others, he now fears to remain with his companions (FR 2.x.403). The gentle phrases he now employs as he realizes what he must do—"the Ring must leave them before it does more harm" and "now Boromir has fallen into evil"—reveal the pity that Frodo has so quickly come to feel for the man of Gondor, quite unlike the purely harsh words he had had for Gollum when he rejected out of hand Gandalf's suggestion that pity was in order (2.x.401, 1.ii.59). Then, too, he had scorned the idea that seeing Gollum would move him to pity, but here seeing does precisely that, not only for Boromir but potentially for others, too. And so, fearing what the Ring could do to others, Frodo flees the Company, only to run straight into the tale's foremost example of the evil one could fall into because of the Ring. Although readers of *The Lord of the Rings* can easily forget this, only three days pass between the end of "The Breaking of the Fellowship" (26 February) and the start of "The Taming of Sméagol" (29 February; RK App B 1092).

Notice, however, that Frodo does not seem to see the Ring's effect on himself. He sees his friends and comrades as susceptible to something that makes at least *some* of them—evidently Legolas and Gimli—untrustworthy. Nowhere does he wonder what it is doing to him, although the very first thing Gandalf had taught him was what the Ring does to its possessor. Indeed, his self-deception here is visible in his thinking that with the Ring at work he can trust *any* of them, regardless of how fond of them he they might be, and regardless of whether they were Hobbits. After all, as the history of Déagol and Sméagol demonstrates, the allure of the Ring changes everything, sometimes in an instant (FR 1.ii.53). Moreover, the rapid shift of Frodo's thought from preventing the Ring from doing more harm within the Company to distrusting some of his companions marks an undermining of friendship, the very thing Gandalf said they should trust in when he answered Elrond's objections to Merry and Pippin (2.iii.276).

Previously his reluctance to take anyone with him was entirely about protecting them (FR 1.iv.86–87, v.104), but as the reference to trust suggests, it is now at least in part about protecting himself and his possession of the Ring. If this seems an extreme judgement, consider the following. On the night Bilbo left Bag End, he threatened Gandalf with his sword because he did not trust him and thought he wanted the Ring for himself. In Rivendell in the morning, Gandalf saw that that Frodo might become a beacon of starlike beauty, but later that day, when desire for the Ring came between them like a shadow, Bilbo and Frodo both saw things that dismayed them in each other's faces. In Lothlórien, Frodo offered the Ring to Galadriel because he did not feel adequate to the task, but once she declined to take it, he not only immediately asked her about using it himself but never responded to her warning not to try. Here, too, the good and the bad are woven together. Even the clarity of vision he has just gained is quickly dimmed, and what begins as a concern for the evil of the Ring at work in the Company ends with the seeds of distrust. What, after all, is the whole question of trust bound up with if not the fear that someone else will try to take the Ring for himself as Boromir has just done? From Gollum's cry of hatred and loss as Bilbo disappears with his Ring in *The Hobbit* to Bilbo's threatening Gandalf with his back to the wall and with his hand on his sword, from Frodo's urge to strike Bilbo for reaching for the Ring to Boromir's "I am too strong for you, halfling," the fear of this threat persists, and underlying it is one simple sentence toward which all roads lead for everyone who feels the pull of the Ring: "The Ring is mine."

Frodo is here in part seeing, in part experiencing, the truth Galadriel uttered when she told them how precarious their Quest was and how essential it was for them all to keep faith with it and each other for there to be any hope at all (FR 2.vii.357). As I indicated above (page 101), she is referring here as much to Frodo as to Boromir. But Frodo does not fully understand her words because he does not seem to see the Ring's subtle effects on himself, how its gravity pulls him over the edge from concern for his companions to suspicion of his dearest friends. Galadriel, however, understands the temptation of the Ring perhaps better than any other character, including Gandalf (S 84). For she grasps precisely where the Ring will take her, beyond the longing to preserve and heal that was the purpose of the ring she wields to the desire for domination and retribution (FR 2.vii.366). Her powers of enchantment conjure for Frodo just such a fallen Galadriel, who unites in herself beauty and terror, love and despair.

Similarly, in a letter drafted years later Tolkien explained what would have become of Gandalf's "pity for weakness and the desire of strength to do good," had he accepted Frodo's offer of the Ring: "Gandalf as Ring-lord would have been worse than Sauron. He would have remained 'righteous,' but 'self-righteous.'" In a marginal note on the draft, he went further still: "Thus while Sauron multiplied . . . evil, he left 'good' clearly distinguishable from it. Gandalf would have made good detestable and seem evil" (*Letters* no. 246, p. 333). The contrast of Galadriel and Gandalf with Sauron is here apposite. Before his body was destroyed in the downfall of Númenor, Sauron had been fair to look upon and winning in his ways, a giver of gifts and a teacher of great lore, thus making evil seem good and seducing Elves and Men. Afterward, he could no longer assume a pleasing form, so that his "new guise [was] an image of malice and hatred made visible" (S 280–81). Much the same was true of Morgoth, who could no longer appear fair or heal his wounds after he had transferred so much of his power into Arda (*Morgoth* 399–401; S 154). In Galadriel's moment of transfiguration, hers is a terrible beauty because of what the power of the Ring would make of her (FR 2.vii.366; see also vii.373).

So, given the remarkable beauty with which Sauron, no doubt intentionally, imbued the One Ring when he put so much of his power into it, we may reasonably infer a connection between that beauty and that power.[4] It is, however, a deceptive beauty that seduces and destroys any good that the appearance of beauty seems to promise. Even what might seem the greatest of gains is also a loss: "All shall love me and despair" (FR 2.vii.366). Through his experiences with the Ring so far, Frodo has gained a larger perspective and grown in understanding and courage; he has also grown more suspicious of the motives of even his dearest friends and desirous of using the Ring for its true purpose, not invisibility but domination. Yet the day on which the Fellowship is broken is also the last day Frodo will wear the Ring until he reaches his destination. This would seem a good thing.

CHAPTER SIX

From the Emyn Muil to the Dead Marshes

THE PITY OF FRODO

With the entry of Gollum in "The Taming of Sméagol" we come to consider the following question: given that the portrayal of Gollum in the first three books of *The Lord of the Rings* is negative, dark, and monstrous, why does Frodo pity him?[1] The narrator has taught the reader to regard Gollum with fear and loathing just as Frodo does, and thus Frodo's pity, when it comes, may seem right in a high moral sense but terribly wrong in visceral, practical terms. Like Sam, the reader was not expecting this change of mind toward an enemy who, the hobbits believe, would happily kill and eat them. Yet, if Frodo has descended to a point at which he can see Bilbo as Gollum on the day they meet again after so many years, it would seem he has also risen enough to understand the import of what Bilbo saw when he had Gollum at his mercy.

We can detect this change in Frodo in the interplay of the wording of the text. For in the moment the hobbits first spy Gollum, the narrator dehumanizes him, likening him to a spider and a "prowling thing of insect-kind" as he crawls headfirst down a sheer wall, and calling him "it" several times (TT 4.i.612–14).[2] There is also a hint of Frodo's denial that Gollum could be a hobbit in the statement that "no hobbit" could have made this descent. This is in keeping with Frodo's previous references to him as "the very Gollum-creature" and "that vile creature" whom he wished Bilbo had killed long ago (FR 1.ii.54, 59). Yet, as he comes closer and as Frodo and Sam begin to talk about him, they use the masculine third person pronoun rather than the neuter, and the narrator at once follows suit. As if to signal the change in Frodo, "the black crawling shape" of the next paragraph's first four words is almost immediately defined as "he," which appears in its various forms eight times in the eight lines of the paragraph, after which Gollum begins to speak. By contrast in the paragraph directly before Frodo and Sam's discussion, the narrator uses *it* and *its* eleven times in eleven lines, as if the narrator and characters were in subtle dialogue about their changing perceptions.

Within the story, we also see Frodo the character in dialogue with his former self when he, too, gains the chance Bilbo had let slip, of inflicting the death he deserves on this vile creature. For, having resolved that he will do what he must, he and Sam turn the tables on Gollum (TT 4.i.612–14). In Frodo's case, however, Sting, not the Ring, gives him the upper hand at first. With his sword at Gollum's throat, he and Sam play a new version of Bilbo's moment of choice. Frodo's words (and Sam's) echo Bilbo's frantic thoughts about whether he should kill Gollum, whether it was right to do so, whether the harm Gollum meant to do was relevant since he had not yet attempted it. Even Sam's hostility to Gollum doesn't outweigh his sense of fairness once his "miserable enemy lay groveling on the stones whimpering" (4.i.614). As Frodo recognizes that they cannot "kill him outright. . . . not as things are"—that is, they cannot execute him now that he is their captive—he also recalls the conversation about Gollum he had with Gandalf, or a version of it (4.i.615). Crucially, he remembers how the wizard had answered his declaration that Gollum deserved death. "*Deserves* death! *I daresay he does. Many that live deserve death. And some die that deserve life. Can you give* that *to them? Then* be not *too eager to deal out death* in the name of justice, fearing for your own safety. Even the wise *cannot see all ends*"(4.i.615; italics Tolkien's, roman emphasis mine). Yet he does not remember it precisely as it was: "*Deserves* it! *I daresay he does. Many that live deserve death. And some that die deserve life. Can you give* it *to them? Then* do not be *too eager to deal out death* in judgement. For even the very wise *cannot see all ends*" (FR 1.ii.59; italics Tolkien's, roman emphasis mine). Now, it is nothing new that these two passages do not correspond exactly. The remembered conversation condenses and omits much. We could easily argue that this is a realistic touch, since memory is selective both in what it recalls and what it forgets. We could also suggest, as Christopher Tolkien does, that the original conversation and the memory of it "remain different in detail of wording, perhaps not intentionally at all points" (WR 97). Thus, the discrepancy might owe itself to chance rather than choice.

I would argue otherwise, that the differences are intentional and significant. For we have just seen above the subtlety with which Tolkien uses words, specifically *he* and *it,* to suggest the change in Frodo's perception of Gollum *once he saw him*, and Frodo will single out the decisive importance of having seen him in replying anew to the plea for pity Gandalf had made. The differences between the original conversation and the conversation as Frodo here recalls it do far more than attribute to Gandalf words he never said, such as "fearing for your own safety." To be sure, *Frodo* had mentioned that he was frightened, but Gandalf ignored the fear Frodo adduced as a motive. Rather, Gandalf argues from higher ground. Here Frodo puts these words in his mouth, empowering Gandalf to directly reject the validity of his fear as a reason to kill Gollum summarily. Yet, if this were all, we might allow that Frodo, with far more to fear now than he had a lifetime ago in the comfort of his parlor, has simply conflated the fear he had admitted he felt then with his recollection of Gandalf's answer to his fear. Memory rewrites history all the time. Or, as Christopher Tolkien suggested, his father simply did not quite recall what he had written.

But this is not all. The changes alter the tone of Gandalf's statement and lifts it into a higher moral register. It begins with the change of *it* to *death* in the first sentence and *it* to *that* in the fifth sentence, which through increased emphasis on *death* and *life* lend greater weight to his rejection of the claim of Gollum's deserts. In the sixth sentence the words *be not* have a biblical formality entirely lacking in the colloquial *do not be*. In the same sentence the shift from *in judgement* to *in the name of justice* exchanges an action that could be good or bad for a dishonest appeal to an almost personified concept of right and wrong. For not all judgements are just. Nor are all motives creditable, as the antithesis established by the juxtaposition of the social *in the name of justice* and the selfish *fearing for your own safety* demonstrates. The seventh sentence, with *For* and *very* removed, sharpens the sting of Gandalf's rebuke with its gnomic brevity and suggestion of folly.

If Tolkien rewrote Frodo's recollection in a fit of absence of mind, it is indeed surprising that he contrived to produce a memory in which Frodo portrays Gandalf as more severe and himself as more blameworthy, a memory that is a more honest and more abstract assessment of the issues at stake, a memory so potent that Frodo can only acquiesce to its demand that he set aside fear in the Emyn Muil just as he did upon Amon Hen (FR 2.x.401, 403).

> "Very well," he answered aloud, lowering his sword. "But still I am afraid. And yet, as you see, I will not touch the creature. For now that I see him, I do pity him."
>
> Sam stared at his master, who seemed to be speaking to someone who was not there. Gollum lifted his head.
>
> (TT 4.i.615)

Is it simply that Frodo sees a "poor wretch" groveling before him? No, because even as Bilbo had done long ago Frodo also sees that Gollum is "full of wickedness and mischief," and even an angry, vengeful Sam recognizes misery at once and in fact adopts Frodo's "poor wretch" himself, referring to Gollum twice that way in "The Passage of the Marshes" (TT 4.ii.615, 614, 623, 624). It has been a long journey for Frodo from truculent denial that seeing Gollum would make a difference. What, then, is it about seeing him that compels Frodo to pity him and show him mercy? A single word tells us: *Sméagol*. When Frodo almost immediately calls him by his true name, as Gandalf had done when—and only when—telling Sméagol's tale, he is implicitly admitting that Gollum is in fact a Hobbit, an assertion he had also hotly denied. He had declared the very thought of it abhorrent (FR 1.ii.54). What Frodo finally sees, as he stands poised with his sword at Gollum's throat, is a Hobbit.

Much that Frodo has seen and experienced has readied him to finish now the conversation he had begun with Gandalf then. In this, the burden of the Ring as it slowly but inevitably pulls him in, turning friends and loved ones into objects of mistrust, fear, and violent impulses, is interwoven with his dedication to the errand he has taken on himself, first to save the Shire but then, from the moment at the Council of Elrond he declared his intention to take the Ring, to save all of Middle-earth. More than that, we see the awakening of his courage at the barrow but also the faint first stirrings of sympathy even for the evil in his characterization of the wight's song as one of bereavement (FR 1.viii.141). Nor is this the first time he has done so. While still in the Shire, he had heard the loneliness in the wail of the Nazgûl (1.iv.90). Clearly, he does not lose sight of their evil when he recognizes their wretchedness, no more than Gandalf does when speaking of the slaves of Sauron to Denethor (RK 5.iv.814). For chief among those slaves, of course, are the Ringwraiths—not that Frodo the character ever pities the Ringwraiths in the moment, but the narrator here reflects the perspective of a Frodo who is far older in suffering and recognizes the bereavement of those alone in the darkness. Although Frodo's possession of the One will lead him to think of defying and even challenging the Ringwraiths, it is also because of the Ring and his wound from the Morgul knife that he sees slaves of the Ring for what they are.[3] Witnessing what the pull of the Ring did to Boromir and briefly losing himself only three days earlier have opened his eyes. He can no longer deny that one of those slaves is a Hobbit, just like Bilbo and himself.

A related aspect of the conversation with Gandalf was the effect of the Ring on its bearer and whether it could be healed. Frodo feared for Bilbo and hoped he would recover eventually, while Gandalf pitied Gollum and hoped he, too, might be healed (FR 1.ii.48, 55). The wizard had even suggested that Bilbo's voice stirred within Gollum pleasant memories of the time before the Ring, and he took this as a sign that recovery was not impossible (1.ii.54–55). Gandalf's words here recalled for Frodo not only the riddles Bilbo had posed to Gollum but also his sudden vision of all that Gollum had lost, a vision that turned him from murderous fear to pity and mercy. With all this in mind, Frodo accepts the example of Bilbo, and in refusing to kill Gollum, like Bilbo he refuses to become Gollum.

But what does he become? It is easy to overlook just how paradoxically stern and commanding Frodo is once he chooses pity. Sam sees it in the oddness of his mood, though Gollum misses it, regarding Frodo's mercy and insistence on his help—because "one good turn deserves another"—as an opportunity for his cunning (TT 4.i.615). Frodo is having none of this. He is never fooled. Straightaway, he abandons the appeal to gratitude based on what *he deserves* of Gollum, and he turns instead to self-interest, forcefully argued by the challenge to reclaim the name Sméagol and admit that he has been to Mordor. Though "such frankness, and the open speaking of the names [i.e., Sméagol and Mordor] seemed to hurt him," Frodo keeps pressing Gollum for the truth until he, too, addresses someone who is not there, picking up the thread of an earlier conversation he had had with Sauron, only giving it a new ending (4.i.616). Just as Frodo had moved from defiance to agreement, Gollum now moves from acquiescence to defiance. Yet the selfishness of his self-interest is plain: "shaking his [fist] towards the East" he cries out, "We won't [find the Ring].... Not for you" (4.i.616). *Not for you.* Unrelenting, Frodo ignores Gollum's words and suggests they might find Sméagol if they go to Mordor, and he demands to be shown the way. He then waits for the treachery Gollum's words promise. When it comes, he moves beyond gratitude and self-interest.

To what? First he dominates Gollum physically by binding him with Sam's elven rope, but the very touch of it torments him, just as the torture Sauron had inflicted on his hands had done. That Frodo did not wish to harm Gollum despite his deserts offers some comfort, but that he is willing to do so to secure his cooperation is disquieting after his profession of pity (as is the fact that Sauron, too, had tortured him). Though unplanned, it marks a further unhappy shift in attitude, which had begun with the faint hope that he had earned Gollum's gratitude, to the acceptance of the use of pain as a necessary, if regrettable, means to gaining his end. But he does not stop there. Frodo swiftly moves from physical compulsion by means of the rope to spiritual domination by exacting a promise from Gollum, which, it seems fairly clear, Frodo meant from the first to use the power of the Ring to enforce. Gollum understands him at once. His offer to swear "on the Precious," however, is answered indignantly: "Frodo drew himself up, and again Sam was startled by his words and his stern voice. 'On the Precious? How dare you?' he said" (TT 4.i.618).

We say "how dare you" not to those who have suggested merely a bad idea but to those who make a comment or request we find insolent because we believe they have gotten above themselves by making it. In this case Gollum's offer to swear with his hand upon the Ring. So Frodo's response is not quite consonant with the explanation he offers, that seeing or touching the Ring would be bad for Gollum, or that the Ring would twist his oath, true though these claims are. It harmonizes rather with the way Frodo accepts the implication that he is "the master of the Precious" by which he compels Gollum to swear. In Rivendell, when Bilbo had stretched forth his hand for the Ring, Frodo had a vision of him as Gollum-like creature; and Gandalf had chastised the impervious Pippin for suggesting that Frodo was master of the Ring (FR 2.i.225). Here, though Frodo pities Gollum's desire to touch the Ring, his own desire to dominate Gollum makes the power of the Ring outwardly manifest. When Gollum claims that "he must swear on the Precious," Frodo's response illuminates not only the newfound kinship between them but also the position of undisputed mastery of the Precious Frodo asserts—and Gollum seemingly accepts—within their new relationship:

> "No! not on it," said Frodo, looking down at him with stern pity. "All you wish is to see it and touch it, if you can, though you know it would drive you mad. Not on it. Swear by it, if you will. For you know where it is. Yes, you know, Sméagol. It is before you."
>
> For a moment it appeared to Sam that his master had grown and Gollum had shrunk: a tall stern shadow, a mighty lord who hid his brightness in grey cloud, and at his feet a little whining dog. Yet the two were in some way akin and not alien: they could reach one another's minds. Gollum raised himself and began pawing at Frodo, fawning at his knees.
>
> "Down! down!" said Frodo. "Now speak your promise!"
>
> (TT 4.i.618)

That it is Sam who perceives this manifestation attests to its reality, if not its verity. However it may seem to Sam, Frodo has not grown into a tall and mighty lord, and Gollum has not shrunk into a whining, fawning dog. In much the same way, the orc who sees Sam in Cirith Ungol with the Ring in his hand will see him as more than he is (RK 6.i.904). And yet, there is much here that is telling. Frodo's pity is now "stern," and he a "stern shadow," while Gollum is again dehumanized—both described and addressed as a dog, now and later (4.i.618-19, iii.622, 634-35; vi.687). Frodo indeed speaks like a "a mighty lord" with his "it is before you." But, though his tone here recalls that of Aragorn at the Argonath, he is not Aragorn (FR 2.ix.393).[4] What Sam sees is a lie. Only his perception of the kinship between Frodo and Gollum is true, but he does not grasp the underlying truth that what the Ring has done to one hobbit, it will do to another. The distance between king and cur is not so great, nor again is that between "one good turn deserves another" and "how dare you."

We have already seen a similar lying vision between two of even closer kinship, in Rivendell when Frodo saw Bilbo as Gollum. To be sure, though what Frodo saw was inside his own head, it is still a manifestation of the Ring's power to produce such an effect. Then, too, there is the hint that Bilbo saw something untold in Frodo's face, from which he shielded his eyes and which allowed him an understanding he had lacked before, much as Sam gains here with his master and Gollum. Answering the scene with Bilbo in Rivendell, moreover, is the moment in "The Tower of Cirith Ungol" when Frodo sees Sam as an orc (RK 6.i.911-12). In this same chapter Sam has already appeared to an orc in a guise grander than his own, and in "Mount Doom" he will again see Frodo and Gollum "with other vision" (6.i.904, iii.943-44).

We shall scrutinize each of these scenes in its proper context below. For now it is enough to see that the power of the Ring can have this effect on people looking at the Ring-bearer as much as on the Ring-bearer himself. It seems akin to the thoughts of power and glory that come to those who feel the pull of the Ring, inasmuch as both thoughts and visions are lies, an inevitable means by which the will to power and the mechanism of power come together.[5] In this scene, Frodo trades one lie for another. The now untenable assertion that Gollum could not be a Hobbit yields to the equally false notion that he is the master of the Precious. By announcing, "It is before you" without revealing it, Frodo identifies the Ring with himself and reestablishes the distance between himself and Gollum in a new guise.

Some might object to this reading on the grounds that Frodo has shown Gollum pity precisely as Gandalf wished him to do. True enough. But it is also true that Gandalf said the pity Bilbo felt and the mercy he showed protected him from the worst the power of the Ring might do (FR 1.ii.59). Frodo has not begun his ownership thus, plus he has used the Ring for invisibility and shown himself inclined to use it for more than that. Only three days ago, atop

Amon Hen, the Ring allowed him to see a vast perspective of the world, and he did not seem averse to enjoying this vision until Sauron became aware of him and he came to realize using the power of the Ring was stripping him of his identity. Feeling that loss, and having just seen Boromir lose himself, brought him to pity Sméagol. His resistance, born of fear and hatred of all involved—himself, Bagginses, the Ring, and Sauron—creates a situation in which Frodo uses the power of the Ring to dominate him and compel him to swear an oath by the Ring itself. The course of his pity does not run true because of this, precisely as Gandalf feared his own pity would be perverted if he attempted to wield the Ring (1.ii.61).

There is no question here that Frodo pities Gollum, that he has no wish to harm him, that he wishes to help him regain his identity. There is also no question that no good intention will defend him from the pull of the Ring forever, no matter how decisive a role Bilbo's pity may play in the end. Frodo is "still afraid," however. That and his errand drive him onward, and, taking a page from Aragorn's book, he means to make Gollum useful (FR 2.ix.384). Since he has no other way of binding Gollum—gratitude, self-interest, and elven rope all fail—he uses the Ring to do so, invoking its power by identifying himself with it and calling it to witness. This may not be the power of the Ring he asked Galadriel about, but he is nonetheless using its power to dominate the will of another. He even invokes the Ring verse, which makes the Ring more dangerous to him, for all his good intentions. In the summary of *The Lord of the Rings* in the 1951 letter to Milton Waldman, Tolkien leaves no doubt that Frodo has used the Ring here: "Gollum reappears, and is 'tamed' by Frodo: that is by the power of the Ring he is cowed to a Caliban-like servitude" (no. 131, in RC 746).[6] Given Tolkien's comments about "attempting to conquer Sauron with the Ring," however noble we may think Frodo, his use of the Ring to compel Gollum to help him destroy the Ring is a case of the means unjustifying the ends (*Letters* no. 66, p. 78; see also no. 183, pp. 242–43). Only a few days earlier he had declared his understanding of the Ring to Boromir: "What is done with it turns to evil" (FR 2.x.398). If the Ring was at work in the Company before he and Sam left, it is still at work now; they have brought their peril with them.

That Frodo's journey with the Ring should encompass a complex spiritual evolution, in which one step up is often followed by two steps back, is entailed by the nature of Arda Marred. From the Music of the Ainur onward, the interplay of light and darkness, as it were, has been an intrinsic and inextricable aspect of the way in which the World and the Will of Ilúvatar work. Evil may not be the Will of Eru, but he turns it into his instrument to realize a greater whole. This he told Melkor before the World was made, and this he showed Ulmo in the beautiful metamorphoses of water that Melkor's excesses made possible (*S* 17, 19).

As Verlyn Flieger has notably observed, this interplay not only informs the fabric of the legendarium as a whole, it proceeds from Tolkien's personality and worldview, which had its own inner tensions, between light and darkness, hope and despair, (dys)catastrophe and eucatastrophe (*Splintered Light* 1–31). Burdened with an ultimately irresistible power that can only turn what is done with it into evil, Frodo cannot fail to be accompanied in his progress by the corruption of his will and the desolation of his heart even as he suffers into greater wisdom and nobility. Whether he will gain anything in the end, or lose everything, we shall see.

THE EVIL WE BRING WITH US

The portrayal of Gollum in the first two chapters of *The Lord of the Rings* and the significantly revised fifth chapter of *The Hobbit* left little to be desired. He is vengeful, monstrous, treacherous, murderous, and cannibalistic. By "A Long-expected Party," Bilbo has long since forgotten the glimpse into the misery of Gollum's life that allowed "an act of virtue [to] become a part of Fate" (Spacks 58). He now recalls only the threat. Even Gandalf cannot deny that, pity notwithstanding, Gollum deserves death for his crimes. He is perfectly aware that Gollum shares the traits of malice and vindictiveness with Sauron himself. After the tales Frodo has heard, it is hardly surprising that he feels no pity for him and abruptly dismisses Gandalf's claims that he should. Those tales of Gollum have likewise prepared the reader not only to see Gandalf's pity for the lofty feeling it is but also to share Frodo's loathing for Gollum and understand his refusal to see Bilbo's pity as an example to imitate.

This portrayal receives silent reinforcement even before Gollum is mentioned again. Frodo's vision of Bilbo as a creature very like Gollum reaching for his Ring is almost premonitory, in terms of both Gollum's appearance when he finally does arrive on stage and of what the Ring might do to Frodo (*FR* 2.i.232). The fear of becoming Gollum is as present here as the fear of Gollum himself. Discussion of him at the Council of Elrond only deepens the impression of vileness and treachery that the reader has been led to expect. Aragorn is certain that Sauron had let him go with a purpose, and Boromir recognized his capability for doing evil (2.ii.255). Even when the elves of

Mirkwood begin to pity him, he proves himself cunning and untrustworthy, merely awaiting an opportunity to escape and the help of orcs to facilitate it (2.ii.255–56). Aragorn's rebuke of the elves of Mirkwood for their negligence, no less than his cryptic confession that he was "not gentle" with Gollum, underlines the lesson of the elves' failure: trust and pity this "creature," this "thing," if you will, but you do so at your own peril (2.ii.254).

We can see then that "Many Meetings" and "The Council of Elrond," with which book 2 begins, parallel book 1's "A Long-expected Party" and "The Shadow of the Past" both structurally and in their portrayal of Gollum. They also parallel each other in that the tales they tell of Gollum are Bilbo's and Gandalf's, Aragorn's and Legolas's, that is, of someone other than Frodo, for whom he remains a more personalized version of the monster of whom the Woodmen of Mirkwood spoke in terror (FR 1.ii.58). But Gollum will soon become more than a story because in "The Shadow of the Past" he is a prisoner of the elves, but in "The Council of Elrond" he has escaped captivity and vanished. Legolas's dismay and Aragorn's harsh reproach accentuate the danger he poses, just as the question Boromir had asked—"to what doom did you put him?"—reminds us of Frodo's more pointed assertion of Gollum's deserts.

While Frodo keeps silent for the moment, Gandalf says that Gollum "must do what he will," which mirrors both the statement Frodo will make at the end of "The Council of Elrond"—"I will take the Ring"—and in "The Breaking of the Fellowship" when he chooses to leave the Company after escaping Boromir and the Eye of Sauron—"I will do now what I must" (FR 2.ii.270, 2.x.401). In both of Frodo's statements, the first-person future *will* (rather than *shall*) signals his intention, choice, desire even, to embrace necessity or moral obligation, to accept the Ring as his burden, whereas Gollum has no choice. The necessity of the Ring is always upon Gollum; it precedes and dictates his desire.

This convergence of choice and necessity is hardly chance. It suggests the eventual convergence of Frodo's and Gollum's paths, just as the news of Gollum's escape from the elves did. Gandalf hints at this when he repeats the suspicion he first uttered when he told Frodo about the Ring, that Gollum "may play a part yet that neither he nor Sauron have foreseen" (FR 2.ii.256; see also 1.ii.59). If we are to consider these matters, however, we must not ignore what the Ring "wants." Whether we construe it as I have, as a metaphor expressing the Ring's inherent natural tendency to return to its proper place, or take it as evidence that the Ring is to some degree conscious, bringing the Ring to Mordor entails taking it in the direction it "wants" to go. The closer it gets, the more powerful it will become, and *this* convergence of the Ring's power and its "desire" can have no good effect on the bearer, or on Gollum, who wants the Ring for himself. Frodo is growing stronger and wiser as his journey progresses, to be sure, but any comfort we may draw from that is dubious. The power of the Ring devours such qualities, or Elrond, Gandalf or Galadriel would have been ideal choices to bear it.

Since Frodo fears Gollum, it is hardly surprising that he becomes progressively aware of his presence in ways that lead him to question whether he is dreaming. His first twinge of awareness comes in Moria as a sense of "evil following," a perception made possible, it is suggested, by the effects of the Ring and his Morgul wound, which have already enabled him to see the Ringwraiths without putting on the Ring (FR 2.iv.311-12). He thinks he hears footsteps behind them in the dark (2.iv.312, 314). Upon seeing what he believes are eyes, he thinks he must have been dreaming (2.iv.318). Even in Lothlórien, when he tells Gimli he thinks he hears the footsteps and sees the eyes, he does not insist on his perceptions (2.vi.337). He remains silent and alone with what he carries and what he fears.

Later that same night in Lórien, Frodo once more senses danger, hears noises and sees "pale eyes" again—only now Haldir also spots Gollum (FR 2.vi.345). His perceptions confirmed to be neither dreams nor imaginings, he concludes that their pursuer is in fact Gollum (2.ix.383). Yet still he keeps silent, withholding information about a peril not only to himself and his errand but to all of his companions. Not until this pursuit repeats itself on the Anduin, when Sam sees Gollum who comes so close that Frodo draws his sword, does Frodo share the truth with the rest of his companions (2.ix.382-84). That Strider already knew who was following them *and* that he has been trying to capture him shines a light on Frodo's secrecy and silence. At first glance, it is amusing to learn that Strider already knew (of course), but Frodo's withholding his suspicions about Gollum until now serves no good purpose. As Frodo realizes at Amon Hen, "the evil of the Ring is already at work even in the Company" (2.x.401). There he will be thinking of Boromir first of all, but then as now, as it always has been, the pull of the Ring is working on him first of all, isolating him even when it is accomplishing nothing else. The same isolation we see in his keeping secrets from Strider is more clearly and more dangerously visible in the fact that none of the other Company members aside from Sam could see the depth of Frodo's fear of his task, and even Sam does not understand him well enough—in justice to Sam, he cannot—if he thinks that even in terror Frodo could ever throw the Ring into the Anduin

(2.x.403). Galadriel's warning was not idle. Though Frodo senses the evils ahead and following, he does not fully perceive the evil he brings with him as he chooses to turn away from the Company toward Mordor and Gollum.

THE BURDEN AND THE EYE

Until now, references to the Ring's seeming weight have been few, and only one of these links the sense of its weight to the burden Frodo feels (FR 2.iv.312). That sensation first came to Frodo in Moria as a feeling of imminent evil. Now the evil that dogged his steps, namely Gollum, has overtaken him and become real to him in ways that he was not before. By means of the Ring, however, Frodo has pressed him into service. Is it a coincidence that the burden of the Ring increases after he uses it to dominate Gollum? To be sure, the Ring grows more powerful as they come closer to Mordor, and that growth is perceived as an increase in weight, but Frodo's first experience of this in Moria suggests that proximity to Mordor is not the whole answer.

Another part is the proximity of evil. In Moria, Gollum had been behind and the Balrog ahead. Here, in "The Passage of the Marshes," they have already seen phantom apparitions of dead Orcs, Elves, and Men, and no sooner do they emerge from the mere they were crossing when they saw them than a Black Rider passes overhead, momentarily paralyzing Frodo, Gollum, and Sam with fear (TT 4.ii.627–30). The wraith also circles back, as if he detected the presence below him of something he could not identify, much the same as the Witch-king does later in Morgul Vale (4.viii.706–07). Obviously, they do not realize that it is the Ring, which suggests that in previous encounters they were guided by the pull of the Ring as much as by the knowledge that a hobbit was carrying it. If we consider also the "rous[ing]" effect on evil creatures that the presence of the Witch-king near the Old Forest and Barrow-downs apparently had, evil seems to resonate with evil (UT 348). Since, then, the weight of the Ring does not vary in fact, but only in seeming, this resonance must occur on a spiritual plane.

We can also see that possession of the Ring erodes the identity of its bearer, as it has for Gollum, whose confusion of pronouns and names and of *Precious* (the Ring) with *precious* (himself) can be dizzying, and as it has already begun to do with Frodo, who even in "The Shadow of the Past" has a moment of confusion. When he was about to hand Gandalf the Ring, it seemed to grow much heavier, which the narrator took as a sign of unwillingness for the Ring to be touched, but cannot (or will not) say whether Frodo or the Ring itself is unwilling (FR 1.ii.49). At Rivendell, Frodo did not want to let Bilbo see the Ring, and his impulse to strike Bilbo when he reached for it must be seen as an extension of this reluctance. An even more profound loss of identity afflicted him upon Amon Hen, so much so that he briefly did not perceive himself as himself or even know what he was saying. The confrontation with Gollum here and now, Gollum whose identity is dubious, and the challenge to reclaim his lost identity as Sméagol pose for both Gollum and Frodo the question Bombadil asked with a word order and punctuation that emphasized the elements he was inviting Frodo to consider: "Tell me, who are you, alone, yourself and nameless?" (1.vii.131).

If, moreover, in "The Shadow of the Past" the Ring seems to grow heavier because of Frodo's reluctance to let Gandalf handle it, what does its increasing weight suggest here and now? That he already has an unacknowledged desire within him not to destroy it? What a grand self-deception that would be, but such is the lot of those who bear or would bear the One. It would be consistent with the corruption Rings of Power work on mortals, the desire Frodo deceptively expressed to Galadriel (see on pages 99–100), and his use of it to compel Gollum's service. It would also be consistent with his allowing Gollum to identify him, implicitly, as "the Master of the Precious." If Frodo's recovery of his name at Amon Hen is one possible answer to Bombadil's question, "Master of the Precious" is surely another. In such a context, it makes sense that the perception of greater weight derives from his use of the Ring on Gollum.

Yet we may well ask if Frodo is actually using the power of the Ring here. This question may be unanswerable, but it may not matter. Frodo could merely be manipulating Gollum, that is, using the Ring's power *over him* rather than the power of the Ring itself. If so, he is engaged in precisely the sort of "train[ing of] his will to dominate others" Galadriel had told him he would need to do before he could use it (FR 2.vii.366). Frodo is at the very least taking advantage of Gollum's subjugation to the Precious, which he asserts will hold him to his promise, just as Bilbo had leveraged the rules of the Riddle Game to compel Gollum to show him the way out as promised. Tricksy hobbits indeed. No one here is honest, and yet no one is deceived. Frodo knows full well that Gollum will be constrained only so long by his promise, and, even as Frodo is pressing and frightening him, Gollum is trying to twist his words and get his hands on the Ring (TT 4.i.622–23, 24). Frodo indeed predicts the treachery that will nevertheless come of his promise. The way the Ring transfigures Frodo, however, as he stands over a fawning Gollum suggests that its power is somehow in play.

One could argue that "The Disaster of the Gladden Fields" sheds light on this question, since a conversation between Isildur and Elendur, his son, indicates that Isildur had for some time been attempting to wield the Ring and that only now did he concede that doing so was beyond him. For when Elendur asks him, in desperation, to employ the Ring to command the orcs attacking them, Isildur answers that despite his efforts to master it, to do so "needs one greater than I now know myself to be" (UT 273–74). I would not, however, rely on this text, since Tolkien wrote it quite near the end of his life, at least twenty-five years after "The Taming of Sméagol." Not only do we have no evidence that Tolkien had this in mind in 1944 (or at any point before publication), but when he wrote this account twenty-five years later, he was also busy repeatedly reinventing Galadriel to retcon her history before the end of the Third Age. The same may well be true of "The Disaster of the Gladden Fields," as part of an endeavor to explain that is was not cowardice but prudence, at the last, that led Isildur to put on the Ring and run away: it could not be allowed to fall into the orcs' hands.[7] Yet I would argue that this account attempts not so much to extenuate Isildur's desertion as to invoke pity for the tragic error of thinking he could use the Ring.

In *The Lord of the Rings,* Isildur's apparently cowardly desertion of his men when all is lost forms an elegant counterpoint both to Frodo's refusal to abandon his friends in the barrow or in the final race to the ford of Bruinen when he was all but lost in the wraith world (FR 1.xii.211–15, 2.i.219–22), and to Aragorn's equanimity in face of death and ability to command the dead themselves, ironically as Isildur's heir (TT 3.vii.539–41; RK 5.ii.781–90). In "The Disaster of the Gladden Fields," Isildur rues his decision to keep the Ring, against Círdan and Elrond's advice, and means to turn it over to the Keepers of the Three. Whether he could have done so remains a matter of grave doubt. The Ring's pull on the mighty is greater than upon the weak, and he has already refused to destroy it once when he had the best chance anyone would ever have. Two of the Keepers of the Three stood beside him that day, but he would not heed them when they urged him to cast it into the fire. It is not even plausible that any of them would take it, nor, as Gandalf later tells Saruman, could more than one hand keep or wield it. If Isildur genuinely believes this, he is quite deceived.

Sauron was mostly dead, and his servants mostly scattered or destroyed; the Dúnedain were everywhere triumphant; the thing to do was to take the

Ring back to the undefended fire not so far away. But Isildur marches off in the wrong direction. He passes Lothlórien by—because of the weather—without stopping to entrust the Ring to Galadriel, the Keeper of Nenya, or even to consult her (UT 272). His actions are the equivalent on a much more consequential scale of Bilbo and Frodo intending to let go of the Ring, only to find it somehow right back in their pockets. Isildur allows us to doubt whether he would have been able to realize his intentions. Whatever he wishes, he is again deceived if he thinks he can ever willingly let it go. He is as powerless as Bilbo or Frodo to let go of it solely of his own volition, however much he "plays with the idea of passing it on" (FR 1.ii.55).

Most fascinating here is that a man as commanding as Isildur was unable to use the Ring for more than invisibility, though he had had it for two years and had been trying to wield it. In *The Lord of the Rings,* the presumption is that the Ring can be used, but it is a bad idea to do so. Only evil and destruction come of it in the end. Gandalf, however, also notes, "We could not learn how to wield the full power [of the Ring] all in a day" (RK 5.ix.879). We also know from him that the Ring confers power in proportion to its keeper's stature, and that Gollum seems to have acquired his mean powers quickly. To do something more needs not only more time but greater *stature* (see on pages 44–46). So, Frodo may well be harnessing some of that power against Gollum here, and we will see his ability to do so grow. Isildur's inability to wield the Ring may have more to do with the unique circumstances in which he obtained the Ring directly from Sauron's hand and his own unique reaction to putting it on than with any lack of greatness of soul or strength of mind.

So, does "The Disaster of the Gladden Fields" shed any light that helps us understand the Ring better? To the extent that its information is consistent with what we find already in *The Lord of the Rings,* it does. Where it departs most significantly is in its attempt to explain Isildur's flight as counsel rather than cowardice, which seems at odds with the inference drawn so easily (and perhaps so wrongly) from *The Lord of the Rings.* Yet "Disaster" is Isildur's story, telling of his downfall even as he repents for his refusal to destroy the Ring. In *The Lord of the Rings,* that Isildur fled and lost the Ring in the river is what matters.

As a point of reference, however, Isildur's story reminds the reader of the peril of using or attempting to use the Ring. The Wise counseled Isildur to destroy it, and he did not listen, preferring to think of it as a weregild to be paid him and a weapon for him and his heirs to wield. The Wise have also advised Frodo that the Ring must not be used and must be destroyed, that no good can come of it. Yet in the Emyn Muil and thereafter Frodo stands over Gollum attempting to use the Ring to destroy the Ring. In doing so, he allows himself to be referred to as "the Master of the Precious," for which Gandalf would have rebuked him as sternly as he did Pippin for hailing Frodo as "the Lord of the Ring" (FR 2.i.226). Here, too, as when he met Gildor in the Shire, Frodo is "astray bearing a great burden without guidance," but his need is now greater by far in the Dead Marshes with Gollum as his guide (1.xii.210).

Nor is the increasing burden of the Ring all he must contend with. As the narrator immediately reminds us, there is something worse.

> But far more he was troubled by the Eye: so he called it to himself. It was that more than the drag of the Ring that made him cower and stoop as he walked. The Eye: that horrible growing sense of a hostile will that strove with great power to pierce all shadows of cloud, and earth, and flesh, and to see you: to pin you under its deadly gaze, naked, immovable. So thin, so frail and thin, the veils were become that still warded it off. Frodo knew just where the present habitation and heart of that will now was: as certainly as a man can tell the direction of the sun with his eyes shut. He was facing it, and its potency beat upon his brow. (TT 4.ii.630)

Since the day Gandalf undeceived Frodo about uncle Bilbo's magic ring, we have watched Frodo become steadily more acquainted with a larger world. On one level, he comes to learn more of the history and troubles of the world, which hobbits, himself included, seek to fence out of the Shire. On another, more significant, level the perceptual horizons of his world, of his reality, have been rolled back by his experiences with the Old Forest, Bombadil, and the Barrow-wight; with the Ring, the Black Riders, and the Morgul knife; with Lórien, Galadriel, and the Mirror. The enchantments of Faërie and the sorcery of the Enemy have made more of his heaven and his earth. Yet, though he has seen the Eye in Galadriel's mirror and felt it while wearing the Ring on Amon Hen, he has never before perceived it as he does now, with his mind in the normal waking world. We cannot even say that he sees the Eye "in his mind's eye," because the metaphors he uses here are of shadows, veils, and eyes shut.

We may put this, too, down to the resonance of evil with evil as the Ring nears Mordor, and Frodo's use of the Ring on Gollum should also be a factor. For, if putting the Ring on allows the "hostile will" to penetrate more easily the shadows and veils that obscure him, we cannot imagine that wielding it has no effect (TT 4.ii.620). The Ringwraiths, for example, knew precisely which of the hobbits had the Ring the moment he put it on. Before that, even at close range, they had little more than an inkling that some power was present. We have just seen the same with the wraith flying above them in "The Passage of the Marshes." The Ring also promotes a connection between its keeper and others who bear or have borne a Ring of Power. Galadriel, even if she can conceal her mind from Sauron at a distance, cannot hide Nenya from Frodo in his presence, as if seeing the Eye means he had crossed a perceptual threshold.

Gollum has also been feeling the Eye all along. After saying that he "probably" was feeling it, the narrator removes all doubt as to his opinion: "But what went on in his wretched heart between the pressure of the Eye, and the lust of the Ring that was so near, and his grovelling promise made half in the fear of cold iron, the hobbits did not guess: Frodo gave no thought to it" (TT 4.ii.630–31). From the moment the hobbits take him prisoner, Gollum repeatedly—and wrongly—asserts that Sauron and the Ringwraiths see and know everything (4.i.616, ii.625, 630, 633, 635). That he and Frodo have this experience in common further expands the reader's understanding of the kinship between them that Sam sees. They are joined not just in the burden of the Ring but in suffering the unrelenting pressure of the mind that seeks to discover it in addition to the terror that, once discovered, the Ring will surely be lost to them forever. Yet the overwhelming fixation each of them has on the Ring and the Eye must compromise whatever strength such a bond might create. We may well wonder, then, if the statement that Frodo did not think about what Gollum was suffering is more than mere narrative but reflects a judgement passed by the narrator on the character—whether the character is or is not his earlier self—for failing to see or, having seen, failing to attend to the torment endured by one for whom he at last felt the pity Gandalf had believed to be of the greatest import. Later moments that hint at regret for opportunities, real or not, that were lost through inattention or misunderstanding suggest the same may be true here.[8]

The terror Frodo felt when Gandalf told him The Shire was no longer beneath Sauron's notice now seems small. If we consider that the burden of the Ring, of which we have heard so much, is *the lesser* of the two evils oppressing him now, we may glimpse both the enormity of his temptation and the nobility of his resolve. For the relentless tidal brutality of the assault on his mind can be seen in the very structure and punctuation of the sentences describing it. The repeated colons, including one nested inside another, focus the attention of the reader on the "potency [that] beat upon his brow." Yet the blows are unfocused because the Eye looks but does not see. That the

Eye sees everything is another deception of the Ring, but without the Ring it cannot do so—or else the story would have ended, as Galadriel's account of her battle against the Eye suggests (FR 2.vii.364–65). Gollum's haunted conscience, long steeped in the mad notion that he was being watched, had him shaking his fist at the Yellow Face long before he ever shook it at the Eye (1.ii.54; TT 4.i.616). "The wicked flee when no man pursueth" (KJV, Prov. 28.1). He cannot imagine that the Eye can look without seeing.

For all their kinship, however, for all their ability to "reach one another's minds" (TT 4.i.618), Frodo is not Gollum. He did not begin his ownership of the Ring by murdering Bilbo; he received it as a free gift from a somewhat badgered Bilbo. Neither of them used the Ring for any purpose more nefarious than avoiding people. And if Frodo at first rejected the pity and mercy Gandalf urged upon him, he has a strong sense of what is just, with which Gandalf agrees in principle, if not in execution. Yet it is with Frodo as Chesterton said it was with children, who "are innocent and love justice, while most of us are wicked and naturally prefer mercy" (91). Through suffering and temptation, Frodo has grown indeed. Innocence and fear no longer bar the twice-blest tempering of justice. Gollum, though still vile and monstrous, is now also undeniably a Hobbit; and it was Hobbits and the Shire that Frodo set out to save when he took up this Quest.

Frodo's attempt to win Gollum's assistance by suggesting that Gollum might find Sméagol again and be cured as Gandalf hoped, is noble and necessary— *and not impossible*—but pays too little heed to Gandalf's caveat about stirring the ghost of Sméagol by evoking memories of days before the Ring came. The evil part of him will strike back (FR 1.ii.55). It seems safe to say, however, that Gandalf's hope in no way involved resorting to the compulsion of the Ring, if Gollum refused to help. Frodo knows he is taking a great risk here and that the Ring will devour him all the sooner if he uses it (2.x.398, 1.ii.47). Nevertheless, he uses it. He knows that the promise will hold Gollum only temporarily (TT 4.iii.624). If, moreover, sunlit memories of Sméagol's days will anger Gollum, what rage will the sight of another wielding his Precious provoke? What rancor will have gripped this creature of malice when he has to suffer another to be Master of the Precious? Nevertheless, Frodo "trusts" him, relying, inter alia, on the power of the Ring to dominate Gollum to counterbalance the pull of the Ring on him for a time. *For a time.*

CHAPTER SEVEN

From the Black Gate to Ithilien

TWO THOUGHTS AND ONE GOLLUM

Frodo does not believe he and Sam are likely to survive the destruction of the Ring (TT 4.ii.624). Even before he left Bag End, he thought his Quest had no return (FR 1.iii.66). Now in the heart of the Dead Marshes he poignantly dismisses Sam's concern that they have only enough food to get them to the fire: "If the One goes into the Fire ... are we ever likely to need bread again?" (TT 4.ii.624). This is how long he needs Gollum's promise to endure, for the few weeks it will take them to reach Mount Doom and destroy the Ring. Although Frodo is not fooled by Gollum—as his knowledge that the promise will not last attests—he is here underestimating the Ring's hold over Gollum.

In truth, he cannot do otherwise because he has not suffered or done the things Gollum has. He has not lost his identity or the memory of the sunshine and green grass, though his experience atop Amon Hen indicates he is heading that way. He may have momentarily desired to strike Bilbo when he reached for the Ring, but he did not do so, unlike Gollum, who murdered Déagol the moment he saw that his friend wanted for himself this greatest of all secrets, a treasure fished from the Anduin's timeless waters. Sméagol leapt at the chance and so became Gollum, lost in an instant. Frodo, when given the Ring, is amazed by a gift he neither desired nor expected to receive. His comment on its usefulness marks a transition, a dismissal of Bilbo's motives and an acceptance of the power of the Ring to the limited extent he then understands it, as uncle Bilbo's magic ring of timely invisibility (FR 1.i.36).

Invisibility, however, is an outward sign of an inner transformation, which whether quick or slow is inevitable. So, too, is the fading a mortal bearer of a Great Ring undergoes as he is devoured (FR 1.ii.47). Even Bilbo's famous jest about bread and butter is, without his realizing it, a sign that the Ring is reducing him to the meal that Gollum could not (1.i.32; ii.47; Hillman "Not Where He Eats" 141). Another even subtler indication that Frodo is slowly losing his identity to the Ring may be found in the narrative's shift in perspective in book 4 from Frodo to Sam, who becomes more and more important to the tale and its telling as Frodo increasingly fades beneath the burden of the Ring and the pressure of the Eye after he uses the power of the Ring to dominate Gollum. That struggle soon deprives him of the emotional substance of his memories so essential to identity (RK 6.iii.938–39), a connection Gandalf's attention to the memories Bilbo stirred in Gollum also emphasized. With Frodo's mind so preoccupied and his identity becoming compromised, both errand and tale necessarily come to depend on Sam. It is no accident that book 4 begins with "The Taming of Sméagol" and ends with "The Choices of Master Samwise," a chapter whose very name attests to his now central role.

We have already seen Sam play his role as witness and living memory in "The Taming of Sméagol," when he saw the power of the Ring manifested in the transfiguration of Frodo and Gollum and grasped the link between them, and then in "The Passage of the Marshes," when he noticed the effect of the burden on Frodo and put him first, even enlisting Gollum's aid, while neglecting the "dark cloud that had fallen on his own heart" (TT 4.ii.631). But Sam is also a witness to the torment of Gollum, whose identity the Ring has so shattered that his conflicting impulses toward it manifest themselves as two "thoughts" in a conversation with each other, which Sam overhears while pretending to be asleep. "For a moment Sam thought that he was trying to rouse Frodo; then he saw that it was not so. Gollum was talking to himself. Sméagol was holding a debate with some other thought that used the same voice but made it squeak and hiss. A pale light and a green light alternated in his eyes as he spoke" (TT 4.i.632). *Thought* is an intriguing word choice here, and how we understand it will affect our grasp of the Ring's effect. It would be so easy to say that Tolkien means quite simply *personality*. Though he uses *personality* in his letters, he would likely have considered the modern use of the term unsuitable for the tone and diction of *The Lord of the Rings*.[1] Two statements in Letter 181, moreover, suggest that *personality* refers in any event to the whole and *thought* to a constituent part: "I did not foresee that before the tale was published we should enter a dark age in which the technique of torture and disruption of personality would rival that of Mordor and the Ring and present us with the practical problem of honest men of good will broken down into apostates and traitors" (234). With this we must compare: "By temporizing, not fixing the still not wholly corrupt Sméagol-will towards good in the debate in the slag hole, [Gollum] weakened himself for the final chance when dawning love of Frodo was too easily withered by the jealousy of Sam before Shelob's lair" (235). What Tolkien here calls "the Sméagol-will" is the same as what the narrator calls a "thought" in "The Passage of the Marshes," and *will* seems part of what *personality* comprises. *Thought* also refers to a part of the whole in Frodo's experience upon Amon Hen, where the Voice he hears in his mind is called "another thought," which implies that the Eye, too, is a thought. The Voice is no more all of Gandalf than the Eye is all of Sauron. I would further argue that "Never! Never!" and "Verily I come, I come to you!" and Frodo's confusion about these phrases reveal in him an early stage of the same kind of disintegration we see afflicting Gollum in "The Passage of the Marshes" (FR 2.x.401). Frodo, however, is whole enough for now to reassert himself and not be ruled by any of the "thoughts" that come to him on the Hill of the Eye of the Men of Númenor. Once he remembers who he is, that is.

He also started off with a will far more fixed toward good than Sméagol did. In the same letter, Tolkien passes a damning verdict on Gollum, who murdered Déagol within minutes of seeing the Ring because he had a "mean soul" and had already become "a mean sort of thief" (*Letters* no. 181, p. 234). Being of such a "mean" *stature* (see pages 44–46), Gollum fell at once. Thus, now that the "Sméagol-will" has been roused by Frodo's kindness, as it was by Bilbo before him, he is so divided from himself that he has been reduced to competing intentions. No whole self exists to overrule the two warring "thoughts" and choose a way of his own.[2] Atop Amon Hen Frodo can still do this; at the bottom of the slag-hole Gollum cannot.

This scene also marks the fulfillment of Frodo's warning to Gollum that the Ring would prove "more treacherous than you are. It may twist your words" (TT 4.i.618). Again, he has just seen Boromir's thinking warped by the Ring's pull on his fears for Gondor and his *honest* desire to save it until he sees himself as a conquering hero and in time a king. The way oaths and promises can bend or break those who make them was well known to Elrond (*Shaping* 37–38, 70, 150, 155; see also *S* 274), which is why no oath bound the Company. Boromir's fall into evil—so Frodo thinks, not knowing the end of his story—provides him with all the evidence he needs to recognize the truth of the temptations that Gandalf and Galadriel faced. Boromir, too, imagined himself starting out well. Frodo no doubt meant it when he told Gollum that he might find Sméagol again if they went to Mordor, but he will soon have much harsher words for him.

What Sam witnesses here is "the terrible call of the Ring" playing itself out in the struggle between two parts of Gollum, the one wholly lost, with the other not far behind. The narrator has alluded to this earlier, making the point that both of the other hobbits were too preoccupied to notice his suffering (TT 4.ii.630–31), and above we noted that invisibility and fading outwardly mark an inner change. Here that inner change, that shattered identity, is made manifest in his hands, which alternate between reaching for Frodo's throat and drawing back; in his changing eyes, which shine with a pale or green light as the different thoughts speak; and most of all in his words, which illuminate the difficulties of the cure Gandalf hoped for. Within Gollum, a shard of Sméagol does still exist, who responds to kindness and minds the solemnity of his promise. The larger part of him, the Gollum-will, is moved by malice and the desire for revenge.

Yet, if we think that what we see here is as simple as Good Sméagol versus Bad Gollum, or even Slinker versus Stinker, we are missing a crucial point: lust for the Ring drives them both. Where they differ is in the lengths to which each of them is willing to go to get it and what to do once it has been recovered. The Sméagol-will resists the idea of breaking his promise but allows himself to be persuaded by the self-serving twisting of its wording, which Frodo predicted, and to be daunted by the anger that Gandalf foresaw. One objection after another falls once the Gollum-will reinterprets the terms of the oath: "If we was master [of the Precious], then we could help ourselves, yes, and still keep promises" (TT 4.ii.633). The Sméagol-will acquiesces far too willingly to the Gollum-will's intention to harm Sam. He offers not a word of opposition to the dodgy assertion that "the nice hobbit" will not be harmed, "not if it doesn't please us." His fear of Sauron is answered by the fantasy of "Gollum the Great." His fear that Frodo and Sam will kill him if he tries to take the Ring becomes a plea for time—"Not now. Not yet"—that only reveals his desire to make the attempt. Finally, though the Sméagol-will protests in horror at the suggestion of help from Shelob, he has no answer to the debate's final argument, the Gollum-will's cry of pure lust: "Yes! We wants it! We wants it!"

The Sméagol-will has no answer, because this is no less his desire. That he does not desire the Ring is the one lie he cannot tell himself. Once a person is captured by the gravity of the Ring, no fear or morality can successfully resist its pull. If this is true of both Gandalf and Gollum, what hope can Frodo truly have of ever fulfilling his Quest? (*TT* 4.ii.624). If one hobbit will murder another to get the Ring, and if Gandalf with the Ring would have made good as bad as evil, how can Frodo not be overborne and thus in that final moment corrupted? (*Letters* no. 246, p. 333). His dispirited words to Sam a few days before Gollum's debate show that he may already suspect on some level that he, too, will succumb to the desire for the Ring. The three questions that must be answered in the negative, and the three incredulous conditional statements in seven sentences convey his doubt and the darkness falling within him just as surely as Gollum's debate reveals torments which both his "thoughts" are feeling: "To do the job as you put it—what hope is there that we ever shall? And if we do, who knows what will come of that? If the One goes into the Fire, and we are at hand? I ask you, Sam, are we ever likely to need bread again? I think not. If we can nurse our limbs to bring us to Mount Doom, that is all we can do. More than I can, I begin to feel" (*TT* 4.ii.624).

Verlyn Flieger has called Gollum "the emblem of Frodo's growing division from himself, a division that we do not see in its entirety until the final moment at the Cracks of Doom" (*Splintered Light* 151). This division, as we have seen from the beginning, is signaled through details often quite small in themselves, and just so the characters of Gollum, Bilbo, and Frodo have been intended to be viewed side by side. Indeed, Gandalf encourages Frodo to see Gollum and Bilbo side by side as Hobbits and as bearers of the One Ring, so that he may learn pity and fear. Now that Frodo and Gollum are face to face, as Bilbo and Gollum were in "Riddles in the Dark," the apposition of their characters enables us to glimpse more of the division of Frodo from himself of which Flieger spoke, though I suggest that the division is better described as being "within himself."[3] What is more, we see the same "appositive characterization" at work in the debate of the Gollum-will and the Sméagol-will. Here we see the Sméagol-will trying to "transcend a foe who is, in essence, *himself*, or a self he has the potential of becoming" (Stratyner 80). Bilbo faced and Frodo is now facing the same battle the Sméagol-will is fighting against the Gollum-will.

What's remarkable, given the lust of both wills for the Ring, is that there is any bit of Sméagol left at all after five centuries of murder in the darkness. This hobbit toughness (*FR* 1.ii.55) proves an interesting counterbalance to Tolkien's reading of him in Letter 181, that the Ring was too much for his already "mean soul." While something in his character led him to fall so quickly, something in his nature allowed this last piece of him to survive, stained with blood and guilt, but not perhaps beyond the hope of a cure (1.ii.55). Unlike the proud and great men who became the Ringwraiths, he did not fade. Their fate, too, is apposite with his own, as their repeated, terrifying presence above the Dead Marshes suggests.

Earlier in "The Passage of the Marshes" Sam had mused that "three precious little Gollums in a row we shall be if this goes on much longer" (TT 4.ii.628), referring of course to their slow, stooped, sometimes crawling, progress behind their guide. Yet Sam's soul is often prophetic in ways he does not understand. When still in the Shire he foresaw that a great darkness lay before them and that he was meant to walk beside Frodo through it (FR 1.iv.87). He has been on that road in earnest since he and Frodo crossed the River Anduin. As one, moreover, who will be a Ring-bearer himself, he walks behind Frodo and Gollum metaphorically and literally.

Earlier still he had noted the oddness of his Master's mood, the unaccustomed sternness that would endure no contradiction from him. There would be no pert "begging your pardon, Mister Frodo . . ." this time.[4] While this hardly amounts to a silencing of Sam, it does underline that Frodo is his Master, too, precisely as he is asserting his mastery over Gollum and accepting the implication that he is the Master of the Precious. At that moment he had also perceived the important link between Frodo and Gollum (TT 4.i.618). Now at this moment, listening to Gollum's debate, he discerns another, that the most threatening hunger which Gollum feels is not a hunger of the body. He does not, however, put the two truths together and grasp that what he thinks of as "the call of the Ring" and what the narrator calls "the lust of the Ring" affects both Frodo and Gollum. It is in this that their kinship chiefly lies. Unlike Bilbo at Rivendell, Sam does not yet understand.

He knows danger when he sees it, however, and he pretends to wake up just as he had pretended to be asleep, concealing by one pretense what he had learned by the other. In using this deception even as the now ascendant Gollum-will is reaching for a sleeping Frodo's throat, Sam has the benefit of the Sméagol-will's fear that the hobbits together would be too watchful and too much for him (FR 4.ii.633). Yet pretense and concealment do not end here. There is no sign in the text that Sam informs Frodo *at this time* of what he has overheard. Clearly Frodo learns it later, but for now Sam keeps it to himself, no doubt to avoid increasing the burden on his master. However good Sam's intentions, we again find the Ring surrounded by deceit.

CHOICES AT THE BLACK GATE

When the hobbits arrive at the Black Gate, Frodo and Sam see at once that entering here is impossible. Reproached by Sam for bringing them here, Gollum replies that this was where Frodo had said he wanted to go: "[Frodo's] face was grim and set, but resolute. He was filthy, haggard, and pinched with weariness, but he cowered no longer, and his eyes were clear. 'I said so, because I purpose to enter Mordor, and I know no other way. Therefore I shall go this way. I do not ask anyone to go with me'" (TT 4.iii.637). *Purpose* is an unusual verb. "Obsolete" for centuries in eight of its ten senses, "archaic" in the other two, it seems an ideal verb for Tolkien ("Purpose, v."). Even in the twentieth century in the hands of masters of prose such as James Joyce and Iris Murdoch it strikes the ear as old-fashioned and formal if not wholly pompous. In "The Dead," Joyce writes "Gabriel, feeling now how vain it would be to try to lead her whither he had purposed, caressed one of her hands" (*Dubliners* 221). Six decades later, Iris Murdoch tells us in *Nuns and Soldiers* that "when she was being converted she was already purposing to be a religious" (57, chapter 1). Tolkien's use of it here fits in well with Murdoch's and Joyce's, but it is when we compare its use in *The Lord of the Rings* and elsewhere in the context of his characterization of Frodo that we begin to see "purpose" as more than an archaic-sounding synonym for "intend."

To begin with, this verb never occurs in *The Hobbit*, predictably. In *The Silmarillion*, however, we find it no less than twelve times. Again, this is not unexpected. Its language is far loftier and more formal than *The Hobbit* or *The Lord of the Rings*. In *The Silmarillion* it marks characters who are either of a high stature and power, or think they should be: Ilúvatar (42), Melkor (73, 79, 107), Varda (100), Celegorm and Curufin (173 twice, 177), Sauron (174), Maedhros (190, 253), and Túrin (221). Their purposes may be cosmic or vile, but are never trivial. It is also used exclusively by the narrator; no character ever utters it.

In *The Lord of the Rings* we find it is much, but not entirely, the same. In the first place "purpose" is found exclusively in the mouths of characters. Galadriel says it first in the courtly beginning of the Company's presentation to the Lord and Lady of the Galadhrim: "Yet not in vain will it prove, maybe, that you came to this land seeking aid, as Gandalf himself plainly purposed" (FR 2.vii.357). Both she and Gandalf and their purposes match what we see in *The Silmarillion*. Frodo and Faramir's discussion of how Boromir's boat survived Rauros, which both find inexplicable in normal, worldly terms, is also full of similarly lofty, courteous speech; and Frodo's declaration that "Boromir purposed" to return to Gondor through Rohan parallels Galadriel's about Gandalf both in his intentions and failure to realize them. Faramir also perceives the connection between the boat's survival and the land where it was made—a land which was "a corner of the Elder Days. ... where ancient things still lived on in the waking world" (FR 2.vi.349)—and more particularly with Galadriel, "the Lady that dies not" (TT 4.v.667). Such language may befit Galadriel, but for Frodo we may well wonder.

Consider how "I purpose to enter Mordor, and I know no other way" transforms "I will take the Ring, though I do not know the way" into a far more commanding declaration of intent than he had expressed at the Council of Elrond (FR 2.ii.270). This harmonizes not only with the overall description of Frodo in this paragraph as resolute and unafraid, but with the "tall stern shadow, [the] mighty lord who hid his brightness in a cloud" that he had seemed to Sam to be when he used the Ring to tame Sméagol at their first meeting (TT 4.i.618). Frodo, "Master of the Precious" and "mighty lord," will reveal himself yet more before this day is done.

Gollum, moreover, on the morning after the debate of his two "thoughts," reproved by Sam and shocked by Frodo's open declaration of his (for Gollum) inconceivable purpose, responds with fear, lust for the Ring, and disgruntled mockery. For to him entering Mordor can only mean taking the Precious to Sauron, who will "eat us all, if He gets it, eat all the world" (TT 4.iii.637). Gollum suggests that Frodo instead "give [the Ring] back to little Sméagol," which Frodo notices but for the moment ignores, reiterating his determination to enter Mordor by the only way he knows. Gollum desperately allows that there may be another way:

"You have not spoken of this before" [said Frodo].

"No. Master did not ask. Master did not say what he meant to do. He does not tell poor Sméagol. He says: Sméagol, take me to the Gate—and then good bye! Sméagol can run away and be good. But now he says: I purpose to enter Mordor this way. So Sméagol is very afraid. He does not want to lose nice master. And he promised, master made him promise, to save the Precious. But master is going to take it to Him, straight to the Black Hand, if master will go this way. So Sméagol must save them both, and he thinks of another way that there was, once upon a time. Nice master. Sméagol very good, always helps."
(TT 4.iii.638)

To the petty resentment he feels at not being consulted by Frodo, Gollum adds mockery as he parrots back at him the high-sounding words of a master who, as he sees it, has to be saved from himself. (Sam, by contrast, will try to talk sense to his master, but he never mocks him.) Caustic remarks and mockery are of course nothing new from Gollum, and much of his fawning on Frodo is likely as insincere as Sam thinks it. In general, his sarcasm has been directed at both of them, and has made pointed fun of their dangerous ignorance and their distrust of him.[5] If, however, we compare his use of Sam's words against him back in "The Passage of the Marshes"—"Yes, yes, and Sam stinks!" (TT 4.ii.629)—with his use of Frodo's here, there is a difference between them. With Sam, it is banter—"the same to you." With Frodo, in a context where Gollum is openly questioning his master's judgement and implying that his own is better, openly mocking him with his own choice of a verb more suitable for figures of the Elder Days than for three stinking hobbits is a sign that both Frodo and Gollum have crossed a line.

For Gollum, we saw this passage in the end of his internal debate the night before, when the lust for the Ring of both his "thoughts" twisted the words of his promise. For Frodo it was adumbrated in his use of the Ring to dominate Gollum and in his threatening him with Sting to get him to move when the Ringwraiths flew over ahead and froze him in fear (TT 4.ii.635). This threat, which also took place the night before the Black Gate, is far different than the threat he made in the Emyn Muil. There, Sam's life was in jeopardy and Frodo's response justified (4.i.614). Had he in that instant simply struck Gollum down without warning in defense of Sam, not even Gandalf could have said that he was "eager to deal out death in the name of justice, fearing for [his] own safety" (4.i.615). To use violence, however, or the threat of it merely to compel obedience is an act of terror more suited to an orc chieftain, like Uglúk in book 3, or to a master of slaves, like Sauron, than it is like the brave hobbit who would not abandon his friends in the barrow a few months earlier or who held out to Gollum the hope that Sméagol might be found again, only a little while after he had threatened him to save Sam's life. Between that threat and that hope came pity; between that hope and this threat came the increasing burden of the Ring, made to dominate others. Just as Gollum is pulled in different directions by his different "thoughts," much is in flux within Frodo between the effect of the Ring and his sense of his mission.

Scholars have discussed the differing speech patterns of and pronouns used by Gollum and Sméagol, but Frodo's language is also revealing.[6] Even now it betrays him. As he solemnly pronounces what he purposes, he sounds much more like the Frodo of the Cracks of Doom than the Frodo of the Council of Elrond. That is to say, he doesn't sound like the Frodo we have known so far. As recently as his capture of Gollum, just a week earlier, Frodo did not speak thus. To be sure, as we saw when he compelled Gollum to swear by the Ring, he spoke gravely and more than a bit pompously (TT 4.i.618). His tone, however, throughout the rest of this long scene is far more familiar and even friendly. Before the Black Gate, moreover, he follows up his statement of purpose with a third threat, in which he again speaks as to a despised minion:

"I did not mean the danger that we all share," said Frodo. "I mean a danger to yourself alone. You swore a promise by what you call the Precious. Remember that! It will hold you to it; but it will seek a way to twist it to your own undoing. Already you are being twisted. You revealed yourself to me just now, foolishly. Give it back to Sméagol you said. Do not say that again! Do not let that thought grow in you! You will never get it back. But the desire of it may betray you to a bitter end. You will never get it back. In the last need, Sméagol, I should put on the Precious; and the Precious mastered you long ago. If I, wearing it, were to command you, you would obey, even if it were to leap from a precipice or to cast yourself into the fire. And such would be my command. So have a care, Sméagol!" (TT 4.iii.640)

Frodo recapitulates his warning about swearing by the Ring but lets Gollum know with devastating effect that he has given himself away, not to Sauron but to the current Master of the Precious, who would, if necessary, put on the Ring and bid him leap to his death. A twofold threat now hangs over Gollum, from the Ring *and* from its master. Few could imagine a domination so perfect that it had the power to command suicide, but here and now Frodo imagines just that. This is far beyond Frodo's desire to strike Bilbo at Rivendell and beyond his asking Galadriel about using the Ring.

Yet there is a link and a progression from one to the next. The threat of death so far seen in Frodo's sword now merges with the will to dominate others embodied in the Ring, to become, as it were, the blade held to Gollum's throat. Sam and Gollum now see something in Frodo they had not seen before, because they had "confus[ed Frodo's] kindness and blindness" (TT 4.iii.640). By means of the Ring, Gollum is reduced to gibbering terror. Sam, although he sees something more—"a look in his face and a tone in his voice"—than he saw in the Emyn Muil, so admires Frodo and so loathes Gollum that he is blind to what is going on within his master (640). Never having borne the Ring himself, he can be surprised by Frodo's sternness and approve the vicious threat he has made. Gollum, in his terror and his kinship, has the clearer understanding of Frodo at this moment. That Frodo is then kinder to Gollum, though still insistent, shows he too perceives the line he has crossed in his use of the Ring.

Yet like Boromir on Amon Hen, Frodo has not fallen. For the Man of Gondor, his attempt to seize the Ring was a moment of madness brought on by fear and despair for his homeland, from which a literally fortunate fall saves him (*RK* 3.v.496, 5.iv.813). He recognizes what he almost did, deeply repents it, and pays for it. Yet his death is not so much a redemption as a confirmation that he is the Boromir the Fair of whom Aragorn and Legolas will sing and whom Faramir will see preserved as if by miracle in the Elven boat (*TT* 4.v.666). Boromir's words to Frodo were full of fear, doubt, and despair, as they faced the choice between Mordor and Minas Tirith, much like Frodo's thoughts here as he must decide between the Black Gate and the nameless way Gollum has just suggested, which existed "once upon a time" and may still (4.iii.638). Having terrified Gollum as Boromir had terrified him, Frodo also turns back, recrossing the line from the cruel menace of his threat to the patience and kindness with which he usually treated Gollum.

A cynical view might suggest that Frodo is playing "nice master, wicked master" with Gollum, but from what we have seen of those caught between a desire to do good and the pull of the Ring their shifts are far more impulsive than studied. Bilbo gets angry enough to threaten Gandalf with his sword when the wizard prods him; and Boromir does attempt violence when Frodo rejects his arguments. Both are suspicious and make accusations of treachery. Even in the case of the overheard desires of the Sméagol-will and the Gollum-will the inclination to do good swiftly yields to the plots and passions of violence. Nor should we forget that Sméagol attacked and killed Déagol not simply from behind, as he might have done—and would later prove quite proficient at doing—but only after Déagol denied him the Ring (*TT* 4.ix.726). When Bilbo reached for the Ring, in a heartbeat Frodo went from overjoyed to see the beloved, old hobbit to ready to strike the creature he suddenly seemed to have become (*FR* 2.i.232).

Outside the Black Gate, Frodo states his purpose, and in a seeming panic Gollum asks him for the Ring back. After these examples, we might expect this Frodo to respond swiftly and harshly. But that does not happen, because Gollum wrong-foots him by playing to his purpose of entering Mordor through the Black Gate. His unanticipated suggestion of an alternative shakes

Frodo's outward resolution and briefly turns his gaze inward to his fears as he gauges Gollum's tale and trustworthiness.

It is the daylight terror of the Black Gate, and the despair of seeing his vision on Amon Hen realized in the arrival of another army to strengthen Mordor, that first moves him to choose to trust Gollum and even to believe that it is their fate to help and trust each other. Yet, Frodo's rebuke shows that any trust is transactional, depending on Gollum's continuing to keep his promise. First, Gollum must answer them about this other way he has suggested. That interrogation, however, leaves Frodo in further doubt about Gollum's truthfulness, behind which, as Gollum has just demonstrated, lies the desire to reclaim the Ring. He wonders about the efficacy of any choice he might make, given the vast strength of Mordor: "And here he was a little halfling from the Shire, a simple hobbit of the quiet countryside expected to find a way where the great ones could not go, or dared not go. This was an evil choice. Which way should he choose? And if both led to terror and death, what good lay in choice?" (TT 4.iii.644). As if to confirm him in his doubt and despair, as he sits with Sam and Gollum "under the weight of doom," the Ringwraiths circle high above, adding their own weight of horror and dread (4.iii.644). Then the arrival of another army to swell Mordor's brooding strength adds to Frodo's fear and despair (4.iii.646). At this moment, however, Frodo laughs from the depths of despair, for Sam's "old fireside rhyme of *Oliphaunt*" brings the Shire vividly back into his mind, a place that had come to seem long ago and far away. The simple Hobbit verse of a sort Ted Sandyman would have laughed to scorn—oliphaunt or dragon, it's all childish nonsense to him—affords Frodo something resembling the relief and recovery Tolkien says Fairy-stories provide (1.ii.44). For Frodo regains a "clear view," just as he had upon Amon Hen, not perhaps of "things as they are" but of "things as we are ... meant to see them" (OFS ¶ 83, p. 67).

Frodo thus comes to see his errand as he must, as he had on Amon Hen and in Rivendell, as he had in the spring of the previous year, when he set out to save the Shire. The good in choice lay in the scant difference between despair and the slimmest, most foolish of hopes. To attempt the Black Gate now that he sees the impossibility of doing so would mark him with a despair as great as Fingolfin's when he hammered on the gates of Angband and challenged Morgoth to single combat. In stepping back from the harshness of his words and going forward with Gollum, Frodo is again embracing the pity Gandalf had urged upon him. He will spare the one deserving of death and trust the one unworthy of trust. He is also once more accepting of the "fate" he had taken upon himself in the Shire only last spring, though to him it seems "so remote now... like a chapter in the story of the world's youth" (TT 4.iii.644). He even suggests again that Gollum can choose to be who he wishes to be (4.iii.640).

Yet, while Frodo thinks of himself as "a little halfling from the Shire," he also entertains the grandiose and scornful thought that he is going "where the great ones ... dared not go," which resonates with Boromir's derisive "I doubt if they are wise and not merely timid" (FR 2.x.398). That's the Ring talking, in both cases. While Frodo steps back from the harshness of his words to Gollum, he does not repudiate his threat to use the Ring to order him to commit suicide and is relentless in the pressure he puts on Gollum for answers. Boromir, by contrast, wept for what he had said and tried to do and fought to the last to protect Merry and Pippin. He considered his death just atonement for his attempt to take the Ring (2.x.414).

Frodo's identity is of course not the only one in question as they hide outside the Black Gate. For this conversation with Frodo marks the last occasion Gollum ever uses the words *I, me,* and *my*. From this point on, he will speak only in that welter of names (Gollum and Sméagol), pronouns (*he* and *we*), and pet names (precious and Precious) with which we tend to associate him. Frodo and the narrator call special attention to Gollum's use of *I* here; In doing so, he invokes the prior uses of *I* as evidence for the interpretation Frodo the character gives it now and recalls Sam's observation that Frodo and Gollum shared a connection even when they seemed most different (TT 4.i.618). At the same time, however, Frodo has been so preoccupied with his own struggle that he has overlooked Gollum's entirely, and he will fail to notice that Gollum ceases to use the very characteristic of speech to which he has just drawn the reader's attention (4.ii.630). We have also just witnessed Frodo go farther than he has yet gone in threatening a reluctant, evasive Gollum with the Ring but then be brought back by Sam's reminder of the Shire; and we have seen the Gollum-will and shared lust for the Ring prevail over the Sméagol-will in the two "thoughts" conversation, pulling him back from the positive changes Sam and Frodo had both noticed and mistrusted (4.i.618–19, ii.622). Some attention here to Gollum's use of the first-person pronoun will help clarify Frodo and Gollum's relationship to each other and to the Ring as it continues to break down their identities and challenge their senses of self on the journey from the Black Gate to Mount Doom.

In a 2006 article, Gergely Nagy states, "Frodo's rapid slide lower and lower into inaction and automatism in Mordor already signals how the Ring is at work again" ("Lost" 66). Now it cannot be denied that Frodo declines with increasing swiftness once inside Mordor, but we can see that the power of the Ring has been affecting him increasingly along the way. While Frodo and Gollum will in Ithilien have spells of what we might loosely call revival or recovery, where they rally, the Ring is always "at work." It never stops. There is no "again." And if his entry into Mordor will accelerate his descent yet more—as it will—his use of the Ring to dominate Gollum has already precipitated him down this slope. Since "what is done with [the Ring] turns to evil," as Frodo told Boromir only a few days before he met Gollum, his attempt to use it to control Gollum can only end badly, despite his sincere desire to fulfill his Quest and to help Gollum (FR 2.x.398). That we see Frodo saying one thing to Boromir one day and doing another to Gollum a few days later is one more subtle aspect of the Ring's power, much like Frodo's finding pity for Gollum because of Boromir (2.x.399).

The suggestion of automatism should also be scanned, since it connotes that in Mordor Frodo will exhibit no conscious or voluntary control over his actions ("Automatism, n."). It neglects the emphasis we shall see placed on the force of will Frodo and Sam exert in Mordor to keep going. As Sam will recognize, but for their doggedness they might have lain down and died together already (RK 6.iii.939, 935). The silent plodding that the word *automatism* misrepresents is in truth the fiercest act of will when all that remains of what and who you are is the purpose for which you came, the Quest you set out to fulfill, and the moral choice to throw all else away rather than surrender to Sauron. If we consider what rouses Frodo on that final journey—Sam's offer to carry the Ring, Gollum's attempts to take it, and the breaking of his will in the moment he claims the Ring and thereby challenges Sauron—and compare it to what most rouses Gollum, we shall see how very fierce a sense of self persists even in those whose identity has been shattered by the power of the Ring. As all else is stripped away, the struggle between will and desire increasingly defines them.

The first-person singular pronoun is key here. As Nagy also notes, Gollum's relationship with Frodo helps restore for a time some of Gollum's "lost" self, but the text shows there is more to it than that ("Lost" 61–62). One way this brief, partial recovery manifests itself is in his use of *I, me,* and *my.* There are eleven distinct moments in which he employs these words of himself, and these moments contain twenty-six instances of *I* and seven of *me* or *my*. In two of the eleven, Gollum says *I* three times, but he is quoting Frodo every time he does so (*TT* 4.iii.638, 642). In another two, the first and the last such moments, Gollum is quite emphatic about himself and his agency, using *I* eleven times and *me* or *my* four times (4.i.616, 643). In the remaining seven moments, we find twelve *I*s and three *me*s. Let us turn to this last group first, since it shows the improvements Nagy and many others have noticed.

After Gollum says "I promise.... I will serve the master of the Precious," his use of *I* expresses, remarkably and perhaps surprisingly, a sense of history, both recent and remote, and even a pride in the usefulness of his experiences to their present errand (*TT* 4.i.618).[7] Within this grouping Gollum also four times begins a clause with *Sméagol* as the subject, and once with *we* before correcting himself, consciously, and starting over with *I*:

"Sméagol went this way once: I went this way." (*TT* 4.ii.620)

"Sméagol will stay here: I will stay here." (4.ii.621)

"But Sméagol has used his eyes since then, yes, yes: I've used eyes and feet and nose since then." (4.ii.625)

"When Sméagol was young, when I was young." (4.ii.628)

"We tried once, yes, precious. I tried once." (4.ii.628)

However, after a Ringwraith passes overhead, Sam wakes to overhear the conversation between the Sméagol-will and the Gollum-will, in which the next *I* leads back to *Sméagol*: "I don't know. I can't help it. Master's got it. Sméagol promised to help the master" (*TT* 4.iii.633). Aside from a *me* the Sméagol-will uses a few lines later, we don't encounter *I*, *me*, or *my* again until he begins quoting Frodo outside the Black Gate (iii.638). We might also compare his telling Frodo at that same point that "Sméagol found" the other way into Mordor with his earlier "I found it, I did" when speaking of the path across The Dead Marshes 4.iii.638, ii.619).

With fear of Sauron thrown into the scales by two more flyovers by Nazgûl, "the terrible call of the Ring," as Sam calls it, begins to counter whatever good Frodo's pity and kindness has done (*TT* 4.ii.634–35). This reversal, recognized by Sam, answers the question Frodo posed several days earlier about "what kind of a change" they had seen in Gollum "and how deep" it might prove to be (4.ii.622–23). The fear that Sauron will get the Ring back can only whet the lust for the Ring that both the Gollum-will and the Sméagol-will feel.

Let us now turn to our other two groupings, starting with the first and last moments when Gollum uses *I*, and then incorporating the moments he uses *I* in quoting Frodo, which occur at different points in the same conversation as his last uses of *I* to refer to himself. It bears repeating that almost half (eleven of twenty-three) of the instances of *I* occur in these first and last moments, and more than half of *me* and *my* (four of seven). This concentration is very much in response to the particular topic in both of these moments, a topic now critical since the hobbits have learned they cannot enter through the Black Gate.

The first moment comes almost as soon as they meet Gollum in "The Taming of Sméagol," directly after Frodo and Sam have subdued him initially. Frodo's insistent questioning about Mordor—"So you have been there?... And you're being drawn back there again, aren't you?"—sets him off. But what starts with the jumbled pronouns we expect soon takes a curious turn: "Then suddenly his voice and language changed, and he sobbed in his throat, and spoke but not to them. 'Leave me alone, gollum! You hurt me. O my poor hands, gollum! I, we, I don't want to come back. I can't find it. I am tired. I, we can't find it, gollum, gollum, no, nowhere.... I can't find it. Ach!' He got up and clenched his long hand into a bony fleshless knot, shaking it towards the East. 'We won't!' he cried. 'Not for you'" (TT 4.i.616). The intensity of Gollum's feeling and of his sense of self is perfectly obvious, and it is equally so that this *I* defines itself in opposition to Sauron's *you* over the issue of *it*, that is, the Ring. As he says these words, Gollum doesn't even seem aware that Frodo and Sam are present: Gollum's *I* is alone with Sauron's *you*. So, first of all, this *I* already exists prior to Frodo's seemingly beneficial master-servant relationship with him. Note also that Gollum does not say *Sméagol* here at all, though Frodo has just addressed him by his original name when telling him that he is on his way to Mordor. Rather, Gollum stops his ears, "as if such frankness, and the open speaking of the names, hurt him" *the names* in the plural, that is, Sméagol and Mordor (TT 4.i.616). His direct reply, which precedes the passage quoted directly above, addresses the mention of the name Mordor, but not at all his own. Gollum's *I* thus seems in context to respond to Frodo's insistence on Mordor and Gollum's familiarity with it. We know, moreover, that Gandalf's knowledge of the name Sméagol can only have come from his interrogation of Gollum the previous year. So, while Frodo's continuing to address him as Sméagol was surely beneficial, it is the kindness underlying the gesture that affected Gollum. It is that kindness which the Sméagol-will singled out in resisting the Gollum-will. Merely hearing Frodo utter his true name once or twice cannot be reasonably said to have liberated Sméagol from the murder-haunted darkness in which Sméagol had hidden for centuries.[8]

Not until Frodo mentions Sméagol a second time, suggesting they might find him again in Mordor, does Gollum even acknowledges the name, but his response is dismissive. Sméagol is long gone: "they took his Precious, and he's lost now" (TT 4.i.616). Gollum only uses *Sméagol* independently when the idea of swearing an oath strikes him and Frodo responds with interest. From this follows the first midsentence revision of subject, as Sméagol takes a master: "'We promises, yes I promise!' said Gollum. 'I will serve the master of the Precious. Good master, good Sméagol, *gollum, gollum!*'" (4.i.618).

If we turn to Gollum's final *I*, he is again quite vehement. Although he now addresses himself directly to Frodo, who once more presses him about his escape from Mordor, he returns to the same issue, his own interactions with Sauron regarding the Ring:

> "And did you escape out of the darkness, Sméagol? Were you not rather permitted to depart, upon an errand? That at least is what Aragorn thought, who found you by The Dead Marshes some years ago."
>
> "It's a lie!" hissed Gollum, and an evil light came into his eyes at the naming of Aragorn. "He lied on me, yes he did. I did escape, all by my poor self. Indeed I was told to seek for the Precious; and I have searched and searched, of course I have. But not for the Black One. The Precious was ours, it was mine I tell you. I did escape."
>
> (TT 4.iii.643)

It is essential to note here that in revisiting this issue Gollum again answers a question Frodo never asked at all. In their first conversation, Frodo never spoke of any errand but his own, and here he hints at an errand but never names it. Since Gollum will never again employ any form of the first-person singular, we may well think he has come full circle back to where he began with Frodo a week earlier—for the whole brief span in which we see him using *I* is no more than this.[9] That their conversation outside the Black Gate is meant to mark an ending, at least to any progress he might have been making, receives support from the commentary Christopher Tolkien offers on this passage in *The War of the Ring*. There we learn Frodo's mention of Aragorn and Gollum's response to it were not at first present and that Frodo's means of assessing Gollum's truthfulness here—precisely his use of *I*—underwent meaningful revisions (WR 124, 124n11). The first text read: "Gollum used *I*, as he had hardly done since he had been frightened out of his old bad wits away back under the cliffs of Emyn Muil." It then became "Gollum used *I*, and that seemed usually to be a sign, on its rare appearances, that Smeagol [sic] was (for the moment) on top." In the final text, the pronoun "seemed usually to be a sign, on its rare appearances, that some remnants of old truth and sincerity were for the moment on top" (*TT* 4.iii.643). Not only is the *I* always present, but its significance evolves. Starting from a preexisting usage linked to his prior habits and indicating a lack of fear, it becomes a sign of the dominance of one personality over the other, and ends in the resurfacing of something akin to the truth. Beyond fear and bad old wits, beyond domination, these qualities hark back to the Sméagol before he saw the Ring and to the last bit of him that Gandalf said had survived the centuries with the Ring (*FR* 1.ii.54). The evolution in his portrayal here underlines the persistence of the sense of self even in one whose identity is as shattered as Gollum's is and who may well be deceiving himself when he insists that he escaped Sauron on his own. That story seems as firmly fixed in his mind as the birthday-present narrative.

Two points remain. First, if we consider the evidence of the Witch-king, whose will and sense of self are hard to dispute, we shall see certain commonalities. Not only do his actions demonstrate his indisputable sense of self, as when he takes the lead at Weathertop, the Ford of Bruinen, and the gates of Minas Tirith, but his words confirm that he, too, thinks of himself at times as *I*. He cannot call the siege of Minas Tirith "my hour" otherwise (*RK* 5.iv.829). Yet, even when he refers to himself in the third person, he does so in the grand manner, vaunting his sense of his own superiority with his contemptuous *thee* and *thy* to Éowyn (5.vi.841). He shares a perspective and a pronoun here with the Ring-nurtured fantasies of his fellow slave, "Lord Sméagol? Gollum the Great? *The* Gollum!" (*TT* 4.ii.633).[10] We see a strong will and sense of self defined with respect to the Ring. To what extent that fantasy is a delusion depends on the bearer's stature. Of the great, Tolkien indicated, Rings of Power make a Ringwraith, and of the small a Gollum (*Letters* no. 212, p. 286). This accords with their stature. "Samwise the Strong, Hero of the Age" is but one bad choice behind them on this journey (*RK* 6.i.900).

Finally, there is one other moment when Gollum speaks in the first-person singular, but it is not in *The Lord of the Rings*. The very first time he speaks in *Riddles in the Dark*, in both the 1937 and 1951 texts of *The Hobbit*, Gollum sneaks up on Bilbo and, though addressing himself, hisses in Bilbo's ear: "Bless us and splash us, my precioussss! I guess it's a choice feast; at least a tasty morsel it'd make us, gollum!" (*H* 120). For all Tolkien's revisions in this chapter to make the Gollum of *The Hobbit* a better fit to the Gollum of *The Lord of the Rings*, he saw no reason to remove this *I*. So, Gollum's *I* is not only prior to his relationship with Frodo and his acquaintance with Bilbo but is also singled out at the moment of its disappearance as an important clue to the survival of a key ingredient of his sense of self. In noting this clue, Frodo follows the lead of Gandalf, who told him that finding truth in Gollum's words required sifting because he was a liar to himself and to others (FR 1.ii.56). That *I* who falls silent outside the Black Gate, whether it represents the Sméagol-will or the original Sméagol, also wants the Ring for himself. When properly sifted, the words *not for You* and *not for the Black One* mean "for me" (TT 4.i.616; iii.643).

The sudden, total disappearance of *I* points to a renewed dishonesty and a conscious withdrawal from the master from whom Gollum now means to take the Ring. We have already seen him begin plotting with himself to get Frodo within Shelob's reach (TT 4.ii.633). Moreover, earlier in that conversation, the Gollum-will had pressed the Sméagol-will for answers about what "master" was doing and how they were going to get the Ring back from him and keep it from Sauron, to which the Sméagol-will replied much as he had responded to Sauron when Frodo first pressured him about Mordor: "I don't know. I can't help it" (TT 4.ii.633). So, before the Gollum-will gets the final word, the Sméagol-will speaks to him about Frodo as he speaks to Frodo about Sauron. Outside the Black Gate, on the same day as Gollum last uses *I* in his own voice, he quotes Frodo's own words back to him, "But now he says, 'I purpose to enter Mordor,' and to Sam, 'But if master says *I must go* or *I will go*'" (TT 4.iii.638, 642). Just as the *I* had pretended to acquiesce to Sauron's demand that he seek the Ring, now the *I* is complaisant to the "master of the Precious" and his purpose of entering Mordor, and for the same reason: to get the Ring back for himself.

Subject to the Ring far longer than Frodo, haunted by the murder of Déagol for five hundred years, Gollum has neither the desire nor the will to renounce or destroy the Ring, but that is a far cry from having no will or desire at all. Sauron might terrify Gollum, and by allowing him to escape Sauron might have tricked Gollum into serving his end, but he cannot merely daunt him into lasting servitude. For the pull of the Ring has already enslaved him far more thoroughly than Sauron without the Ring ever could. This is consistent with a fact Frodo knows well, that Gollum's oath will hold him in his service for only so long. Even with the Ring, the power of command Frodo at times presumes he would have over Gollum will fail to overcome his lust for it.

Gollum's initial retreat on Mount Doom is a tactic, and Frodo's final threat there a failure. Enslavement by the Ring trumps service in fear.

Gollum's choices, his words, thoughts, and actions show that however splintered his identity may be and however enslaved to the Ring, he has nevertheless a strong sense of self. His refusal to carry out Sauron's wishes (once safely out of reach) and the definition of his *I* in opposition to Sauron's *you* prior to his establishing a relationship with Frodo provide ample foundation for this assertion. The renewal of his dishonesty is as much choice as failure. Sméagol had begun turning away from Frodo and toward Gollum and the Ring during the two "thoughts" conversation. Outside the Black Gate the very next day, Frodo's cruel reminders that he would never get the Ring back can only have confirmed him in that turn back toward the darkness. The words "Gollum, or Sméagol, if you wish," may emphasize that Frodo in his better moments believes Gollum has the ability to choose between these two shards of himself that the desire for the Ring unites, but Frodo is locked in his own struggle with identity, self, and the Ring at this very moment (TT 4.iii.640). Here, outside the Black Gate at the halfway point in his dark journey with Gollum, Frodo needs to believe that there is some good in choice.[11]

Evil is not "without echo in the hearts of the good," to borrow a phrase of Tom Shippey's which suits the difficulty the Ring poses both for those in the tale and its readers (*Author* 142). For the power to dominate inherent in the Ring stirs within those hearts a confusion of echoes where ends and means and necessity and will and desire become guides as uncertain as they are powerful, and even for the wise and worthy Háma the Doorward, sorting the good and the bad and the right and the wrong would seem an impossibility (TT 3.vi.511). Frodo grows stronger as he bears his burden, but in doing so he also grows more subject to its pull. Good also can echo in the hearts of the evil, although retracing one's steps back to the light is always a harder task. Yet Frodo's kindness does affect Gollum, and even Saruman and Gríma Wormtongue pause to consider turning from their downward paths when offered the chance (3.x.582–83; *RK* 6.viii.1019–20). The complex ambiguities and reversals of these struggles are as hard for the reader to parse as they are for Sam, who, like us, wishes to see the best in Frodo. "The Black Gate Is Closed," a masterful chapter, manifests how thwarting Frodo's inner journey is.

JUDGEMENTS IN ITHILIEN

If much of what we have seen in the first three chapters of book 4 traces a descent for Frodo, the next three will show his path turn upward again. For the pity he showed Gollum is Frodo at his best and confirms Gandalf and Bilbo's good opinion of him. Soon, though, and in the name of his Quest, he uses the Ring to dominate a Gollum whom he would not kill and could not set loose. With use, the burden of the Ring increases until in doubt and despair he terrorizes Gollum with the threat of what he, as Master of the Precious, would compel him to do if it came to it. This is Frodo at his worst. His vaunting of his possession of the Ring and his power over Gollum here is little different than Boromir's boast of his superior strength when he tried to seize the Ring (FR 2.x.399). That neither Boromir nor Frodo can make good on his threat reveals once more the deception at the heart of any experience of the Ring.

The green memory of the Shire, stirred by Sam's recitation of "Oliphaunt" in the choking wasteland before the Black Gate, marks a turning point. It allows Frodo to reclaim some of his humanity and with it some small hope. For his wish that the "third turn may turn the best" is for more than the transactional trust that has subsisted between him and Gollum thus far, an outcome possible only if they also "find Sméagol" and Gollum reclaims his humanity (TT 4.iii.647).

Parallel to Frodo's ascent in these chapters is his departure from "the desolation" outside the Black Gate and entry into the "dishevelled dryad loveliness" of "desolate" Ithilien (TT 4.iv.631, 650). No one who has read *The Lord of the Rings* with the least attention needs to be reminded of this shift we see in the two phrases just quoted, from a wasteland where "nothing lived" (4.ii.631) to a garden where no one lived ("Desolate, adj. and n."). Tolkien's remarkable selection of the word "dryad" here evokes the immanent loveliness of the land by conjuring the reader's understanding of the minor deities who lived in the woodlands of Greek mythology. For the Old English for *dryad* was *ælfen*, and the narrative has been hinting at fairy tales for some time (Hall 78–88; "Ælfen, n."). Thus, the relief and recovery Frodo first experienced on hearing Sam recite "Oliphaunt" will continue in Ithilien.[12] But there are no Elves in Ithilien. To Frodo and Sam, its woodlands smell of the Shire, that is, they smell of home, unlike the similar woods through which Bilbo passed on his approach to Rivendell eighty years earlier (H 90–91). For the first time in quite a while, the hobbits' hearts are lightened.

Sam and Frodo also feel themselves "reprieved" by being there, another remarkable choice of words (TT 4.iv.648–49). Tolkien uses *reprieve* only here, at the beginning of a section that ends with another, more formal, reprieve, as Faramir and Frodo revisit the question of Gollum's deserts, and, in fact, Faramir spares Frodo and Sam the full weight of the law of the land (4.vi.689–93). For even to walk in Ithilien earns death for those not in Gondor's service. It is a measure of the horrors from which they have just emerged that two hobbits of the benignly anarchic Shire do not see this situation as the world turned upside down.

Yet it *is* just such a world. Here Sam prepares a bit of home cooking for Frodo as he sleeps just uphill from the horrific scene of an orc meal (TT 4.iv.651). Though the narrator never says what kind of creature's remains these are, the reader knows full well these bones belong to no beast, and the rhetorical inversion of the natural order of such events—that is, putting the feast before the slaughter—places the emphasis on the horror perpetrated here, a horror whether in the midst of war or in the seeming peace of Ithilien. Sam knows the nature of this feast, but Frodo sleeps on in ignorance, dreaming dreams of comfort that he will not recall.

Here, too, Sam and Gollum banter like old comrades about coneys and taters, despite their dislike of each other. Both look upon the sleeping Frodo. Sam sees the same light welling from within him more clearly than he had seen it—we now learn—back in Rivendell (TT 4.iv.652). That light had then allowed Gandalf the hope that Frodo would become a living beacon of hope, like the light of the silmaril which the star Eärendil bears or like the glass which Frodo himself now bears, carrying water that shines with the light of that star (FR 2.i.223). What Gollum sees as he looks at Frodo over Sam's shoulder we never learn—much as we never learn what Bilbo saw in Frodo's face in Rivendell which led him to understanding and regret—but if he sees the same light Sam does, he has not addressed it but turned away (2.i.232; TT 4.iv.652). Juxtaposed with Sam's expression of love and the light of Frodo, it reminds us of the isolation of the Ring and the longing for lost things that lie hidden even in the darkest heart.

Unlike Lothlórien, Ithilien is not, for all its loveliness, an enchanted forest or perilous only to those who bring their peril with them. Like the Ring, its beauty is part of its peril. Sam, so quick to detect the danger immanent in the enchanted Old Forest, misjudges the risk he is taking by building a fire here despite the warning of the charnel pit down the hill and the protests of Gollum who is not deceived at all by Ithilien's homely beauty. Though Gollum now recalls a time when he had a home, his memories are wistful and remote, something Frodo's have shown signs of becoming; they lack the immediacy that give Sam's power. The meal is as much about getting home as it is about hunger, about the spirit as much as the body.

The peril their cooking fire brings down upon them comes not from the enemy but from the Men of Gondor, the dispossessed rightful inhabitants of this land, and their laws. Their discovery of Frodo and Sam sets up a trial of sorts in which Faramir judges and spares not only Frodo and Sam but also Gollum. This trial replays both Frodo's conversation with Gandalf at Bag End in "The Shadow of the Past" and Bilbo's moment of pity and mercy. Here, however, Frodo plays Gandalf's part, urging Faramir to show Gollum mercy, whatever his deserts, and arguing that Gollum is "not altogether wicked" (TT 4.vi.691). Unlike the Frodo of "The Shadow of the Past," Faramir does not judge in haste or fear or kill without need (FR 1.ii.59; TT 4.v.665). So far from fearing for his own safety, he fears for Frodo's. In trying to be just, he knows wisdom can only see so far (TT 4.vi.68; FR 1.ii.59). So he, who rightfully may and should deal out death in judgement, suspends the Doom of Death he has pronounced on Gollum for as long as he is with Frodo and faithful to his promise to serve him.

In Frodo's dealings with Faramir and Gollum, we see how he has grown since he summarily declared that Gollum deserves death, never considering that the world is about more than the deserts of one person, whether good or evil or not altogether wicked. The suffering of bearing the burden of the Ring and of the Quest to destroy it has broadened his perspective, as have his other experiences along the way, especially his dreams and visions in the house of Tom Bombadil and in Lothlórien. He can now pity Gollum and show him mercy and counsel others to do so. He can stand up for the bond that Gollum's promise and his own use of the power of the Ring have imposed on the both of them. It may be Frodo's wisest insight so far that at Henneth Annûn he recognizes, or becomes able to admit to himself, that Gollum serves him in fear (TT 4.vi.686).

Yet Frodo no longer remembers even the dreams that comfort him, and his memory of the home he set out to save is beginning to be left behind, just as Lothlórien seemed to him to be slipping away as they left it (TT 4.ii.634, iv.655; FR 2.viii.377).[13] Soon he will have no living memory of the Shire, which will leave him alone with the Ring (RK 6.iii.937–38). That isolation from home and from even the memory of home again underlines the importance of Bombadil's still unanswered question to Frodo about his identity. Frodo's bond to Gollum, moreover, rests on his being acknowledged not merely as master—as with Sam—but as the Master of the Precious. In this latter role, his third use of the Ring to compel Gollum to obey him at the pool below Henneth Annûn is as petty and cruel in its expression as his threat before the Black Gates was proud and cruel. So, far from being the stern lord Sam had seen in the Emyn Muil and at the Black Gate, Frodo petulantly warns Gollum that he will have the Ring choke him on the bones of the fish he is eating (TT 4.vi.687).

Above, we noted Frodo's words to Gollum: "The third turn may turn the best" (TT 4.iii.647). More recently Sam, when trying to enlist Gollum's aid gathering herbs to go along with the stewed rabbit, gives this phrase its more familiar form, "third time pays for all" (4.iv.654). If the third time doing something is supposed to have significance, what, then, are we to make of this moment here, when for the third time Frodo uses the Ring to dominate Gollum? By Frodo and Sam's own standard of judgement, Frodo's behavior here should tell us that Frodo is on the road to losing himself, just as the good turns Gollum has done so far seem to signal that he has at times come closer to finding Sméagol.

Directly after Faramir learns to his astonishment that Gollum had long borne the Ring, Anborn asks permission to shoot him and invokes the law that enjoins them to kill all who come uninvited to this place. Faramir's reply— "This is a harder matter than it seems"—aptly characterizes the complex interplay of good, evil, and the pull of the Ring's power in Gollum and Frodo alike (TT 4.vi.685). Gollum is not wholly evil, and Frodo, as we have seen, is not wholly good (4.vi.691). In Ithilien, they both stand in the dock before one for whom the Ring seems to possess little allure.

CHAPTER EIGHT

From Ithilien to Cirith Ungol

THE RIDDLES ANSWERED

When Faramir appears amid Ithilien's dryad loveliness, questions of law, punishment, and justice appear with him. Unlike Frodo in Bag End, who condemned Gollum unheard and unseen because of his many evil deeds and because of his own fears, Faramir is charged with enforcing a law that demands summary death for deeds that seem far less criminal than Gollum's. So harsh a law has arisen because of the war with Sauron, and the reader has already encountered laws much like it, though less extreme, in Lothlórien and Rohan (FR 2.vi.347). Éomer's duty there was quite similar, and he wondered openly, "How shall a man judge what to do in such times?" (TT 3.ii.438).

Faramir may not wonder, though the complexity of justice is plain to him. Unlike Éomer, and, more importantly, unlike his own brother, he does not fear or misunderstand what Men no longer know, such as the Golden Wood and its White Lady. Like Aragorn, he knows that no one passes through Lothlórien "unchanged," and he seems to suspect that Boromir brought with him a peril that slept in his very heart (TT 4.v.667). To judge by Faramir's comments on Boromir and Lórien, the awakening of just such a peril within themselves is too often the lot of Men in Faërie. Yet Faërie is not to blame, as Sam would agree (4.v.680). So, far from blaming Galadriel for his brother's death, he credits the survival of the boat carrying Boromir's body to her power. That it is Faramir who providentially sees this boat, preserved as if by enchantment—"almost filled with clear water, from which came the light.... Dreamlike it was, and yet no dream"—further marks him off as a different sort of man than both Éomer and Boromir (4.v.666). He often dreams of the great wave that drowned

Númenor, and it was to him, not his brother, that the riddling dream of Isildur's bane came frequently (RK 6.v.962; FR 2.ii.246). It was he, as we shall see, who may well have guessed the identity of Isildur's bane.

What this man who dreams dreams sees when he looks on the boat that bears his dead brother moves him to feel awe and pity and grief, as if Boromir's sacrifice hallowed the boat, a sacrifice made necessary by the differences between him and his brother. For Boromir was a brave, noble, and accomplished warrior whose desperation to save Gondor and whose childhood fantasy of being king gave the gravity of the Ring purchase in his heart. Here the desire of their father, Denethor, is also relevant.[1] For he wished the Stewards of Gondor to remain the rulers of Gondor, as they had been for nearly a thousand years (RK 5.vii.854). Faramir, however, wants to serve and not to rule; that is, he wishes to see the Stewards resume their ancient place as the servants of King and country, not as its rulers (TT 4.v.671–72). For that, the King must return. Unsurprisingly for Faramir, he will first encounter Aragorn in a dream in the Houses of Healing and on waking will know him at once to be the King (RK 5.viii.866). We may well wonder if the Aragorn Faramir meets in his dream is the same man with the star on his brow whom Bombadil conjured for the hobbits in their vision upon the Barrow-downs.

Such a readiness to serve rather than to rule or dominate others and to accept what has been lost, not just the life of Boromir, but downfallen Númenor, the knowledge and acquaintance of the Elves, and the ancient values and wisdom of Gondor seems to confer upon Faramir a resistance to the Ring. Faramir's wish for Gondor, moreover, similarly and predictably rejects domination for his country as well as for himself (TT 4.v.671–72). When Faramir says to Frodo that he would not pick up the Ring if he found it lying by the highway, his words tell us that his heart still dwells in a golden age of peace and prosperity (see on page 31).

At first, of course, Faramir does not know that "this thing" he has forsworn is the One Ring, but his reaction on learning so is remarkable. Amused at the heartbreaking irony of Frodo's plight and Boromir's "too sore a trial," with a smile, he says: "So that *is* the answer to all the riddles!" (TT 4.v.680–81, emphasis mine).[2] The grim mirth and pain with which he rehearses the events that have left the One Ring within his grasp frightens Frodo and Sam, who think momentarily that Faramir is about to take the Ring from them. Then he laughs, and the spell, so to speak, is broken. Faramir has proven his quality. That he regards the words he uttered about the Ring in ignorance to be as binding as an oath "make him appear lordly and generous as a king of old, gracious, gentle" (RK 5.iv.812). These words are of course said to Faramir in reproach by his father, who wished Faramir had followed the law rather than justice and had brought him the means, as he thought, of defending Gondor. So far from the reproach Denethor will mean them to be, they are just praise of Faramir and a just measure of Denethor's departure from the path of wisdom.

Here we should recall two other moments from early in the tale. At Bree, Strider also terrifies the hobbits by demonstrating that the Ring was his for the taking, if he wanted it. But with a smile and a laugh, he, too, proves his quality. Strider is "not such a man," as Faramir will say of himself (TT 4.v.681). Far from it. The rightful King embraces service to a cause greater and longer lasting than his own and is willing to lay down his life to save it (FR 1.x.171).[3] Earlier still, Tom Bombadil, the Master who, free from the burden of possessing and dominating, can mock the power that frightens the wise, seems entirely immune to its effects. It cannot strip Tom's identity from him, and it cannot deceive him. Thus, he neither vanishes with the Ring on nor does he lose sight of Frodo when he wears it.

Yet, their laughter does not argue a lack of seriousness. Aragorn and Faramir are mocking themselves and the irony of their situations. Aragorn knows that he "look[s] foul, but feel[s] fair (FR 1.x.170–71). Faramir, of whom also Sam has suspicions—"Fair speech may hide a foul heart"—is astonished that what seemed a far-fetched guess has proved correct and led Sam and Frodo from his brother to him (TT 4.v.675). Bombadil, however, is mocking the Ring, but not just because he can; Gandalf unequivocally states that the Ring has no power over him (FR 2.ii.265). Rather, his mockery is the most serious part of the expansion of Frodo's horizons, showing him that the Ring is not almighty, that some things are forever beyond its reach. Directly after Tom teaches them about the road they must take across the Barrow-downs to get back to the everyday world beyond his country, Frodo has the last of his fully told dreams or visions in which he is in a ship sailing on the straight road to the country that lies beyond the sea.

Gandalf, however, also unequivocally states that no mortal can withstand corruption and domination by the power of the Ring (FR 1.ii.46). His own particular fear of it, and the effect it has on Boromir, both show that neither mortality nor possession are prerequisite to being overcome. What does this mean for Faramir, who is so winning and admirable in rejecting the Ring, twice, that he seems as untouchable by its power as Old Tom? Since Bombadil is sui generis, it can only mean that the Ring would possess Faramir, too, in the end. He may have the love, sense, courage, and virtue to reject the Ring, as Sam will later do, but there can be no doubt what would have befallen Sam in the end had Frodo in fact been dead when Sam took the Ring from him.

For all Faramir's honor and honesty—he is as open about his brother's failings as about his love for him—his reaction to the boat he sees carrying Boromir suggests that in the end he is not above self-deception. For when Frodo declares that what he saw must have been a vision, Faramir adduces the separate discoveries of the shards of Boromir's horn as proof that the boat was not a vision (TT 4.v.667). But the return of the horn does not prove the boat either real or illusory. Faramir's inference does not follow. If anything, the tangible reality of the horn shards and their arrival separately from the ghostly looking boat suggest the opposite. That he is willing to believe otherwise is far more important in this context than the truth about the boat; his need to believe that he saw what he thinks he saw prompts him to construct a suitable version of the truth, not unlike a birthday present or a victory in the riddle game. However, Faramir's love of Boromir and experience with the funeral boat, whether actual or a vision, fortifies him against the pull of the Ring when he learns of its connection to Boromir's death. So, while he is no doubt a paragon, he remains a mortal man doomed to die. That he is not perfect makes his rejection of the Ring more admirable, even if also more precarious than it seems at first glance.

Faramir's remarkable conduct here begs for two further connections to be made. First, Frodo has previously offered the Ring to Gandalf, Aragorn, and Galadriel, because he felt inadequate to the burden. Yet here in a situation that evokes Gandalf's discovery of how to prove the Ring's identity, and that echoes Aragorn's grim jest about taking the Ring in Bree and Galadriel's relations with her guests who are also utterly in her power if she chooses to use it, Frodo does not offer the Ring, the burden of which has only increased, to the noble man whose guest he finds himself.[4] Why? The thin line between the full acceptance of his burden and the desire to use its power is the edge of the knife to which Galadriel referred.

Second, Faramir's desire for the King to return and his adoption of a regal graciousness naturally draws our attention to the king who is returning, as does his unknowing imitation of Aragorn's behavior. Aragorn also twice rejects the Ring. At Bree, he couches his rejection in terms of his identity. Rather than wanting the Ring or taking it from Frodo by force, he is willing to die to save the hobbits, if need be. At Rivendell, he refuses to accept the Ring as his legacy, even though he is Isildur's heir. He is, however, not slow to assert his right as Isildur's heir to use the palantír or to compel the Dead of Dunharrow to fight for him (RK 5.ii.780–81). In his use of the Stone of Orthanc and on the Paths of the Dead, Aragorn displays a will that can overmatch that of Sauron himself and command the Dead, provided he is asserting his claim to something that is his by right. The One, of course, is not, as he acknowledges. Yet, strength of will is an essential component of wielding the Ring, and seeing him use that strength to dominate Sauron and the Shades of Men allows Legolas to see the potential greatness and terror of Aragorn as Ringlord (5.ix.876).

The "real Aragorn" is the "true king" and knows better than to try. He knows what is his to claim and what is not. He knows the difference between being one thing and being seen as another. He knows what it is to serve unnoticed and what it is to command. He knows, as Charles Williams's Arthur did not, that "the king [is] made for the kingdom, [not] the kingdom... for the king" (39). Armed with these truths, he will not be easily or quickly deceived by what the power of the Ring seems to offer. Faramir is like him in this, as Boromir was not. Nor was Frodo. When he sees himself in the mirror the day he wakes up in Rivendell, the day he veers between being seen as a beacon of hope and seeing his beloved uncle as a monster he wishes to strike, he fails to recognize that at fifty years of age he should not look "remarkably like" he had two decades earlier, before he had come of age and into his inheritance as Ring-bearer (FR 2.i.225). The thoughtful look he sees in the eyes of his reflection does not penetrate what should be the Ring's most familiar effect. By noting how remarkable Frodo's present resemblance is to his younger self, the narrator may well hint at what should be a troubling and instructive discrepancy between his age and his appearance, but the Frodo of that moment seems far more attentive to the terrors those eyes have seen and to the pleasures he anticipates once he leaves his room. He thinks that, like Bilbo long ago, he has reached the end of his adventure and that he may now rest (2.iii.272; H 360). Yet the Ring's most obvious deception has just escaped him. The power of the Ring has skewed his vision.

That was then, before the desire to take on himself the Quest to destroy the Ring and before the desire to use it to control others, before the madness of Boromir and the pity for Gollum, before the despair and cruelty of the Black Gate and Ithilien's shallow respite, before Frodo's use of the Ring to threaten Gollum and to save Gollum. If Frodo's determination to see the Ring destroyed has cozened him into using the Ring to further that goal, that is the way of the corruption worked by the gravity of the Ring. As we have seen in "The Forbidden Pool" (above on pages 152–53), it can make kindness cruel and faith treacherous (TT 4.vi.686–90). For Frodo, full acceptance of his burden may well mean accepting what the Ring is going to do to him while resisting its pull to the last.

A HOBBIT'S GOT TO KNOW HIS LIMITATIONS

At the crossroads, when Frodo sees the flowers growing round the fallen statue's brows, he takes it for a sign that a day will come when Sauron fails (TT 4.vii.702). He here shows a prophetic quality and a hopeful resolve in strong contrast to the despair he had felt before the Black Gate. From this last moment of Ithilien's loveliness, made more poignant by its precarity in the falling darkness, Frodo takes a measure of defiance, which the immediately renewed burden of the Ring overwhelms but doesn't quite drown. For, turning eastward and crossing the road, he walks out of the Ithilien of Faramir and enters a darker Ithilien, a forest dominated and warped by the sorcery of Minas Morgul.

Morgul, of course, means "black magic" or "sorcery," and the Tower of Sorcery was once the Tower of the Moon, Minas Ithil, which lent its name to the land on both sides of the road. When Faramir longs for Minas Tirith to become Minas Anor once more, he is wishing for the time before Minas Ithil fell to the Ringwraiths (TT 4.v.672).[5] Unlike the light of sun and moon evoked in the names Minas Anor and Minas Ithil, Minas Morgul is full of light, but it is a corpse-light, a tower tall but not high, loathsome not fair, ruled by the Witch-king, who is a slave to the One Ring. Frodo even suggests to Faramir that if the Ring went to Minas Tirith, it would become a second Minas Morgul (4.vi.692). Faramir does not disagree.

What Frodo encounters as he approaches Minas Morgul is perhaps the clearest demonstration we have of the narrow difference between power used to dominate and power used to preserve or inspire. In Lórien, Galadriel conjures to hold back the tides of time, and her enchantments succeed so well that in the Golden Wood the Elder Days live on, and, as is often the case for mortals in Faërie, the passage of a month seems but a few days. The spells of Morgul, however, corrupt what was good and beautiful of old and seem to slow time "so that between the raising of a foot and the setting of it down minutes of loathing passed" (TT 4.viii.703). In Lórien, the waters of the Nimrodel comfort the grieving with their music and refresh the weary with their touch; the stream in Morgul Vale has no voice, and its "vapour" disorients and dispirits them. Morgul's pale, white flowers are likened to something out of a nightmare and reek of death; Frodo will remember the white niphredil of Lórien as in a waking dream long after he has left the Golden Wood.

Yet, however kindly the intent, the desire to preserve entails domination. Whether the domination aims at controlling the fundaments of nature by withstanding the passage of time or at saving the Shire from the Dark Lord, any desire of this kind leaves the would-be preserver more vulnerable to the pull of the Ring's power. Indeed, Saruman's fall may well be evidence of just how profoundly he had once wanted to save Middle-earth, if his corruption took place at such a distance. Gandalf's statement to Denethor that "were [the Ring] buried beneath the roots of Mindolluin, still it would burn your mind away" should be viewed in the same light; and Gandalf says this directly after telling Denethor that he had refused the Ring even as a gift because he knew what it would do to him (RK 5.iv.814). By contrast, we may again consider Faramir: with no hope of victory, he sees Gondor as without a future, and when he tells Frodo what he "would see," he expresses a wish he believes unattainable (TT 4.v.671–72, 677). This attitude, a peculiar mixture of love, hopelessness, and a desire to serve what he loves, confers an initial resistance to the draw of the Ring. Peculiar, but not unique. For Faramir and Sam are very much alike in this regard, as we shall see when even Sam's quality is put to the proof.

Bombadil alone affords the Ring no purchase. Although unexpectedly possessed of vast Knowledge, Tom has no interest in Rule and Order, such as Saruman had (FR 2.ii.259). With such power, Saruman argued, he could govern the world for its own good. But that is a measure of his dishonesty, with Gandalf and almost certainly with himself, and of how one can fall to the Ring despite never being anywhere near it. Tom is Master because he just stands back and lets it all be. He has been here since the beginning and watched it all. He accepts that there is evil, but takes no steps against it without immediate cause. Justin T. Noetzel has not unreasonably called him a "pacifist-unless-provoked" (171).[6]

As Tom Shippey has said of Bombadil, however, "what he *is* may not be known, but what he *does* is dominate" (Road 106). He makes short work of evil, whether it occurs naturally (Old Man Willow) or unnaturally (the Barrow-wight), but he treats the two differently. While he destroys the evil produced by dark forces, he merely compels the evil born of age-old resentment to release its victims. And there he stops, but we should note that he does more than rescue the hobbits. He gives them advice he hopes will guide them safely and blades designed to destroy Ringwraiths, and thanks to Gildor and Farmer Maggot he was expecting them. He helps to prepare them for a wider world than they have yet known and for the greater tasks that lie beyond the borders of his land, not least by showing them that the power of the Ring has limits even if the hobbits cannot grasp them. In doing all of this, Tom avoids the mistake the Valar made when, fearing for the Elves and desiring to protect them from Melkor, they summoned them to Valinor (*S* 52; see also Flieger, *Splintered Light* 77).

Even the desire for control implicit in wanting to preserve a fading world or save others from death and slavery leaves one vulnerable. Thus, Boromir starts out talking about saving Gondor and ends up talking about himself as its savior and king (FR 2.x.396–98). Thus, when Sam tells Galadriel he wishes she would take the Ring, she quite humbly disabuses him (2.vii.366). Thus, Bombadil, who has no such desires, has a power vis-à-vis the Ring (Gandalf notwithstanding) that unnerves Frodo who does have such desires.

In the dark Ithilien ruled by Minas Morgul, Frodo comes face to face with the will to dominate expressed through Morgul-spells, is momentarily overwhelmed, and is nearly lost because of it. The fascination it exerts roots all three hobbits in their tracks as soon as they set eyes on that ghastly city, whose lighthouse-like tower draws them in rather than warning them off (TT 4.viii.703–05). All of them have trouble looking and moving away while the city remains in sight, but Frodo, already struggling with the perceived weight of the Ring and perhaps more sensitive owing to the sorcerous wound he had received on Weathertop, rushes toward the city, "as if some force were at work other than his own will" (4.viii.704).

Clearly some other force *is* at work; Sam and Gollum are sharing much, if not all, of Frodo's experience. That other force can drive the moods and the actions of those it acts on (see RK 6.iii.946). Why, then, does Frodo the narrator muddy the waters by casting doubt on it with "as if"? He also implicates the Ring, the increasing burden of which he has already mentioned. As soon as he turned away from the road to Minas Morgul, he says he felt the Ring resisting him. We have already seen, however, that the perception that the weight of the Ring changes is a moral or spiritual reality, not a physical phenomenon. Frodo has also in the past confused the effect of his own fears with the work of the will of others, whether he believes that force is the Ring or someone or something else (FR 1.ix.157). Recall, moreover, Frodo's inability on Amon Hen to tell whether he was rejecting or embracing Sauron's imminent discovery of him and his alternation between the kind and the stern Master of the Precious in handling Gollum. Given all this and the already nightmarish effects of the bewitchment he and his companions are struggling against, the resistance Frodo perceives here may well be his own as much as the result of some resonance between the Ring and Minas Morgul.

This nightmare now takes a stranger, more alarming turn. For Frodo, this day's journey began with a touch of hope and defiance as the last rays of the setting sun illuminated the golden coronal upon a king's fallen statue and now nears its ending with the appearance of another king, the pale king of the Ringwraiths, his "dark head crowned and helmed with fear" (TT 4.viii.706). The very realization that this is he makes Frodo begin to relive what the Morgul blade had inflicted on him, ensorcelling and paralyzing him. Even more than at Weathertop, he feels commanded to put on the Ring.

Much of this is a dagger of the mind, however. The Witch-king cannot know that Frodo and the Ring are near, or else he would never have ridden away. That he senses something is unquestionable, but unlike the Black Rider in the Shire, he has no clue what it is or even in what direction it may lie. He is also, therefore, quite unlikely to be the knowing source of the urge to put on the Ring, as he was on Weathertop. Nor does the narrator state or imply that the Witch-king issued the command; that is our inference, a poor one logically as we have seen. Frodo (and Bilbo before him) has a history of using or wanting to use the Ring to escape everything from unpleasant relatives to the Barrow-wight and the Black Riders. Even when he knows what the Ring is, he cannot often tell whether the urge to put it on comes from within him or without. At Weathertop, one of the few instances where it is obvious to the reader, Frodo is doing the will of the enemy when he dons the Ring, but he does not see that until later.

Here Frodo sees something quite different, which will repay our scrutiny:

> But great as the pressure was, he felt no inclination now to yield to it. He knew that the Ring would only betray him, and that he had not, even if he put it on, the power to face the Morgul-king—not yet. There was no longer any answer to that command in his own will, dismayed by terror though it was, and he felt only the beating upon him of a great power from outside. It took his hand, and as Frodo watched with his mind, not willing it but in suspense (as if he looked on some old story far away), it moved the hand inch by inch towards the chain upon his neck. Then his own will stirred; slowly it forced the hand back, and

set it to find another thing, a thing lying hidden near his breast. Cold and hard it seemed as his grip closed on it: the phial of Galadriel, so long treasured, and almost forgotten till that hour. As he touched it, for a while all thought of the Ring was banished from his mind. He sighed and bent his head.
(TT 4.viii.706–07)

Two words, so easily and so often overlooked, set up a chilling counterpoint to the phial of Galadriel: *not yet*. Without these two emphatic words the tenor of this passage would be quite different. Without these words we would see a Frodo who is wiser, stronger, more mature, whose *will* is not to resort to the Ring, but to use the light to fight the darkness. When we say, "not yet," however, we declare our belief that "if it be not now, yet it will come" (*Hamlet* 5.ii.166–67). When we emphasize these words by placing them at the end of the sentence, we indicate that what we anticipate is also something we desire, and we relish the thought that someday we will have what we desire. Those final words declare Frodo's desire to put on the Ring to use it, to reveal himself rather than to hide, and to challenge the Witch-king, who had wounded and humbled him. By their position, they manifest a grim determination.

It has been a long road for Frodo, from Bag End where he was terrified by the thought that Sauron knew the Shire existed, to Morgul Vale, where he looks forward to the day he will be strong enough to face the Witch-king. His near deadly encounter with him at Weathertop, his literally laughable attempt to defy him at the Ford of Bruinen, his subsequent desire to use the Ring, his use of it to dominate Gollum despite Galadriel's warning, and his acceptance of being called the "Master of the Precious" are all steps on this journey. So, too, is the dissolution of his identity and the growing division within himself, which we have seen before and see again here in his hand moving independently of his will, in his perception of his mind as not entirely the same as himself, and in the remote perspective he has on what his hand was doing.

What, then, is moving Frodo's hand? Not the Witch-king, nor Sauron, for reasons even more obvious than the Witch-king. Nor the Morgul-spells which have troubled Frodo and his companions since they passed the crossroads and began heading for the Morgul Vale but whose effect is now lessening as the hobbits climb the stairs. The mover must be something in the relationship between Frodo and the Ring, in the accelerating pull that the Ring's gravity exerts on his desire to use the Ring and for the power to face the Morgul-king. His "not yet" suggests that he believes time will soon come. In view of this desire and the self-deception that surrounds the Ring, it seems likely that it is this desire that moves Frodo's hand.[7] The addiction model is here quite apposite. It is common for alcoholics and other addicts to personify the alcohol or drug which they both loathe and long for, and they speak of the pressure to give in to the yearning *as if it were coming* from outside themselves, when of course it is doing nothing of the kind.

Frodo does make a choice here that shows that he has also grown wiser and stronger. He diverts his hand from the Ring around his neck to the phial of Galadriel in his breast pocket. Instead of daring to face the darkness with darkness, he chooses the light that penetrates and blinds the darkness—his own and the Witch-king's—and turns aside both his and his enemy's thought from the Ring.[8] But the Ring and the phial are so close to each other in Frodo's bosom that it brings to mind the knife edge of Galadriel's warning (FR 2.vii.357). Frodo's "not yet" and his reaching for the phial equally mark his path and his peril.

AND BE A VILLAIN

Even before the army emerged from Minas Morgul, Frodo had been insisting he needed to rest, that he was "not yet" ready to go on (twice at TT 4.viii.704), but not until now does the reader learn that at some point Frodo has lost consciousness. "Then at a great distance, as if it came out of memories of the Shire, some sunlit early morning, when the day called and doors were opening, he heard Sam's voice speaking. 'Wake up, Mr. Frodo! Wake up!' Had the voice added: 'Your breakfast is ready,' he would hardly have been surprised. Certainly Sam was urgent. 'Wake up, Mr. Frodo! They're gone,' he said." (TT 4.viii.707) So how much of what we have seen is a dream, and where does the outer nightmare of the Morgul-spells blend into the inner nightmare of the Witch-king? To be sure, Frodo has dreamt before, but the dreams we have witnessed have a distinct beginning, and the others have been identified as such. Here we have something out of Dostoevsky, which we can recognize as a dream only when it ends and whose beginning remains in doubt.

It starts, I would argue, directly after Frodo touches the phial when "Frodo sighed and bent his head" and ends with the answering "Frodo raised his head, and then stood up" (TT 4.viii.707). Of far greater significance, however, than the point at which the dream begins is the fact that its beginning is so easily overlooked, suggesting that for Frodo waking and sleeping have both become nightmares with little to distinguish between them (see Flieger, *Question of*

Time, 196–99). The dream unveils the nearly frantic despair toward which his reasonable fears and unreasonable self-recriminations drive him. We cannot read his "who can now hold the fords when the King of the Nine Riders comes?" and forget that Frodo tried and failed to hold the Ford of Bruinen against the Witch-king, or that he declared but a moment ago that he was "not yet" strong enough to face him (TT 4.viii.707). Though his heart goes out to Faramir and his friends, his focus is ultimately on himself, as his faulty reasoning leads him to the false conclusion that all will be in vain if there is no one alive to know what he has done, a self-deception he repudiates as soon as he awakens. Yet the despair remains.

The one thing that is different, the one thing that calls him back from this wholly dark world is the memories of the Shire, which Sam's voice embodies for him. Outside the Black Gate we saw how Sam's recitation of "Oliphaunt," a fireside rhyme from the Shire, had lifted his spirits and turned him away from his suicidal intention to try to enter Mordor there (above on page 141). And once they have climbed the stairs of Cirith Ungol, Sam will again raise in Frodo thoughts of the Shire, not memories this time but imaginings of a future in which Sam and Frodo, and perhaps even Gollum, will be the heroes of a Great Tale told to inspire and instruct, just as the Tale of Beren and Lúthien has been told for millennia. Sam's realization that they are "in the same tale" as Beren and Lúthien leads directly to their envisioning of a future in which hobbit children hear tales of Frodo, "the famousest of the hobbits," and "Samwise the stouthearted" (TT 4.viii.711–12). As hobbits are wont to do, of course, they cloak the seriousness of their discussion in humor, and even Frodo laughs for heart's ease, a sound seldom heard on the Stairs of Cirith Ungol (4.viii.712). Sam even seeks to include Gollum in their mirth and wonders whether he fancies himself "the hero or the villain" in their tale, but Gollum is nowhere to be found (4.viii.712).

It is precisely this question—hero or villain—that Gollum faces in serious form on his return. He does so in a moment, moreover, in which all the loathing to which the reader has been schooled since the book began is forgotten, and the narrator grants the reader a vision like that which Bilbo received in the dark at the roots of the Misty Mountains long ago. For Gollum comes upon Frodo and Sam asleep, unaware, as entirely at his mercy as he had been at Bilbo's, but the peace and love apparent in them stirs something in him.

> Gollum looked at them. A strange expression passed over his lean hungry face. The gleam faded from his eyes, and they went dim and grey, old and tired. A

spasm of pain seemed to twist him, and he turned away, peering back up towards the pass, shaking his head, as if engaged in some interior debate. Then he came back, and slowly putting out a trembling hand, very cautiously he touched Frodo's knee—but almost the touch was a caress. For a fleeting moment, could one of the sleepers have seen him, they would have thought that they beheld an old weary hobbit, shrunken by the years that had carried him far beyond his time, beyond friends and kin, and the fields and streams of youth, an old starved pitiable thing.
(TT 4.viii.714)

Just as thoughts and memories of the Shire have twice recalled Frodo from the darkness of his despair, it is the loss of memories of the very same kind that have helped make Sméagol, a hobbit, into a "thing" called Gollum. Gandalf spoke of these forgotten memories to Frodo in "The Shadow of the Past," citing Bilbo's ability to stir them in Gollum through human conversation as a reason to hope that Gollum could one day be cured, as unlikely as that might seem, and it is from this corner that Sméagol now reaches, longing for "such forgotten things" as he has seen Sam and Frodo share with each other and as in part they have both attempted to share with him (FR 1.ii.54). For even Sam was not all unkindness.

In Letter 181 Tolkien speaks of this moment as "the final chance when dawning love for Frodo was too easily withered by the jealousy of Sam" (*Letters* 235). Though Tolkien wrote this letter in 1956, more than a decade after he composed this passage, his assessment surely suits the context of the scene, with Sam and Frodo's friendship well established, with the touching position Gollum finds them in, and with the use of the word *caress*, connoting nothing if not the physical expression of a gentle affection. In Letter 246, from 1963, Tolkien again speaks of Gollum's "new love" and of his repentance being "blighted" by Sam's "fail[ure] to note the complete change in Gollum's tone and aspect" (330). Although Tolkien goes on to speculate about what might have happened had Sam reacted other than he did, he is unequivocal that Gollum's "love ... could not have wrested mastery from the Ring." This passage, too, is consistent with the earlier letter and with the text, and the continuity of thought attested by the carryover of the botanical metaphor ("withered," "blighted") from the first letter to the second reinforces that consistency.

In this moment, as he turns back and reaches out, Gollum is close to choosing, in the terms of Sam's unanswered question, to be the hero, or, as Frodo put it when they first met, to find Sméagol again. But if pity cannot save a

Gandalf or a Frodo from the Ring, can love save such a thing as Gollum? Or perhaps the better way to put the question, since Gollum is already lost, is to ask if love can *redeem* him from the Ring. Not in any easy or simple way, to be sure, not even if the change in him that flickers in this moment had been apparent to Sam. The change was still too shallow in its roots not to be withered by Sam's hostility and scorn, and no doubt Gollum's guilt plays a role. For Sam is of course right to suspect him of being up to no good. He is. That much is certain.

Yet, if pity is important despite its ultimate ineffectualness against the pull of the Ring, so is love, so much so that we bear witness to this "crucial" moment, as Tolkien calls it, in a scene that is wholly convincing and powerfully evocative of the reader's pity but which might, nevertheless, take place only in the narrator's imagination (*Letters*, no. 194, p. 255). For neither Frodo nor Sam was awake to watch it unfold, a fact to which the narrator explicitly draws our attention through the contrafactual condition depicting what the sleepers could have seen, had they not been sleeping. Frodo and Sam, however, are the only narrators the book claims, and even if we were to suppose another, what motive could they have had to construct such a scene? Why would they wish to give even this tiny rehabilitation to a character otherwise portrayed as murderous, treacherous, cannibalistic, and consumed by malice? (*TT* 4.vi.691). We might, however, imagine a motive for the narrators we know, and I believe the final chapter of *The Lord of the Rings* offers us a parallel.

In "The Grey Havens," Frodo turns the book over to Sam, telling him that the ending is for him to write (*RK* 6.ix.1027). While there is some uncertainty about how much Sam wrote, he must at the very least have written everything from the time Frodo gave him the book onward.[9] For our purposes, however, that is enough, since we find our parallel after this point. Frodo's moving approach to Eressëa cannot have been witnessed by Sam or anyone else remaining in Middle-earth. So, where does it come from? Remembering Frodo's final dream or vision in the house of Tom Bombadil and knowing where Frodo was headed, Sam grants Frodo the happy ending to his tale which he believes he was cheated of in life. As with the scene of Gollum's near repentance, the description has the power to compel belief. It lifts Frodo's final journey to the mythic heights foreseen in his vision in the House of Tom Bombadil. Nor do we question its truth.

In the same way, we do not question the truth of the scene on the stairs. Frodo, we know, came to pity Gollum despite his initial protests against the idea. Sam, too, will do so before long (*RK* 6.iii.944). Like Frodo, Sam had been a vocal opponent of pity and mercy at first, although his words had also been far fiercer than his deeds. We need only recall the looseness of the rope he tied around Gollum's ankle, not to mention the offer of fish and chips (TT 4.iv.617, 654). He does glimpse the end of Gollum's "caress" or "'pawing at master,' as he thought" (714). The double qualification of "pawing at master," first with quotes and then by "as he thought," suggests the truth of the "caress," the wrongness of Sam, then, and the subsequent change of heart that arose from bearing the Ring himself. Once his pity was aligned with Frodo's, Sam would have a very different perspective than he had when he woke to find Gollum had returned. Then, too, Sam's conscience had pricked him into trying to apologize almost at once.

In this connection, note also that the last mention of Gollum in the tale comes just after the Ring's destruction, when Frodo humbly concedes that without Gollum all would have been lost: "So let us forgive him!" (RK 6.iii.947). In the direct line from Bilbo's pity to Frodo's, from Frodo's to Sam's, and thence to forgiveness, this scene makes that pity intelligible to the reader by showing the loathsome Gollum almost repenting of his betrayal out of love for Frodo, and the admirable Sam blighting that repentance for the same reason. But neither of them can take back what he has done and felt. Gollum's momentary choice to be the hero is answered by a moment of inadvertent villainy by Sam. We feel for them both.

Frodo, when he later came to write this scene, drew on what Sam told him (just as Sam would later do for him in "The Grey Havens") and included both the "pawing" version Sam thought he saw unfolding as he opened his eyes and the "caressing" version, which he realized, too late, was the truth. It was not the first time of course that Frodo had heard two versions of a story about Gollum from another hobbit. To adapt a phrase of Gandalf's, the stories were too much alike for comfort in their portrayals of Gollum. From this likeness, Frodo constructs a scene that rehearses Bilbo's discovery of pity, but here the horror at Gollum's lost chance to find Sméagol again is most immediately our own—the readers'—not that of any character in the story. As in "The Grey Havens," the momentary removal of the narration from a limited perspective to a seemingly omniscient one makes the incident both more real and more remote. Just as Sméagol's mention of love before murdering Déagol and Frodo's desire to strike Bilbo have already suggested, in the end, love is no more impregnable than pity. If this truth crept past us before, it is because we were focusing on the corruption worked by the pull of the Ring's power. Where love's roots are deep, it may stay the hand of a Frodo; where its roots are not deep, a Sméagol may speak love but use none. On the stairs of Cirith Ungol, with our perspective reversed, we see how hard a task it is to retrace our steps even for love. All the weight of Sam's precipitate hostility notwithstanding, Gollum's inability to face and admit the truth of Sam's accusation—he *has* been sneaking *and* a villain—is as much to blame for his inability to repent and prove the hero. While he holds on to that lie, his love and desire to repent cannot be stronger than his guilt or his desire for the Ring.

CHAPTER NINE

Hobbits in Darkness

THE LIGHT ALONE IS NOT ENOUGH

High in the Mountains of Shadow, after their long, steep climb to Shelob's lair, Frodo and Sam meet the deepest darkness, an evil of another kind than Sauron's and as indifferent to power and domination as Tom Bombadil.

> "Master, master!" cried Sam, and the life and urgency came back into his voice. "The Lady's gift! The star-glass! A light to you in dark places, she said it was to be. The star-glass!"
> "The star-glass?" muttered Frodo, as one answering out of sleep, hardly comprehending. "Why yes! Why had I forgotten it?"
> (TT 4.ix.720)

Why indeed? It's an excellent question, the answer to which cannot simply be that Frodo's wits are befuddled because he is "walk[ing] *as it were* in a black vapour wrought of darkness itself" (4.ix.718, emphasis mine). Only two days earlier he had been bewitched by the vapors rising from the enchanted Morgulduin, but, as he fought the urge to put on the Ring, he had instead put his hand on the phial, which had gone largely forgotten until then also (4.viii.707, ix.720). Now, in the midst of another dreadful peril, he wonders why he has forgotten it again.

The vapor was literal in Morgul Vale; in Shelob's lair it is metaphorical ("as it were"). Yet, what the metaphor attempts to describe seems a kind of Manichean darkness, a darkness more a presence than an absence. It numbs and blinds body and mind, stripping away memory, time, and space until only night, everlasting and all engulfing night, and *will* and *desire* remain (*TT* 4.ix.718). The darkness of Shelob shows that there is no simple answer to what evil is in Tolkien's Secondary World, because neither the Augustinian-Boethian notion that evil is the privation of good nor the Manichean idea that evil is a coherent force opposing good suffice to describe the human experience of it which, even in the Primary World, defies every attempt to comprehend it fully and explain it.[1] Tom Shippey is surely correct when he states, "The uncertainty over evil in a way dominates the entire structure of *The Lord of the Rings*. All the characters would find decisions much easier if evil were unquestionably just Boethian or Manichean" (*Road* 145). So, too, would scholars. Ursula K. Le Guin wrote that Tolkien did not have "an *answer* to the Problem of Evil," but that was because "like all great artists he escapes ideology by being too quick for its nets, too complex for its simplicities, too fantastic for its rationality, too real for its generalizations" (176). With this, I believe Shippey would agree: Tolkien's "ideas were often paradoxical and had deep intellectual roots, but they appealed at the same time to simple things and to everyday experience" (147).

Shelob, visible, wholly alive, and neither Sauron's slave nor familiar, gives evil a present substance much harder to descry in the shadowy wraiths and in a Dark Lord glimpsed only in Frodo's mind's eye or Pippin's misadventure with the palantír (*TT* 4.ix.724). In Shelob, we see in person, as it were, that evil in Middle-earth is also incarnate and can be as unconcerned with domination as Tom Bombadil is in his goodness. (It may be no accident that Sam in this hour, faced with the indifferent evil that is Shelob, thinks of the indifferent good that is Bombadil.) Her malice, moreover, not only outdoes the spells of Minas Morgul but almost accomplishes in a brief hour what the Ring has not yet done across long years (*TT* 4.ix.723). For the *will* and *desire*, which are all that Frodo and Sam have left in that darkness, do not by themselves constitute an identity, not without memory and sensation of the world and time. But they alone have power here. At first it is only through them that the hobbits keep moving forward at all. Crucially, however, the power of the Silmaril's light does not become truly effective against the darkness until Frodo exerts his *will* to turn and fight, knowing both that flight is impossible and that the phial is not in itself a sufficient weapon (see Milbank 77). Nor was it meant to be a weapon, but "*a light when all other lights go out*," a distinction underlined by the flash of his drawn sword as he advances upon Shelob (*TT* 4.ix.720).

What the light reveals, however, is not Eärendil or Beren (*TT* 4.ix.720, 721). Rather it is "Frodo, hobbit of the Shire," hardly a heroic epithet to match Beren One-Hand or even Eärendil the Mariner (4.ix.721). Yet it is not mockery. For they are all part of the same tale, as Frodo and Sam's conversation on the stairs has recently pointed out; and the narrator describes Sam in similar language when he uses the star-glass to rout Shelob finally: "Samwise the hobbit, Hamfast's son" (4.x.729–30). In both cases, moreover, each of them first cries out in a language he does not know, as if "another voice spoke through his," and reverts to his hobbit-self (4.ix.720, x.729–30). Only once they have recovered themselves do they find the fire of spirit to set the light of the Silmaril ablaze.

The phial was made for precisely this occasion, clearly foreseen by Galadriel, when Frodo and Sam would walk in "the shadow of death" (Sind. *nguruthos*) in a "phantom world of horror" (*TT* 4.x.729). An enchanted object, it remained mostly forgotten until needed, much like Sam's elven rope, to which he gave no thought until its moment arrived, and which then came when needed (4.i.608, 611). This seems quite the opposite of what generally happens with the Ring, which is very often on its bearer's mind. Increasingly is this the case with Bilbo. Within a short time of finding it, he forgets he has it in his pocket, and by the time he leaves the Shire sixty years later, it is he is constantly fretting over it (*FR* 1.ii.49). Recall also that Bilbo will again ask Frodo about his Ring when the hobbits stop in Rivendell on their way *back* to the Shire and that Frodo will say to Farmer Cotton two years after the Ring's destruction: "It is gone for ever ... and now all is dark and empty" (*RK* 6.vi.987, 6.ix.1024). The Ring's power leaves a mark that survives the Ring.

If, moreover, the pull of the Ring acts on the will and desire, we must ask why Frodo never even thinks of it when everything but will and desire has been taken from him. When required to face Lobelia Sackville-Baggins, for example, or the crowd in the common room of The Prancing Pony, Frodo wants to put on the Ring and vanish. To escape from Boromir, he does so. Here, however, faced with death for himself and Sam, with the failure of his Quest, and quite possibly the night of the world, it doesn't cross his mind at all. So Frodo neither thinks of the thing he cannot otherwise forget nor remembers the thing that was meant to be remembered at precisely this time. The former is good but also strange and perhaps not unconnected to his experience in Morgul Vale, where "there was no longer any answer to that command [i.e., the pressure to put on the Ring] in his own will" (*TT* 4.ix.706). The same cannot be said of his hand, that tool of his desire, though he is able to rouse his will to redirect it to the star-glass. That desire would have proved fatal, if an external intervention had not reminded Sam of the phial beforehand. By this, of course, I mean Sam's vision of Galadriel, which is proved to be more than memory by Frodo and Sam crying out invocations in a language they did not know (TT 4.ix.721, x.729).

For all the nudges and winks that more than chance is at work in the tale of the Ring, Providence tends to preserve its anonymity through coincidence and leaves it to others to detect its influence and see in the events a pattern. Only once before have we seen anything like what we see here (above on pages 107–08). On Amon Hen, Frodo briefly lost himself to the pull of the Ring, and Sauron was about to locate him, when he heard a voice—Gandalf's—telling him to take off the Ring, an intervention that allowed him to reclaim his identity and remove the Ring in time. The parallel between these two moments is striking: all is about to be lost when someone not physically present intervenes to enable Frodo to escape catastrophe. Where they diverge is also significant. For here Sam, not Frodo, is prompted by vision and voice to remember the star-glass, and he in turn reminds Frodo. Here, too, the source of the reminder is never identified. If the evidence of the text points to any character, it is to Galadriel, but Tolkien was in no way averse to mysteries and identification may matter as little as determining the *nature* of Tom Bombadil as opposed to his *function* within the story (on pages 84–85).[2]

Far more important, I would argue, is why such an indirect intervention—to Frodo through Sam—is necessary. The night, the darkness, the evil that Shelob inhabits and that inhabits her is a power different from Sauron's. He seeks to dominate and to enslave, not destroy. Even a Dark Lord needs subjects. Shelob wishes to destroy and consume *everything*. To say that Sauron will "eat all the world" if he gets the Ring back, or that the One and the Nine devour their mortal keepers, is to speak in a metaphor. To say that Shelob lusts to devour all life is if not wholly literal not quite a metaphor either. There is too much of Ungoliant in her for that. Allison Milbank's likening of Shelob to an "arachnic black hole" owes its humor to its truth (78). The narrator sums up the attraction she held for Gollum and its effect with a rare indulgence of religious language. "Already, years before, Gollum had beheld her, Sméagol who pried into all dark holes, and in past days he had bowed and worshipped her, and the darkness of her evil will walked through all the ways of his weariness beside him, cutting him off from light and from regret" (TT 4.ix.723). Shelob's malice reduces Sméagol to an apposite of Gollum, whom we have seen as two nearly distinct "thoughts," and leaves him blind to what might help save him. Her evil is so overwhelming, while remaining indifferent to power, that it suggests evil is intrinsically dominating, no matter what it desires. We might, therefore, recast Tom Shippey's comment on Bombadil (above on page 160) to characterize Shelob: what she *is* may be unclear, but what she *does* is dominate. Without regret, however, whatever love Gollum may be beginning to feel for Frodo lacks the strength to overcome his lust for the Ring and his anger at the pitiless suspicions of Sam, who, though unkind, is right to assume Gollum is up to no good. Sam cannot get past the truth of what Gollum deserves, and Gollum cannot get past the truth that he deserves it. The light that comes through the chink in Gollum's darkness, to borrow Gandalf's metaphor, may well inspire fond memories of lost days and a desire to belong once more, but it cannot cure or conquer the evil part of him: it can only make it angrier. A repentance without regret is as impossible as a repentance that seeks to "retain th' offence" (*Hamlet* 3.3.56).

We must also give thought to *what* Gollum almost repents in the scene on the stairs. From our first encounter with him in "The Taming of Sméagol," what we see suggests that the regret he is cut off from begins with the murder of Déagol and continues on through all the deeds he keeps locked away in the dark rooms of his mind. Haunted he may be, but so, too, is Claudius, and he cannot repent. When he looks back, moreover, he looks to pleasant things like tales told in the evening by the Great River, not to killing Déagol on its banks. Even when he speaks of Bilbo, the Baggins he hates most of all, he refers to his cleverness in guessing the answer to the riddle of the fish, not how this disappointed his own present hopes of a meal. We have also seen, however, that, as early in his journey with the hobbits as the two "thoughts" scene in "The Passage of the Marshes," he does not wish his recovery of the Ring to involve harm to Frodo; and it is then that the idea of betraying Frodo and Sam to Shelob first arises as a solution that leaves no blood on his hands. As Gollum's glance back up the hill and the shaking of his head in "The Stairs of Cirith Ungol" indicate, it is this betrayal he is on the point of repenting when Sam wakes up. It is, then, repentance, not of a past, but a future evil, which fails to flower.

This same darkness also cuts Frodo off from remembering the light from which he had drawn strength only two days earlier and which was meant to give him hope in just this peril. In the night of an evil that cares not for such things, the Ring, too, becomes invisible, sunk in the deeper shadow. Sam, though with "darkness" around him and "blackness" within, is prompted by touching the hilt of his barrow blade to remember Bombadil (TT 4.ix.719). Just as sunlight had come flooding into the barrow when old Tom broke down the door to rescue them, so now a light blazes in Sam's mind (4.ix.730). It resolves itself into a vision of Galadriel, whose light Haldir had said "perceives the very heart of the darkness" (FR 2.vi.352). And so it does here: by filling his mind with the white light of Galadriel's gift, it sets Sam free from the black night Shelob's evil has brought to his heart. He can thus rouse Frodo from the stupor into which he has fallen.

The thoughts and images in Sam's mind here are quite revealing, for both Bombadil and Shelob are their own masters, one wholly good, one wholly evil. Neither is interested in dominating the wills of others. Shelob wishes to devour all life; Tom lets even Old Man Willow and the Barrow-wights be, unless they provoke him by acting themselves. Even then, he destroys only the unnatural evil, though perhaps *banishes* would be the better description of what he does to the Barrow-wight. The Ring has no power over Bombadil and Shelob because of their fundamental indifference to its purpose. Between these poles are Galadriel and Sam, both of them vulnerable to the Ring's pull, since both live in a world where such power seems useful. Yet, both are capable of choice. Galadriel's temptation we have seen; Sam's we shall see before long.

If Sam's vision is Galadriel's doing, she addresses him rather than Frodo because she knows Sam's love for him and his commitment to their Quest, the very things she tested him for in Lórien with both mind and mirror. Frodo is also more stunned by the evil of Shelob: "'The star-glass?' muttered Frodo, as one answering out of sleep, hardly comprehending" (TT 4.ix.720). Whoever the source of the vision, the vision itself points to the need for illumination, but the failure of the star-glass by itself to drive off Shelob shows that Frodo remains in the dark. The light needs desperate courage to dispel the darkness, just as it did for Eärendil. Frodo's recognition of this is the illumination he requires.

In this moment, with the pull of the Ring somehow suspended and no thought of it in his mind, Frodo is perhaps for the last time fully capable of free choice, just as he was at Amon Hen; and he chooses to give himself entirely to the light and to attack the darkness rather than merely attempting to hold it back. The heroic register of this passage draws attention modestly to its subject, "Frodo, hobbit of the Shire," ironically so, humbly rather than proudly, suggesting identity rather than ambition or temptation, so different from the words of Saruman to Gandalf, or Boromir to Frodo, or indeed from Frodo's own words to Gollum at the Black Gate or in the Emyn Muil (TT 4.ix.721).

This is Frodo's finest hour. He knows Gollum has betrayed him and that, as Gollum's master, he has failed to either tame him or help him find Sméagol. He knows that despite his courage he is not ready to face the Witch-king but believes he someday will be. He knows, finally, that it does not matter whether anyone will ever know what he does or suffers to destroy the Ring. Ever so briefly, the tangle of truths and lies like truth that enmesh the Ring-bearer is undone, and as in the moment on Amon Hen he is himself again and he chooses freely (FR 2.x.401). The words the narrator uses to describe him here both take up the claim of Elrond that "this is the hour of the Shire-folk" and reach for an answer to Bombadil's question (2.ii.270). Yet, as the narrator also allows us to see, he has underestimated this creature of darkness, who disregards what Sauron thinks important and over whom he can only pretend to have sway. No sooner does Frodo hand off the phial to Sam than Shelob returns. Frodo thinks they have escaped and mistakes the evening shadows of Mordor for a "a morning of sudden hope" (TT 4.ix.723). He runs deliriously toward Mordor, as deceived by his joy now as before he was stupefied by Morgul's spells. This time, however, the enemy for whom he is not yet ready knows where he is.

This moment in Shelob's lair is also the last time on the hither shore Frodo is ever free of the Ring. How is this so? He doesn't think of the Ring here at all, whether as a means of escape, as in the barrow, or as a weapon with which to defy the enemy, as in the Morgul Vale. Instead, he reveals himself and advances. He submits himself entirely, not as the Master of the Precious or even as the Ring-bearer, but as himself to the light and to his mission, just as Eärendil had done; and he too pierces the Shadows. "Frodo, hobbit of the Shire" may not be the answer to Bombadil's question, but it is the closest he ever comes—perhaps the closest he or anyone ever could come—to answering it.

SAM BETWEEN TRAGEDY AND FAIRY-STORY

Of the characters who bear the Ring, Sam Gamgee alone gets to think it over before he takes up the burden. He is also the only one who questions taking it up at all. Isildur and Gollum come by it through violence, the one calling his precious spoil a weregild, the other a birthday present. Bilbo picks it up without a thought but contrives an elaborate story to prove he won it. Frodo, though surprised by Bilbo's legacy, at once turns his thoughts to how useful it might prove. Timely disappearance may have once seemed the most enjoyable perk of his inheritance. But the instant Sam confronts the implications of Frodo's death for him and the Quest, his shock demonstrates how he sees himself and his situation as categorically different from Mr. Bilbo and Mr. Frodo: "What? *Me* take the Ring from *him?*" (TT 4.x.732)

This difference is even more fascinating because Sam's actions immediately prior to his debate about whether to take up the Ring offer a parallel to Frodo's actions in the tunnel: he thinks of the glass; invokes the aid of Elbereth in a language he does not know, as if another voice were speaking through his; and then calls upon Galadriel. Underscoring this parallel is the description of him as "Samwise the hobbit, Hamfast's son," to match "Frodo, hobbit of the Shire." And it was that Shire and that Frodo whom Hamfast's son saw when he looked into Galadriel's mirror. The memory of this vision returns to him now, to be interpreted anew as revealing to him his master's death.

He made his first choice—to go on to the end—long ago, the night they met Gildor and his company in the woods of the Shire (FR 1.iv.86–87). He admitted he did not know to what end his road led, but the sorest trial of that road waited until now. For a moment, he relishes the thought of a Quest of his own down the path of vengeance, to corner and kill Gollum for his treachery. He knows, however, that revenge was not completing what he had started and that Frodo would still be dead (1.iv.86–87). Vengeance does not mean that everything sad will come untrue.

He then contemplates other alternatives, the counsels of his despair: suicide whether by falling on his sword or by leaping off a cliff. For someone as fascinated by heroic tales as Sam is, these specific means of suicide, which repeat the deaths of Túrin and his sister Nienor, suggest that he is still measuring the tale he is in against the older tales, just as he had when discussing the Tale of Beren and Lúthien with Frodo only two days earlier (S 223–26). To be sure, since Sam has limited means with which to kill himself, one might doubt that the examples of Túrin and Nienor play a silent role here. Yet when he learns a little while later that Frodo is not dead, Sam imagines a heroic last stand over Frodo's body, a deed worthy of song, though there would be no more songs (TT 4.ix.735). In this he would be like Húrin, the father of Túrin and Nienor, but he would know that day would never come again (S 195). He has no delusion that the invisibility conferred by the Ring will deliver victory. It's more a matter of how many orcs he can take with him.

Thus, I would argue that even in despair Sam construes his own tale in terms of the Great Tales, and this allows him to reject anger, vengeance, and suicide and to accept grief. He sees that the path between doing something not worthwhile (vengeance) and something that was "to do nothing, not even to grieve" (suicide) leads to another path, which he regards as by far the worst. He sees he must take up the Ring and the Quest. It is nevertheless a very close call with heathen despair and a necessary counterbalance to the hope he finds in the star of Eärendil after rejecting the Quest and the Ring and choosing to do the right thing for all the wrong reasons.[3] Here we see Sam weighing the Tale of the Children of Húrin, which is a Tragedy, rather than the Tale of Beren and Lúthien, which is a Fairy-story, because he sees himself *at this moment* as being in a Tragedy (or would, if he possessed those terms to think in). Like Bilbo poised on the brink of Tragedy with his sword in his hand, Sam chooses wisely and avoids the mistake (*hamartia*) that would make him a tragic figure. Because of this wisdom, Sam's born of love as Bilbo's was of pity, Sam will be able to return to the Fairy-story Great Tale of Beren and Lúthien once he understands that Frodo is not dead. Knowing the choices made by Túrin Turambar, the self-proclaimed Master of Fate, Master Samwise chooses the road that leads toward the eucatastrophe of Fairy-story rather than the catastrophe of Tragedy.

But it is significant that he comes to this conclusion only after two other understandings presented themselves to him serially. This is a sequence of thought quite unlike his subsequent review of the reasons for taking the Ring and abandoning his master's corpse unburied in the road, a step he is loath to take. In considering this latter course Sam rationally and intentionally weighs what will happen if he does not leave Frodo behind: "Let me see now: if we're found here..." (TT 4.x.732). He convinces his mind, but so great is his love for Frodo that he never assents in his heart. As he says, paradoxically, in the moment he turns back: "I can't be their Ring-bearer. Not without Mister Frodo" (4.x.735). He says this, moreover, while wearing the Ring to hide from the orcs and while still believing that Frodo is dead. At no point in this sequence does Sam exhibit any desire for the Ring for himself; rather he manifests all the profoundest sense of his own unworthiness to take up this burden, which it has become his duty to bear.

The love, humility, and duty Sam shows here as he debates both course and conscience lend him a strength to resist the Ring for long enough, even though its pull has grown much greater now that it is so close to the source of its power. If we compare it briefly with the argument the two "thoughts" Gollum had with each other, not only does Gollum's insanity become clearer, but so do the malice, resentfulness, and low cunning that made him fall so far so quickly after the briefest exposure to the Ring. Gollum wants the Ring, and he will allow Frodo to be killed by Shelob, so that he can get it without technically breaking the promise he swore by the Precious. Whatever love Gollum might have begun to feel toward Frodo, his lust for the Ring has broken every bond since he first saw it in Déagol's hand. Sam has the Ring but doesn't want it, and he is willing to risk the whole world to stay by his dead master's side.

The chapter is called "The Choices of Master Samwise," and the two most important of these are the choice to take up the Ring and the Quest and the choice to turn back. The first, like the decisions against vengeance and suicide, is moved by reason; the second arises from his heart alone. Both are correct. Had Sam not taken the Ring and left, all would have been lost, since the Ring would have been found; had he not turned back, recklessly casting the fate of Middle-earth into the balance, all would have been lost, since Sauron would have "pluck[ed] out the heart of [Frodo's] mystery" (*Hamlet* 3.2.353–54). Like Aragorn in "The Departure of Boromir," who followed his heart rather than his reason, seeking to rescue Merry and Pippin rather than to follow Frodo and the Ring, Sam made his final choice with his heart, right but for the wrong reasons. Like Bilbo in "Riddles in the Dark," the temper of his heart allows him to begin his possession of the Ring with an act antithetical to the nature of its power to dominate. As Bilbo began with pity and mercy, Sam begins with love and sacrifice. Each follows with actions that save others from imprisonment and death at great risk to themselves.

Yet Gandalf stressed that in the end there was no resisting *a* Ring of Power, let alone *the* Ring of Power (1.ii.46). Its effect on Frodo's will was such that he could not throw it into his hearth in Bag End, and for all his valor Boromir slipped into a fugue of ambition and hopelessness that threatened the life of someone half his size. Here, now, on the threshold of Mordor, the Ring is far more powerful than it was at Bag End or on Amon Hen. Sam, moreover, is beset by anger and "black despair" before he thinks of or touches the Ring (TT 4.x.730). To be sure, he rejects the actions to which these feelings prompt him, but deciding against vengeance and suicide is no anodyne for the emotions, which creep back in when he discovers that Frodo is not dead and his anger turns inward. The last stand Sam momentarily imagines—in which he would use the invisibility conferred by the Ring to maximize the number of orcs he can kill—turns on its head Bilbo's revulsion at the unfairness of attacking Gollum from behind while invisible. Heroically framed "The Last Stand of Master Samwise" may well be, but it could also be the first hint that the Ring is already affecting him perniciously.

This is speculation, no doubt, but grounded in the other signs we have seen of the Ring's subtle effects. When Sam realizes that he is trapped by two bands of orcs, approaching from both directions, he asks himself, like Frodo in the barrow, "How he could escape, or save himself, or save the Ring" (TT 4.x.734). Sam is not the first to speak of saving the Ring, but the only two others who have done so, Gollum and Frodo, are both also Ring-bearers, whose interest in the Ring is no simple matter.[4] Gollum's understanding of the promise he swears by it is crucial. He twists the meaning to allow him to betray Frodo, so that he can save it for "ourselfs," and when he finally grasps that Frodo has intended all along to save the Ring only in order to destroy it, he explodes into truly desperate violence (4.ii.633). By that moment, however, Frodo, too, means to save the Ring for himself (RK 6.iii.943). Sam's speaking of saving himself and the Ring in the same breath is no step in the right direction. Recall that Sam "bent his own neck and put the chain upon it, and at once his head was bowed to the ground with the weight of the Ring," a phrase that suggests not only movement but submission like that of an animal to the yoke (TT 4.x.733).[5] Since the Ring was made to dominate the wills of others, it is an apt description of the true relationship between the Ring and every Ring-bearer but Sauron. It also illustrates the predicament of any Ring-bearer trying to fulfill this Quest. For if everything done with the Ring turns to evil, as Frodo said to Boromir, what of Sam's use of the Ring here? It is to himself that the evil is done (FR 2.x.398).

What does not require speculation is seeing that the Ring's immediate impact on Sam differs from the experiences of Bilbo and Frodo. As soon as he hangs the Ring around his neck, it is a burden that bows him to the ground, making it difficult for him to get to his feet and leaving him surprised that he can walk once he does. When discovery by the orcs seems imminent, he puts the Ring on without any "thought or decision" but also without any feeling of external pressure to do so. He finds that his perceptions of time and of the world around him are vastly changed. Not only can he hear the voices of prisoners beneath the tower of Cirith Ungol, but also the "murmur" of water in the Morgul Vale on the far side of the mountains, even though the stream that flowed there had been described as "silent" (TT 4.x.734, 4.viii.704). The darkness of Shelob's lair, once he reenters it, no longer seems as dark, although he does feel as if he's in a fog. Time dilates, but not as it had done in the Morgul Vale, where every step seemed to take "minutes of loathing"; here "a moment was filled with an hour of thought" (4.x.734). His will grows stronger as his weariness increases. He feels alone in this world, with the Ring a burning weight on his hand, but he is not alone, and he knows it: "Somewhere an Eye was searching for him."

As Hammond and Scull have noted, the hardening of Sam's will as he wearies beneath the burden of the Ring is "a clear echo" of the famous lines in the Old English poem *The Battle of Maldon*, lines which Tolkien rendered as "Will shall be the sterner, heart the bolder, spirit the greater, as our strength lessens" (RC 498; B&M 6).[6] Yet given Tolkien's position on these lines, this allusion is no simple echo. For he has argued that they are crucial to reading the poem as he believes the poet meant it to be read, since they exist in tension with a comment the poet made earlier about the *ofermod* or "pride" (of Beorhtnoth, the English commander (Gordon ll. 89-90; M&B 27-35). His sense of fairness toward the enemy leads to his own death, to the deaths of the warriors of his household (*heorþwerod*), and to a signal defeat for the English.[7] His men, as the lines quoted above indicate, embrace their heroic deaths around their dead lord out of love and loyalty, regardless of any larger effect the deaths may have. The courage of the *heorþwerod* is praiseworthy but tragic because it is their lord's pride that sets the stage for it. The ethos of chivalry and the heroic northern spirit, Tolkien argues, is here viewed with a critical eye by the poet, who is "above chivalry, or even heroism" (M&B 32). Like the *Beowulf*-poet before him and the *Gawain* poet afterward, the poet of *Maldon* questions the heroic code.

Tolkien notes that "The words of Beorhtwold have been held to be the finest expression of the northern heroic spirit" (M&B 28), but goes on to criticize this spirit when it is misdirected, as he believes the *Maldon* poet does here: "For this 'northern heroic spirit' is never quite pure; it is of gold and an alloy. Unalloyed it would direct a man to endure even death unflinching, when necessary: that is when death may help the achievement of some object of will, or when life can be purchased only by denial of what one stands for. But since such conduct is held admirable, the alloy of personal good name was never wholly absent" (M&B 28). Sam's death as he envisions it is the worst possible outcome: so far from achieving some necessary end, he will be delivering the Ring up to Sauron. He is also quite right to recognize that there would be no songs at all, let alone one to praise the good name he should merit as a faithful retainer defending his lord's body with his last breath; but the idea of his love and loyalty being immortalized in song is not without its allure.

With the Ring on Sauron's hand, however, there would then be no Master Samwise whose choices the very title of this chapter commemorates; no Master Samwise whose tenacity gets the Ring to the fire; and no Master Samwise to end as master of the house in which he had begun as a servant and whose "Longfather Tree" in the Red Book of Westmarch affirms the gentling of his condition (RK App. C. 1105).

What has *Maldon* to do with the Ring? First, of course, the hardening of Sam's will is presented as at least concurrent with and proportional to his growing weariness. While the text does not explicitly say that the Ring is causing Sam's will to harden, the context, in which we find other effects detailed, suggests that we should regard it as also owing to the Ring. Gandalf, moreover, explained that "at last every minute is a weariness" for a mortal who possesses a Ring of Power even if he does not use it to become invisible (FR 1.ii.47). At the very least, we have a correlation between the onset of weariness and the hardening of the will. But that does not in itself establish causation.

What of the Ring and the will then? Does the gravity of the Ring break the will of its bearer or change it, pulling it in a given direction? We may well ask, rhetorically I think, whether we believe Gandalf's or Galadriel's will would be less strong if they had the Ring? Does Gollum seem in any way weak-willed? Or does Frodo, whom we have seen trying to use the Ring to bend Gollum to his will, despite Galadriel's warning that using the Ring would require him to train his will to dominate the wills of others, an act which would destroy him? What of the Witch-king—no soul more lost to the Ring than he—whose overpowering "will" must be severed from his "undead flesh" before he can be killed? (RK 6.vi.844). What is the "spell" that "knits" them together if not the power of his ring, which is as enslaved to the One as he is to Sauron? The strength of his will is very closely bound to the power of his ring. So, rather than breaking the will of its bearer, the Ring cozens and corrupts the bearer's purpose to the domination of the wills of others, so that Gandalf's pity and desire of strength to do good would become an irresistible hateful sanctimony. Since the power of the Ring is greater than the power of any possible bearer within Middle-earth, every will becomes the will to power, and every moral choice of the Ring-bearer in the end the choice to dominate others.

Second, the debate we see within Sam in this chapter is about what his duty is and to whom he owes it. His love and loyalty to Frodo have no finer expression than when Sam sets his barrow sword beside Frodo "as it lay by the old king in the barrow" (TT 4.x.731). This action's significance for Sam's view of Frodo becomes even clearer when we note that the text does not mention a king lying in the barrow until now. It is absent from "Fog on the Barrow-downs," both published and in draft, as well as from the manuscript of "The Choices of Master Samwise." So, whether we want to view this detail as a late addition by the narrator or the late invention of the detail by Tolkien, its introduction here and now means that Sam thinks Frodo deserves to be treated like a king. He has felt something similar before. When Frodo was using the Ring to compel Gollum to swear by the Precious, Sam momentarily saw him as "a mighty lord" (4.i.618; see also 4.iii.640).

In *Maldon*, as Tolkien sees it, the poet is questioning the very issues that Sam is trying to work out. Beorhtnoth's men, however, have no conflict approaching Sam's, whose dilemma collapses the distinction between Beorhtnoth and his men. Once Sam concludes that Frodo is dead, he sees that he must become the Ring-bearer in order to fulfill his duty and tries to convince himself to do just that, and that his duty to Frodo is done, superseded by his duty to the world, which will be covered in darkness if he fails. Sam inherits the Quest in ways that Beorhtnoth's men never inherit their lord's mission. Once Beorhtnoth is dead, some of his men flee, as Bowman points out, apparently believing their entire duty at an end; others will not desert Beorhtnoth even in death (98). Not one gives the least thought to the mission that brought them here, the need to defend their land from invaders (100).

The heads of those who stay to die over Beorhtnoth's body may be as full of the heroes of song, as is that of the bard Torthelm in "The Homecoming of Beorhtnoth Beorhthelm's Son," who needs reminding that it is "Beorhtnoth we bear not Beowulf here" (*M&B* 15). Beorhtnoth's men are also already proven warriors of status, members of their lord's *heorþwerod*. Sam, however, is not, no matter how keen he may be for tales of such times, and no matter how much he measures the tale in which he and Frodo find themselves against the deeds of the heroes of old (FR 1.i.24). Indeed, he emphatically denied any desire to be either wizard or warrior when Frodo playfully suggested that he would end up becoming one or the other (1.xi.208).

Yet from the scene in which we first saw Sam, "half chanting" that the Elves were "sailing, sailing, sailing" away and talking of dragons in a Bywater bar, we have known him to be of a passionate and Romantic nature (FR 1.ii.44–45). When his temptation comes, it will proceed from this nature. The lies the gravity of the Ring pulls from him will take their shape equally from the tales of the old days he has loved his whole life and from his love of the life of the earth he has tended for just as long. Despite his protest that he wished to be neither a wizard nor a warrior, he looks across the ashen solitude toward Orodruin and Barad-dûr and envisions a future for himself even greater and more glorious than Boromir had imagined upon Amon Hen (1.xii.207). He would be both wizard and warrior:

> His thought turned to the Ring, but there was no comfort there, only dread and danger. No sooner had he come in sight of Mount Doom ... than he was aware of a change in his burden. As it drew near the great furnaces where ... it had been shaped and forged, the Ring's power grew, and it became more fell, untameable save by some mighty will. As Sam stood there, even though the Ring was not on him but hanging by its chain about his neck, he felt himself enlarged, as if he were robed in a huge distorted shadow of himself, a vast and ominous threat halted upon the walls of Mordor. He felt that he had from now on only two choices: to forbear the Ring, though it would torment him; or to claim it, and challenge the Power that sat ... beyond the valley of shadows. Already the Ring tempted him, gnawing at his will and reason. Wild fantasies arose in his mind; and he saw Samwise the Strong, Hero of the Age, striding with a flaming sword across the darkened land, and armies flocking to his call as he marched to the overthrow of Barad-dûr. And then all the clouds rolled away, and the white sun shone, and at his command the vale of Gorgoroth became a garden of flowers and trees and brought forth fruit. He had only to put on the Ring and claim it for his own, and all this could be.
> (RK 6.iii.900–01)

The surge of Sam's thought here is breathlessly swift, from fear to a realization of the Ring's awesome might. From this heady feeling of power, a series of unspoken lies underpins the mad illusions tempting him: that *he* has the will to master the Ring; that with it *he* is a threat to Sauron; and that *he* can freely choose between forbearing the Ring despite the torment and claiming it for his own. Yet even that seeming choice vanishes into the final lie, that "all this could be," which for the reader at least echoes what Satan said to Christ on a high mountain, as he showed him all the kingdoms of the earth: "All these things will I give thee, if thou wilt fall down and worship me" (KJV, Matt. 4:8–9).

Briefly the Quest disappears, and Frodo disappears, and even Sam himself. For it is not Sam Gamgee, Hamfast's son, or Master Samwise who stands poised in this high place. No, it is "Samwise the Strong, Hero of the Age," who will cast down Sauron and make the desert bloom. Yet just as the Ring has struck him the harder for being so close to the place of its making, so his strength has not been worn down by the long, hopeless burden of spirit Frodo has borne. "Love of his master" and "plain hobbit-sense" allow his humility and his reason to shrink the hero back down a terrified halfling gardener (RK 6.i.901). Thus, unlike Beorhtnoth, whom *ofermod* moved to make a grand and foolish choice, Sam can in this moment see through the lies of glory and renewal grown from his fantasies by the power of the Ring. He rejects the choice of Beorhtnoth as he had previously done that of Beorhtnoth's *heorþwerod*.

With the Ring, however, there seems no step forward without at least one step back. Sam's moving refusal of the Ring and heroic rescue of Frodo are quickly, though subtly, countered: "Now it had come to it, Sam felt reluctant to give up the Ring and burden his master with it again" (RK 6.i.911). Since he is returning the Ring to his master, the Ring-bearer, we might have expected "give back" here, connoting the propriety of the restoration. But what we get is "give up," whose implications of surrender and sacrifice, especially after "reluctant," suggest that at some level Sam wishes to keep the Ring for himself, and that not wishing to burden Frodo is an unconscious rationalization. This of course can only cast doubt on his present offer to help bear the Ring "if it's too hard a job." Despite his love and loyalty, the power of the Ring has already begun to corrupt his purpose. He would not have remained able to give up the Ring for long. He would soon have withheld it and used it to bend Frodo to his will—for Mr. Frodo's good, of course, just as Frodo had tried to do for Gollum's. For the One beats down all love, all kindness, all pity.

THE LIMITS OF PITY

In "Many Meetings" when Bilbo attempted to touch the Ring, Frodo momentarily saw his beloved uncle as a frightening Gollum-like creature and wished to strike him. In "The Tower of Cirith Ungol" as Sam is passing the Ring to him and offering to help him carry it, Frodo sees him as an orc "leering and pawing at his treasure" (RK 6.i.912). Only evil creatures or things "leer"; only Gollum and orcs "paw"; and Frodo is not the only Ring-bearer to regard the Ring as his treasure.[8] In "Many Meetings," only the look on Frodo's face (whatever it may be) communicates his reaction, and only, as far as we can tell, to Bilbo. In "The Tower of Cirith Ungol," Frodo's reaction is so much more extreme—seizing the Ring and calling Sam a thief, "eyes wide with fear and enmity"—that he horrifies himself and brings Sam to tears. Now in the tower, as Bilbo had in Rivendell, Sam says "I understand" in response to Frodo's reaction (6.i.912). Now, too, as Anna Smol has keenly observed (51), Frodo seems not to shine with the light Gandalf and Sam had seen in him, but "he looked to Sam as if he was clothed in flame" (RK 6.i.911).

Again, we see the Ring alienating its bearer from his own, doubly so in this instance. For Sam, though reluctant, feels no desire to strike Frodo when he snatches the Ring from him, but Sam is progressing far more quickly. Within hours of taking possession of the Ring, he has begun to be unwilling to give it up. Frodo, by contrast, had possessed the Ring for seventeen years by the time he saw Bilbo in Rivendell, and only six months before that he had handed the Ring to Gandalf when the wizard asked to see it. He had done so reluctantly, however, and found himself unable to tell whether it was he or the Ring who did not wish Gandalf to touch it, an uncertainty of identity that Sam does not appear to share.

At Rivendell, Bilbo defused the moment by understanding at last what he had never been able to fully grasp before: the power of the Ring over Frodo and over himself. Until now, despite living many years without the Ring, he has not seen what Gandalf had been on about. The surprise he expressed to Frodo here about all the fuss over his Ring shares a perspective with his annoyance the night he had left Bag End that Gandalf kept "badgering" him about it (FR 2.i.239, 1.i.33). What he sees in Frodo's face in the Hall of Fire undeceives him. This insight, much like his glimpse into the horror of Gollum's existence long ago, allows him to avert an evil. As hobbits often do when words are not enough, Bilbo passes quickly to humor, but it is a wise humor that situates his understanding and regret in the context of their story before turning "back again" to the talk of home in which Hobbits take such comfort (FR 2.i.232; see also TT 2.viii.557–58).

In Mordor, however, the vehemence of Frodo's reaction leaves him begging Sam's indulgence, and Sam's understanding is the more injured because he is the more blameless. No light words follow as Frodo looks forward without hope, and no talk of home can offer comfort because Frodo looks back without memory. During his captivity, as he tells Sam the next day, he had tried to recall the Shire but failed (RK 6.ii.918). Even his most recent thoughts of the Shire have been vague and dim. In the Morgul Vale, he hears Sam calling him to wake up, but his voice seems to come from far off "memories of the Shire" wording that suggests that Frodo's memories themselves are themselves fading (TT 4.viii.707). Later, during their famous conversation about the

Great Tales in "The Stairs of Cirith Ungol," he playfully imagines a future hobbit child asking his father to tell him more about Sam, now envisioned as a hero of the same kind of tales he had once heard at Mr. Bilbo's knee; but memory and imagination are not the same thing, and despite this flight of mirth here Frodo expects the tale he and Sam are in to be the kind that ends sadly (4.viii.712). Without a memory of the past, he cannot imagine a future like the one Sam does, a future that emerges from the past, but in which he "wak[es] up to a morning's work in the garden" (4.viii.712). Unlike Sam, Frodo is not present in the future he imagines.

This scene from "The Tower of Cirith Ungol" soon replays itself in "Mount Doom," but now with powerful echoes of Bilbo's clash with Gandalf in "A Long-expected Party." Because "in his pity he could not keep silent" (*RK* 6.iii.937), Sam again offers to help his master bear the burden, and Frodo snaps for a moment, threatening him in word and deed exactly as Bilbo had done Gandalf: "His hand strayed to his sword-hilt" (6.iii.937; *FR* 1.i.33).

Above I noted what I called Frodo's finest hour (on pages 175–76), as he advanced on Shelob with his sword in one hand and Galadriel's star-glass in the other. Here we see something quite different. Just as Bilbo had recovered somewhat in the years since his confrontation with Gandalf, so Frodo has grown worse since his own clash with Bilbo in Rivendell. In a matter of days, he has descended from the heights of his false hope in the moments before Shelob stung him to an abyss of terror and shame when he thought the orcs had seized the Ring; from the joy of his rescue, which learning that Sam had taken the Ring only heightened, to an equally sudden reversal for much the same reason; and then from apologies and pleas for understanding to another threat, more apologies, and more pleas. So slender has the difference between claiming the Ring and claiming the burden become: "But then quickly his voice changed. 'No, no, Sam,' he said sadly. 'But you must understand. It is my burden, and no one else can bear it. It is too late now, Sam dear. You can't help me in that way again. I am almost in its power now. I could not give it up, and if you tried to take it I should go mad'" (*RK* 6.iii.937). How different Frodo's "morning of sudden hope" outside Shelob's lair is from Sam's "morning's work in the garden": the one a precipice of delusion, the other a foundation for resisting the illusions that arise from the pull of the Ring (*TT* 4.ix.723, 4.vii.712). The sting of Shelob, and perhaps of Gollum's predictable failure to prove true, blight almost the last hope Frodo ever feels. Is it a coincidence that memory and hope fail at the same time, given that without memory it becomes harder to imagine a future for oneself? Nor does the renewed and increased burden of the Ring allow for any restoration of either memory or hope, not while the Quest remains unfulfilled. Over and again in the first chapters of book 6, the narrator—Frodo, perhaps, but telling the story from Sam's perspective since his own memory was lost—indicates Frodo's hopelessness from the moment Shelob pierces his delusory hope.

Sam's "quick spirits" allow his hopes to rise and fall with the occasion, an impulsive resilience that makes him more like Bilbo than his master is. Frodo may come close to running down the lane without a hat or pocket handkerchief as Bilbo had done, but he does not (RK 6.ii.919, FR 1.ii.62). His feet are not "eager" but "weary." Sam, for all his native Hobbit fear and distrust of boats and water, hurls himself into the Anduin and the peril of drowning rather than be left behind by Frodo (FR 2.x.405–06). Sam may tell himself that he "never really had any hope," but he is berating himself for not trusting his heart when he does so (TT 4.x.739). His words—"Don't trust your head, Samwise, it is not the best part of you"—are rooted in a legacy of semi-jocular reproach come down to him from his Gaffer. Sam's spirits, moreover, rise and fall even in Mordor where he, too, can feel the enormous pressure of the Eye even while he is not wearing or carrying the Ring (RK 6.iii.934).

Frodo makes one positive reference to hope while in Mordor, if we can count irony as positive. He expresses his hope that Sam had looked into accommodations for their journey, in which we again see a hobbit making light of a serious subject (RK 6.i.913). Given Frodo's expectation from the start that his adventure will end in death whether it succeeds or fails, his jest is really a bit of gallows humor. Otherwise, it is an itinerary of hope denied (6.ii.917, 924 twice, 926, 927, 6.iii.934–35). Several details underscore this despair. First is his inability to find hope in the wailing cries of dismay voiced by the Nazgûl who brings word of the Witch-king's destruction, which itself also affords quite a contrast with his hearing the loneliness in the Ringwraith's cry at FR 1.iv.90. Next, I point out his surrender to Sam of agency over everything but the Ring, and his quiet declaration to Sam after the Ring has gone into the Fire that "hopes fail." Days before they ever draw near the mountain, finally, Frodo has declared all his hope gone, and Sam has seen that his master is "too much occupied with his burden and the struggle in his mind . . . and almost too hopeless to care" (6.ii.918, 927, iii.934).

So, when pity compels Sam days later to offer—hopelessly, as he knows—to carry the Ring for Frodo, it is no surprise that the struggle with the Ring is all that is left in his master's mind. Frodo's reaction bears witness to that very "spirit of Mordor" that he and Sam had seen in the two orcs tracking them:

they might be at odds with each other but are as one when they perceive a threat (RK 6.ii.924–26). Thus, Sam's pity is answered with a threat. As we saw before, memory plays an important role here. In Rivendell, Bilbo could defuse the tension through asking Frodo to share memories that linked them at the most basic level, as hobbits of the Shire. During his captivity in the tower, Frodo tried to remember the Shire but could not, and that divided him from Sam. Here now Sam tries to prompt Frodo to remember the meal they had eaten in Ithilien only days ago, but he cannot: "At least, I know that such things happened, but I cannot see them. No taste of food, no feel of water, no sound of wind, no memory of tree or grass or flower, no image of moon or star are left to me. I am naked in the dark, Sam, and there is no veil between me and the wheel of fire. I begin to see it even with my waking eyes, and all else fades" (RK 6.iii.937). Just as Frodo's threat in this scene goes beyond what happened in Rivendell and the tower, so, too, now with memory: even when prompted he cannot recall the meal they shared in Ithilien only days before, or anything else, it would seem. Sam's own memories seem long ago and far away, but their sensuality remains in the fragrance of Ithilien and the cool mud of the Water between his toes, not to mention Rosie Cotton and her brothers. His memories of the Shire and its people define and identify him as much as his love of Frodo and his hobbit-sense. One potentially significant contrast between Sam and Frodo here is that Frodo's memory of the Shire seems much more closely tied to the place he left behind, or, more abstractly, to the idea of it, than it is to individual people.[9] While he is very much attached to Bilbo, Bilbo left the Shire many years ago. Trebly orphaned, as it were, and one of those queer Bagginses, Frodo was isolated before he took up the legacy that would isolate him yet more; and this isolation and abstraction may well have made his lost memories of the Shire harder to regain or to recover from.

We would also do well to recall how important memories of home were for Bilbo on his adventure, an essential part of which was always the idea of "back again," no matter how much those adventures with dragon and war might have jaded him. As Thorin's dying words recognize, those aspects of home whose memory Bilbo cherishes throughout his journey make him who he is—it is more a matter of *baconitas* than bacon of course—and to forget them is to lose one's identity. Bilbo is at the point of forgetting when he threatens Gandalf, an old friend and a guest in his home, with a sword; Frodo, as he tells us himself, has forgotten them by the time he threatens Sam. He is nearly as "miserable, alone, [and] lost," as Gollum was when Bilbo first pitied him and his "endless unmarked days" (H 133).

The Shire was the very thing Frodo had set out to save, and he has lost it. He also came to see that far more than the Shire was in danger, and to save everyone from Sauron he *chose* to be the Ring-bearer (FR 2.ii.270). Yet, he has lost that, too, having no memory of Ithilien or Faramir. His panic in the tower when he thought the orcs had taken the Ring demonstrates that he still felt the emotional core of his choice, but the equally frenzied jealousy for the Ring which bared its teeth even before Sam suggested sharing the burden (which Sam felt a sudden reluctance to let go) leaves no doubt how thoroughly compromised Frodo's thinking about the Ring and the Quest has become. What Frodo said to Sam about Gollum having a "muddled head" about "saving the Precious" is also proving true for himself (TT 4.viii.713–14).

Even when Frodo apologizes to Sam in the tower, his last words—"You can't come between me and this doom"—may be seen in hindsight to bear an irony that Frodo would not have noticed in the moment. For "come between" is ambiguous here ("Between, prep., adv., and n."). Does Frodo mean Sam is trying to come between him and what is threatening him, or between him and what he desires? By comparison, there is no ambiguity in "come not between the Nazgûl and his prey" (RK 5.vi.841). The threat is obvious, even without the rest of the Witch-king's statement. Given Frodo's mercurial perspective here, however, the only answer to the question seems to be "both." Yet Sam is well aware of the "struggle in [Frodo's] mind" between "the Ring is my burden" and "the Ring is mine." Or else, his master's failure to react when he took the Ring from him would not have seemed proof that he really was dead (TT 4.x.732).

Strait is the way between these two aspects of the struggle, but it grows narrower still. For the claim that "the Ring is my burden" is perilous in itself. To suffer burdens alone is often a source of pride, worn like the crown of martyrdom; and as the Ring grows heavier and Frodo wearier, the vulnerability to pride can only grow. Of course, Frodo is also correct that this burden cannot be shared. It is necessarily his. Nor can we forget Frodo's desire to use the Ring, as expressed to Galadriel and as realized in his dealings with Gollum. The way thus narrows to a vanishing point, at which "Frodo, hobbit of the Shire" will disappear, because he will claim the Ring as his own.

In thinking about Frodo's struggle, we should bear two thoughts in mind. First, Sam experiences no such struggle. Is this owing to his concern for Frodo, whose very corpse (as he thinks it) proves more important to him than the Quest he turns away from, knowing full well the almost certain consequences of his choice? If so, that would certainly fit with what we saw of Bilbo's untroubled use of the Ring to help rescue Thorin and Company (above on pages 58–59). Sam's conflict while he has the Ring is whether to leave his master, and generally his struggle is between hope and despair. He knows the importance of the Ring and the Quest and is willing to take up the burden, but "not without Mister Frodo" (TT 4.x.734).

Second, Frodo has faced this struggle all along, whether contending against a desire he feels to put on or use the Ring or against a seemingly external pressure to do so. When the desire is external, as when the command of the Witch-king upon Weathertop overpowers him, it is obvious to the reader before it becomes so to him (FR 1.xi.195). Frodo may not at first grasp that "in putting on the Ring he obeyed not his own desire but the commanding wish of his enemies," but the narrator understands this very clearly, and tells the scene on Weathertop in such a way that the character's later recognition of what happened there serves to confirm something the reader already knows (1.xii.198).

Note the wording of this recognition. The phrase "obeyed not ... but...." gives a far different impression than if the verb were *yielded to* or *gave in to*. The words chosen connotes conformity along with submission to domination, while the words not chosen generally do not. We yield to or give in to a desire or an impulse or a temptation, but yielding to or giving in to a "commanding wish" just doesn't sound right; and when we see *obey*, we expect *orders* or *commands* to follow, not *wishes*. The phrase *commanding wish* is thus a strange periphrasis for *command*, which would have so simply and perfectly balanced *desire*. It splits the difference between the compulsion and desire he feels but does not wish to yield to or openly admit. Yet in doing so, it betrays itself. It seems be holding the very idea of what it desires at arm's length. Then, too, the wording of the entire clause strongly suggests that Frodo would have regarded obeying his own desire or wish as less problematic: his choice, not the Witch-king's command.

We can see Frodo making a free choice about putting on the Ring in the curious parallel between his behavior in Tom Bombadil's house and in the barrow. In both, Frodo desires to put on the Ring, without the least hint that the desire came from any source but himself. Alarmed in the first case by the Ring's lack of effect on Bombadil, Frodo wishes to prove that Tom has actually given him back the real Ring, *his* Ring, so he dons it and gets up to leave. Where he means to go is never addressed, but he was heading for the outer door, which often passes for a sign of intent. In the barrow, he is so afraid that he briefly wishes to use the Ring to escape, abandoning his friends to their deaths. He chooses not to use the Ring but to stay and fight to save his friends. It is a brave and reckless choice, and it is his own.

Just so, upon Amon Hen Frodo escapes Boromir, necessarily by means of the Ring, and never is he more justified in using it, especially since he thereby saves Boromir from a fate far more grim than the one he meets. Boromir may force Frodo to decide, but it is certainly not his wish that Frodo should put it on and vanish. During his first near encounter with a Black Rider back in the Shire, fear spurred an "unreasoning" desire to put the Ring on and set his hand moving while he came up with reasons, or rationalizations, for yielding to his desire (FR 1.iii.74–75). The second time the Black Rider appears, the desire to don the Ring supplants thought entirely and he is reaching for the Ring "almost before he realized what he was doing" (1.iii.78). There is a process of choice here and an entirely natural desire to reach for something he believes will keep him safe, just as it had Bilbo. Yet, as we have seen (on pages 93–94), there is also the silent and undetected will of the Black Riders bidding him to reveal himself, compromising but not necessarily ruling his choices. Frodo later thought he could have resisted the command to put on the Ring at Weathertop, and Gandalf also seemed to think it possible (1.xii.198, 2.i.219).

When Sam uses the Ring because he cannot avoid discovery by the orcs and rescue his master in any other way, his decisions are likewise justified and likewise his own. Although immediately aware of the Eye of Sauron, and though afraid of the orcs, he puts on and removes the Ring without any apparent difficulty. He feels no compulsion, experiences no unreasoning desire. He also recognizes that wearing the Ring can be a hindrance. For Frodo on Amon Hen, removing the Ring to escape Sauron proves far more difficult than putting it on to elude Boromir. Having swiftly lost himself in his vision of the Eye, he finds that he is not "free to choose" to remove it until he remembers who he is. Once he does, however, the power of choice is his again. Not only can he remove the Ring, but he soon decides to put it back on again to facilitate his departure from the Company (2.x.402).

Several threads come together here. Identity and choice are linked, but the Ring wipes out identity, isolating the bearer, taking away his memories and even his name. Without these he cannot be "Frodo, hobbit of the Shire." Without these, there is only the losing struggle in his mind between "the Ring is my burden" and "the Ring is mine," between purpose and desire. In these two statements, we can also see different overlapping aspects of the will, the rational, often expressed as "will," and the irrational, often expressed as "desire" and manifested in the hand that reaches for the Ring. Frodo has felt the desire to put on the Ring quite a few times, and it is commonly said to be his will that counters the urge, or stops his hand as it gropes toward the Ring. When he cannot stop his hand without Sam's help, as happens on the slopes of Mount Doom the day after Sam offers, a second time, to share the burden, it is a sure sign that the struggle in his mind is nearly over. His "will" has almost lost. As Frodo has already told Sam, he is "almost in its power" (RK 6.iii.937).

We may get a clearer notion of what being in its power means if we turn back again to the Witch-king's command at Weathertop, where the desire to slip the Ring on his finger had gripped him and, despite all his experience so far and Gandalf's warning, "he longed to yield" (FR 1.xi.195). *Longed* is a very strong word. As the description of Frodo's experience shows, this longing reaches beyond his terror and his temptation, beyond the grip of his single-minded desire, and beyond even the compulsion he knew was pushing him toward folly. In *The Lord of the Rings* this word describes a poignant, overwhelming desire for things lost that should never have been lost, things denied that should never have been denied, and things that have seated themselves deeply in the soul: the yearning of the Elves for the Sea, of the Dwarves of Durin's house for Khazad-dûm, of Sam in Mordor for just plain food (RK 6.iii.936), of Gollum most pertinently for the Ring.[10] Longing always indicates a deep, heartfelt desire, but quite often there is a sense of belonging, too, that the thing I desire is in some way mine or inseparable from me, which harmonizes with the point made above (on page 191) that Frodo would have been less troubled if putting on the Ring at Weathertop had been his choice rather than the result of the Witch-king's command. To be in the Ring's power, as the example of Gollum also shows, is to long for the Ring with all the will, both rational and irrational.

An example of the struggle in Frodo's mind that illustrates the convergence of being in the Ring's power and longing to be so comes from his crucial moment atop Amon Hen: he has lost his identity to the power of the Ring, and he cannot tell whether the words he cries out to the Eye are words of longing or denial (FR 2.x.400–01). Indeed, he cannot even tell what words he is uttering, as if the distinction between denial in "*Never, Never*" and the longing in "*Verily, I come, I come to you*" had collapsed. In the difference between his words on Amon Hen—whatever they were precisely—and the phrases "the Ring is mine" and "the Ring is my burden," we may see a shift in focus and a progression. In the first pair, Frodo is focused on the Eye and he fears imminent detection by it, a perspective that consciously regards the Ring as a burden precious to him and his journey as a Quest to destroy it nevertheless. In the second pair, the Ring has taken on a metaphorical life of its own: once in Mordor, the wheel of fire supplants not only the memories of time and place that form Frodo's identity but even displaces the fire-rimmed Eye. The pull of the Ring in Mordor is so great that "all else fades" (RK 6.iii.938). From here, "the Ring is mine" is just a step away. Of course, Frodo's voice will be heard coming from the Ring clutched at his breast, which even Sam now sees as the wheel of fire. For as the Eye is to Sauron, so is the Wheel of Fire to Frodo Baggins, a ring-corrupted vision of "the small hands" that turn "the wheels of the world ... while the eyes of the great are elsewhere" (FR 2.ii.269).

A short step, however, ought not be mistaken for an easy one. The present-tense *fades* denotes an unfinished process, as does *begin* in the previous clause: all else has not yet faded. The Eye still seeks Frodo, whose left hand tries to shield him from that brutal gaze, while his right reaches for the Ring. Frodo's will, his rational purpose, has also not yet faded, but it certainly would have done so without the nourishment provided to his will by *lembas,* the waybread given to the Company by Galadriel (RK 6.iii.935). Even so, lembas can only do so much. Both their wills are failing as they draw near the mountain (6.iii.938). Frodo still has the will to go on with the Quest, but he now lacks the strength to initiate action without Sam's prompting.

In Sam's last internal debate, he seems to concede, implicitly, that Frodo won't be able to throw the Ring into the fire: "When you get there," he asks himself, "what are you going to do? He won't be able to do anything for himself" (RK 6.iii.939). He, too, can now see only as far as the mountain. Behind them is an "ever-darkening dream" of the past, ahead the Power of Sauron "like the oncoming wall of night at the last end of the world" (6.iii.935–56). Yet, Sam's sight grows keener as his perspective narrows and he watches the helpless convergence of the "thoughts" struggling in the mind of his master. Just as his love for Frodo saved him from the Ring, so his experience bearing it himself allows him to pity Frodo's sufferings far more truly than he could have done otherwise. Twice when Frodo threatens him over the Ring, he replies, "I understand," but his choice of words does not just idly echo Bilbo's words in Rivendell, nor is it one of the helpless sympathies we utter when we don't know how to respond to the inconsolable sufferings of another. He has borne the Ring and felt the gravity of its power; he has seen what it does to those he loves and those he loathes; he has heard Bilbo's tale, both the false and the true; he has watched Frodo look on Bilbo with loathing and Gollum with pity. He comes to pity Gollum, but he pities Frodo first.

This pity does not arise from an unexpected and sudden understanding, as Bilbo's did in "Riddles in the Dark." For that was Bilbo recognizing, providentially, a fundamental kinship in the sufferings of another long bereft of the comforts and beauties of life that he so prized in his own. Rather, Sam's pity for Frodo is more akin to Bilbo's in "Many Meetings," which proceeds from his own experience with the Ring, from his knowledge of Frodo, and from the pain of seeing himself reflected in Frodo's eye. Yet Bilbo's understanding in Rivendell is still sudden. Sam grows more slowly into his, beginning in earnest when Frodo uses the Ring to become Gollum's master. Quite soon afterward Frodo first begins to feel the burden of the Ring as "an actual weight dragging him earthwards" (TT 4.ii.630-31). It would be a strange coincidence indeed if Frodo's first attempt to realize the potential of the Ring for domination were not causally linked to the metaphorical burden seeming to become a literal one. His constant weariness and preoccupation do not escape Sam's keen servant eye any more than the torment of Gollum's murderous obsession.

The pity that will not allow Sam to hold his tongue any longer also compels him to see more truly. Gollum, having finally grasped what Frodo's purpose is, attacks him and Sam; Frodo, roused by this threat to "his treasure," throws Gollum to the ground. "Then suddenly, as before under the eaves of the Emyn Muil, Sam saw these two rivals with other vision. A crouching shape, scarcely more than the shadow of a living thing, a creature now wholly ruined and defeated, yet filled with a hideous lust and rage; and before it stood stern, untouchable now by pity, a figure robed in white, but at its breast it held a wheel of fire. Out of the fire there spoke a commanding voice" (RK 6.iii.944). In this vision, Gollum and Frodo are scarcely human any longer: a shape, a shadow, a creature, a figure without pity grasping a wheel of fire. In the Emyn Muil, Frodo had appeared "a mighty lord who hid his brightness in grey cloud" and Gollum "a little whining dog" (TT 4.i.618). Sam's approval of Frodo and contempt for Gollum could hardly be clearer in this first instance of "other vision." Outside the Black Gate, too, Sam had explicitly approved of his master's harshness to Gollum, but not without a faint note of disquiet. The link in Sam's mind between kindness/blindness and sternness/wisdom suggests that he could just as well have called Frodo's behavior here unkind as stern. We should also recall Faramir in this connection, "a man . . . both sterner and wiser" than his brother (4.v.665). This equivalence has a bearing on the description of what Sam saw in the Emyn Muil and what he will see on Mount Doom, because in both visions he sees Frodo as stern and because on Mount Doom the note of disquiet in the description rings louder and truer.

Sternness is of course commonly associated with a kingly or authoritative manner or appearance. Aragorn, Gandalf, Boromir, Faramir, Denethor, Théoden, and Éowyn are all called stern. Yet the word has another sense, one long obsolete and unfamiliar to most people today. In Middle and Early Modern English, in authors from Laȝamon to Shakespeare, it could also mean merciless or cruel ("Stern, adj., n.2, and adv."). We need look no farther than Tolkien's own edition of *Ancrene Wisse* for a most pertinent example of precisely this sense of the word: "Rihtwisnesse, he seið, mot beo nede sturne, ant þus he liteð cruelte wið heow of rihtwisnesse. Me mei beon al to riht wis. Noli esse iustus nimis. In ecclesiaste." ("Justice," he says, "must necessarily be stern," and thus he dyes cruelty with the hue of righteousness. But one may be all too righteous. "Be not excessively just." In Ecclesiastes [7:17].") (p. 138, ll. 16–18).[11] Since the subject of *he says* here is the devil, it seems relevant to our assessment of *sternness* to notice that the very next words in the paragraph in "Mount Doom" describing what Sam sees—*untouchable now by pity*—further argue that Frodo's sternness has gone beyond righteousness toward cruelty. For given the cardinal importance Gandalf assigned to pity and mercy in "The Shadow of the Past," a lesson Frodo refused to learn until his own sufferings and the wretchedness of Gollum taught him better, to be beyond pity's touch cannot be good. Moreover, there is less to Frodo's appearing to be "a figure robed in white" than meets the eye (RK 6.iii.944). For in the Emyn Muil, Sam saw as "a mighty lord" who shone *with a light from within,* as Sam and Gandalf have seen Frodo do before (TT 4.i.618). From within, not from without. Yet here on Mount Doom the most important element in the vision is the wheel of fire. It blazes with a light of its own and it has transfigured the "mighty lord" into an indistinct "figure," an "it" (RK 6.iii.944; TT 4.i.618) rather than a person. The whiteness that robes the figure is also ambiguous and can be quite deceiving. We should not be taken in by it. When Frodo becomes able to see beneath the cloaks of the Black Riders, he sees them and their clothing as gray and white (FR 1.xi.195, xii.213). Saruman the White also appears white, when he is so no longer. We should not forget what Tolkien knew well, that Satan can appear as an angel of light. Moreover, the strongly adversative *but* that follows marks the wheel of fire as by far the more important detail. In the end, the wheel is what remains, and thus it is from the wheel that the voice seems to speak, loud and cruel.

Yet Sam is seeing with "other vision" sights "for eyes to see that can" (FR 2.i.223). If he sees more truly, it is because what he is seeing presents itself to him in a mythic form that can convey truth without necessarily conveying fact, and what we see in visions we often do not interpret correctly at the first or even the second attempt. Thus, in Galadriel's mirror Sam sees Frodo asleep, which isn't quite right, but is less wrong than his second interpretation, that Frodo is not asleep but dead. His vision of Frodo on Mount Doom shows him the truth about what the power of the Ring has done to his master, even if what he sees is not fact, and even if he does not yet understand what the truth means, namely that Frodo is about to claim the Ring and fall. Sam still does not recognize the truth. As Gwenyth Hood so keenly observed in assessing the first time Sam saw "as with other sight" on the night Frodo tamed Sméagol: "It is in Sauron's vision, not that of the Fellowship, that the holder of power is a great lord hiding his power, and the subject commanded is dehumanized" (6).[12]

Likewise, he mistakes the truth he perceives about Gollum, who is "wholly ruined and defeated" but whose "lust and rage" are unyielding. Gollum certainly has been defeated, not by Frodo (as events will show), but by the Ring. He has now come to the point that Gandalf claimed he had *not* reached in "The Shadow of the Past," and the words used to describe it are the same: "wholly ruined" (FR 1.ii.55). His true ruin is moral, his true defeat spiritual, which Sam does not understand until, sword in hand, he takes Frodo's place standing over Gollum. Like Bilbo and Frodo before him, the judgement of death is now his to execute. Sam, however, comes to his moment by a path broader and longer than those by which Bilbo and Frodo did theirs. Sam's experience as Ring-bearer has been brief but profound, multiplied by the increase in its power near Mordor. He has watched Frodo suffer and change more and more because of the Ring, side by side with Gollum, whose torment and struggle he has also witnessed, whose treachery and violence he has endured. He has surrendered the Ring with only the slightest reluctance and without the badgering Bilbo needed. Face to face with Gollum now and with a free hand at last, Sam finds that the pity which compelled him to seek to spare Frodo the torment of the Ring, if only for a little while now, requires him to show Gollum a mercy he does not deserve. To be sure, Sam does not love his enemy, but the sufferings he has witnessed and the temptations he has felt allow him to look upon this "creature," this "thing lying in the dust" before him, with a pity that Frodo no longer can (RK 6.iii.944).

In leaving Gollum and pity behind, Frodo has critically also left Sam behind. They both seem aware that something has changed between them, that a gap is opening. "Frodo looked at him as if at one *now* far away. 'Yes, I must go on,' he said. 'Farewell, Sam! This is the end at last. On Mount Doom

doom shall fall. Farewell!'" (RK 6.iii.944, emphasis mine).[13] If we recall that we are getting the story here from Sam's point of view, we shall see that the first sentence conveys Sam's impression of how Frodo was looking at him *now*. The words Frodo speaks reveal his sense of the finality of their parting and a regret that it must be so. They are strangely formal, however, sounding less like his normal tone of address to Sam and more like Théoden's manner when he releases Merry from his service or Denethor's when he dismisses Pippin (RK 6.ii.800, 801, 803–04, iv.825–26). In fact, Frodo's words are more formal than the Steward's or the King's, which may be bad in itself. As commanding as Théoden and Denethor may be, they are not remote.

Consonant with his dismissal of Sam is Frodo's unconcern for what Sam may intend to do to Gollum. From their first meeting, Sam has been suspicious even when not openly hostile. He recommended tying Gollum up and leaving him behind in the wilderness, a certain death as both Frodo and Gollum see (TT 4.i.614). At Henneth Annûn, he wished he had dared bid Faramir shoot Gollum when they had the chance (4.v.684). Any lessening of his hostility toward Gollum, such as we see in their banter in "Of Herbs and Stewed Rabbit," or in the attempt to include Gollum in the discussion of the Great Tales in "The Stairs of Cirith Ungol," is swept away by the treachery in "Shelob's Lair," which turned Sam's thoughts to murder even before he came to believe Frodo dead (4.ix.726). With such a history anyone—including the reader—would naturally have expected that Sam meant to do what he in fact began to do, to attack an unarmed Gollum with his sword and kill him. Yet Frodo, who has spared Gollum and tried to help him find healing, now shows himself utterly indifferent to what happens to him or Sam next. Can the Frodo of Mount Doom even remember the Frodo of the Emyn Muil or the Frodo who pleaded with Faramir to show Gollum mercy? No.

Or is it, as one might argue, that Frodo has other things on his mind? Indeed, he does: the "wheel of fire" he still clutches to his breast. In this, the last moment before he falls, he can see little else in a faded world, stripped of memory and identity. What remains is his determination to complete his Quest, to bring Doom to Mount Doom, and the delusion that he can do now what he could not in his parlor at Bag End a year earlier. But the thrill of the Ring's power leads its bearers to ask "what could not [we] do in this hour" if we could claim it for our own, and to believe that we know the answer (FR 2.x.398). Boromir thought as much; so, ironically, did Sam. When Frodo's strength inevitably fails in the Chambers of Fire, "the Ring is my burden" becomes "the Ring is mine"; the delusion that he can throw the Ring into the fire transforms into the delusion that he has no need to do so. Even the idea that when he speaks of doom falling on Mount Doom, he still means the doom of the Ring's destruction is an assumption, however.

"'I have come,' he said. 'But I do not choose *now* to do what I came to do. I *will* not do this deed. The Ring is mine!'" (*RK* 6.iii.945, emphasis mine). In chapter 6 (on page 121) I noted Frodo's use of *will* rather than *shall* when he says, "I will take the Ring." The word suggests intent, purpose, and desire, rather than merely asserting a fact about the future. He was claiming the burden of the Ring for his own for the purpose of destroying it, but no desire connected to the Ring is safe, no purpose beyond corruption. Here, *now* in the Sammath Naur, Frodo uses *will*, thus signaling his intent and the fulfilment of what has become his desire. To claim the Ring is of course to challenge its maker, a fact Sam grasped even as the illusion of Samwise the Strong teetered on the brink of delusion (6.i.900). Yet, only minutes earlier Frodo's accidental glimpse of the Dark Tower became a brief vision of the Eye, and this sufficed to strike Frodo to the ground even though the attention of the Eye was elsewhere and it never even saw him (6.iii.942). Only days before that, in the Morgul Vale, Frodo "knew that the Ring would only betray him, and that he had not, even if he put it on, the power to face the Morgul-king—not yet" (*TT* 4.viii.706). *Not yet* has become *now,* even as he turns to face an opponent of vastly greater power. In view of Frodo's dismissal of Sam and indifference to Gollum, however, his mention of only the Ring and his desire for it, but not of the Lord of the Rings himself, may well signal the "rashness" and "pride of the new Ringlord" (*RK* 5.ix.880).

In discussing the scenes on Mount Doom in *Sauron Defeated* Christopher Tolkien notes the ease and speed with which his father's long contemplation of this moment allowed him to write it. Changes were few, but for our argument one is quite significant. Frodo originally said, "But I cannot do what I have come to do" rather than "I do not choose now to do." Now Christopher Tolkien points out, "Since it was already a central element in the outlines that Frodo would *choose* to keep the Ring himself the change in his words does no more than emphasize that he fully willed his act" (38). From Christopher Tolkien's perspective, this change is of little importance. He argues that it reveals no new understanding of Frodo and the Ring. Yet Judith Klinger's close attention to these words suggests that the emphasis they place on Frodo's choice has more to tell us.

Klinger asserts quite reasonably that Frodo's four brief sentences are "excessive[ly] repetitious," containing four instances of *I* and five of *do/deed*.

She characterizes Frodo's *I* as a "peremptory subject," which is "isolated and engaged in a monologue that allows for nothing beyond itself" (136–37). She also astutely observes that the "double negation embedded in these lines" tends to undermine grand egotistical isolation of all those first-person pronouns.

Klinger's points are strong and well taken. The "peremptory subject" does allow for nothing beyond itself, but, however firmly the peremptory subject speaks as if no challenge to its claim were possible, the peremptory subject is wrong. At least two will be sure to challenge its assertion, one of whom Frodo might overcome (though he will not), the other of whom he cannot overcome. That it makes no allowance for anything beyond itself shows how self-deceived, indeed delusional, Frodo has become under the influence of the Ring. More than that, however, the peremptory subject also allows for nothing, we might say, within itself. If the double negations hint at the existence on some subconscious level of Frodo, the Ring-bearer, who chose to take on himself the burden of destroying the Ring for everyone's sake, then the claim of the peremptory subject is challenged from within as well as beyond itself. Like the Gollum of whom Gandalf spoke in "The Shadow of the Past," the Frodo who claims the Ring has not been "wholly ruined," even if his will has been overwhelmed by the lust for the Ring that the irresistible power of his burden stirs in the hearts of all it reaches (FR 1.ii.55).

Building upon Tom Shippey's suggestion (*Author* 140) that Frodo's phrasing accurately reflects the resolution of his struggle, namely that "Frodo does not choose; the choice is made for him," Klinger posits that "the power of action claimed by the subject 'I' is drawn into question by the counter-voice of the subjected, and this voice, by using the double negative, retains a final trace of opposition" (356). In support, she points out that "Frodo generally shows no penchant" for the rather pompous and self-obsessed language used here. The struggle reflected here cannot "evolve into a dialogue." For "what these lines articulate is a collapse of boundaries: between Frodo and the Ring, between will and choice on the one hand and the compulsion to do on the other."

While I find this reading ingenious and intriguing and agree that it would be quite persuasive if the Ring should be, as Klinger assumes without examination throughout her article, a conscious entity wielding an agency of its own, we have seen, however, that the evidence of the text, when scrutinized from "A Long-expected Party" onward, provides ample reason to doubt and in my view to reject such an understanding of the Ring. It is rather the power of the Ring with which we tempt ourselves, as Gandalf indicates immediately and emphatically when Frodo offers him the Ring: "With that power I should have power too great and terrible" (FR 1.ii.61). Even before considering how vulnerable his pity and desire to do good make him, he believes that so much power would compass his downfall.

Yet I would still agree that what we hear in those negatives is the last trace of "the counter-voice of the subjected," but rather than expressing the final opposition of "the subjected," the words "But I do not choose now to do what I have come to do. I will not do this deed" express the final answer of the peremptory subject to the subjected, that is, to the Frodo who said, "I will take the Ring . . . though I do not know the way." The speaker is not the Ring itself but rather the Frodo who asked Galadriel about using the Ring; who, desperate to see the Ring destroyed, has repeatedly used it as a means to dominate Gollum to that very end; and whom we have seen speak, in just such moments, the very sort of unnecessarily inflated and self-obsessed language he utters here at the Cracks of Doom.[14] Klinger is thus correct to state that Frodo does not generally speak in this way but has overlooked the importance of the times when he does (356).

For in the Sammath Naur comes Frodo's two "thoughts" moment, the crisis of the struggle between "the Ring is my burden" and "the Ring is mine." Borrowing from Tolkien's discussion of what "the Sméagol-will" and "the Gollum-will" (above on pages 131–34), and recalling the changes we have seen in Frodo, we might well view his two "thoughts" here as "the Ring-bearer-will" and "the Ringlord-will." Frodo's crisis, like Gollum's in "The Passage of the Marshes" and in "The Stairs of Cirith Ungol" (above on pages 167–69), ends with the subjugation of one "thought" to the other. The forcefulness of desire triumphs because both the Sméagol-will and the Gollum-will lust after the Ring, because their argument is over means, not ends, and because will and desire can never be wholly separate. The struggle between the Ring-bearer-will and the Ringlord-will on Mount Doom reaches its climax in Frodo's exceptionally compressed statements of choice and will as he claims the Ring. These words mark the domination of the will of Frodo, Hobbit of the Shire, by that of Frodo, Master of the Precious, much as Gollum's embittered hiss of "Sneaking, sneaking!" marks the passing forever of the moment when the Sméagol-will might have repented of the plot initiated by the Gollum-will to betray the hobbits to Shelob (TT 4.viii.715).

What this emphasis brings to our attention once again, however, is the significant role of the will and choice. The Ring's power to dominate others or to attain a goal—whether good or evil—through such domination is so great, and as such so alluring, that sooner or later anyone with the opportunity to do so *will choose* to claim the Ring and use it. No matter how aware that no good can come of it, no matter how strong or well-intended a person may be, that much power is too precious a gift to reject. The temptation—to see it through the lens Gandalf did—proves too great to be resisted; the lie is too attractive for disbelief. The will affirms the command of the desire and chooses to grasp the Ring for which the hand is reaching. The very attractiveness of the temptation lies at the heart of the Ring's precious beauty.

As deceived as Frodo may be in his choosing, as incapable of defeating Sauron even with the Ring, the mere act of claiming it shakes Barad-dûr "from its foundations to its proud and bitter crown" (RK 6.iii.946). These foundations, it will be recalled, had been laid using the Ring and could not be destroyed while it existed (FR 2.ii.244). This is the most significant demonstration of the Ring's power we have seen thus far and emphasizes the intimate connection between the power with which Sauron imbued the Ring and the works he wrought with it. Small wonder, then, that feeling this power would create the illusion that Sauron might be overthrown using it. In this connection, the refusals of the Ring by Gandalf and Galadriel become even more revealing. Each of them is wise enough to reject it on moral grounds, because of the evil they would do and become if they had it, but neither of them questions whether they would succeed in defeating Sauron. It is assumed, but they are deceived. Of those so tempted, Sam alone recognizes or openly acknowledges that his challenge to Sauron's authority would be brief.

Sauron, "the Power in Barad-dûr," is also shaken by the claim. In this, we again see how intimate the link is between the Dark Lord and the Ring because he has transferred so much of his native strength into it. Frodo's claim is of course a further reminder, if one were needed, that Dark Lord's fate is tied to his Ring's, but for Sauron, learning "the magnitude of his folly" is both literally and metaphorically apocalyptic. It is a bitter and precious irony, moreover, that Sauron discovers how deceived he has been in very much the same way as Celebrimbor had, by "hearing" the Ring claimed at the Sammath Naur (FR 2.ii.253–54). Folly is not done with him, however. For just as Sauron could not conceive that his enemies might wish the Ring destroyed, it appears he does not grasp that they would find themselves unable to do so if they reached the fire. Similarly, only on the slopes of Mount Doom does Gollum recognize what his now "wicked master" purposes to do; he, too, believes Frodo can accomplish it; and he, too, knows that the destruction of the Ring means the end of him.

Poised between the two of them here, as he was between the Voice and the Eye on Amon Hen, Frodo chooses a path that is neither willing surrender nor steadfast rejection, but open challenge.[15] Before, Frodo regained control by remembering who he was, which enabled him to remove the Ring and escape Sauron's notice. Now he has forgotten everything that made him who he was, which includes both the terror of the Dark Lord's power and the love of the Shire that made him willing to sacrifice everything he had and, as it turns out, everything he was to save it. By the very way he speaks to Gollum and Sam, he shows that he sees himself as that figure "untouchable now by pity" whose voice seems to come from the Ring itself; who no longer merely sees the wheel of fire, but holds it burning in his hand. When he speaks, his voice channels its power. Without his identity, without being "Frodo, hobbit of the Shire," without any answer to Tom Bombadil's question, his will can in the end be nothing other than his desire. Gollum's attempt to take the Ring from Frodo sets the "the dying embers of his heart and will" ablaze, and, as they fight and as Frodo comes at last to the Sammath Naur, the struggle in his mind between "the Ring is my burden" and "the Ring is mine" resolves itself (RK 6.iii.943). The burden has become the Precious. The Ring-bearer-will and the Ringlord-will have merged.

It was always going to end this way, with Frodo's fall. From the first, Gandalf knew Frodo would be unable to cast the Ring into the fire. The Quest was just a fool's hope, as he says. For pity could not save Frodo from the Ring any more than it could have saved Gandalf. Yet, in the end pity might just save him from evil. Only it cannot do so alone. No single created being in Middle-earth has enough pity and strength to succeed in this Quest. Bilbo's pity, Frodo's, and then Sam's—each founded upon its predecessor, each with its own role to play in its moment—together create the circumstances in which the Ring can be destroyed in *this* moment, inadvertently and providentially, by the most unlikely person imaginable, and the one least deserving the pity and mercy which all three hobbits of the Shire have shown him.[16]

"Nothing is evil in the beginning," said Elrond to the council (FR 2.ii.267). "Even Sauron was not so. I fear to take the Ring to hide it. I will not take the Ring to wield it." Thus, good becomes evil. This much is also clear from the beginning. Gandalf feared what he would become and what he would do, if he had the Ring. That vast power to dominate others and impose one's will on them is not too great for him to wield but is too great for him or anyone less powerful than Sauron to wield and remain his own master. For most, merely possessing it is too much, even locked away unused (RK 5.iv.814).

For some, that descent is easier than for others, the work of a moment, as it was for Sméagol; for Frodo every step downward is bitterly contested, as he tries to resist the temptation to use a power whose usefulness grows more enticing as his strength lessens. The way of the Ring to his heart or anyone's is through the power it seems to offer to realize their intentions, whether good or bad. Recall Frodo's reaction to inheriting the Ring, a thought so simple and so easily overlooked, but which summarizes every temptation to arise from the Ring's power: "It may be useful." His road began there with the small and seemingly innocuous desire to avoid unpleasant relations, but it did not seem harmless to Gandalf, who at that time had little more than a bad feeling about the Ring. Frodo's appraisal of the Ring's usefulness, combined with his inability to throw it into the hearth, opens wide a gate that in retrospect makes his Quest seem the fool's hope Denethor said, and Gandalf agreed, it had always been (RK 6.iv.813, 815).

Yet, though the Quest may be a fool's hope, and defeat the most likely outcome, there is more than one failure possible for Frodo. He may fail by losing the Ring to death or capture, which comes so close to happening that even he believes it has occurred. He may fail as we have seen him do, when he can no longer resist the allure of the power he has inevitably come to desire. Or, he may fail as Sméagol failed Déagol, his friend whom he loved. In the barrow, Frodo was tempted to put himself and the Ring before the lives of those he loved. Without question, that would have been a moral failure, a choice of evil while he still had the strength and clarity of mind to choose good. In that case Frodo would certainly have "come to evil." As we know, Gandalf held that instance in the barrow to be "perhaps the most dangerous moment of all," and it was almost certainly Frodo's rejection of the temptation there that caused Gandalf to think Frodo would likely not come to evil in the end (FR 2.i.219). This type of failure also threatens Frodo's relations with others. As I noted in discussing "Many Meetings," on the same day Gandalf muses about Frodo's behavior in the barrow, Frodo feels an urge to strike Bilbo because he reached out for the Ring. More darkly still, Frodo taunts and threatens Gollum outside the Black Gate when he asks for the Ring back, and in Mordor he twice threatens Sam with his sword in response to Sam's offer to help him bear the burden.

As close as he comes to a fall, however, Frodo never carries out his desires or threats. Unlike Sméagol with Déagol, he does not strike Bilbo or murder Sam, even though they appeared inhuman to him in the moment he saw them as a threat to his possession of the Ring. Conversely, he does not kill Gollum when he has the chance—and justification since Gollum is throttling Sam—because his own experience of the Ring has led Frodo to see him as a person, not a creature, and to pity him. It is at first curious that Frodo does not kill Gollum in their initial encounter on Mount Doom, in which he has the upper hand and all pity is gone. Stranger still is how alike his threats here and outside the Black Gate are: death in the fires of Mount Doom. It is almost as if he recalls the first threat while making the second and wishes to remind Gollum of it, too. Though he cannot remember wind or water, tree or grass or flower, the evil thought that with the Ring he has the power to command Gollum to cast himself into the Fire has not faded.[17] That he remembers all too well. But Frodo's words here outside the Sammath Naur indicate that he regards Gollum as a despised nuisance. Contempt spares Gollum now, just as pity had done before and will soon do again.

Even so, it is the power of the Ring that has turned Frodo's pity into contempt and on which is founded Gollum's unquenchable "lust and rage." What is the significance of a moral force that can succeed only with the timely assistance of chance that was no chance at all? Its quality is not denied by failure, nor by its success in setting the stage for eucatastrophe. For pity, "defeat is no refutation" (M&C 21). In Letter 246, from 1963, Tolkien noted that Frodo's "exercise of patience and mercy towards Gollum gained him Mercy: his failure was redressed." The difference between *mercy* and *Mercy* matters. Earthly pity and mercy could not accomplish the destruction of the Ring, but they were repaid in Pity and Mercy. The Pity of Bilbo is as plain as Gandalf can put it. The redress is that Frodo fails but does not fall. He is delivered from evil.[18] Yet the limits of the pity and mercy of this world are revealed.

CHAPTER TEN

From the Black Land to the Undying Lands

DELIVERANCE AND FORGIVENESS

In seizing the Ring from Frodo and perishing with it, Gollum saves him from evil. What he intended, of course, was to save the Precious from Frodo and to possess it again, to the extent that he could be said to possess a thing that so wholly possessed him. His last words as he falls into the fire—"Precious, precious, precious! ... My Precious! O my Precious! ... *Precious!*"—may not be as eloquent as those of Milton's Lucifer, but in their climactic simplicity they are just as telling (RK 6.iii.945). What comes afterward for Frodo reveals much, because the Ring's effect does not end with the Ring.

Frodo has escaped from becoming another Gollum, or, as infinitely unlikely as it seems, from becoming a new Sauron, a new Dark Lord like Gandalf and Galadriel feared they would have become. It does not matter that the latter would not have happened; it matters that when Frodo claimed the Ring he envisioned taking Sauron's place. His words and behavior from the moment Gollum attacks him the first time until the Ring is destroyed demonstrate that he was certainly not thinking of the good he could do with the Ring. In the Sammath Naur—"the heart of the realm of Sauron and the forges of *his ancient might, greatest in Middle-earth*; all other powers were here subdued" (RK 6.iii.945, emphasis mine)—there can be no resistance to the pull of the Ring, which is the product and the repository of so much of that ancient might that Sauron cannot survive if it perishes; and we fail to grasp the measure of Sauron's strength, if we do not also keep in mind that without the Ring the Dark Lord is still far too strong for his foes.

The gravity of that power is matched only by the fascination of its beauty. It soon bewitched Isildur. He told Elrond and Círdan that he would take the Ring as weregild and an heirloom but privately reflected more on how "*precious*" its appearance made it: "*I will risk no hurt to this thing: of all the works of Sauron the only fair*" (FR 2.ii.243, 252–53). It gladdened Déagol's heart and cost him his life because Sméagol, too, found the Ring "bright and beautiful" (1.ii.53). Bilbo and Frodo were far from blind to its loveliness, and Frodo, like Isildur long before him, shrank from the idea of harming *this thing*, in substance so "very fair and pure," in color so "rich and beautiful," in shape so "perfect," in itself so "admirable" and "so altogether precious" (1.ii.60). The treacherous and compelling beauty of the Ring is reminiscent of the fair guise its maker wore before his death in Númenor but which he could never resume afterward. Was the part of himself that made Sauron able to appear fair inseparable from the part he put into the Ring, so that once his old body perished he could not even simulate beauty in his new one? He literally did not have it in him to do so any longer. The power and beauty of the Ring, both of which come from its maker, were too much for Isildur three thousand years earlier; they are too much for Frodo now. One does not simply walk out of Mordor.

Yet at first Frodo seems to have put his ordeal wholly behind him, a point Tolkien makes about the text in a 1963 letter: "[Frodo] appears at first to have had no sense of guilt ([RK 6.iii.946–47]); he was restored to sanity and peace. But then he thought that he had given his life in sacrifice: he expected to die very soon. But he did not, and one can observe the disquiet growing in him"(*Letters* no. 246, p. 327). Let us consider first what the text itself shows us. Although Frodo is convinced that he and Sam are about to die, to Sam's eye Frodo seems to have been restored to himself as he was before they had left the Shire (*RK* 6.iii.947). To be sure Frodo was never sanguine about surviving the Quest, but to expect death when inside an erupting volcano is scarcely (if at all) pessimistic. At the same time, Frodo's conviction that this is the end for them opens and closes this final, brief scene in "Mount Doom," but within the frame of Frodo's talk of "the end of all things" endings, we find Sam's joy at his master's return and grief for his wounded hand, Frodo's admission that the Quest would have failed without Gollum, and his quite remarkable desire for them both to forgive Gollum (6.iii.947).

How changed he is here, not merely from the grand pitiless figure of minutes earlier but also from the "dear master of those sweet days in the Shire." The Frodo Sam looks back to with such partial fondness was nevertheless also the one who, though thoughtful and dear to his friends, denied Gollum his humanity and condemned him to death unseen, refusing to heed Gandalf's pleas for the value of mercy. Although Frodo's inexperience and fear no doubt informed his judgement, Gandalf saw no reason to excuse him on that account. As Frodo's reminder in "Mount Doom" that the wizard had foreseen that Gollum might have a part to play shows, all that Frodo has suffered and done has taken him beyond pity and mercy to forgiveness. This is what it is to become "a glass filled with a clear light for eyes to see that can" (FR 2.i.223). Despite his faults and mistakes, he always had this potential. His willingness to leave the Shire to save the Shire, never expecting an adventure like Bilbo's or even to return alive, demonstrates this potential. That he could not comprehend the road before him any more than any of the other hobbits could is true; and it is also true that until quite near the end he does not appear to have grasped that the Ring was turning the good in him into evil (2.iii.276). Even after seeing what was happening to Boromir and had happened to Gollum, he doesn't seem to think himself in their company. Only in the Tower of Cirith Ungol when he momentarily sees Sam as an orc greedy for his treasure do his eyes begin to open, and he begs Sam's forgiveness. Yet that doesn't stop the transformation of good into evil, because the transformation is inevitable.

Many a character in *The Lord of the Rings* begs or asks forgiveness. Sam hopes he will be forgiven for leaving Frodo behind in the pass and hopes again when he forsakes the Quest to return to his apparently dead master's side. Faramir does the same for pressing Frodo too hard about Boromir and Isildur's bane in front of his men. After stealing the palantír, Pippin asks pardon of Gandalf, as Merry does of Théoden on disobeying his order to stay behind. Both the wizard and the king grant it readily. Twenty-four times in the course of the book characters ask, grant, or receive forgiveness for various infractions, the most serious of which I have outlined above.[1] Otherwise the forgiveness is a matter of form or courtesy, and a handful of times it is humorous, as when Bilbo's generosity leads his neighbors to "forgive him his oddities" or when Gollum sarcastically remarks that "he always forgives, he does, yes, yes, even nice Master's little tricksess" (FR 1.i.21; TT 4.vii.696).

Not even Gandalf, however, *advocates* forgiveness. Although he urges Frodo to pity Gollum and show him mercy and expresses the admittedly wan hope that he may one day be healed, he goes no further. Gandalf's use of the names Sméagol and Gollum repays scrutiny here. The wizard calls him Sméagol only when telling of how he came by the Ring and became Gollum. It is also true that Gandalf can only have learned that Gollum was once called

Sméagol during his interrogation in Mirkwood. Once Sméagol has murdered Déagol and been cast out, he is simply Gollum. Gandalf can refer to Sméagol's grandmother, but Gollum apparently has none. She cast him out like Cain (FR 1.ii.52–54). This usage reveals the abyss that has opened between Gollum and Sméagol because of the Ring and explains Gandalf's near despair of finding him a cure. Pity and mercy may seem the most he can hope for.

Frodo's experience is more complex, in that both he and Gollum are so gravely affected by the Ring. In a period that cannot be as long as a single hour, he has dominated and dismissed Gollum only to be maimed and defeated by him. Yet now, with his hand still bleeding, he forgives Gollum unrepentant. The turnabout here parallels his sudden pity in the Emyn Muil for a creature whose throat he has just threatened to cut. But that is not all. For he has already gone farther than Gandalf's small hope by suggesting to Gollum that it may be possible to "find [Sméagol] again" if he helps them get to Mordor (TT 4.i.616). That he is well aware of the difficult course he has proposed for Gollum, we can see in his own use of *Sméagol* and *Gollum*. Frodo *addresses* him as Sméagol, but *refers* to him as Gollum when speaking to Sam. By maintaining the distinction, he indicates his agreement with Gandalf, that there was "not much hope" Gollum could ever be cured. We may also see it dimly in Frodo's varying treatment of him, which is a mirror to the struggle in his mind. Even now, though, even as he forgives him and urges Sam to do the same amid the cataclysm unfolding around them, he calls him Gollum, not Sméagol. It is the last time he is ever mentioned in the tale.

He has come far, this hobbit of the Shire. As Tolkien said in his reading of his text, Frodo was "restored to *sanity* and peace," and what Sam sees when he looks at him confirms that Tolkien wrote it to be so: he is "himself again," not mad and burdened by a war between his will and his desire (*Letters* no. 246, p. 327; *RK* 6.iii.945, 947). The Quest is achieved in a eucatastrophe. In such a context, we will do well not to overlook the words Tolkien chose to describe the effect of that sudden turn: Frodo "appears at first to have had no sense of guilt... he was restored to *sanity* and peace." First, *appears* suggests that there is more (or less) here than meets the eye. Second, to be restored to these mental and spiritual states is to recover them; Recovery is of course one of the most valuable benefits the eucatastrophic endings of fairy stories have to offer; and no one needs to be able to "look at green again and be startled anew (but not blinded) by blue and red and violet" (*OFS* ¶ 82, p. 67) more than Frodo, who has "no memory of tree or grass or flower left" now (*RK* 6.iii.937–38). The rub is that, as Frodo and Sam discussed in "The Stairs of Cirith Ungol," what makes a good ending for those listening to a story is not always a happy ending for the people in the story. Thus it is with Frodo.

The Ring is gone. The Quest is over. But the wounds Frodo came by through bearing the Ring remain. His mutilated hand is only the most evident of these, for now. Consider Bilbo. When he relinquished the Ring, he felt better immediately and laughed from heart's ease; yet the Ring still affected him. Witness his urges to return from Rivendell to the Shire and fetch it, complete with rationalizations justifying his desires, and his reaching for the Ring in the Hall of Fire (FR 2.i.231–32). His tenure as Ring-bearer may have been far longer than Frodo's, but it was far less traumatic. And the Ring was still pulling on him seventeen years later. Frodo did not relinquish the Ring; he claimed it for his own. Moments later Gollum violently seized it, quite literally taking a piece of him with it. Frodo may feel relieved of his burden; he may have suffered into the wisdom to forgive; he may be at peace with death; but he is not laughing.

Frodo's peace is neither joyful nor triumphant. Framed as his restoration is in "Mount Doom" by his declarations that this is "the end" and "the end of all things," statements the narrator emphasizes by returning to precisely this moment and these very words several pages into the next chapter, "The Field of Cormallen," the peace he feels is mixed with sorrow and acceptance but absent of hope (RK 6.iii.947, iv.950). When Sam asserts that it is "not like me" to give up on survival and a return home, Frodo replies, "It's like things are in the world. Hopes fail. An end comes" (RK 6.iv.950). He is talking about not just their own immediate situation. Rather, ending in failure is the way of things, a view that encompasses his own failure to destroy the Ring and contains the seeds of guilt and of the realization that in the end he chose the Ring.

By contrast, Sam faces the end he sees approaching for himself and his master by means of the Great Tales he has spoken of since the beginning. The tale they are in will continue without them; and his curiosity about what will happen shows he draws comfort from the belief that life will go on. Still, he is not content that their lives end with their Quest, especially now that he has his old master back. Sam's view is larger than Frodo's. It takes in both the grand comfort of the story they are in and a longing for home that demands he not give up. For all the dreams and visions Frodo has had, for all the chance meetings that were not chance at all, he finds no solace in the larger picture that has been before him since the beginning. Although he knows the Quest could not possibly have been completed without Gollum, he sees no Providence in that fact, just as he could not understand what Gandalf had been trying to tell him in "The Shadow of the Past," that "Bilbo was *meant* to find the Ring, and *not* by its maker" (FR 1.ii.56).

That Frodo does not recognize the hand of Providence even now and that the expectation of imminent death is at worst a matter of indifference to him attest to the spiritual damage he has suffered from the Ring. Beyond all his other hurts—knife, sting, tooth—there is the Ring; and beyond all the torments of bearing it, there is the guilt of succumbing to, claiming, and losing it. Although the struggle in his mind between "the Ring is my burden" and "the Ring is mine" has ended, his recovery of sanity and peace brings him neither escape nor consolation. Not even a eucatastrophe can heal "the dying embers of Frodo's heart and will" (RK 6.iii.943). There is no coming back from "the Ring is mine," certainly not in Middle-earth. But within the narrowing minutes he believes remain in his life, Frodo can be glad that Sam is with him and can accede to his desire to try to survive. This gladness and the forgiveness he urges for Gollum reveal how far he has come from the hobbit who in fear for his life rejected the idea of pity and mercy.

He has come here through suffering and willingness to suffer more, but the price of bearing the Ring has come high. Galadriel warned Frodo that the Ring would destroy him if he tried to use it. If we recall what Gandalf said possessing a Ring of Power does to a mortal, it will be clear that Galadriel did not mean the Ring would kill him. We have witnessed Frodo trying to use the Ring to dominate Gollum. We have heard him entertain the notion that someday he would be strong enough to face the Witch-king. We have seen him challenge the Dark Lord himself by claiming the Ring for his own. At the same time, we have watched his memory and identity being stripped away and the wheel of fire becoming everything to him. Even before the last moment, before he said, "the Ring is mine," he had become a pitiless "figure" filled with scorn, interested only in his own desire (RK 6.iii.944).

It is all too easy, however, for Frodo's state after the Ring goes into the fire to be forgotten or underestimated in the joyous course of the chapters from "The Field of Cormallen" to "Homeward Bound," only near the end of which do we begin to realize just how deep and enduring his wounds are. At first, despite his words on Mount Doom, there seems some slight promise of further recovery. Yet as closer scrutiny reveals, Frodo is surrounded by the joys of others whose hopes are being fulfilled: Aragorn and Arwen, Faramir and Éowyn, the people of Gondor as a whole, Beregond, and even Ioreth, who gets to preen before her country cousin about her acquaintance with Mithrandir and the King (*RK* 6.v.966–67). The list could be much extended, but not by including Frodo. He stands among the crowd, but not of it.

When Sam awakens in Ithilien days after the Ring's destruction, he knows where he is by the well-remembered fragrance of its woodlands, and at first he thinks he has dreamt all that has occurred since he and Frodo were there. When he sees Frodo's wounded hand, he remembers the truth; and when he sees Gandalf, whom he thought dead, he asks, "Is everything sad going to come untrue." To be sure, Sam's question is rhetorical, a joyous bewildered hyperbole. Gandalf does not reply—and need not—to a question whose answer they both know. Frodo's "poor hand" is a sufficient answer to his question, to start with. Sam then expresses to Gandalf the more sober hope that Frodo, despite the wound to his hand, is "all right otherwise" (*RK* 6.iv.952). Here there is no exaggeration. No one knows better than Sam what Frodo has been through. Again, Gandalf remains silent. It is Frodo who responds and with a laugh echoes Sam's own words: he is indeed "all right otherwise." Yet how credible is this, given the hell he has walked in and given his later exhibition of symptoms consistent with what our age would call PTSD and Tolkien's "shell-shock"?[2]

Sam's recognition of Ithilien from his memory of its scent, especially since he has momentarily forgotten the reality of everything that has happened since then, should remind the reader of Frodo's inability to remember Ithilien or anything before it because the Ring has stripped him of precisely the sort of recall that Sam is experiencing. Sam has now twice drawn comfort from a recollection of that idyllic morning of herbs and stewed rabbit. In this context, Gandalf's response to neither of Sam's questions should give us pause when Frodo gives his answer. This would not be the first time that Frodo declared himself all right when he was not (*FR* 2.v.325–26; *RK* vi.335–36). More importantly, the self-deceptions of Ring-bearers about the Ring do not cease simply because they no longer possess it. This was not the case for Gollum or Bilbo. Frodo may well believe what he is saying—indeed he may well *feel* all right. We should not expect the sanity and peace Sam saw in his face to be all a lie or to have disappeared along with the certainty of imminent death. In fact, we can see the truth of his feelings the next morning when he and Sam alike feel "hope and peace" (*RK* 6.v.957). If Frodo ever truly thought that he might be happy in the Shire again—and he later tells Sam he once did (6.ix.1029)—it was likely this morning. Bilbo and Gollum also felt better. Gandalf's silence does not proclaim, but suggests, that all will not be as well as it seems right now.

After Sam's and Gandalf's tears and laughter, moreover, Frodo's response is quite subdued, an impression strengthened by his fading at once into the background while Gandalf and Sam continue their conversation. He speaks only once more, when Gandalf produces the phial of Galadriel, and Frodo's reaction there is as enthusiastic as one could hope—perhaps too much so. In fact, as Hammond and Scull have noted, Tolkien added this moment on to the end of the scene only in the second edition of *The Lord of the Rings* (RC 623-24). Without these two brief paragraphs, the present scene glides placidly into the next with remarks about clothes and washing.

> Then [Gandalf] held out his hands to them, and they saw that one shone with light. "What have you got there?" Frodo cried. "Can it be—?"
> "Yes, I have brought your two treasures. They were found on Sam when you were rescued. The Lady Galadriel's gifts: your glass, Frodo, and your box, Sam. You will be glad to have these safe again."
> (RK 6.iv.952)

Why did Tolkien think it necessary to make such an addition? Was it to remind the reader that the gifts had not been lost? However, there has been no suggestion that they had even been missed. Any reader who thought about it would reasonably assume they were both still in Sam's breast pocket. Or was it to show that Frodo was all right at least at first by showing him excited and happy to regain the phial? This would still have required some hint that the glass had been missed. There is none.

But think of what we have and have not seen in this passage. Upon awakening, Sam realizes where he is through a sense memory, which Frodo had been unable to recall even when prompted. The revelation that the Ring had stripped all such memories from him is one of the most significant and moving moments in *The Lord of the Rings*. So, when Sam accomplishes without thinking what Frodo could not at all, it points to how badly damaged Frodo has been. The connection is not overtly made, however. Similarly, the questions Sam asked and Gandalf did not answer allow and perhaps even expect the reader to infer that the wizard's silence implies something he will not state: that the answer to both questions is no. The quiet role Frodo plays in this scene suggests so much about him precisely by stating so little. Moreover, the lines Tolkien adds bring Frodo suddenly back to the foreground, ending the scene in excitement rather than calm and in a question that never reaches its crucial final word, the word that would name the object of his excitement: "Can it be—?" *What?* Can it be what?

The obvious answer, the one the text gives on its surface, is of course the phial. But it is also true that Gandalf does not allow Frodo to complete his sentence. When Gandalf finishes Frodo's question for him in a scene characterized by unanswered questions and unspoken suggestions that all is not well with Frodo, the reader can consider the possibility that beneath the surface lay the thought of another object he treasured and which could shine through the hand holding it. Being a wizard and therefore subtle, Gandalf does not always say what he is thinking or explain what he has said. On the morning Frodo awoke in Rivendell, we should recall, Gandalf did both. Though he called the barrow "perhaps the most dangerous moment of all" for Frodo, he never says why it may have been so (FR 2.i.222). Then, too, he confesses to himself that he cannot guess "to what [Frodo] will come in the end," but tells Frodo he looks "splendid" (2.i.223).

One might object that Frodo cannot be leaping to the conclusion that Gandalf has the Ring in his hand, because, as he should know, the Ring has been destroyed. Frodo, however, also knew that Bilbo was not a Gollum-like creature and that Sam was not an orc, but because of the Ring's effect on him he ever so briefly saw each of them as such when his possession of the Ring seemed at risk. The immanent power of the Ring induced that effect, just as the pull of gravity induces the effect of weight in a mass. Such illusions thus do not emerge from the Ring itself but from the bearer's jealousy of possessing its power. They take their shape from the fears and desires in the heart of anyone feeling the pull of that power, whether Frodo or Sam, Boromir or Gollum, Gandalf or Saruman. Decades separated Bilbo and Gollum from possessing the Ring, but still their hearts and minds longed for it and still their hands reached for it. It hardly seems likely that Frodo, only days removed from the Ring, would not yearn for it now, especially since he will do so later on.

So much of what we learn in this scene comes to us unsaid, whether by the characters or the narrator. From his knowledge of *Beowulf*, Tolkien was familiar with statements, questions, silences, and answers which mean more than they say. For, as Tom Shippey has shown, both *The Lord of the Rings* and *Beowulf* are full of them ("Beowulfian Speech" 109–26; *Author* 70–71). If we take seriously the narrative conceit that Frodo is both the third-person narrator looking back on his own situation from a not too distant future and a character in his own right, it is Frodo who, by opening this scene with Sam's memories, has silently drawn our attention to his own memories that were lost to the Ring. Sam had woken up believing that everything that had happened to them since Ithilien was a dream, and so he can still visualize it, but once he sees his master's hand, he knows it was no dream. Frodo, however, could not visualize or recall anything before Ithilien, except in the most bare and useless way. Like a man with the index to a book that no longer exists, he has references but no referents. How fully these memories return we do not know. Nevertheless, he has come by the awareness to weave an account which shows that he has recovered to some degree—"hope and peace" may well have succeeded "peace and sanity" for a time—but which suggests that the "dying embers of [his] heart and will" may not be so easily woken from the ashes to which the wheel of fire reduced them.

Above I noted that the happiness of others surrounds, but scarcely includes, Frodo in these chapters. As such it anticipates his withdrawal once he has returned home. "The Field of Cormallen" is very much Sam's chapter, from Gandalf's return to hearing the lay of Frodo of the Nine Fingers and the Ring of Doom, a hearing that unites the entire host "in thought ... where pain and delight flow together and tears are the very wine of blessedness" (RK 6.iv.954). The healing here is undoubted, but Frodo seems somewhat removed from it. He says very little. He tries to decline wearing a sword and points out that he had given Sting to Sam but relents when both Sam and Gandalf refuse to hear of it. This moment points both backward and forward, recalling his travails in Mordor and again anticipating his withdrawal from the doings of the Shire. We can also see this isolation already in his reunion with the other members of the Fellowship. Sam, Pippin, Aragorn, Legolas, and Gimli all speak, but we hear no word from Frodo. Nor, for that matter, do we hear from Merry, whose experience with the Witch-king and the darkness make him an interesting parallel.

It might be unwise to build too much on Frodo's almost total absence from the next chapter, "The Steward and the King." The chapter is not about him. Its attention is on Aragorn and Faramir and Éowyn and the joy of the people of Gondor at the downfall of Sauron and the return of the king. Yet we might make two small observations. In the coronation scene, Frodo appears at the center of events but is overshadowed by them; and the legend of Nine-fingered Frodo is already starting to grow taller than the truth, as Ioreth's remarks to her kinswoman show: "Why, cousin, one of them went with only his esquire into the Black Country and fought with the Dark Lord all by himself, and set fire to his Tower, if you can believe it" (RK 6.v.966; see also S 303–04). And yet, Frodo's name seems unknown or unimportant to her. Within the tale, it is true, these two points do not seem to have great bearing on the Ring's continuing effects on Frodo, except that we have seen from the start that the Ring tends to isolate its bearer, and his remoteness here as an object of curiosity and gossip echoes both Bilbo's and his own "queerness" in the Shire and is consistent with Frodo's slowly fading presence as an actor in the narrative. From "The Field of Cormallen" onward, he is far more of a witness to events or an interlocutor of those who are acting.

The most telling exchange comes from an unexpected quarter. When Frodo tells Aragorn that he wishes to leave Minas Tirith, Aragorn assumes he is eager to return to the Shire. Frodo, however, points out that it is Bilbo who is uppermost in his mind, since he finds his failure to attend the wedding disturbing (RK 6.vi.972–73). Though Aragorn grants his wish and responds to Frodo as a friend, calling him by name, Arwen answers his concern about Bilbo's absence. She, however, addresses him as "Ring-bearer," and reminds him, "All that was done by [the Ring's] power is now passing away." She tells him openly that Bilbo's failing life is not unexpected, given the source of his longevity, but in doing so she also prompts him to recognize what lies ahead for him. Again, a more important point emerges from what is not said.

Having identified Frodo by the role he chose to play, Arwen does the same for herself. She will not be going into the West with Elrond, her father, since she has made "the Choice of Lúthien," which deals in Life and Death, in questions of Mortality and Immortality, just as a Ring of Power does when on the hand of a mortal. Rings of Power, as the Ring verse cannot emphasize enough, offer *"mortal* men *doomed to die"* the delusion of an Immortality resembling the Elves', which first Lúthien and now Arwen have relinquished for the love of a mortal (FR 1.ii.50, my emphasis). Nor is that Immortality all Men have deemed it to be. Elves will not die as Men do. It is not their doom, but they will fade like flowers past their bloom, and the world will fade and die around them. Mortals with Rings of Power also fade, but more swiftly and horribly, into a nightmarish mockery of the Elves' longevity, like characters in a story granted Immortality but not eternal youth. Just as Men try to hold off or elude Death, Elves seek to stay time. They made their Rings of Power to preserve and to heal, but it's a losing battle. Even before the Company had left Lothlórien, the fading had begun there, the last corner of the Elder Days. The long defeat is fought not just against Morgoth or Sauron and Arda Marred but against the very nature of things.

Arwen's future, too, is great with loss. In choosing Aragorn, she has chosen to lose all else she has ever loved or thought of as home. In choosing to take the

Ring and save the Shire, Frodo has chosen to lose the Shire. That is the sweet and the bitter of their choices. In fact, Frodo has already lost the Shire. The peace he knew when death seemed imminent will slip away the more he comes to realize that this is so. The disquiet he feels about Bilbo signals to Arwen that "his hurts grieve [him]" *already* and that "the memory of [his] burden is heavy"; and she sees that in time to come they will do so "still" (RK 6.vi.974). From the troubling persistence of the memory of his burden, we can see that the displacement of his own memories no more reverses itself on the Ring's destruction than the wounds he suffered on his Quest heal themselves.

That Arwen offers him her place on the ship into the West shows that she thinks his healing unlikely in Middle-earth, but of course she never expresses this directly. Frodo's silence acknowledges that he is not "all right otherwise," despite his earlier claim. Arwen is a very late addition to the tale. As Sandra Miesel describes her, Arwen "looms far larger in the plot than in the text" (140). Her "inner power," Nancy Enright adds "is subtly conveyed, but present throughout" (123). Far more important than Arwen's role as Aragorn's queen is her bringing the Tale of Beren and Lúthien full circle by repeating the Choice of Lúthien. As Enright affirms, "what is most crucial about Arwen is her renunciation of Elven Immortality for love" (123). In the same way, Frodo's choice is what is most crucial about him.

Her words to Frodo in this scene are the only words we hear Arwen speak within the text of *The Lord of the Rings*.[3] By linking their choices, she reaffirms the connection between their tales and the Great Tale of Beren and Lúthien, which theirs continue and by which they are contained, and she uses the consequences of her choice to help him find healing from the consequences of his own. To the mortal whose fate beyond the Circles of the World now anticipates her own, Arwen holds out the hope of peace and healing beyond Middle-earth but before death. The white—that is, clear—gem she gives him in token of that hope recalls the clear crystal of Galadriel's phial, which shone with the light of the Silmaril Eärendil had worn upon his brow when he pierced the shadows and reached Valinor. That jewel, set in the sky with Eärendil as the evening star, was seen as a sign of hope from its first rising (*Shaping* 154–55). So it was still when Sam saw it above Mordor seven thousand years later. "The thought pierced him that in the end the Shadow was only a passing thing: there was light and high beauty forever beyond its reach" (RK 6.ii.922).

Whether the light that Frodo follows and carries with(in) him bears any hope for her remains to be seen. Yet, Arwen says Frodo's life is "woven" with hers and Aragorn's, which may not immediately disclose how strong the link between them is. Consider Aragorn's statement in "The Passing of the Grey Company" that the "fates" of the Dúnedain and the Shirefolk "are woven together," a remark relevant at the very least for its parallel phrasing (*RK* 5.ii.780). In Letter 246, moreover, Tolkien puts it more forcefully, saying of Arwen that "her renunciation and suffering were related to and *enmeshed* with Frodo's" (327n, emphasis mine).[4] The date of the letter, September 1963, rightly sounds a note of caution, but the message Arwen sent to Aragorn through Halbarad—"*Either our hope cometh, or all hope's end*" (*RK* 5.ii.775), that is, not the end of all hopes, but the end of all hope—shows how closely connected and how important Tolkien felt the choices of Frodo and Arwen to be from her inception.[5] Consider, too, how songs of the Blessed Realm frame this meeting and their initial encounter in Rivendell, where, as a hymn to Elbereth was being sung, the "light of her eyes fell upon him from afar and pierced his heart" (*FR* 2.i.238). Frodo does not yet know, of course, that he will be going to the Blessed Realm and Arwen will not, nor does he understand his dream of "a far green country" (1.vii.135). Yet the poignance of her glance remains unexplained if it does not lie in the exilic nature of the hymn to Elbereth, in the Choice of Lúthien before her, and in an understanding that the failure of the Quest is the end of all hope.

To Arwen's perception of his pain and her offer of hope Frodo has no answer but silence.

THE MALICE OF SARUMAN

"Many Partings," as its title suggests, portrays more of the bitter than the sweet. Nor are its great joys unalloyed. In the courtly and even more poignant dialogue between Gimli and Éomer about Galadriel and Arwen Evenstar, which directly follows Arwen's conversation with Frodo, Gimli likens them to Morning and Evening but fears that "soon [the Morning] will pass away for ever" (*RK* 6.vi.975). The reader already knows, if Gimli and Éomer do not, that Arwen will pass away in another, perhaps more final sense. Even the gratifying betrothal of Faramir and Éowyn signals the passing of the old world, that the Men of Gondor will continue to grow more like the Rohirrim, Men of the Twilight, matchless in valor and honor to be sure, but less learned and less high-minded (*RK* 6.vi.983–84; *TT* 4.v.679). Not only are the Ring's effects passing away, but so also is the world for and in which it was made. In telling of this transition, the narrator writes Frodo's fading character out of sight until a significant moment occurs.

In "Many Partings," Frodo appears five times. Three of these are of some significance: with Arwen and Aragorn as we have just seen; with Saruman and Gríma Wormtongue; and with Bilbo and Elrond in Rivendell (RK 6.vi.983–84, 985–89). Of the other two appearances, single sentences report that he knew the flash seen in the mist after Galadriel's departure was from her ring and that that he and Sam rode beside Aragorn, a place of great honor (6.vi.984–85, 975). These moments are woven into or together with other passages of an elegiac tone for all that is passing, all that is fading, Frodo not least. Beginning with Arwen's suggestion to Frodo, they culminate in a corresponding suggestion from Elrond as the chapter ends, to which Frodo also makes no reply.

Between these two, Frodo's disquiet about Bilbo is heard again, voiced more forcefully, at the end of the scene in which the party returning north comes on Saruman, the abusive master who with words and blows dominates his cringing, broken servant, Wormtongue. Though everyone who speaks shows Saruman pity and kindness, he responds with the bitterest sarcasm, mocking them as the cause of their own passing (RK 6.vi.983). Ironically, in attempting to seduce Gandalf away from the good a year earlier, he had used the passing of the Elves to argue for a timely betrayal. For, Sauron's victory being inevitable, they had to survive if they were ever going to control or defeat him; and either way, they would be able to achieve their errand. He suggested that they could even *share* the Ring. In the end, they would rule the World of Men, as they should (FR 2.ii.259).

Like an ancient practitioner of rhetoric, to which Dennis Wilson Wise compares him in his 2016 article, Saruman tries to persuade Gandalf that the morally worse argument (expedient betrayal) is to be preferred to the morally better argument (hopeless resistance), by appealing superficially to his desire to do good and the need for strength to accomplish it while secretly relying on the undertow of the Ring's power on the powerful. His argument, however, is bad because he has mistaken his audience. Gandalf has already recognized the way of the Ring to his heart, and domination is not what he desires. In his humility, he knows that the possession of so much power can end only one way. The deceit that surrounds the One Ring is well suited to the rhetor's art, but, as always seems the case, the one most deceived is the one possessing or desiring to possess the Ring. Clearly, too, the allure of that power can cause the fall of the powerful at a distance, if power is what is desired. Gandalf's remark to Denethor about the Ring's effect would have on him even if he never used it also nicely suits the fall of Saruman, who never came anywhere near the Ring (RK 5.iv.814). Thus Elrond, no doubt with Saruman in mind, states that "the very desire of it corrupts the heart" of the powerful (FR 2.ii.267).

Here and now Saruman mocks the passing of the Elves, the very loss he had used with Gandalf to justify joining the enemy as a means to gain access to, and eventually possession of, the Ring (FR 2.ii.259). (It was, of course, a cover for his ambition.) His rhetoric and his voice, however, no longer have their old strength. Nor is the rage with which he responds an attempt to daunt into acquiescence those he cannot persuade (2.ix.567), but, as Dennis Wilson Wise argues in his study of the rage of Saruman here and of Thrasymachus in Plato's *Republic*, it is evidence that his rage has gotten the better of him: "With the waxing of his anger comes the waning of his Voice" (3–4, 11–12). And his anger waxes as the desire for the Ring corrupts him (20–21).

Of the characters who speak to Saruman in "Many Partings," there is only one to whom he does not respond with anger. In fact, when Frodo replies to Saruman's request for pipe-weed that he would give it to him, had he any to give, Saruman wholly ignores him. Frodo no longer has what he wants. Saruman directs his attention to those who do and to those he hates. It is an intriguing encounter, Saruman and Frodo. Both are damaged because of the Ring; both have lost or will lose their homes; both are heading for the Shire; both have or have had mad, servile companions who turn on them in the end. The quiet kindness with which Frodo answers Saruman is in line with his forgiveness of Gollum, but only moments later he is dismissive, almost churlish, to Sam, who suggests they need to be getting back to the Shire. In his insistence that he must first see Bilbo in Rivendell "whatever happens" in the Shire (RK 6.vi.984), Frodo is very much the master putting a "pert servant" in his place (to borrow Faramir's words at TT 4.v.82). He and Sam, for all that they are master and servant, do not work this way. Aside from this moment and Frodo's rebuke of Sam back in the Shire for failing to tell him about the Gaffer's encounter with a Ringwraith (above on page 80), there are only two other occasions on which Frodo addresses Sam impolitely or unkindly (all hobbitry aside). I refer to the moments when Frodo sees Sam as an orc in the Tower of Cirith Ungol and at the foot of Mount Doom when he threatens him with Sting (RK 6.i.911, iii.937). His behavior toward Sam here testifies so powerfully, as we have seen before, to the Ring's effect because of its shocking contrast with the normal ease and affection between them, but we should not let that blind us to less prominent hints of trouble. Nor should we forget that Sam is not the only servant Frodo has in the course of his journey.

For we have seen Frodo threaten Gollum, whom he regards as his servant, with his sword and with the Ring more than once (TT 4.vi.687). In every instance but the first, Frodo compels Gollum to go to Mordor. To be sure, Frodo's peremptory response to Sam's assertion that it's time to get home hardly compares to Saruman's vicious physical and verbal abuse of Wormtongue, but Frodo's twice taunted words to Gollum outside the Black Gate—"You will never get it back"—are by no measure kind. Their full bitterness will soon come home.

Frodo's fears for Bilbo now that the Ring has been destroyed emerge from his love for the old hobbit and from his own experience. Recall how anxious he was, when he learned what Rings of Power do to mortals, that Bilbo would in time recover (FR 1.ii.48). Now, I argue, Frodo worries that Bilbo's suffering will mirror his own even as the full weight of his years descends on him. Yet Bilbo is as all right as a hobbit could be at the age of 130. He eats, writes poetry, and dozes. Not even the other hobbits' tales of their adventures suffice to keep him awake. His desire now is to beat the Old Took. There is no repetition of the scene in the Hall of Fire, no horrid visions, no sudden understandings. By contrast, when Bilbo finally does ask about the Ring, the night before Frodo leaves, the aged forgetfulness with which he inquires is touching and funny, prompting Frodo to call him "Bilbo dear" (RK 6.vi.987). A certain fascination with the Ring may persist, but now he is at peace with having given it up. If hearing what Frodo and Sam have to tell of their journey to Mordor with the Ring cannot keep him awake, if he can forget what has become of the Ring from one moment to the next, then obviously his obsession with it has passed to the extent that it can pass (see below on page 256). Bilbo is neither Gollum nor Frodo. He never suffered as they did, nor, though he came perilously close beneath the Misty Mountains and on the night of his farewell party, did he ever completely lose hold of who he was. Nevertheless, if Bilbo's feet are now at last weary of the Road, as the final version of "The Road Goes Ever On" attests, it is with more than years. Age alone gains no entry to the Straight Road (RK 6.vi.987).

Bilbo is so much himself in fact that Frodo is persuaded that it is time to return to the Shire. His remark to Sam at this point that Rivendell has "something of everything ... except the Sea" reveals that he has been suffering precisely as Arwen guessed he would be (RK 6.vi.986). It is also the first direct evidence that the hope he felt in Ithilien was transitory. As Frodo is about to depart for home, moreover, and at the very threshold of the Last Homely House, Elrond tells him privately that the ship of which Arwen had spoken will set sail before long (6.vi.988). As with Arwen at the beginning of "Many Partings," Frodo has no reply to Elrond at the chapter's end. The balance between the two scenes indicates that the chapter is as much about Frodo starting to come to terms with what possessing and losing the Ring have done to him as it is about the passing of an age.

No sooner does "Homeward Bound" begin than Frodo crosses another boundary at the Ford of Bruinen. It is evident to Gandalf and the other hobbits that he is in difficulty, but now for the first time someone asks him if he is in pain, and he speaks openly. The wound he received from the Morgul blade a year ago to the day hurts him once more. More significantly, he tells Gandalf that "the memory of the darkness is heavy on me," a distinct echo of Arwen's words to him and a frank admission of the irremediable spiritual damage he suffers from because of the Ring (RK 6.vii.989).

> "Alas! there are some wounds that cannot be wholly cured," said Gandalf.
>
> "I fear it may be so with mine," said Frodo. "There is no real going back. Though I may come to the Shire, it will not seem the same; for I shall not be the same. I am wounded with knife, sting, and tooth, and a long burden. Where shall I find rest?"
>
> Gandalf did not answer.
>
> (6.vii.989)

Bilbo, too, had spoken of rest, "evening-rest and sleep to meet" in the last version of "The Road Goes Ever On" but Bilbo's rest is an old man's metaphor (6.vi.987). Frodo has more in common with the speaker of the first version of the poem in *The Hobbit,* someone yearning to get his own life back, like a soldier longing for what Homer called νόστιμον ἦμαρ—"the day of his homecoming" (*Odyssey* 1.354–55):

> Roads go ever ever on
>   Under cloud and under star,
> Yet feet that wandering have gone
>   Turn at last to home afar.
> Eyes that fire and sword have seen
>   And horror in the halls of stone

> Look at last on meadows green
>   And trees and hills they long have known.
>
> (H 360)

Many a man and woman since before Homer's day has had and lost these hopes; and the literature of the twentieth and early twenty-first centuries has been particularly full of them. Some lost the day of their homecoming in battle or on the journey home; others came home and found that fire, sword, and horror—or, like Frodo, "knife, sting, and tooth, and long burden"—had changed them so much that the home they found could never be the home they longed for. Bilbo and Frodo both turn toward home but don't see those hills and trees in the same way. For Bilbo, the Ring was never the burden it became for Frodo. His memories of home remained intact and important to him throughout his adventure, and his memories of his adventure were important to him once he was home again. Frodo's memories were stripped away until all he could see was the Ring, the burden of which he cannot forget. Frodo's words quoted just above answer the question he had asked himself before he left the Shire: "I wonder if I shall ever look down into that valley again?" (*RK* 1.iii.71). The answer is, no, he will never look down into *that* valley or at *that* Shire again: he will never be *that* Frodo again. And he knows this before he ever gets there.

The Shire that he left to save from Mordor, however, has become Mordor, largely but not wholly because of Saruman's involvement in its affairs at first by proxy but now in person. The very first thing Frodo sees upon reaching the gates of Buckland is a sign declaring "no admittance between sundown and sunrise," which both recalls and repudiates the sign on Bilbo's gate in "A Long-expected Party," "no admittance except on party business" (*RK* 6.viii.998; *FR* 1.i.26). And from the locked gates of Buckland to the rat-infested halls of a now comfortless Bag End, Frodo and the others find one example after another of the wanton destruction, corruption, and divisiveness that is "the spirit of Mordor" (*RK* 6.ii.925).[6]

Sam calls it "worse than Mordor.... Much worse in a way. It comes home to you, as they say; because it is home, and you remember it before it was all ruined" (*RK* 6.viii.1017). Frodo replies at once: "Yes, this is Mordor." Note the perspectives of Sam and Frodo here. What makes it "worse than Mordor" is memory. Sam's intention had always been to "see it through" and then return to home to the Shire, and his memories helped sustain him through the darkness.[7] Sam does not see the pain of this homecoming as owing to any change in himself. The Shire "was all ruined." No agent is named; the verb is passive; the subject receives the action, as if the destruction alone matters right now. Sam, however, still has those memories and now the people in them.

With the damage he suffered to his memory Frodo can see the destruction for what it is, but cannot feel it as Sam, Merry and Pippin do. "The memory of the darkness is heavy on me," Frodo told Gandalf. It cuts him off from coming home in the way the others can and in the way he wished to. To whatever degree Frodo regains his lost memories emotionally, the weight of the darkness is greater and will remain so. Frodo saw coming home and being healed as woven together, but his wounds and his burden have changed him too much for him to come home in heart and spirit even if he can in body. As long as his hurts and especially the memory of the darkness remain, Frodo will bring Mordor with him. Love of the Shire and the desire to save it started Frodo down that road, not the desire to follow Bilbo or to go forth carrying a sword rather than a walking stick. Without doubt the thought of those desires stirred his fancy, but not enough for him to pursue the road they opened before him.

But just as the suffering of his burden led him first to pity and then to forgive Gollum, so now on his return home he sees a bigger picture than even Merry, Pippin, and Sam do, let alone the other hobbits. He acts for the good with a quiet resolve so firm that others heed him. Merry will briefly mistake his desire to avoid killing for a lack of will, but, though his blood is up, Merry listens. In later years Frodo's role in this time will be underestimated because the heroics of Merry and Pippin are more dramatic, but during the scouring the other hobbits follow Frodo's instructions, all of which aim at restraint and mercy as much as at putting things to rights. It is Merry who leads in the actual fighting, which marks a change from the original draft of "The Scouring of the Shire." As Christopher Tolkien describes that draft, "Frodo is portrayed here at every stage as an energetic and commanding intelligence, warlike and resolute in action; and the final text of the chapter has been very largely achieved when the changed conception of Frodo's part in the Scouring of the Shire entered" (*Sauron* 93–94).

By reassigning the martial aspects of Frodo's role as leader to Merry, Tolkien is not portraying Frodo as weak or shy of battle. Far from it. His "I will not have him slain" is authoritative and effective in restraining the hobbits who wish Saruman dead.[8] Frodo is also in the battle, but he never draws his sword. Rather, his more precise focus illuminates in this context what has been his purpose since the beginning, namely, to save the Shire, now even from itself, by means of the lessons he has learned about pity and mercy and himself since then. If no hobbit has ever killed another on purpose in the Shire, Frodo knows a hobbit who once did so elsewhere, with the unhappiest of results. He will not have that happen here. To save the Shire at this point means to save the hobbits from their wrath at the ruffians and especially at the hobbits who collaborated with them out of fear.

The last scene of "The Scouring of the Shire" brings the final confrontation of *The Lord of the Rings* as Frodo meets Saruman once more. Here, too, the first draft differs substantially from the final text. In the first draft, Frodo slays Sharkey in single combat, but Sharkey is a man, the chief of the ruffians. Saruman is nowhere to be seen. It is only in the second draft when "Captain Frodo"—as his friends had called him before they left the Shire (FR 1.v.105)—disappears that Saruman appears (*Sauron* 93-104). It is hard to imagine that this is coincidental, given how well the Frodo and Saruman who meet here balance each other and how their meeting brings full circle the ideas of pity and mercy and justice first discussed by Frodo and Gandalf in "The Shadow of the Past." Now it is Frodo who feels pity and argues for mercy, the other hobbits who demand death for the murderer, and Saruman whose guilt cannot be denied but whose sentence ought to be set aside, because "to meet revenge with revenge will heal nothing," and because Saruman's cure, like Gollum's, may not be beyond all hope (RK 6.viii.1018, 1019).

Frodo's cure, too, is doubtful, which Saruman sees just as Gandalf had. There is, however, more revealed here for "eyes to see that can" (FR 2.i.223). When Frodo absolutely refuses to let Saruman be killed despite the wizard's attempt to murder him, Saruman regards him with "a strange look in his eyes of mingled wonder and respect and hatred" (RK 6.viii.1019). In Rivendell the year before, Gandalf had looked at Frodo and could not foresee to what he would come in the end (FR 2.i.223). Saruman now sees that end. It is to wisdom and pity and mercy that Frodo has come at last and to a humility that reveres the lofty height from which Saruman has fallen and the nobility that he has debased through his desire to possess the power of the One Ring. Frodo came to this end through resisting the pull of the Ring until it overcame his strength. Through suffering this conflict with all the pain and wounds attendant on it, and from which he will continue to suffer, he has become the Frodo Saruman wonders at and respects, even as he hates him.

Saruman, too, looks homeward, though not to Isengard, which he has called his home and which has been destroyed (as he sees it) in the same way that he tried to destroy the Shire. When Wormtongue kills him, his spirit rises up like a mist from his body, towering over the Hill, but a wind from the West "dissolve[d] it into nothing" (RK 6.viii.1019). Surely this will recall to the reader Sauron's last moments, as it is meant to do. Yet there is a crucial difference we must not overlook. The spirit of Sauron is reaching out as if to strike at his enemies one last time when the West wind blows it away. The "pale, shrouded figure" of Saruman's spirit looks to the West even as the wind dissolves it. Frodo seems to have been right about Saruman, as Gandalf had been about Gollum. To use Gandalf's words from "The Shadow of the Past," there was "not no hope" that he might be healed. Yet Saruman's hatred and malice, fatally expressed in his cruelty to Gríma Wormtongue, denies him even that.

The "pity and horror" with which Frodo reacts to the "long years of death" swiftly revealed in Saruman's corpse (RK 6.viii.1020) also turns our thoughts back to Gollum and Bilbo: "A sudden understanding, a pity mixed with horror, welled up in Bilbo's heart: a glimpse of endless unmarked days without light or hope of betterment" (H 133). More than once, the narrator has evoked that moment of recognition beneath the Misty Mountains. Gandalf spoke of it in "The Shadow of the Past," and in recalling that conversation in "The Taming of Sméagol" Frodo came to understand what Gandalf had been saying (FR 1.ii.54, 59; TT 4.i.615). In "The Stairs of Cirith Ungol," we received a wondrous, impossible glimpse into the narrator's understanding of the heart of Gollum, who had far outlived everyone and everything he had ever known, all but the Precious (TT 4.viii.714). In "Mount Doom," because of his brief but intense experience of the Ring Sam "dimly . . . guessed" Gollum's torment and pitied him at last (RK 6.iii.944).

That pity and horror, as we have seen, mark out the witness to a Tragedy who has also stood on the brink but whose response to the possibilities before them has saved them. If we consider Bilbo's near failure at Bag End, Frodo's actual failure on Mount Doom, and Galadriel's desire that Frodo "must depart, for now we have chosen," we shall again see that where the Ring is concerned the test or temptation is never truly over (FR 2.vii.365). Even with the Ring destroyed, those choices and their consequences persist. Saruman's lust for the power of the Ring was so great that he fell without ever coming within reach of it. If his declared end of "Knowledge. Rule. Order." is ideological trumpery and not to be trusted, it also suggests the original good intentions that may have paved his road to hell (2.ii.259). Gandalf and Galadriel knew themselves well enough that they avoided falling into the trap that in the end they would have set for themselves.

All Saruman has now is malice and revenge, motives Frodo didn't understand when Gandalf adduced them as sufficient to explain why Sauron would wish to destroy the Shire and enslave its inhabitants (FR 1.ii.48). As with pity and mercy, Frodo has since come to a better understanding, seeing the uselessness of vengeance for healing and the harm that killing Saruman "in this evil mood" would do to the hobbits (RK 6.viii.1018). Saruman may warn that dire consequences will come of killing him, but Frodo knows these will arise from the indulgence of their evil mood, and acting in wrath and hatred, not because Saruman has cursed them and their land.

In Gandalf's assertion to Frodo that Saruman "could do some mischief still in a small mean way" (RK 6.vi.984), the mischief of which he speaks is not the "high-spirited or playful naughtiness" we so often use this word to describe but the more serious evil or harm that malice has long inspired ("Mischief, n." III.8, II.2a–b). Leaving the dishes for the Sackville-Bagginses to wash is petty mischief on Frodo's part; it is not to be compared to the widespread destruction Saruman visits on the Shire in general and on Bag End in particular (FR 1.iii.60). No harm he does there is "small" or "mean," but he has become both in spirit. He sees kindness and mercy as cruelty, to be repaid with spite, whether it is Merry giving him pipe-weed or Frodo saving his life. The wisdom he concedes to Frodo he can only interpret as calculation, as if Frodo had spared him because he reckoned that being indebted to the hobbit's mercy would gall him the most.

Saruman threatened that "if his blood stained the Shire, it would wither and never again be healed," but it is he who has "withered altogether" as Gandalf noted after their last meeting (RK 6.viii.1018, vi.972). It is he who will never be healed. Frodo, however, has grown. Gandalf and Saruman both say so. Frodo's journey to pity has been tortuous. At first, he refused to acknowledge Gollum could be a Hobbit, like him, and could see nothing but the justice his misdeeds deserved. By the time he met Gollum, he had learned better and was able to pity him. The progressive erosion of his strength and identity under the burden of the Ring as he came closer to Mount Doom left him "untouchable now by pity" even as his will was about to break (6.iii.944). Given the importance of pity, moreover, losing it may have lost him all. Yet it was his failure and defeat that regained him the pity he had lost. And more. For in pitying Saruman and showing him mercy, Frodo shows that he has grown beyond pitying someone who is like him and someone he saw whom he could become. His pity extends now to one whose nature before his fall Frodo believes to have been far above him or any other mortal.

REMEMBERING THE DARKNESS

No passage attests the Ring's hold on its bearer more dramatically than the death of Gollum. "Dancing like a mad thing" and shrieking its name over and over as if in ecstasy, he falls into the fire; only minutes earlier he had whimpered that he would come to "dusst" with the Ring destroyed (RK 6.iii.946, 944). At this point, he has not held the Ring in seventy-eight years, but possession regained sparks a joy that renders death meaningless: even at the last he cries "*Precious!*" Bilbo kept the Ring for sixty of those years, and began his tenure with mercy, not murder; yet it held him hard until its unmaking. With Boromir and Saruman, we have seen how its corruption can work at a distance and how, as with Sméagol and Déagol, the briefest glimpse can turn love into murder.

With the Ring destroyed, everything sad did not come untrue. Nor does it now. The significance of Frodo's role in the scouring is his refusal to let the hobbits act out of malice and revenge as Sauron and Saruman and Gollum did. Eighteen months earlier, Gandalf had not replied when Frodo asked why Sauron would desire revenge on the Shire—"Revenge? ... Revenge for what?" (FR 1.ii.49). Such motives are not always easily explained because they are not entirely rational. Gollum's desire for vengeance on Bagginses and on Sauron has a plausible basis. Saruman's assertion that Galadriel "always hated me" however, does not (RK 6.vi.982; see also FR 2.vii.357). His revenge on the hobbits is a petty, irrational transference of his hatred to them because others, like Gandalf and Galadriel, are beyond his ability to harm directly. Such reasoning and motives dovetail with the desire for the Ring. Suffering, however, has taught Frodo the wisdom to see the peril here. Malice will find a pretext for the evil in the heart. Thus, Saruman's sneer at "hobbit-lordlings" (RK 6.viii.1018). Thus, Sméagol and his birthday present. Understanding this compels Frodo to fight to keep the hobbits from killing Saruman, the ruffians, or, worst of all, other hobbits.

It is a part of Frodo's fading after the Ring goes into the fire, moreover, that little rouses him, as if the weariness was not lifted with the burden. So, we should note when something does rouse him. He became quite excited when Gandalf told him he had a "treasure" for him (on pages 213–14 above); and he was adamant that he must see Bilbo in Rivendell before returning to the Shire (RK 6.vi.984). The passion of his insistence that Saruman be spared even after his attack reveals both how dangerous he considers this moment to be for the hobbits and how far he has come in feeling the importance of pity and mercy, beyond Bilbo even. For Gollum had not tried to kill Bilbo only seconds before. Frodo knows that, if the hobbits kill Saruman "without need" and "in this evil mood," his blood will stain not the land proper, but its people (FR 1.ii.59; RK 6.viii.1019). The Shire will wither from its roots, which will be far more the hobbits' doing than Saruman's. Because of Frodo's intervention, however, the Shire will instead be healed.

To save the Shire was of course Frodo's original Quest, and the destruction of the Ring was the means to doing so. David M. Waito has argued that this Shire Quest "overarches the Ring Quest" and that "the main conflict of Tolkien's novel is not to destroy the Ring, but to "scour" or save the Shire" (155–56). I argue that the Quest changes not in purpose but in scope when Frodo chooses the burden of the Ring at the Council of Elrond. He does so because his perspective on the Shire and the rest of Middle-earth has broadened as the result of all he experiences, good and bad, on the way to Rivendell. He knows now in his heart what before he knew only in his head, that Gildor spoke the truth when he said to him that he "cannot for ever fence [the wide world] out" of the Shire (FR 1.iii.83). Casting the Ring into the fire and saving the Shire or "the wider world" are causes too closely interwoven to be spoken of apart. Against such an evil, saving the Shire is possible only by saving the world. Clearly, the one encompasses the other. It is not an alternative. Yet, if we bear in mind that Frodo's Quest begins thus, as Waito and I have tried to do, and that he never expected to survive, his return thoroughly damaged to a Shire still in need of saving will hardly seem anticlimactic or irrelevant even if some may find it unexpected. It underlines not only the wisdom he has won from the conflict between "this is my burden" and "the Ring is mine" and the courage with which he has faced despair but also the conviction growing within him that unlike Bilbo he will not remain "very happy to the end of his days" (H 361). Even before the narrative becomes more explicit about Frodo's sufferings at home, the truth of the words he will before long say to Sam will have been established. Thus, when Sam says he thought Frodo would live happily ever after, Frodo responds: "So I thought too, once. But I have been too deeply hurt, Sam. I tried to save the Shire, and it has been saved, but not for me. It must often be so, Sam, when things are in danger: some one has to give them up, lose them, so that others may keep them" (RK 6.ix.1029).

From the death of Saruman to the departure of Frodo measures a little less than two years, during which Frodo falls ill three times, at regular intervals that mark the dates on which he was wounded by the Witch-king at Weathertop (6 October 1420) and by Shelob (13 March 1420, 1421). This illness had already affected him when he crossed the Bruinen on 6 October

1419. The date and place are significant, of course, but perhaps not as much as the fact that, turning for home at last, he "feels the first return of the pain" and despairs of finding rest in the Shire. For now he must face the truth that his home cannot heal him and that his longing for the Ring is unabated; or perhaps it is that his home cannot heal him *because* his longing is unabated: "It is gone for ever ... and now all is dark and empty" (RK 6.ix.1023).

Frodo had insisted on going to Rivendell to see Bilbo before returning to the Shire because he was worried about him now that the Ring was gone. Bilbo, however, showed no sign that he felt the profound sense of loss Frodo so obviously does. Without the Ring, the preservation and longevity bestowed by his long possession of it were rapidly slipping away, but he had long ago let go of the Ring of his own free will. He had stopped possessing it entirely when he looked at Frodo's face and understood what it was doing to him. Frodo, by contrast, sounds more like Gollum speaking of Sméagol and the Precious, but with one difference (TT 4.i.616; vi.686). The Ring no longer exists. What remains is that part of Frodo which responded to the pull of its power and has not let go. His every wound merges into the torment of the loss of the Ring, so that even when it is the anniversary of his wounding by Shelob or the Witch-king, those pains are not foremost in his mind. He fades not physically but personally. If we set Frodo's experiences beside those of Gollum, whose possession of the Ring was from its outset marked by murder upon murder, it becomes clear how remote a chance Gollum had of being cured, his moment of near repentance on the stairs of Cirith Ungol notwithstanding.

If we turn again to Letter 246, Tolkien continues his reading of his own text:

> I think it is clear on reflection to an attentive reader that when his dark times came upon him and he was conscious of being "wounded by knife sting and tooth and a long burden" [RK 6.vii.989] it was not only nightmare memories of past horrors that afflicted [Frodo], but also unreasoning self-reproach: he saw himself and all that he [had] done as a broken failure. That was actually a temptation out of the Dark, a last flicker of pride: desire to have returned as a "hero," not content with being a mere instrument of good. And it was mixed with another temptation, blacker and yet (in a sense) more merited, for however that may be explained, he had not in fact cast away the Ring by a voluntary act: he was tempted to regret its destruction, and still to desire it. "It is gone for ever, and now all is dark and empty," he said as he wakened from his sickness in 1420. (*Letters* pp. 327–28).

Can we, if attentive, see this in *The Lord of the Rings* as it was written over a decade earlier, or is Tolkien imposing a later "meaning" on the text? Of the temptations to which he refers, the latter is without doubt present. It is impossible to understand Frodo's words in 1420 as expressing something other than regret, desire, and perhaps shame. The seed of the former—to return as a hero—lies hidden in Frodo's awareness that he could not have destroyed the Ring without Gollum, and we may suspect it in how commanding Frodo is during the Scouring. We should not mistake Frodo's desire to avoid bloodshed for weakness or passivity. His entering the battle without a sword in his hand, in order to save enemy lives, is quite heroic. How perfectly it answers and corrects the threats he and Bilbo made when they felt the Ring threatened! Surely, had he retained in "The Scouring of the Shire" the martial character ultimately transferred to Merry, and had this been followed with Sam's pain in "The Grey Havens" at seeing how little people marked and honored his master's deeds, the former "temptation out of the Dark" would not be so easily eclipsed by its "blacker and yet ... more merited" companion (RK 6.ix.1025).

The comparison is to the former temptation—that is, there is no reason for him to feel like a failure quite simply because the power of the Ring was too much for him. He had borne it farther than anyone could have hoped. The second temptation, however, was not a matter for "unreasoning self-reproach" (*Letters* no. 246, p. 328). It was a consequence of his choosing not to destroy the Ring, and of the loss of it against his will to Gollum and the fires of the Sammath Naur. We should not forget that Frodo saw the Ring as useful from the beginning. Despite Gandalf's warnings about the Ring, it seemed to Frodo a means, first of all, of avoiding undesirable social encounters and then of escaping from the enemy. The pains of this error led him not to forswear all use of the Ring but to desire to read the thoughts of others by means of it, which Galadriel identified at once as an ability requiring the domination of the wills of others. If Frodo wished to do so to defy the enemy (as he tried but failed to do at the Bruinen), he never said so. In fact, he neither explained why he wished this ability nor denied a desire for domination. His assertion to her, moreover, that as the Ring-bearer he is "permitted" to use the Ring is at best unevidenced. Despite Galadriel's stern warning that any attempt to use the Ring to this end would destroy him, and despite the terrifying lesson of its effects on Boromir, Frodo soon began trying to dominate Gollum by means of the Ring, or, if there is a difference, by the fear of it. Clearly this is a dangerous road to step into, leading as it does to Sauron's Road. Thus, the second temptation is more merited in this sense, that it fits the desire.

Tolkien's commentary in Letter 246 offers a perceptive and consistent analysis of Frodo's progress to this moment so near the end of his journey. "The memory of the fear and the darkness" of which Arwen speaks is but the beginning or adumbration of what he suffers because he has borne the Ring, that is, because he has lived so intimately with the pull of that much power. Just as gravity warps space, so power warps us. Even with the source of that pull removed, the momentum imparted by it to that on which it pulls remains, as if it still reaches out and grasps at the source that is gone. Frodo's spiritual pain, both merited and unreasoning, manifests itself through his wounds and through his inability to return home. He will not find his "home afar" in the "meadows green / And trees and hills they long have known," as Bilbo did and as Frodo's companions do. He will have to look beyond them, to "a far green country under a swift sunrise" (RK 6.ix.1030).

In a tale in which lies and self-deceptions play so significant a role, in which a ring found "by chance" in the darkness becomes a ring won in a game of riddles, in which a ring won by murder becomes a birthday present, Frodo's coming to the far country where he would find healing is worthy of note. For just as no one could have witnessed Gollum nearly repent upon the stairs, none in Middle-earth could have heard the singing across the water that Frodo heard or seen the swift sunrise that Frodo saw. This portion of the story, however, was written, or perhaps only first written, by Sam. So, the narrative burden has fully shifted, completing the transition that first began to be obvious in the Dead Marshes when the burden of the Ring and the pressure of the Eye hastened his isolation as "Master of the Precious" (TT 4.ii.630–31). Sam, however, now *the* Mister Gamgee of Bag End, who has risen through the most heroic service to be master of the house in which he served, recognizes the mythic truth of Frodo's vision in the house of Tom Bombadil. Revealed then so it could be recorded now, the vision establishes the happy ending which Sam felt Frodo had been denied in losing the Shire. Frodo will at last leave Mordor behind, and go "sailing, sailing, sailing over the Sea" (FR 1.ii.44), which allows Sam to become whole himself and return home completely.

The vision proves to be a true myth.

CHAPTER ELEVEN

Pity and Power in Time

THE TRAGEDY OF THE INCARNATE

In his famous essay *Beowulf: The Monsters and the Critics* Tolkien says of the hero Beowulf: "*He is a man, and that for him and for many is a sufficient tragedy*" (M&C 18). Extending the reach of this characterization, Anna Vaninskaya writes, "These words, italicized in the original, can be emblazoned at the head of Tolkien's entire fantastic oeuvre" (154). In his essay, Tolkien lays out his understanding of *Beowulf*, its Christian poet, and the legendary past he was writing about, an age whose "days were heathen—heathen, noble, and hopeless" (M&C 22). That hopelessness is rooted as deeply as Yggdrasil because the final defeat of men and gods alike is inevitable. It is how the world ends. Their nobility, however, reveals itself in their fighting on regardless, in doing deeds worthy of song even if no one is alive to hear it, because they find in that "*defeat no refutation*" of their "Northern courage" and of the worth of their struggle against the darkness (20–21).[1]

We can see this nobility in Théoden, Éowyn, and Éomer during the Battle of the Pelennor Fields. The old king has no regrets because he is dying well, having done great deeds himself. Éowyn, "one without hope who goes in search of death," defies the Witch-king to defend her own (RK 5.iii.803). Éomer, the young king, "laugh[s] at despair" and sings his defiance of the doom that seems to be approaching them all (5.vi.847). At the same time within the city, Denethor, the Steward of Gondor in whom "the blood of Westernesse runs nearly true" is yielding to despair (and madness) and failing this test (6.i.758). Anna Vaninskaya rightly calls him the "great exemplum of heathen hopelessness in the novel" (177). And just as the *Beowulf*-poet reproaches those who turned to the heathen gods in despair when their own strength proved too little to defeat Grendel (170–88), so Gandalf rebukes Denethor by likening him to "the heathen kings" of old when he chooses death for himself and his son, Faramir, a comparison Denethor has already embraced on his own (RK 5.iv.825, vii.852).[2]

Yet Gandalf acknowledges the truth that led Denethor to despair: "Listen to the words of the Steward of Gondor before he died . . . *against the Power that has now arisen there is no victory*" (RK 5.ix.878; see also 5.vii.853). In the end, as long as the Ring exists, no courage, no strength, no will in Middle-earth can defeat Sauron without becoming Sauron, and the Quest to unmake the Ring has never been more than "a fool's hope," another point Denethor made and Gandalf conceded (6.iv.825, vii.852). That much power will crush or corrupt anyone in the end. It is as evident in the struggle within Frodo as it is on the battlefields of Gondor. No one who partakes of the substance of Arda Marred, whether by nature or adoption, or who seeks to order it, change it, or to keep it from changing can successfully resist. Only Bombadil, who takes Arda as he finds it, is beyond the pull of the Ring, and even he could not stand against Sauron; what makes him immune does not make him a savior (FR 2.ii.265).[3] The rest of us must simply fail: "The power of Evil in the world is *not* finally resistible by incarnate creatures, however 'good'" (*Letters* no. 191, p. 252).

This courage to face an ineluctable universal defeat is, as W. P. Ker, followed by Tolkien, called it, "perfect because without hope" (Ker 57–58; *M&C* 21). The pity Gandalf urges on Frodo is analogous. It cannot defend the Ring-bearer against the pull of the Ring any more than courage can succeed against the assault of Sauron. Yet its hopeless perfection also defies all refutation of its worth. Pity, however, opens a door that strength and courage, reinforced by grace, can keep open for a time. The pity Bilbo felt for Gollum, which Frodo and Sam, too, came to share, and the mercy they each chose to show him allowed the hope, however increasingly slim, that he could be healed, and preserved each of them from becoming another Gollum. More than that, as Gandalf intimated in "The Shadow of the Past," pity may well have a role to play in a much larger and providential plan. Doom, as Tolkien knew, is as effective an agent of man's tragedy as the *hamartia* (ἁμαρτία, *M&C* 15) Aristotle spoke of in the *Poetics*, and which Tolkien here explicitly acknowledges in his lecture on *Beowulf*. Doom hung over Túrin Turambar, but it was his character and mistaken choices that brought it down upon him and so many around him.[4] Bilbo was "meant" to find the Ring, and his "sudden understanding" may have been granted by Providence, but his revulsion at the thought of killing Gollum was all his own and it came first. His choice both embraces his doom and avoids the mistake, the ἁμαρτία, that made Sméagol into Gollum.

As he told Gollum's sad story in "The Shadow of the Past," Gandalf said Gollum was "bound up with the fate of the Ring" and had "some part to play yet" (*FR* 1.ii.59). It is in precisely this connection, as we know, that the pity of Bilbo would prove critical. So, it is reasonable to think Gollum, too, was meant to have the Ring and to keep it hidden away until Bilbo came along. His embrace of his doom, however, made his story a tragedy at once. Just as sparing Gollum was all Bilbo, so the murder of Déagol was all Sméagol. Bilbo leapt "in the dark" (*H* 133). Sméagol leapt into darkness. Seeing something he wanted, he went straight to murder to obtain it. As A. C. Bradley pointed out in his lectures on Shakespeare, when the Witches prophesy that Macbeth will be king, "[their] words... are *fatal* to the hero only because there is in him something which leaps straight into the light at the sound of them" (320, emphasis mine).[5] Doom and ἁμαρτία are compounded in the sudden tragedy of Sméagol (and Macbeth and Túrin, son of Húrin). Yet the slow descents of Bilbo and Frodo nevertheless establish that their keeping of the Ring also "ends in night," a phrase Tolkien uses to describe the heroic world as the *Beowulf*-poet perceived it (*M&C* 23). It is just as apt here.

The Doom that the *Beowulf*-poet had in mind was Death, so Tolkien reminds us: "that man, each man and all men, and all their works shall die" (*M&C* 23). Even the man of perfect courage cannot prevail against "his inevitable overthrow in Time" (18). As a Christian, the *Beowulf*-poet knew that "beyond [Time] there appears a possibility of eternal victory (or eternal defeat), and the real battle is between the soul and its adversaries"; but he also knew that the *hæleð under heofenum* of whom he wrote and thought never learned the "solution of [Man's] tragedy" (22, 23). The gospel—the evangelium—had not reached them that beyond Death there was, shall we say, "more than memory" (*RK*, App. A I.v.1063).

Death and Immortality are of course part of the nature of things in Arda. Rings of Power challenge these parameters. They offer, or seem to, escape from Death to "mortal Men doomed to die." Consider how the Ring-verse twice harps on the nature of Men, which it never does for Elves, Dwarves, or the Dark Lord. Its association of them and their Rings of Power with things of this world (sky, stone, darkness), however, is noteworthy since Arda is not the true home of Men. The Elven Rings are named for fire, water, and adamant. Rings of Power keep mortals in this world against their nature and in rejection of the Gift of Ilúvatar to Men (Death). Yet it was "the chief bait of Sauron" (*Letters* no. 212, p. 286). The result is a twofold horror. For, as Amy Amendt-Radeuge has suggested, "the Ringwraiths represent the latent recognition that while dying may be the most terrifying experience known to humanity, not dying deprives us of being human altogether," and in menacing Éowyn with "the houses of lamentation" the Witch-king describes a fate very much like his own ("Better Off Dead" 70, 79).

For the Elves, by contrast, the Rings of Power are tools to heal the ever-fading world and preserve it from the stain of Time. In Lórien especially the result is like a dream, perhaps even a Faërian Drama, in which someone else is dreaming the dream.[6] Yet the dream isolates the Golden Wood from the world around it, sundering Elves from Men, and from more than Men. Even Treebeard, "the oldest of all living things," sees "they are falling rather behind the world in there" (TT 3.vii.558, iv.467). It is a dream doomed to pass away. For the Three Rings of the Elves can no more confound Time than the Nine Rings of Men can humble Death. Like Death and Time, the One Ring is impossible to resist for long, but with that failure comes a darker fate: "Neither strength nor good purpose will last—sooner or later the dark power will devour" the possessor (FR 1.ii.46). Gandalf would become a Dark Lord no less than Sméagol became Gollum. The greatest virtues are as much meat for the Ring's consumption as the greatest malice.

In *Beowulf*, the futility of all heroism against Death, Time, and the monsters finds no solution. The poet and his audience may know what it is, but salvation is not his theme. The poem begins and ends with the funeral of a hero. If the riddle of Scyld's origins and his final, mysterious destination hint at something beyond the Fields of Time, the funeral given him is nonetheless just as heathen as Beowulf's is at the end.[7] It is the poet who suggests in his own voice that God sent Scyld to found a dynasty "*folce to frofre*"—"to comfort the people"—who had long been without a king; and it is the poet who makes heroes such as Beowulf and Hrothgar seem "noble pagans" deserving of more than fading memory in this world and damnation in the next (1. 14). The characters in the poem who mourn Beowulf, however, look forward to a world of pain and destruction without their king to protect them. Like those who turned to their heathen gods in despair of defeating Grendel, the survivors of Beowulf should also "expect no comfort" ("*frofre ne wenan*": *Beowulf* 1. 185).

The Lord of the Rings begins with a different ceremony, a birthday party, but one also followed by a departure to no one knows where (though most hobbits do think Bilbo is dead: FR 1.ii.42); it ends with another such departure, now also on a ship into the West, a journey whose completion can be glimpsed through Sam's imagination and faith in Frodo's vision. There Frodo will receive the healing he could not find in the Shire, while Sam, turning back to the homeland he has made bloom again, will become whole and happy and much honored. *The Lord of the Rings* thus ends in hope and sorrow. Unlike in *Beowulf*, some who remain behind in Middle-earth "can say for certain who received that ship's burden" (*Beowulf* ll. 50–52). Sam for one knows very well where the ships of the Elves went "sailing, sailing, sailing over the Sea," and it is he who will hand down the story whose readers will have no doubt that Frodo's vision and Sam's imagination are true (FR 1.ii.44).

EUCATASTROPHE HALLOWS LEGEND

The poet's weaving together of pagan and Christian in *Beowulf* supplied Tolkien with a clear paradigm for subcreating a world "fundamentally religious and Catholic" but by definition "heathen." Tolkien and the *Beowulf*-poet use this paradigm differently, however. The poet imagines for us a world in which the heroes are pagan, but not exactly, and speak of one god almost as if they were Christians. The tragedy of Beowulf and Hrothgar is not that they will die but that their virtue and nobility bring them to the threshold of a salvation they almost certainly cannot attain because they do not know of Christ. It is a desperately poignant portrayal of heathens with whom the poet and others felt a deep connection. As Fulk, Bjork, and Niles have pointed out in their introduction to the fourth edition of Klaeber's *Beowulf*, this "representation of pagan society as something only intermittently reprehensible suggests a sense of continuity between the people depicted in the poem and those of the poet's day" (lxxiv). And the full spectrum of this continuity is on display throughout the poem.

For the poet makes no doubt that "holy God," "the wise Lord, the Ruler of the heavens" "decided aright" in the fight between Grendel's mother and Beowulf, who suddenly spots the sword with which he kills her (*Beowulf* ll. 1550–69). In telling his tale to Hrothgar, Beowulf is less effusive, saying he was "shielded" by god, "allowed" to see the sword and "guided to draw it," while at the same time taking pains to explain inoffensively why the sword Unferth had generously lent him wasn't up to the job (ll. 1655–64). Recounting his exploits to Hygelac upon his return home, he is even more subdued and heathen: "I was not yet doomed to die" (l. 2141).

The differences of perception allow a clearer vision. The *Beowulf*-poet sees God as the judge whose righteous judgement empowers the hero's victory.

Beowulf sees himself as not yet doomed to die, and, it seems, "shielded" by god from death for that reason, just as he was also "spared" because of his courage, as men not doomed to die often are (ll. 572–73). Whether prompted or allowed to catch sight of the sword, the courage and strength to use it were Beowulf's own. The failure of Hrunting, Unferth's storied and otherwise worthy sword, to achieve anything against Grendel's mother may be seen in this context to underscore the suggestion that Beowulf needed more than his own prowess to defeat her. "Valour needs first strength, and then a weapon" as Boromir is quick to point out (FR 2.ii.26x). Beowulf obtained that weapon only because of divine intervention. Rather like Bilbo, we might say he was *meant* to have it, but he still had to find it. Against Grendel, Beowulf's unarmed courage was enough; against his mother it was no more effective than Unferth's sword. When the dragon comes, however, God does not save or shield Beowulf, nor, it seems, will he protect Beowulf's people from their enemies after his death. For now it is his time, and in this world night still wins.[8] Its people know little or nothing of a larger and more significant spiritual contest beyond the Fields of Time. They remain forever poised in that moment of humane "fusion" between a myth that was wholly true and a myth that was not (M&C 20).[9] Whatever feelings this portrayal may evoke in us, the poet's first audience will have felt pity for their virtuous but damned ancestors, and it was pity of this kind for the unredeemed heathen that generated over a thousand years of speculation and casuistical shenanigans to find a way to salvation for those who never saw the path. Aristotle and Homer were the heathens the scholars debating this matter had in mind, at least as examples; the less philosophically inclined would have held their thoughts closer to home, with their kin and their kind.

Tolkien takes the *Beowulf*-poet's paradigm further in several ways. First, the differing fates and natures of Men and Elves add a perspective, that of the *longaevi*, who to their sorrow see all fade and die around them while they live on. For us, the audience, the tale is as much a fusion of the mortal and immortal perspectives as *Beowulf* is of the heathen and Christian. Both sets of perspectives are in fact present. For the people of Middle-earth, existing long before the evangelium, are also heathen. Aragorn is no less likely damned than Beowulf. Even if we view Aragorn as a type of Christ the King, as, for example, Bradley Birzer does, applicability does not equal salvation (69–70).[10] The relapse, so to speak, of Denethor in his despair into heathen practices known "before ever a ship sailed hither from the West" recalls both the coming of Scyld and the Danes' turning back to "the hope of the heathens" in their despair (RK 5.iv.825). Tolkien's remarkable use of "heathen" in this context only underscores the status of his "heroes under heaven" as parallel to Hrothgar and Beowulf, virtuous indeed but not saved, closer to the light than those who came before but still in darkness.[11] As Tolkien wrote in Letter 165, "the 'Third Age' was not a Christian world" (220).

We also find the fusion of mortal and immortal, of Elf and Man, to begin with as The Children of Ilúvatar, who are allies and friends though their paths are divergent, but also in the Half-elven and the descendants of Lúthien and Beren, who play a decisive role throughout the legendarium. Tolkien has thus redeemed the Elves, pulling them back from the brink of the abyss that awaits the race of Cain, which is where the *Beowulf*-poet had found, and left, them (Hillman et al., "Eldar" 51). We might also wonder if the fusion of mortal and immortal in the line of Lúthien marks an early stage in a line of thinking analogous to the revelation found in scripture that is, to a more complete fusion of mortal and immortal that will span the Fields of Time and the Timeless Halls, the Levels of Nature and of Grace (see below on page 245), and help to heal the hurts of Arda (see on pages 260–61).

Second, although in Arda, too, there is a shadow that Men and Elves cannot hope to defeat, its victory will not wait until the world ends but "will be swift and complete: so complete that none can foresee the end of it while this world lasts" (RK 6.ix.879). The power of the Ring, moreover, acts as a bridge between the monsters and us, threatening to reveal that we, too, are or can easily become the monsters we fight. In "One Ring to bring them all and in the darkness bind them," the word *them* refers first and most obviously to the power of the One over the other rings but also to the purposed dominance of the One over those who wield the others. In the darkness there can be orcs and worse on both sides.[12]

Finally, to prevent Sauron's otherwise inevitable domination of the world with or without the Ring, Providence takes a hand, orchestrating "chance" events and meetings, so that in the critical moment the pity of Bilbo, not the power of the One Ring, *rules* the fate of many.[13] We must not, however, view that pity too narrowly. For it does not just allow Gollum to be alive to take the Ring from Frodo. It puts the Ring in Frodo's hands in the first place, which necessarily ends in Frodo's claiming the Ring for his own. This claim lifts Gollum beyond the limits of his starved and ruined strength, enabling him to best Frodo, who had handily defeated him only minutes earlier and whom we might expect to have even greater power over Gollum now in the Sammath Naur than he has ever had before. The threat Frodo had made outside the Black Gate that, wearing the Ring, he could successfully command Gollum to hurl himself into the fire, now seems just another self-deceit under the Ring's influence. It shows how fathomless Frodo's deception of himself in the Morgul Vale was, to think that "not yet" adequately described how far from ready to face the Witch-king he was.

This stunning double reversal, in which Frodo's will—his intention—is overcome and he falls (however briefly) into evil and in which Gollum's actions are the best thing that could actually happen, both fulfills the promise Gandalf saw in Bilbo's pity and confirms the certainty of failure he perceived in his own. The deciding factor is that Bilbo and Frodo were "*meant* to find" (and bear) "the Ring, and *not* by its maker" (FR 1.ii.56). Even if Frodo the character does not understand what Gandalf is suggesting, the narrator does. Through a grand and subtle design Eru Ilúvatar has intervened not to fight the darkness for his Children but, indispensably, to shepherd the eucatastrophe that Frodo, Gollum, and Sam together bring about on Mount Doom, a eucatastrophe that arises as much from who they are individually at that moment as from the will of Ilúvatar.

Such an intervention is missing from the world of the noble pagans of *Beowulf,* though not from the world of the Christian poet and his Christian audience, not at least as Tolkien sees it. For in his view, evangelium begins and ends in eucatastrophe, which "denies (in the face of much evidence if you will) universal final defeat, and in so far is *evangelium,* giving a fleeting glimpse of Joy, Joy beyond the walls of the world, poignant as grief" (OFS ¶ 99, p. 75). "The birth of Christ is the eucatastrophe of Man's history. The Resurrection is the eucatastrophe of the story of the Incarnation. This story begins and ends in joy" (¶ 104, p. 78).

The phrase "universal final defeat" should recall our thoughts to the *Beowulf* essay. There, too, Tolkien made a connection between this notion and the concept that the evangelium meant the story could end otherwise, and also "beyond the walls of the world." Victory or defeat within time matter little sub specie aeternitatis: "the real battle is between the soul and its adversaries" (M&C 22). The "sufficient tragedy" of Man, which in *Beowulf: The Monsters and the Critics* Tolkien identifies as the theme of *Beowulf,* finds its complement only in *On Fairy-stories,* where Tolkien propounds eucatastrophe as the sine qua non of evangelium, and that eucatastrophe is itself evangelium to the extent that it denies the tragedy of Man (18).

The gospel then is not just a fairy story come true. It is the reason fairy stories end in eucatastrophe. For they reflect the truth of the original fairy story, the evangelium. That a man of such deep faith argues thus attests the fundamental consequence this truth holds for him and for his work. Through it, faith informs art and art faith. Whether we take Middle-earth as meant to be a fictional or a historical antecedent to the history we know matters little. As a Roman Catholic, Tolkien was not required to believe that the stories of Genesis and Exodus, for example, were literally true, nor was truth of this kind essential to their relevance and interpretation. Typologically, Eru's intervention in the Tale of the Ring could serve as another, even earlier, antecedent to God's intervention in the evangelium.

However, just as every Bible story that can be read as a type has a life of its own, so, too, does Tolkien's. Without help, there is no hope of defeating the monsters who seek to dominate or destroy us here, no hope of winning the eternal spiritual battle beyond the Fields of Time, no hope of prevailing against Sauron, no hope of resisting the Ring, no hope of conquering Death or Time. Without help, moreover, we will ourselves become the monsters because the power of the Ring also suggests that this tale could end differently. For using the Ring would not just make possible Sauron's overthrow but would also necessitate his replacement. Ironically, a victory by means of the Ring would be just such a refutation as the perfect, hopeless courage of the long defeat denies.

By taking what the *Beowulf*-poet provided and aligning it with the Incarnation and the Resurrection through eucatastrophe, Tolkien created in his Secondary World an "analogy of revelation," as Northrop Frye would term it: "In the mythical mode the encyclopaedic form is the sacred scripture, and in other modes we should expect to find encyclopaedic forms which constitute a series of increasingly human *analogies* of mythical or scriptural revelation" (56).[14] Glen Robert Gill is right to point this out (269), adding that Frye's approach allows us to resolve the paradox noted by Shippey, namely that a work so "fundamentally religious" as *The Lord of the Rings* "contains within it hints of the Christian message, but refuses just to repeat it," and "the whole story furthermore aspires in places to mythic meaning.... The aspiration is limited only by Tolkien's refusal to reach out to, to do more than hint at ... 'true myth,' or gospel, or revelation, or ... *evangelium*" (*Author* 210, 222–23). Eucatastrophe permits us that limited hint of revelation, that "piercing glimpse of joy" (*OFS* ¶ 101, p. 76) which may be all that a fairy-story can bear, as Shippey (*Author* 223) concludes. For it "rends indeed the very web of story" (*OFS* ¶ 101, p. 76).

The analogy of revelation in *The Lord of the Rings* brings us to Pity just as revelation proper does in scripture. Its manifestation may be different, but the lesson is the same. When considering the failure of Frodo's strength on Mount Doom and the eucatastrophe that completes his Quest, Tolkien indicates in Letter 246 that we must not "forget that strange element in the World that we call Pity or Mercy, which is also an absolute requirement in moral judgement (since it is present in the Divine nature). In its highest exercise it belongs to God" (326). Note the beautifully inclusive *or* that holds Pity and Mercy to be two sides of the same coin, and the *strange* that marks these qualities as foreign to our world, yet also present because of their presence *in the Divine nature; strange,* too, because of the difficulty of exercising judgement morally, by tempering the just punishment of our deserts with Pity and Mercy. Gandalf tried to teach Frodo this from the first, but until Frodo suffered himself and saw Gollum all he could do was insist on the death Gollum deserved for his crimes.

Note, too, Tolkien's capitalization of Pity and Mercy here, which reproduces Gandalf's usage in "The Shadow of the Past." Gandalf and Tolkien are talking of a Pity and Mercy that, even as human pity and mercy, long remain beyond Frodo's grasp. We see his lack of understanding even in the moment he comes to pity Gollum. Remembering Gandalf's words to him as he looks down on a Gollum entirely at his mercy, Frodo thinks Gandalf was speaking of a pity and a mercy far more ordinary than the Pity and Mercy the old wizard meant (TT 4.i.615). For Gandalf, the pupil of Nienna, this was another moment when he could not put what he meant any more plainly (see also FR 1.ii.55). Frodo could not "hear" the capital letters at that moment, but obviously the narrator does, a perception which has added weight if the narrator is Frodo. He has suffered into enough wisdom "to perceive the complexity of any given situation in Time, in which an absolute ideal is enmeshed" (*Letters* no. 246, p. 326). He can now see the difficulties posed by the coming together of Justice, Pity and Mercy, and Healing in the cases of Gollum and Saruman. If Frodo is at a loss to solve the claims of these ideals, he can at least forgive Gollum and show mercy to Saruman in the hope he will find healing.

Nor is Frodo the only one in the legendarium to weigh such concerns. For in "Laws and Customs among the Eldar," the Valar do so as they try to sort out the marriage of Finwë and Miriel. Though written several years after the publication of *The Lord of the Rings* (Morgoth 304), this text presents statements of Manwë and Nienna that substantially agree with, and shed light on, the positions Gandalf took in "The Shadow of the Past" about what Gollum deserved, why he should be pitied and spared, and how there was still some hope that he might be healed. Healing, moreover, now also capitalized, is explicitly linked to Justice and Pity.

> "In this matter [said Manwë] ye must not forget that you deal with Arda Marred—out of which ye brought the Eldar. Neither must ye forget that in Arda Marred Justice is not Healing. Healing cometh only by suffering and patience, and maketh no demand, not even for Justice. Justice worketh only within the bonds of things as they are, accepting the marring of Arda Marred, and therefore though Justice is itself good and desireth no further evil, it can but perpetuate the evil that was, and doth not prevent it from the bearing of fruit in sorrow."
> (239)

> "In the use of Justice there must be Pity, [said Nienna] which is the consideration of the singleness of each that cometh under Justice."
> (241)

For Gandalf or Frodo then to have given Gollum the death he justly deserved would not only have obviously precluded any possibility of healing but would have allowed new evil to arise from the old. Just as it was for the Valar considering the problem of Finwë and Miriel, for Gandalf and Frodo the condemnations of Gollum and Saruman, however legitimate in terms of Justice, would be inadequate in terms of Healing.[15] For Ilúvatar, however, Justice and Mercy may become one. As Amy Amendt-Radeuge points out in *The Sweet and the Bitter*, not only is Gollum's fall into the Cracks of Doom with the Ring a just punishment for his crimes, but it also "ends a life that has gone on too long, that has lost all its meaning and purpose, and breaks the circle of enslavement and betrayal which has held Gollum for so long. 'Deserves death' is not always an indictment" (43). Tolkien would seem to agree about Gollum, "over whom the Ring that he no longer possesses has a power that nothing but Death could heal" (Hammond and Scull quote this in *RC* 747).[16]

Thus, if in a fallen world Justice itself, equally regardless of its good intent and the deserts of evildoers, avails nothing against Evil, and if incarnate beings cannot conquer evil, the Pity and Mercy that can do so must come from beyond Arda Marred. Divine Pity and Mercy are as much a part of revelation as of Tolkien's "analogy of revelation." They are the difference between Gandalf's "the Ring-bearer has fulfilled his Quest" and Denethor's "we are all to burn" as well as between the redemption of sins and the hope of the heathens (RK 5.iv.949, vii.850). Yet, a crucial distinction remains. In *The Lord of the Rings* divine intervention is largely anonymous and indirect, operating through this or that "chance-meeting, as we say in Middle-earth" or through the Ring falling out of Gollum's pocket at just the right time and place for it to be found by the "unlikeliest person imaginable" (*UT* 326; *FR* 1.ii.55). Even the most obvious direct intervention—Gandalf's return from death—is glossed over in the passive voice.[17] By contrast, no intervention could be more direct and personal than the Incarnation of Christ, no conquest of Evil and Death more complete than the Resurrection. Tolkien is not telling that tale, nor would he: "The Incarnation of God is *infinitely* greater than anything I would dare to write" (*Letters* no. 181, p. 237).

Yet, as a devoted Roman Catholic, Tolkien would have heard God's Mercy prominently invoked in the Kyrie every time he attended Mass, and he would have joined in that ancient responsorial invocation: κύριε, ἐλέησον—kyrie, eleison—Lord, have mercy. "In Christianity," as David Konstan notes in the chapter on Divine Pity in his *Pity Transformed,* "no formula is more familiar than [this] invocation . . . addressed to Jesus" (105) To someone as alive to language and his faith as Tolkien was, the survival of the Kyrie in Greek from the early centuries of the Church into the Latin Mass of the twentieth century would not have escaped his notice, nor would he have overlooked the central importance this survival suggests for the role of God's Pity and Mercy in the world.[18] In singling out Pity and Mercy in "The Shadow of the Past," in Letter 246, and in "Laws and Customs among the Eldar," Tolkien is affirming for his subcreation what is implicit in the Kyrie and explicit, for example, in Aquinas who states that Mercy is "proper to God" and arises from his love for us (II-II q. 30, arts. 2, 4).

He is also allowing that Divine Pity and Mercy need not have worked the same in all times and places, that is, with a focus on Redemption and Forgiveness and Life Everlasting.[19] Though the contest on the Fields of Time may be less important than the spiritual battle, it is not without value. Nothing in *The Lord of the Rings* or elsewhere in the legendarium suggests that Tolkien considered it unimportant to fight the evils of this world. Quite the contrary, in fact. The strong feelings and convictions he expresses elsewhere about the two world wars and other evils show that it would be foolish to think he saw the spiritual battle alone as worth fighting.[20] Moreover, the questions of Power and Death and Immortality that Tolkien thought *The Lord of the Rings* had as its theme hold the stage in this world, not the next. It is this world in which Men wish to remain and this world the Elves wish to preserve, and it is these two completely intelligible desires that expose them to the corruption of power vast enough to seem to offer solutions to death and immortality. Pity alone can defend us against corruption of this kind.

In his essential study, *Pagan Saints in Middle-earth,* Claudio Testi persuasively argues that the pagan and Christian elements in the legendarium are, paradoxically, in harmony with each other. To this end Testi identifies "two conceptual levels in defining the structural framework of the *Legendarium,*" that is, Nature and Grace (67). On the Level of Nature is all that "rational creatures" are capable of "thanks exclusively to their own innate capacities and abilities"; on the Level of Grace are the "'gifts' or certain revealed truths...that would be impossible [for Man] to obtain solely with his natural abilities" (68). The discreet interventions of Divine Pity and Mercy seem to most witnesses internal to the story to operate on the Level of Nature but in truth have their origin on the Level of Grace, as some like Gandalf and Elrond descry. When the Level of Nature and the Level of Grace intersect, eucatastrophe occurs.

In a note written long after *The Lord of the Rings,* but edited and published only recently by Carl F. Hostetter, Tolkien maps out the interplay of "Fate (or Eru's plan)" and Free Will between these levels in the very context—that is, Bilbo and Frodo and the One Ring—where he has also stressed the critical importance of Pity and Mercy:

> The Downfall of Númenor was "a miracle" as we might say, or as [the Eldar said] a direct action of Eru within time that altered the previous scheme for all remaining time. They would probably also have said that Bilbo was "fated" to find the Ring, but not necessarily to surrender it; and then if Bilbo surrendered it Frodo was fated to go on his mission, but not necessarily to destroy the Ring—which in fact he did not do. They would have added that if the downfall of Sauron and the destruction of the Ring was part of Fate (or Eru's Plan) then if Bilbo had retained the Ring and refused to surrender it, some other means would have arisen by which Sauron was frustrated. Just as when Frodo's will proved in the end inadequate, a means for the Ring's destruction immediately appeared—being kept in reserve by Eru as it were.
> ("Fate" 185; see also 187n1)

Hostetter has pointed out that Tolkien set down these comments no earlier than 1968 (187n1). Letter 181, however, which Tolkien drafted early in 1956, shows that Tolkien had been thinking in very much these terms for quite some time. "But the One retains all ultimate authority, and (or so it seems as viewed in serial time) reserves the right to intrude the finger of God into the story: that is to produce realities which could not be deduced even from a complete knowledge of the previous past, but which being real become part of the effective past for all subsequent time (a possible definition of a 'miracle')" (235). Above I posited that eucatastrophe arises from the intersection of the Level of Grace and the Level of Nature. In the paragraph just quoted we see this phenomenon delineated as "'a miracle,' as we might say," and as the Eldar would have understood it within the legendarium. Aquinas said that "grace does not destroy nature, but perfects it." He does so by way of explaining the idea that the reason we possess of our very nature should serve faith: "Yet sacred teaching employs even human reason, not indeed to put Faith to the proof, because through this the merit of Faith would be destroyed; but to make manifest other matters which are handed down in this teaching. For since Grace does not destroy nature, but perfects it, it is fitting that natural reason serve Faith; just as the natural inclination of the will bows down to Charity" (1.1.8 ad 2). In the same way eucatastrophe as evangelium does not nullify legend but hallows it. The Oracles did not all fall silent with Christ's birth, as Milton had it. Rather, Vergil's Eclogue 4 becomes a prophecy of the Incarnation. The story of Beowulf, because the poet builds into its telling his and his audience's awareness of the eucatastrophe that the Spear-Danes and Geats never know, becomes an elegiac tale told by and for Christians that illustrates how their pagan ancestors battled on undaunted against the fall of a night that only Christ could overcome. The poet and his audience look on from a world so transformed by evangelium that, as Fred Robinson has shown, old pagan words with new Christian meanings superimposed upon them open the sad, ironic distance between the damned but noble heathens of the past and their heaven-bound redeemed descendants (29–59).[21] Thus, eucatastrophe as evangelium casts its light even into the heathen darkness, making manifest other truths which the evangelium also illuminates. Among these truths is Death, the *Beowulf*-poet's theme, which the layering of Christian and pagan perspectives reveals in chiaroscuro, a "little circle of light" in which the *hæleð under heofenum* are besieged by darkness (*M&C* 19).

PERFECT IN ITS HOPELESSNESS

I noted above (on page 244) that in *The Lord of the Rings*, Tolkien is not telling a tale of open and direct divine intervention like that which we find in the evangelium. Nevertheless, into the background of this story of indirect intervention he weaves a different story of direct and open intervention against evil, namely the "Akallabêth" in *The Silmarillion*, which recounts the drowning of Númenor three thousand years earlier.[22] The perception of depth established by references to the past, as almost always in *The Lord of the Rings*, communicates a meaningful connection between past and present. The story of Frodo and that of Númenor's downfall only seem different stories; so, too, the Tale of Lúthien Tinúviel, as Aragorn and Sam both know well (FR 1.xi.191–94; TT 4.viii.711). Questions of Death and Immortality run through this tale from its beginning with Beren and Lúthien to its putative end with Aragorn and Arwen.

For corrupted by their fear of Death and seduced by Sauron's promise of life everlasting to those who worshipped Melkor, the Númenóreans brought the wrath of Ilúvatar down on themselves when they attempted to wrest Immortality from the inhabitants of the Blessed Realm. Númenor's destruction, with its evocation of both the biblical flood and Plato's pagan myth of Atlantis, is an example of "*dyscatastrophe*, of sorrow and failure: the possibility of [which] is necessary to the joy of deliverance" (*OFS* ¶ 99, p. 75). This dyscatastrophe, however, which quite literally changes the shape and nature of the world, also brings deliverance (if not joy) to the Faithful, the Númenóreans who rejected the heathen turn their people had taken and so received Mercy. For a great wind out of the West blows their ships to safety in Middle-earth. In the eucatastrophe of Mount Doom, we see its mirror image. For the cloud of darkness that towers up like a wave from Mordor in that moment briefly seems about to visit similar destruction on the Men of the West. So it appears from the battlefield outside the Morannon, and Faramir, looking out from the walls of Minas Tirith far off, sees in it that "great dark wave climbing over the green lands and above the hills, and coming on, darkness unescapable" (RK 6.iv.948, v.962). But it is not. Again, a great wind arises from the West, not to deliver the faithful remnant as it had done an age before but to make clear by scattering the last impotent shadow of Sauron's evil that the darkness has already been escaped, and that the Shadow was, as Sam had perceived it, "in the end a small and passing thing" (6.ii.922).

Twice evoking, in the moment of his ultimate downfall, the Great Wave that drowned Númenor and killed Sauron—not to mention the Mouth of Sauron's sneer about "the downfallen West" (RK 5.x.889)—provides more than an artistic stroke suited to capture the characters' emotions at their crest, and more than a clever rhetorical antithesis to limn the balancing of the scales. It's even more than another reminder that Tales like that of Beren and Lúthien never end as tales. What it does is link two catastrophic interventions at opposite ends of a spectrum, the dyscatastrophic and direct intervention of Ilúvatar at the end of the Second Age, and the eucatastrophic and indirect intervention at the end of the Third. This link is implicit in the passage quoted above (on pages 245–46) from Letter 181 and Tolkien's comment published by Hostetter, which pair the miraculous alteration of the world by Eru in the Second Age and the subtler touch of his hand in the Third.[23]

We also saw that Tolkien believed the eucatastrophe of fairy stories was so powerful because it partook of the truth revealed through the eucatastrophes that begin and end the evangelium, that is, the Incarnation and the Resurrection of Christ. Between the dyscatastrophe and the eucatastrophe we find paired here I would argue that there is a similar connection, which two passages of the famous Letter 131, dated 1951, disclose.

> [The Second Age] ends with the overthrow of Sauron and destruction of *the second visible incarnation of evil*. But at a cost, and with one disastrous mistake. Gil-galad and Elendil are slain in the act of slaying Sauron. Isildur, Elendil's son, cuts the ring from Sauron's hand, and his power departs, and his spirit flees into the shadows. But the evil begins to work. Isildur claims the Ring as his own.
> (p. 157, emphasis mine)

> [In the Third Age w]e are to see the overthrow of *the last Incarnation of Evil*, the unmaking of the Ring, the final departure of the Elves, and the return in majesty of the true King, to take over the Dominion of Men, inheriting all that can be transmitted of Elfdom in his high marriage with Arwen daughter of Elrond, as well as the lineal royalty of Númenor.
> (p. 160, emphasis mine)

An incarnation is as much at the heart of this story as the story of the evangelium; only here it is the "Incarnation of Evil" in Sauron, who brings about a Second Fall of Man by exploiting Men's fear of Death, which is itself a result of the First Fall under the influence of Morgoth (evil's first incarnation). In the first version of "The Fall of Númenor," Sauron even preaches a kind of gospel of Melkor: "[He] preached a message of deliverance, and he prophesied the second coming of Morgoth. . . . [He] promised them undying life and lordship of the earth" (*Lost* 15). The preaching of the dysangelium even continues at greater length in the second version with Sauron's Sermon on the Mount (26). The Second Fall, however, goes beyond disobedience and even apostasy. It is insurrection. Even so, the terrible wrath that Númenor brings down on itself is not absent of Pity and Mercy to rule the fate of many, in the short and long term. For, as we know, the Faithful escape to Middle-earth, where together with the Elves they overthrow and kill Sauron, himself newly reincarnated after his death in the drowning of Númenor. More than that, the Númenóreans who assailed the Undying Lands did not die—"it is said"—but "lie imprisoned" beneath the mountains of Aman until the Dagor Dagorath, the Last Battle on the Fields of Time (*Lost* 16; *S* 279).[24] While the part they will play is undisclosed, sleeping armies and sleeping kings are commonly expected to return in their people's darkest hour to defend them against evil.[25] Like the Dead Men of Dunharrow, who also, contrary to the nature of Men, remain bound within the Circles of the World for their transgressions, their punishment contains the opportunity for repentance and amends.

The long, long perspective before us in Tolkien's description of the succession of ages gives way in the narrative of *The Lord of the Rings* to a focus on the single consequential moments in which Pity and Error shift the balance. With "one disastrous mistake," that is, taking the Ring for his own instead of destroying it, Isildur changes the fate of the world and marks his own story as tragic (*Letters* no. 131 p. 157). That he presses his claim to the Ring as a matter of justice for the deaths of his father and brother does not just recall the troublous mortal conviction that Death was not the Gift to Men the Eldar said it was; it should also remind us of Gandalf's insistence to Frodo that our inability to restore life to those who do not deserve death must give us pause when judging those who do. Isildur's insistence on justice in the form of weregild, moreover, leads to new evil by allowing Sauron to reincarnate once more, and augurs darkly for Isildur himself since *weregild* now joins *birthday present*, *I "won" it*, and *I found it* as dubious grounds for a claim of ownership. It may also have kept fresh the pain Isildur had felt since touching the Ring, if the limited harm Bilbo suffered because of the pity with which he began his possession of it offers any guidance. The connections between Pity, Mercy, Justice, and Healing argue forcefully that it does. In a larger sense, even the failure to destroy the Ring because of justice may well have also prevented the Three Elven Rings from healing the hurts of the world as the Elves speculated they might be able to do if the One were no more (FR 2.ii.268).

With Isildur's mistake, we are brought back down from what we might call the miraculous to the level of individual choices, virtues, and failures that rule the fate of many because of the way they fit in with Eru's plan. That mistake, of course, receives ample attention from Gandalf, Elrond, and Aragorn at the council, and it offers far more than a lesson in the history and provenance of the One Ring. For Isildur, Elrond suggests death was the better outcome (FR 2.ii.243). When Gandalf quotes Isildur's scroll, he establishes more than the identity of the Ring. The disclosure that Isildur held the Ring fair though he knew it was evil and thought it "precious ... though I buy it with great pain" corroborates the judgement of Elrond (2.ii.253). To Aragorn as Isildur's heir his true inheritance is not the Ring, which he refuses, but "to repair Isildur's fault" (2.ii.251). Tolkien thus establishes the starting point for the crucial narrative of the Third Age and expresses it in terms we have seen before—the decision of a moment that changes the fate of the world and the mistake, the *hamartia,* that marks the story of Isildur as tragic.

The Council of Elrond, to which those present have been "called, I say, though I have not called you to me" in order to "find counsel for the peril of the world," seeks to harmonize moral choice—the expression of the will—with Providence or Eru's plan (FR 2.ii.242). It replays with a different result the debate Elrond and Círdan must have had, however briefly, with Isildur on the slopes of Mount Doom three thousand years earlier. Frodo's "I will take the Ring," Isildur's "this I will have as weregild," Elrond's "I will not take the Ring to wield it," and Gandalf's "Nor [will] I" are all moral choices to be weighed together in the scales of this Council, as is Aragorn's "it does not belong to either of us" (FR 2.ii.270, 243, 267, 246). Isildur "took [the Ring] for his own"; Frodo takes it as "burden" (1.ii.52, 2.ii.243, 270). As we have seen, however, the line between "the Ring is my burden" and "the Ring is mine" cannot in the end be maintained. Yet choosing "freely" to accept the Ring as a burden brings the expression of the will into sufficient harmony with Providence to "send the Ring *to* the Fire," as Elrond puts it, at which point Providence will see to it that it goes *into* the Fire (2.ii.267, emphasis mine).

Elrond's choice of preposition here seems almost prescient, given Frodo's failure at Mount Doom, which in that moment Frodo expressly declares to be his choice (RK 6.iii.945). Sending the Ring "to the Fire" dovetails nicely with Frodo's use of "into the Fire," since he is little inclined to believe he will get the Ring "into the Fire" (TT 4.ii.624; see also RK 6.iii.939). He comes to have no doubt, however, that, wearing the Ring, he can command Gollum "to cast [himself] into the Fire" or even cast him "into the Fire" himself (TT 4.iii.640; RK 6.iii.944). The triumph of Frodo's delusion of command and his movement beyond pity are revealed together and directly precede his recasting his inability to put the Ring "into the Fire" as his free choice, even though it has long been evident that he could not directly act to harm it (FR 1.ii.60). With his knowledge of Isildur's choice and Frodo's failure even to cast the Ring into his useless hearth, Elrond's phrasing may in the end be more discreet than prescient.

Elrond's remarks at the council about Frodo's choice to take the Ring are hedged with four conditional statements in nine sentences. In these, he questions his own understanding of what he has heard and the conclusion he has reached based on his understanding; he muses on the ironic paradoxes of wisdom; and he declares the necessity of free choice to the correctness of Frodo's decision. His use of *task* and *burden* emphasizes the difficulty and, more importantly, the only useful attitude Frodo could have toward taking the Ring. Yet Elrond recalls all too well how badly Isildur had chosen, Ring in hand. Could anyone in Middle-earth besides Bombadil make a wholly free choice while in possession of the Ring? Elrond's belief that Providence has called them together does not guarantee that they will make the correct decision about what to do with the Ring. Boromir asks: "Why should we not think that the Great Ring has come into our hands to serve us in the very hour of need?" (FR 2.ii.267). And Boromir's question is entirely reasonable, because the Ring has done precisely that. Its coming *is* providential, but that providence will serve the enemies of Sauron only if they reject the power that could give them victory.[26]

Nor does Elrond's confidence that something greater is at work remove his fears and doubts about the plan to destroy it. This is only natural, because on the Level of Nature the plan is hopeless folly. As with pity, however, which affords no defense against the Ring on this level, but which is answered by Pity from the Level of Grace, the foolish hope of destroying the Ring instead of using it against Sauron or losing it to him is answered by a greater Hope, that somehow things will turn out right if they make the morally right choice instead of the merely logical or expedient one, choices such as we see Aragorn making in Rohan and Sam at Cirith Ungol. This is the "encouraging thought" Gandalf finds hidden in Bilbo's discovery of the Ring.

This greater Hope is, of course, what they call *estel* in Middle-earth. In the "Athrabeth Finrod ah Andreth," Finrod describes it as a "trust" "founded deeper" than *amdir*, the ordinary hope that is "an expectation of good, which though uncertain has some foundation in what is known" (*Morgoth* 320). *Estel* is thus a certainty founded on things not seen. Outside the legendarium

Tolkien may well have called this "faith," since it closely resembles what the author of the Letter to the Hebrews says: "῎Εστι δὲ πίστις ἐλπιζομένων ὑπόστασις, πραγμάτων ἔλεγχος οὐ βλεπομένων." "Faith is the substance of things hoped for, the evidence of things not seen" (KJV 11.1). "Trust" is of course also a common rendering of πίστις (*pistis*), and Austin M. Freeman has recently argued with some force that it is the better English translation (157).[27] The word ὑπόστασις (*hypostasis*), moreover, suggests those deeper foundations to which Finrod refers. Its literal meaning, "as an act, standing under, supporting" grows into "foundation," into "confidence," and into the "substance" out of which something is made (Liddell et al. 1895). "Faith" or "Trust" is also a matter of Will, and therefore of choice, which is the sharp edge of the knife when confronting a power that corrupts the will of the possessor.[28]

The Council of Elrond establishes itself on the foundation of Eru's plan—a plan that is never explicit, not implied but to be inferred—and seeks a path forward trusting that "it is so ordered" that they do so despite the peril inherent in anyone taking the Ring. This testifies both to the interaction of Divine intervention and Free Will necessary to the plan and to the domination of all other wills, which is the final cause of the One Ring.

Yet rejecting a power great enough to challenge Death and Time while exposing himself to it, as Frodo does, and embracing pity and folly, no matter what pain or sacrifice doing so entails, prepares the way for him to become what he must become to be a sufficient instrument of Providence. I say *way* advisedly, as in *road*, which is among the most common metaphors in *The Lord of the Rings*. Elrond embraces it wholeheartedly even before Frodo asserts that he does "not know the way" and Elrond replies that if he does "find a way, no one will" (FR 2.ii.270). The literal roads and routes already discussed and rejected give way to a dozen references explicit and implicit to the road or way they must take in the ten sentences Elrond utters culminating in "We must send the Ring to the Fire" (2.ii.267).

With these words about the *way* and the *road* Elrond expresses not only his uncertainty about what will happen if the Ring-bearer gets the Ring that far, but his *trust*, or *estel*, that freely choosing this road is as correct a choice for the council as Frodo's freely choosing to accept this burden is for him. The unforeseen road can only have an unforetold end, but "trust" is "the proof of things not seen." In his commentary on Hebrews 11.1, William Lane argues persuasively for a clearer and more powerful understanding of the Greek: "*Now faith celebrates the objective reality [of the blessings] for which we hope, the demonstration of events as yet unseen.*"[29]

Free choice stands in the same relation to domination as "the Ring is my burden" stands to "the Ring is mine." At the heart of the choices made at the council, as Tolkien came to see from reading his own work, lies the acceptance of Death for Men and of Fading for the Elves. Men will die and leave the world; Elves will live on, but will fade with the world until the end when all that was is no more than memory. These things will, of course, happen whether Elves and Men accept them or not. While Galadriel's statement of her choice is famous (FR 2.vii.364), Aragorn's declaration of his own in "The Tale of Aragorn and Arwen" is somewhat less so: "Now, *I will* sleep," and "let us not be overthrown at the last test" (RK App. A I.v.1062, emphasis mine). Yet both are significant for them and their people. Rejecting the Ring allowed Aragorn and Galadriel to remain who they were. At the same time, Lothlórien is borne back into the past, and the Elder Days come to an end with the passing of their "latest king" (FR 2.viii.376; RK App. A I.v.1062). Later ages will need no wizard or elf-lord or King of Men with a star on his brow, because evil will no longer be incarnate in Middle-earth. While Ilúvatar's Children will still struggle with the evil and temptation to it that they find within their own hearts, the unwinnable contest on the Fields of Time has been won.

This helps explain a passage I have always struggled to understand. In Lothlórien, Haldir asks Merry to tell him about the Grey Havens and the Sea. Merry's confession that he has never before been beyond the borders of the Shire prompts a statement about the world from Haldir which is as Elven in its beauty as it is in its ambiguity: "The world is indeed full of peril, and in it there are many dark places; but still there is much that is fair, and though in all lands love is now mingled with grief, it grows perhaps the greater" (FR 2.vi.349). Through relinquishing "the fair" for themselves in order to overcome the Shadow for everyone, the world "grows perhaps the greater." Galadriel later declares that love and regret will not stop the Elves from "cast[ing] all away" so that "what should be shall be" (2.vii.364). Similarly, Frodo saves the Shire and more than the Shire for others, while losing it for himself. Aragorn, "the last of the Númenóreans," lays down his life when he should, giving back the gift as he rejects the Shadow and the Twilight one last time and lets go what he loves most, trusting that there will be more than memory. In the mingling of love and grief the world becomes the greater (RK App. A I.v.1062).

The pity of Bilbo and the Divine Pity that answered it made this possible. Gandalf urged it on Frodo from the beginning. Like Elrond, he avoided being explicit about the role of Providence, employing the "divine passive" to suggest agency but name no names—"I can put it no plainer than by saying that Bilbo was *meant* to find the Ring, and *not* by its maker" (FR 1.ii.56).[30] Frodo's failure to understand what Gandalf is driving at highlights the freedom of choice he enjoys in first rejecting and then embracing claims of pity, just as his choosing to take the Ring to the Fire does, despite his fear and ignorance of what he is getting himself into, despite his temptation and desire for the Ring, and finally despite his enduring conviction that he will not survive his Quest even if he somehow manages to get the Ring into the Fire. While the hand of Ilúvatar or the Valar remains hidden—and it is usually impossible to tell which is acting given chance and the divine passive—free will has more room to choose within the parameters of the circumstances Chance has arranged.[31]

THE PITY OF ARWEN AND THE DOOM OF ELVES AND MEN

The Lord of the Rings' final moment of pity comes in "The Tale of Aragorn and Arwen." In Letter 181 Tolkien identifies it as "part of the essential story," though told only in the appendices because the narrative proper centers on the hobbits, "that is, primarily a study of the ennoblement (or sanctification) of the humble" (237). That ennoblement begins, however, with the revelation of the pity of Bilbo, which recontextualizes *The Hobbit* and serves as a counterpoint to the pity of Arwen. Both are essential but outside the main narrative of *The Lord of the Rings*. We saw Arwen's pity first in Minas Tirith, when she offered Frodo the possibility of healing beyond the sea. That was the pity of one person who had twice witnessed the irremediable pain of another, both Frodo's and that of Celebrían, her mother, and who saw that healing for them could only be found elsewhere than in Middle-earth. It was not just the sons of Elrond who never forgot the sufferings of their mother (FR 2.i.227).

The pity she discovers in "The Tale of Aragorn and Arwen" is of another order, as her eyes open to the reality of what is, "as the Eldar say, the gift of the One to Men" (RK App. A I.v.1063). In her beloved's imminent death, Arwen confronts only now "the loss and the silence" she judges the Doom of Men to be, and puts on their sorrow as she puts on their Mortality. She exchanges the scorn she had felt toward "wicked fools" for a Pity that embraces an entire fallen world. It is all too easy to see despair in Arwen's devastating sorrow, but that would be to misunderstand her. As Aragorn dies, she calls him by his elvish name, "Estel! Estel!" In grief, she cries out, yes, and in pain—how could she not?—but not in despair. Anna Vaninskaya, noting that "Arwen's final cry is 'Hope!'" has called this "a desperate cry, more appeal than assurance, an invocation" and said that "[Arwen's] ability to hope seems sure to follow" Aragorn into death (172). "So it seems," I would reply with Aragorn. But it is not so. For Arwen's last words, however grief-stricken, however stunned with sorrow, once more embrace the Choice of Lúthien with its promise of release from bondage, and her last deeds answer his: "'So it seems,' he said. 'But let us not be overthrown at the final test, who of old renounced the Shadow and the Ring. In sorrow we must go, but not in despair. Behold! we are not bound for ever to the circles of the world, and beyond them is more than memory, Farewell!'" (*RK* App. A I.v.1063). Thus then, just as he had done, she bids farewell to her son and daughters. She returns to Lothlórien, to Cerin Amroth, where many years earlier she and Aragorn had passed the test and pledged their love and their lives to each other, renouncing alike the Shadow and the Twilight (App. A I.v.1060). Her return to this place reaffirms that choice. She shall no more live on without Aragorn than Lúthien did without Beren. Nor would she wish to. Lothlórien is also "the heart of Elvendom on earth," where the Elder Days "still lived on in the waking world," or so it had been before time swept it away and Galadriel and Celeborn departed (*FR* 2.vi.352, 349). That was the price of passing the tests Galadriel and Arwen faced. It was a world that had to be allowed to fade into only memory or turned away from to look for more than memory. For the "Evenstar of her people" to set in the now springless Winter of Lothlórien is also fitting (*RK* App. A I.v.1059). It is a reaffirmation of more than the choice Arwen had made. It declares the correctness of the choice the Elves had made, to reject Sauron and all the empty promises of power, whether to dominate the wills of others or to hold back time and preserve what was meant to fade within time. It is to "cast all away rather than submit" (*FR* 2.vii.365). All except Hope, perhaps. If, as Anna Vaninskaya has told us, Galadriel's "acceptance of the end of her time in Middle-earth is the Elvish equivalent of Aragorn's acceptance of his mortality," then Arwen Halfelven's laying down of her life in Lothlórien unites mortal and immortal in embracing the correct attitude toward the individual dooms of the Children of Ilúvatar (191).

Yet though Arwen's sorrow was not despair, we must allow it to have been profound. "The light of her eyes was quenched, and it seemed to her people that she had become cold and grey as nightfall in winter that comes without a star" (*RK* App. A I.v.1063).[32] In a letter written in 1963 Tolkien indicated that Arwen could have laid down her life at the same time as Aragorn did but was not yet ready to do so because she still viewed life from her inborn

Elven perspective.[33] The statement of the "Tale" that Arwen "was not yet weary of her days" is weighty indeed (*RK* App A I.v.1062). Such feelings would have only increased her dismay when Aragorn declared his intentions and quickened the bitterness of her recognition that clinging to life did not make Men the merely "wicked fools" she had supposed them to be. Her unwillingness to let go of life just yet also helps to make sense of something Aragorn says just before the end (quoted on page 255). He speaks of "the final test" and their previous renunciation of "the Shadow and the Ring." Now when they had pledged themselves to each other at Cerin Amroth, it was rather "the Shadow and the Twilight" they had rejected, and the substitution here of the Ring for the Twilight might seem to signal a curious shift in emphasis at so late a stage and in a moment Tolkien considers important. But it is not so. For Arwen has just declared to Aragorn her unwavering commitment to the life and death she chose when she embraced the doom of Lúthien; and if she will not or cannot now repent of that choice, she must take care to follow Lúthien in all her footsteps. It is Death *as a gift* he cautions her against rejecting now. Doing so led not only to the downfall of Númenor and the decline of Gondor and Arnor but also, even before that, to the undead horror that the Nine Rings had bestowed on mortal men doomed to die. Though the Rings are gone, the desires within mortals which made the power of the Rings such a trap remain. The desire for the One lingered still within Frodo. It was the most poisonous wound of them all (see on pages 229–30). It had left a persistent black mark on Bilbo and his memoirs, too. If Arwen now understands the desire that left Men seeming wicked fools to her, she is not thereby made immune to it, no more than Frodo for all his suffering and ennoblement was immune to regretting the loss of the Ring. The test, as Galadriel perceived even as she declared that she and Frodo had chosen, does not end. Arwen chooses wisely to let go of the gift, to stop possessing it, and so be free. If these phrases remind us of Gandalf's words to Bilbo about giving up the Ring, that should be no surprise (*FR* 1.i.34).

Thus, within a fading, desolate Lothlórien, a land whose Winter will never see another Spring Arwen's "green grave" remains "until the world is changed" (*FR* 2.viii.375). Here is a preservation that points to a future when the world will be changed and healed. Her evergreen grave works in counterpoint with the long incorrupt body of Aragorn, the ageless beauty of which looks both forward, confirming the truth of the hope he held out—that beyond Death was "more than memory"—and backward, evoking the wisdom of the Númenórean kings who "in glory undimmed before the world was broken" willingly gave back the gift.

If men of later days forget her entirely in the end, it shows only that they did not understand the greenness of her grave, which she chose both over an evergreen memory beyond the Sea and an embalmed memorial of regret in Minas Tirith. We may also doubt whether the claim that she was forgotten is as accurate as it is rhetorically affecting. For "The Tale of Aragorn and Arwen" was written by Barahir, grandson of Faramir and Éowyn, "some time after the passing of the King" in Fourth Age 120, but before Fourth Age 172 when Findegil finished making his copy of the Thain's Book, which included "The Tale of Aragorn and Arwen" (FR Pr. 14; RK App. B 1097–98). So short a span hardly justifies the Romantic melancholy of "and all the days of her life are utterly forgotten by men that come after" (RK App. A I.v.1063).

But memory is not given to mortal men doomed to die as it is to Elves (Morgoth 319). The promise of her green grave and of Aragorn's recapturing in Death the splendor of the faithful kings of Númenor is like that perceived by Legolas in Minas Tirith. When Gimli asserts that "the things that Men begin ... often fail of their promise," Legolas replies that even so they rarely "fail of their seed," which will rise again "unlooked-for" (RK 6.ix.872). Similarly, if we turn to Bombadil's sad reminiscence about the woman who wore the brooch he finds in the barrow along with the sword Merry will use against the Witchking, and if we recall the image he stirs in the minds of the hobbits of "the sons of forgotten kings," we shall see that being forgotten by the "heedless" does not strip "the things that Men begin" of their power or promise (FR 1.viii.146). In "The Tale of Aragorn and Arwen," an immortal once again chooses to accept the Doom of Men out of love and in defiance of evil, just as her ancestor Lúthien had done. The state of Aragorn's body long after Death surely argues that his view is correct, especially since it is neither a treacherous preservation such as the Ring conferred even as it devoured its victims nor a cosmetic preservation such as the false arts of embalming promise. Both of these seek to deny Death, but the preservation of Aragorn's long incorrupt body arises from accepting Death and giving back the gift. It is finally a sign, as we have already suspected, but a passage in *The Nature of Middle-earth* confirms that it is a "sign from Eru for the increase of hope" (273n).

It is the acceptance that *lif is læne*, the phrase Tolkien used to sum up "the deadly seriousness that begets the dignity of tone" found in *Beowulf* (*M&C* 19).[34] Life is transitory, impermanent, a gift on loan from God. The differences in perspective of Elf and Man do not alter the fact that the loan will nevertheless come due for them both (*Morgoth* 311–12). The life, whether measured in one century or ten thousand, must be given back. What is more, from Ilúvatar's transcendent perspective, from his eternal present outside the Fields of Time, all those loans come due at once, but this elusive perspective is the hardest of all for those within time to grasp.[35] In Arwen's return to Lothlórien and in her Death there we see the "mystery" of the Doom of Men and the "anguish" of the Doom of Elves accepted as they are and as they must be, a mingling of love and loss that makes the world greater, and a mingling, too, of Pity and Hope that will bring Recovery and Consolation (*Letters* no. 186, p. 246). As Aragorn saw, rejecting the power that the One Ring (or the Three) seemed to offer to challenge these dooms goes hand in hand with this acceptance. The Choice of Lúthien brings release from bondage; the choice of the Ring brings only enslavement, for oneself and others. The one promises to break the "chains of Death" which the other binds only more tightly around Elves and Men alike (*Letters*, no. 89, p. 100).

It is this acceptance, however, that keeps Arwen's grave green and allows Aragorn with a cry to direct our gaze beyond the transient to a time when the world will be changed. In the same way, Sam's acceptance of Frodo's departure across the Sea and his reenvisioning of Frodo's vision from the house of Bombadil directs our gaze to the fairy-tale ending Frodo could not have in the Shire. Giving Aragorn the name Estel and putting such bittersweet wordplay in the mouths of Arwen and Gilraen, his wife and his mother, as he departs from each of them for the last time in this world were among the very last of Tolkien's changes to "The Tale of Aragorn and Arwen," entered by hand into its final typescript.[36] Christopher Tolkien dates these changes to a time after the publication of *The Lord of the Rings* had become certain (*Peoples* vii, 253, 269–70). In fact, *The Return of the King* was already in proof, and its publication waited on Tolkien's completion of the appendixes in which, of course, "The Tale of Aragorn and Arwen" is found.[37] The lateness of changes by Tolkien argues the significance of the changes, a point well made by Nicholas Birns.[38] That these changes encourage the characters to look forward in connection with the theme of Death and Immortality further suggests the author might be doing the same and perhaps bidding us as readers to follow his gaze, as Aragorn had bidden Arwen to follow his.

Only a "high purpose of Doom" could bring mortal and immortal together in love and Death and what lies beyond (*Morgoth* 324).[39] At least that is the phrase Finrod Felagund employs in the "Athrabeth," the dramatic date of which is a half century before Beren and Lúthien meet, to describe what he sees as a necessary precondition for just such a union (*Morgoth* 324). His words may be prescient, but they offer no comfort in the moment to Andreth, the mortal who loves and is loved by his brother, Aegnor, in vain as it seems to them both. For it is the Doom of the Elves and the Doom of Men that keep them apart, and it is through a discussion of these separate dooms that Finrod and Andreth come to address her mutually unfulfilled love with Aegnor. All of this closely weaves the dooms of the individual mortals and immortals together with the dooms of their races:

> The real theme [of *The Lord of the Rings*] for me is about something much more permanent and difficult: Death and Immortality: the mystery of the love of the world in the hearts of a race "doomed" to leave and seemingly lose it; the anguish in the hearts of a race "doomed" not to leave it, until its whole evil-aroused story is complete. But if you have now read [*The Return of the King*] and the story of Aragorn, you will have perceived that.
> (*Letters* no. 186, p. 246)

The date of this letter, April 1956, locates this statement not long after Tolkien would have made the final changes to "The Tale of Aragorn and Arwen" and roughly contemporary with the earliest possible date in evidence for the "Athrabeth," or at least perhaps the beginnings of its composition.[40] Tolkien's emphasis, however, on this tale as an example of what in his letter he calls "the real theme" bridges any (for him) brief chronological gap between the finishing touches on *The Lord of the Rings* and the composition of the "Athrabeth." It is inviting to see Tolkien moving quickly and directly from "The Tale of Aragorn and Arwen" to the "Athrabeth," but it is not necessary for tracing the continuity of this theme from the one work to the other.

The introductory remarks in the "Athrabeth" twice note Andreth's blood ties to Beren and also stress Finrod's close friendship with this family (*Morgoth* 305, 307). We are thus prompted before Finrod and Andreth's discussion of Death and Immortality even begins to recall that by the time the "Athrabeth" was written *within* the legendarium Finrod would have given his life to save Beren, without which the crucial Choice of Lúthien could never have been made (336). The high doom that brought Beren to Doriath in the first place required many to play roles for its fulfillment in the First Age, even though it was the love and heroism of Finrod, Beren, and Lúthien that opened and defined the drama. Tuor had to choose to obey the summons of Ulmo, which would lead him to Idril. They had to escape Gondolin with their son, Eärendil, who would later meet Elwing, granddaughter of Beren and Lúthien, and possessor of the silmaril. Together, Eärendil and Elwing had to choose to risk everything to reach the Undying Lands and win the aid of the Valar. That Túrin might have escaped his most bitter fate, had he rescued Finduilas, who loved him, suggests that they (or a child of theirs) might have had a part to play if Túrin had not been Túrin (*S* 213). The notice taken of his striking good looks—"his face more beautiful than any other of Mortal Men, in the Elder Days" so much so that he could be easily mistaken for an Elf even among other Elves—also sets up an odd parallel to Lúthien, the "most beautiful of all the Children of Ilúvatar," a parallel that Thingol's declaration to Túrin that "in all your life you shall be held as my son" only makes stronger (210, 165; *Children* 77).[41] It would be strange indeed if this were pointless. Whether Túrin represents the Tragedy of what (he) might have been had he exerted his will differently, or whether the fulness of his parallel to Lúthien can only be seen in the prophecy that in the Final Battle he will return from Death to slay Morgoth, perhaps even with Beren at his side, is hard to say (*Shaping* 165; *WJ* 247). Though if Morgoth's curse upon the family of Húrin and Túrin's life of obstinate tragic misadventure culminate in Túrin's just vengeance upon the Last Day, that would certainly confirm in spectacular fashion Eru's warning to Melkor that none could alter the Music in his despite (*S* 17). Perhaps only through the crucible of such impossible sorrow could Túrin find the strength to destroy Morgoth forever, just as only through her suffering in love could Lúthien find the song to wring pity from Mandos and break the bonds of Death.

Nevertheless, this coming together over and over again of mortal Man and immortal Elf, of Half-elven and Half-elven, demonstrates the essential importance of this high doom to bringing the pity and mercy of the Valar into play against Morgoth. If Andreth and Aegnor had no part in that doom, as perhaps they did not, the heartbreaking failure of their love to bridge the gulf between their peoples has yet a role to play in prompting Finrod to guess that Men, whose immortal *fëar* (spirits), which do not belong to Arda Marred, will somehow bring their mortal *hröar* (bodies), which do belong to Arda Marred, with them when they leave the circles of the world: "And what can this mean unless it be that the fëa shall have the power to uplift the hröa . . . into an endurance everlasting beyond Eä, and beyond Time? Thus would Arda Marred, or part thereof, be healed not only of the taint of Melkor, but released even from the limits that were set for it in the 'Vision of Eru' of which the Valar speak" (*Morgoth* 318). This heady glimpse of a *release* inspires Finrod to the notion that "the errand of Men" was "to heal the Marring of Arda Marred"; and from this he grasps that "by the Second Children [of Eru] we might have been delivered from Death" (318). He sees "as a vision Arda Remade," a world in which Men would be the "deliverers" of Elves from the total Death of *fëa* and *hröa* which they believe awaits them at the world's ending (319). The seeming flaw in Finrod's vision, as he concedes and as Andreth seizes upon with despair, is that Morgoth's interference with Men in their forgotten past seems to have compromised that errand (320). Whether Morgoth "darkened" an "unrest" innate in mortal Men or imposed Death on beings "*born to life everlasting, without any shadow of an end,*" which Finrod refuses to believe him capable of doing, Finrod in his turn seizes upon the idea of Estel, the hope or trust that Eru will not allow his Children to be kept from him (316, 314, 320). Anna Vaninskaya notes well that in this context alone do "Elves draw sustenance for their *estel* from a story of Men" (174–75). And so Finrod builds on the "Old Hope" which some men cherish, that one day Eru will enter his creation in order to heal and remake it into a new Arda where beyond Death there is more than memory for Elves, too, and no longer "*a gulf that divides our kindreds*" (321–23). As Lúthien will later tell a dying Beren to wait for her before leaving the Circles of the World, Finrod here tells Andreth to wait there for him and Aegnor (*S* 186–87; *Morgoth* 325–26).

Finrod's words foreshadow Lúthien's, just as hers foreshadow the ending of "The Tale of Aragorn and Arwen," which we have seen also looks forward to a place beyond Death and memory and a changing of the world. We are, after all, in the same tale still. It seems clear that the release from bondage toward which Finrod and Andreth start groping their darkling way is something resembling the Incarnation of Christ at least functionally, some moment in which mortal and immortal choose to become one and through something resembling the Resurrection overcome Death. For Tolkien, of course, the Incarnation and the Resurrection are the twin eucatastrophes through which divine Pity and Mercy refute the tragedy of Death. But I say "something resembling" advisedly. For in the Secondary World of the legendarium we find a likeness of the Primary World, but not an identity with the Primary World. We must never forget—for Tolkien did not—that the Secondary World is necessarily an *imaginary* world, fashioned by the subcreator in the image of the Primary World, but differing in ways both gross and subtle.[42] These differences allow the subcreator to reflect light back upon the Primary World so that, like Frodo in Lothlórien, we in the Primary World may see it as if for the first time.

The very stuff of Arda Marred, and all that is made from it, including the *hröar* of Elves and Men, is tainted by Morgoth's evil before it is made, unlike in the Primary World, as Tolkien believed it to be.[43] This is as fundamental a difference as there can be: it alters the world not only before "Adam delved and Eve span" but before time itself began. Intimately connected with this taint of evil is another profound difference between the Primary and Secondary Worlds, one we have touched on before. Within Arda Marred, evil is incarnate from its beginning until the end of the Third Age, first in the person of Melkor, and then of Sauron. War against incarnate evil is, to say the least, not only spiritual. In the first two ages it required direct intervention by the Valar and Eru, with devastating costs for Arda Marred and its peoples. Though Men are collectively fallen in Arda Marred just as in the Primary World, Elves are not, and if "The Tale of Adanel" is supposed to be a true account of the Fall of Man—which it may not be—it is a very different account from Genesis (*Morgoth* 345–56). Moreover, while the relationship of Death to Men before that Fall remains uncertain, the "serial longevity" of the Elves is an Immortality only so-called since life for them will end when Arda Marred ends (*Letters* no. 208, p. 267). Thus, Death and Life are profoundly different than mortals of either world can understand. In fact Finrod sounds frustrated, almost bitter, as he tries to get across to Andreth that the Elvish expectation of Death is at least as grim as Man's: "And no one speaks to us of hope" (*Morgoth* 312). What Finrod calls "the errand of Men"—to deliver the Elves from Death and to help remake an Arda cleansed of the evil innate in its primordial elements—can only exist as such in a world so conceived. It is entirely reasonable then to think that whatever form Eru's entry into Arda Marred might have taken, had Tolkien ever gone so far as to imagine it, it would not have simply reproduced the Incarnation. Indeed, consistent with the humility he displayed when mentioning the possibility of telling such a tale, he was also extremely uneasy about any attempt even to speak of the Fall.[44]

The Release from Bondage, however, first attained with Beren and Lúthien and renewed in the promise of "The Tale of Aragorn and Arwen," derives much of its mythic power from the joining of the mortal and immortal through a love sufficient to defeat Death, which Tolkien found in the true myth of the evangelium. The line of Lúthien, "it is said," shall never perish from the world (*FR* 1.xi.193; *RK* 6.ix.879), a prophecy we might do well to construe in connection with Legolas's words about the seed of Men (quoted above on page 257). Here perhaps is a thread such as Tolkien might have followed, had he not thought the telling of a such a tale so far above him. "The Tale of

Aragorn and Arwen" is "part of the essential story" that is "concerned with Death as part of the nature, physical and spiritual of Man, and with Hope without guarantees," but it probably would never be more than a prospect from which to glimpse a future Finrod and Andreth could only guess at (*Letters* no. 181, p. 237).

As tales themselves, "The Tale of Aragorn and Arwen" and the "Athrabeth Finrod ah Andreth" stand at the very margins of the legendarium, but, unlike the many other textual ruins and allusions embedded so deeply in the past of Arda Marred that not even all the characters know the tales to which other characters refer, these two works do not look just to the Great Tales of the past or give a "sense of tales untold." They look beyond both the Circles of the World and the end of Arda Marred to Arda Healed (*Morgoth* 318) to a future whose tales cannot be known by those within the Secondary World except through prophecy, like that of Túrin returning at the Dagor Dagorath, perhaps with Beren One-hand at his side (see page 260). We in the Primary World view those hints of a new heaven and a new earth, as it were, with all the ironic distance that drama can afford spectators who know what those in the drama do not. Or perhaps we only think we know. Perhaps we confuse the parallel trajectory of an imaginary world, a Secondary World existing in mythical time, for what many, including Tolkien, believe to be the trajectory of the Primary World.

In her chapter on Death in Tolkien Anna Vaninskaya points out, "What it is to be a 'Man' in such a world cannot be understood apart from what it was to be an Elf, the two modes of relationship to Time to which God 'doomed' them at their creation gaining all their meaning from their contrast" (157). On this showing, it follows that any approach to an "Incarnation" would have to embrace both Elves and Men, as the "Athrabeth" anticipates, and for this reason it would necessarily have a substantially different theology and realization than the Incarnation in the Primary World. Once accused of "bad theology" for allowing his Elves to reincarnate in connection with their immortal nature within Arda Marred, Tolkien conceded that it might be so in the Primary World as it is, where immortality and reincarnation do not exist, but he countered that God could nevertheless have created beings of such a nature, had he wished to do so (*Letters* no. 153, p. 189). Since within Tolkien's mythology Eru Ilúvatar chose to do precisely that, a theology different from the Primary World's is embedded within the fabric of the Secondary World.

In the next paragraph of this letter, Tolkien asks how two peoples so different—the one immortal, the other mortal—could still be biologically close enough to have children (as of course they do). His answer again shows not only how important he felt the distinct "dooms" of Elves and Men were for his world but also how absolutely essential it had become for the mortal and the immortal to be joined. After briefly weighing the biological issues, he curtly dismisses them and replies: "I do not care. This is a biological dictum in my imaginary world." Thus, even if God should do for Tolkien's "imaginary world" what Ilúvatar did for Aulë's Dwarves (as Tolkien goes on to imagine in the letter), it would not become a part of our world but would remain a separate world of its own.

However fundamentally Christian Tolkien's legendarium is in its worldview, Arda Marred is not in the end our world but a mythology created by a man, who, though steeped in the waters of the *urðabrunnr*, believed himself washed in the blood of the Lamb. Like so many of his generation he saw no conflict between the myths of his cultural and intellectual heritage and the religion of his ancestors.[45] Each had truths to tell, and the one that was true by its truth awoke the other and gave it the power to speak. Tolkien was thus uniquely placed both to understand the *Beowulf*-poet, and, like him, to create a mythology whose foundations (*fundamenta*) are sunk in the deeps of Christian reality and yet sustain the "ancient works of giants," the *eald enta geweorc*, whose tales can exemplify truths about the tragedy of incarnates in Time. It is thus ironic that Tolkien, who could understand the *Beowulf*-poet because he, too, had a foot in each world and could build on that understanding in his own work, should find his work misunderstood in this regard, as scholars and fans alike often argue over whether his world is pagan or Christian. It is also entirely understandable, since few today have the needed background and a heart sympathetic to both faith and myth. If we attempt to minimize or discard either the Christian or the pagan element, we shall necessarily exaggerate the other and cut ourselves off from understanding Tolkien's legendarium as he understood it. To paraphrase something Stephen Halliwell has said about the interpreters of Aristotle, "the serious interpreter" of Tolkien "will wish, as far as his competence allows, to resist this dichotomy" between the Pagan and Christian Tolkien.[46]

That such truths can be applicable to a world always beset with the sufficient tragedy of Man should not surprise us, however, nor that they would have a special resonance with the years of near-apocalyptic warfare during which Tolkien, who knew too well the unnumbered tears of the battlefields of his youth, composed the heart of *The Lord of the Rings*. Of course, a work with Death and Immortality and Power used for Domination as its themes speaks to, and in fact can only be in dialogue with, a Primary World that bodies forth those same themes so bloodily and so well. This is what myth does. Whether it is Sophocles writing of Oedipus in the early years of the Peloponnesian War or Tolkien writing of Frodo during the Second World War, the myth presented in a dramatic or narrative form that ends in tragedy or eucatastrophe weighs the themes imagined in the Secondary World against the those experienced in the Primary World.[47] And the tragic is as present in Middle-earth as the eucatastrophic.

At the heart of Tolkien's myth are the Ring and Pity. The desire to impose our will on others, on the world, on life and time itself, contends with the sorrow of knowing that even the best of us, no matter our intentions, will find ourselves swept away if we set our feet on the path that pursues that desire. The pity of Bilbo, Frodo, and Arwen too easily become lost in the desire to get or keep that which we must let go, as we lose who we are to deceits we practice to justify ourselves: I "won" the Ring; "the Ring is mine"; "Would you then, lord, before your time leave your people...?" (RK App. A I.v.1061). When Tolkien wrote to Christopher on 6 May 1944, a month before the Normandy Invasion, whose operational codename—"Overlord"—bespeaks domination, he felt the weight of myth and of "real life," of Secondary and of Primary Worlds, in the swaying of the balance: "We are attempting to conquer Sauron with the Ring.... But the penalty is... to breed new Saurons" (*Letters* no. 66, p. 78). How close this is in form and movement to Gandalf's debate with Denethor over the folly of using, or even possessing, "this thing" (so named *eight times* in this scene, as if apotropaically like "the Unnamed" for Sauron), which would have stolen Boromir from his father far more painfully and finally than death had and even the mere possession of which unused would have driven Denethor mad (RK 5.iv.812–14). The pity implicit in Tolkien's application of his myth here to his reality is all of a piece with the pity Gandalf expresses in this scene for "even [Sauron's] slaves," chief among whom were the Ringwraiths, his greatest weapons (6.iv.814).

We hear a similar sorrow and pity in Tolkien's letter of 9 August 1945: "The news today about 'Atomic bombs' is so horrifying one is stunned. The utter folly of these lunatic physicists...!" (*Letters* no. 102, p. 113). Later in 1952, when Britain detonated a bomb of its own, we hear it more explicitly: "Such is our life. Mordor in our midst. And I regret to note that the billowing cloud recently pictured did not mark the fall of Barad-dûr, but was produced by its allies—or at least by persons who have decided to use the Ring for their own (of course most excellent) purposes" (no. 135, p. 165). In 1945, however, after six years of a war for survival, the horror and pity Tolkien felt at the bombing of Hiroshima and Nagasaki were balanced against the recognition both that the use of such power could end the war and that God took a harsh view of such uses of power (no. 102, p. 113). He knew well how easily one might hold such power to be "a gift to the foes of Mordor" and how blandly one could assent to "deploring maybe evils done by the way" in the name of doing good (FR.2.x.397, ii.259). Frodo came to pity both Boromir and Saruman, the characters who said these words, but only because Tolkien who wrote these words had pitied them first.

These are but two examples of Tolkien seeing the applicability of the truths of his myth to the reality in which he lived. And pity is at the heart of the challenge these myths lay before us. Tolkien's recollections of "being caught in youth by 1914" (FR xxiv), his passions and fears about the war that came again in 1939, his concerns about its aftermath throughout the world are as incandescent in his wartime letters to his son Christopher as they are in the Dead Marshes, in the cataclysmic destruction of Sauron, and in the return of the Ring-bearer to a land that no longer seemed his own and that needed a healing that only pity could bring. That pity is the true gift given to the foes of Mordor.

The alternative to trying to use the Ring against Sauron is to surrender to failure and to hope in the Pity of Bilbo. This surrender entails far more than the defeat and death Frodo expects to be his lot from the beginning. The draw of the Ring's power strips him of everything that makes him the sort of person who, despite his terror of Sauron, would take up this burden for the sake of others. This power isolates him, despoiling him of his identity, his memory, and even his name. It takes from him the world he set out to save and twists his thinking until "the Ring is mine" seems the right conclusion. This is what Frodo is surrendering to when he makes the moral choice to assume the burden of the Ring and take it to the fire. And though he does not understand this when he chooses to be the Ring-bearer—as Gandalf suggests (FR 2.iii.276)—he never relents in pursuing that choice. He fights it until he can't any longer, and, as was inevitable, he chooses to claim the Ring. Yet it is only through losing every last bit of himself in the struggle between his will and his desire that he can get close enough to the Fire for the Pity of Bilbo to rule the fate of many.

From the earliest days of the legendarium, Pity is present and helps to shape the narrative. In "The Music of the Ainur" of 1917, and in the version of "The Ainulindalë" that Tolkien wrote not long before starting *The Lord of the Rings* in late 1937, we find its seeds already planted.[48] For in the Third Theme, Ilúvatar's remarkable answer to the discord of Melkor is a music of sorrow and beauty, not wrath: "a beauty ... mingled with an unquenchable sorrow" that compels the "rival" discord of Melkor to "supplement" it and "harmonize" with it or to be "taken by the other and woven into its pattern" (*LT* 1.54; *Lost* 157). By this time, too, Nienna has been significantly reimagined, from a cold "mistress of Death" who judged Men and spread mists of despair to a Vala with "Pity in her heart," whose mourning and tears bring comfort to the souls in Mandos (LT I.66, 76–77; *Lost* 206; *Shaping* 115). It will not be until Tolkien returns to the Silmarillion material after completing *The Lord of the Rings* that he will connect Nienna's pity and sorrow to the Third Theme and to Justice, and tell us that Gandalf learned pity from her (*S* 43, 46; *Morgoth* 146, 241–42). The years Tolkien spent exploring the theme of Pity at close quarters in *The Lord of the Rings* while the Primary World tore itself apart around him changed the legendarium, making it more immediate and personal than the Silmarillion material probably would have been otherwise. But by examining this theme from a halfling's perspective, from three and a half feet off the ground, he also brings the intersection of the Level of Grace and the Level of Nature more nearly within our ken, and all the themes—of Death and Immortality, Fate and Free Will, Power and War, the Noble and the Humble, Love and Home, Justice and Mercy—all become manifest through eucatastrophe and tragedy, all for those with eyes to see that can, whether his characters, his readers, or himself.

Notes

INTRODUCTION

1. Thus, Lewis wrote in Tolkien's obituary in *The Times* (3 September 1973): "His standard of self-criticism was high, and the mere suggestion of publication usually set him upon a revision, in the course of which so many new ideas occurred to him that where his friends had hoped for the final text of an old work they actually got the first draft of a new one." The Tolkien Society reprinted the obituary in full in *Mallorn*, vol. 8, 1974, pp. 40–43. Lewis's comment appears unsourced in Humphrey Carpenter's biography of Tolkien (138).

2. Larger thematic concerns do not of course go entirely without mention beforehand. Gollum's near repentance touches upon pity (*Letters* no. 96, p. 110). Letter no. 66, p. 78 addresses power. For more on Power and the Machine, see no. 75, p. 87; no. 109, p. 121.

3. On the *Beowulf* lecture, see Simon Cook, *Apprenticeship* and Michael D. C. Drout's introduction to *B&C*. For *On Fairy-stories*, see the version edited by Verlyn Flieger and Douglas A. Anderson. Tolkien of course later reworked much of his 1939 lecture as he prepared it for publication in *Essays Presented to Charles Williams* in 1947.

4. While in half of these occurrences *Pity* comes first in a sentence, Gandalf clearly has *Pity* rather than *pity* in mind, editorial conventions notwithstanding. Compare this with the obviously conventional capitalization at *RK* 5.vi.841.

5. For the Elves' attempts to preserve the world from "fading" as "embalming." see *Letters*, no. 131, p. 151, and no. 154, p. 196. Men, of course, in their desire to be immortal like the Elves become embalmers of themselves: *TT* 4.v.677; *RK* 5.iv.825–26; *S* 266.

6. In this context I use *temptation* with great care and with no suggestion of conscious agency on the part of the Ring. Temptations, as Aquinas notes, may be internal or external. The fallen need no external tempter. They can tempt themselves because their will is not aligned with God's. The unfallen, like Christ, whose will is one with the Father's, are tempted only from without, as Christ is in the desert. The same would have been true of Adam and Eve before the serpent. This distinction will not have been

lost on Tolkien, as concerned as he was with the Fall. On Aquinas's understanding of temptation, see J. Wawrykov (147–49).

7. See these ambiguities in "The Ring Goes South": Were the *crebain* really sent by Saruman? What was the shadow Frodo perceived passing high above? Was the snow the malice of Caradhras, or Sauron's, or just a winter storm? Such questions run throughout the chapter and into the next chapter, "A Journey in the Dark," with the Wargs and the Watcher in the Water.

8. Accepting Frodo as narrator is not without internal problems. While his knowledge of events elsewhere is often explicable through the accounts of those who were there—for instance, Legolas and Gimli telling of the Paths of the Dead—other moments are harder to explain (RK 5.ix.872–78). Knowledge of what the Black Riders were thinking in Buckland was unattainable (FR 1.xi.176–77). The narrator, whoever he was, was imagining it for dramatic effect.

9. Thomas Kullman has much to say of narrative in terms of linguistic and literary theory but nothing about the claims in the text that Frodo is telling the bulk of this story (89–127). He simply denies that the narrator "take[s] part in the story himself" (90).

1. BILBO'S LIE AND THE RING

1. Tolkien began book 4 in early April and had finished it by late May. Christopher Tolkien dates the rewriting of "Riddles in the Dark" to this period, though the revised chapter did not appear in print until 1951. The dating of the composition of book 4 is most prominently attested by the author's own words in the foreword to the second edition (FR xxiii). For the dating of these revisions to *The Hobbit* to this same period, see John Rateliff (in Tolkien, *History of the Hobbit*, xxvii, 731–32).

2. That Tolkien later found it necessary to retcon Isildur's death so that he doesn't look quite so bad is not entirely relevant to the story as Gandalf told it to Frodo. The impression created remains, and no one in *The Lord of the Rings* mentions any extenuating circumstances. Indeed, Tolkien didn't think up such circumstances until years later. Not only am I dealing with *The Lord of the Rings* as written, but I also question whether the tale retold offers extenuation rather than a more tragic portrayal. See above on pages 125–26.

3. Though not published until *The Silmarillion* appeared in 1977, the verses are in "The Lay of Leithian," composed in the late 1920s, even before Thû became Sauron (*Lays* 150, 230).

4. For this point I am indebted to Shawn Marchese and Alan Sisto of *The Prancing Pony Podcast*.

5. On its indestructibility, see *Letters* no. 211, p. 280. The death of Sauron's physical form, which he made and remade himself, differs categorically from the death of Sauron as a being possessed by nature of both body and spirit.

6. Tolkien qualifies *rapport* with quotation marks in Letter 131, p. 153. Despite this "rapport," however, Sauron cannot simply tell where the Ring is, whether another is

wearing it at a given moment, or even if it still exists. Gandalf says Sauron believed the Ring had been destroyed in the War of the Last Alliance (FR 1.ii.52).

7. Even Judith Klinger's thoughtful study, "The Fallacies of Power: Frodo's Resistance to the Ring" assumes the consciousness of the Ring: "The One Ring is an unparalleled entity whose range of activity and influence can be directly known only by those who carry it" or treats it as established fact (359). Thus it speaks of the Ring's "somewhat clumsy attempt" to corrupt Sam and states that "blatant failures on the Ring's part imply that it is quite incapable of comprehending the personalities and private desires of both hobbits" (362).

8. Merry notes he once saw Bilbo use the Ring to avoid the Sackville-Bagginses (FR 1.v.104).

9. Upon the death of their fathers, Meriadoc will become the Master of Buckland, and Peregrin will become the Thain of the Shire (a title the Brandybucks had also possessed centuries earlier, when they were named the Oldbucks). Note also that Sam is not introduced as Mr. in Bree, but Merry and Pippin are (FR 1.ix.153). That he is a servant quite literally goes without saying.

10. See FR 1.iii.83 for Gildor's response to Frodo's view of the Shire as belonging to the hobbits.

11. For a thorough survey, see Kerry 17–53.

12. In a 1966 telephone interview later published in the fanzine *Niekas,* Harry Resnick asked Tolkien how he felt "about the idea that people might identify Frodo with Christ" (43). Tolkien replied: "Well, you know, there've been saviors before; it is a very common thing. There've been heroes and patriots who have given [their lives] up for their countries. You don't have to be Christian to believe that somebody has to die in order to save something."

13. Compare this with John R. Holmes, who notes that "the concept of *praeparatio evangelium* [sic] makes it possible to nurture images and ideas that would be common to heathen and Christian thought" (128).

14. Tolkien flatly denied the departure from Rivendell to 25 December was intentional, and this genuinely seems to have been the truth (Resnick 43). Yet, once the departure ended up on that date due the shifting needs of his chronology he flatly refused to move it ("Chronology of The Lord of the Rings" 39n34; 133).

15. Compare with John R. Holmes in response to the criticisms of Michael D. C. Drout and Hilary Wynne ("Look Back"): "A certain proportion of Christian interpretations of Tolkien will, and should, continue to do what Drout and Wynne inveighed against: preach to the choir, present 'Christian theology as a received truth.' The choir in fact exists, has a long literary tradition, and to the choristers Christian theology *is* a received truth. There is a place for such parochial criticism, just as there is for Freudian readings of Shakespeare" (140).

16. See, for example, John R. Holmes: "For Tolkien (and, he thought, for the Beowulf-poet), there is more similarity than contrast between Jerusalem and Asgard, because the heathen warrior who sided with the (finally doomed) Norse gods against the 'Chaos and Unreason' was on the same side as the Christian God who opposed the same foes" (131). See further the excellent analyses of Simon Cook and Claudio Testi et al.

2. BILBO'S PITY AND THE RING

1. Sara Brown and Simon Malpas have demonstrated the centrality of "home" for the hobbits.

2. Bilbo obtained the Ring in 2941 and revealed its true story to Frodo in approximately 2989, by which time Gandalf already knew it, probably discovering the truth only a short time before Frodo (FR 1.i.40; ii.48).

3. See Jeffrey Jerome Cohen: "We have seen that the monster arises at the gap where difference is perceived as dividing a recording voice from its captured subject; the criterion of this division is arbitrary, and can range from anatomy or skin color to religious belief, custom, and political ideology. The monster's destructiveness is really deconstructiveness: it threatens to reveal that difference originates in process, rather than in fact (and that 'fact' is subject to constant reconstruction and change)" (14–15). Gandalf aims to deconstruct precisely this difference, and the process is being devoured by the Ring.

4. Simon Malpas sees Frodo's confrontation with the idea that Gollum is a Hobbit as undermining Frodo's concept of home: "the dawning recognition that Gollum, perhaps the most resolutely homeless character in the text, is himself a Hobbit shatters the entire ontological consistency of Frodo's self-identity" (96).

5. Like Gandalf, Galadriel did not at first exist in the wider legendarium. She sprang from Tolkien's head only after the Company reached Lórien (*Treason* 233, 250). Yet she was not fully formed, and her subsequent protean transformations—the last recorded the month before Tolkien died (231)—make interpreting her a more complex matter (UT 231, 228–67). See Christopher Tolkien: "a history of Galadriel can only be a history of my father's changing conceptions, and the 'unfinished' nature of the tale is not in this case that of a particular piece of writing" (9).

6. See Gandalf's account of his interview with Gollum, whom Aragorn captured after he left Mordor (FR 1.ii.57) and Tolkien's observation in "The Hunt for the Ring" that Sauron perceived Gollum's desire for revenge on Bilbo and meant to make use of it (UT 357). Christopher Tolkien argues that "The Hunt for the Ring" was part of the writings his father referred to in a letter of 1964 (not, alas, in *The Letters*) as being extant at the time of the writing of *The Lord of the Rings*, and originally intended for inclusion (UT 11).

7. Malice is ascribed directly to Sauron at 1.ii.49, and Gollum is said at 1.ii.53 to have used his invisibility in its service. Later, at 2.ii.254, Gandalf speaks of the Ring as full of Sauron's malice, and at 2.ii.255 Strider attributes Gollum's unexpected strength to the extremity of his malice. See TT 4.i.622, vi.688–89, 691; RK 6.iii.943.

Besides Sauron (FR 2.ii.269; TT 4.iv.659; RK 5.iv.808, ix.879, 6.i.898, 6.iii.935, 942), we also find malice attributed to Old Man Willow and the trees of the Old Forest (FR 1.vii.130); Caradhras (2.iii.293); orcs (2.ix.386); Wormtongue (TT 3.vi.520); Minas Morgul/The Nazgûl (4.vi.692; RK 5.iv.823); Shelob (TT 4.ix.719, 720, 724, x.728, 730); the Witch King (RK 5.iv.822, vi.841); the Watchers at the Tower of Cirith Ungol (RK 6.i.902, 903, 914); Saruman (RK 6.viii.1018). Matthew DeForrest does well to point out the association of malice "with ancient things that turned to evil . . . as well as those like Gollum ... and Wormtongue ... who served them" (235). See, finally, the words of Legolas (*TT* 4.v.491) and Treebeard (4.iv.468), referring most likely to the Huorns (4.ix.565).

8. As Matthew DeForrest demonstrates, Théoden's treatment of Gríma Wormtongue shows both pity and mercy (230). The king explicitly states his pity and shows mercy by not executing Wormtongue as Gandalf admits would be just (*TT* 4.vi.519–21). When Gandalf suggests that Wormtongue be allowed to prove his worth, the King agrees. Though Wormtongue chooses poorly, healing is held out to him just as it is to Gollum.

9. *Spirits* appears thirteen times to describe mood (*FR* 1.iii.68, 77; iv.91; vii.132; xii.204, 206; 2.iv.311, 314; *RK* 5.iv.807; 6.i.904, 911; ii.919; viii.1014). *Spirit* twice means *courage* (*RK* 6.viii.1013; A 1046). *Spirit* appears twelve times in the sense of *soul*: *FR* 1.ii.52; vii.130; xii.214; *TT* 4.x.730; *RK* 5.iv.825; viii.867, 869; ix.876, 879; 6.1.902; ii.922; A 1037.

Frodo, Sam, and Pippin see "not a soul" on the road only moments before their first encounter with a Black Rider (*FR* 1.iii.74). There's no little irony here.

3. THE 1951 *HOBBIT* AND "THE SHADOW OF THE PAST"

1. Verlyn Flieger ("Tolkien's French Connection" 210–11): "Frodo's journey is in a different key from Bilbo's, and not only because Tolkien spent more time and care developing *The Lord of the Rings* than he did *The Hobbit*, but also because he was conscious of a different authorial purpose. Bilbo had *aventures*—dangerous escapades exciting for their own sake, ending in peace and prosperity for Elves, Men, Dwarves, and Bilbo himself. Frodo goes on a *quest*—a journey as perilous for soul as for body—with a fixed purpose, a goal beyond itself. And while Frodo's quest, like Bilbo's adventure, ends in peace, the peace will not include him, for his quest has left him unable to enjoy it. Unlike ... Bilbo, Frodo gets no happy ever after."

2. I would like to thank Verlyn Flieger for raising the question, in conversation, of Bilbo's theft of the Arkenstone in the midst of his clearly good deed.

3. On other aspects of *The Odyssey* and *The Hobbit*, see Reckford (5–9).

4. Bilbo's assertion that only keeping the Ring saved him from Gollum suggests he had already told Gandalf about Gollum's motives (*FR* 1.i.34). This agrees with Frodo's assertion about Gollum's intentions (1.ii.54).

5. Together with Gollum's remarkable grandmother we might also think of Belladonna Took.

6. On Plato's and Tolkien's approaches to myth, see the indispensable article of Gergely Nagy, "Saving the Myths." On the *Timaeus*, see Camacho and Cook.

7. His respect for the classics and Shakespeare are both on display in *Letters* no. 156, p. 201, where he takes pains to point out how admirable such works are while also noting that his own work does not measure up to them. On classical influence in general, see Scull and Hammond (*C&G* 1.242–44) and most recently Hamish Williams.

8. And in fact, the tradition reaches back beyond Aristotle. See Stephen Halliwell (*Aristotle's* Poetics 109–20).

9. What precisely Aristotle meant by *katharsis* is unclear, but it refers to a kind of cleansing or purification. Note, then, the parallel in "On Fairy-stories," where Tolkien speaks of Recovery as regaining a "clear view," from "clean[ing] our windows" (*OFS* ¶ 83, p. 67). On *katharsis*, see Stephen Halliwell (*Aristotle's* Poetics 168–201, 350–56).

4. FROM BAG END TO RIVENDELL

1. That the Sea later proves to be something else for Frodo is beside the point here about the beliefs of Hobbits. Sam also sees the crossing as a transition between one life and another (*FR* 1.v.99).

2. Elsewhere I have studied the use of parenthetical comments throughout *The Lord of the Rings*, which seem a decidedly hobbitish narrative touch ("Parenthesis").

3. It is uncertain whether the Nazgûl still possess their Rings or Sauron has them. While one reference in *The Lord of the Rings* indicates the Nazgûl have them (*FR* 2.ii.250), two others state the opposite (*FR* 1.ii.51. 2.vii.366). Two passages in "The Hunt for the Ring" (*UT* 338, 343) and one in the *Letters* (no. 246, p. 331) agree with this statement. Also, Frodo might be expected to have seen the rings on their fingers at Weathertop and the Ford, since he was wearing the Ring in the first case, and nearly a wraith in the second.

4. "As þe See" Digby 102 in J. Kail (18). Even in a strictly physical sense "astray" commonly refers to those who, like soldiers or domesticated animals, require guidance, just as Gildor indicates Frodo does. See "strai" (*Strai—Middle English Compendium*) and "astrai" (*Astrai—Middle English Compendium*).

5. On the movement of the hobbits into a wider world, see Hillman et al. ("Eldar" 114–40) and John Rosegrant (24–25). Rosegrant seems to treat all of the hobbits' journey as into Faërie. On the contrary, I would restrict Faërie to certain areas, from the Old Forest to the Barrow Downs, Rivendell, Lothlórien, and Fangorn. That it continues to exist in scattered, fading places contributes to the sense of its loss.

6. *RK* 6.ix.1024: "'It is gone for ever,'" he said, 'and now all is dark and empty.'" On Frodo after the Ring, see especially *Letters* no. 246, pp. 230–31, and chapter 10.

7. See also Tom Shippey's comment: "What he *is* may not be known, but what he *does* is dominate" (*Road* 106). Gandalf also links possession and freedom when admonishing Bilbo about giving up the Ring at *FR* 1.i.34.

8. Appendix B rings subtle changes to Gollum's name. Under 2463, the year he gets the Ring, he is Sméagol; in 2470 and 2941 he is Sméagol-Gollum; from 2944 onward he is just Gollum (*RK* 1087–94). On the use of "Sméagol" and the use of "Gollum," see above on pages 51 and 209.

9. True, Tolkien later wrote a version of Isildur's story that put a better face on his apparent desertion of his men (*UT* 271–87). That does not alter the version in *The Lord of the Rings* as Frodo heard it or as Gandalf told it. There is yet another story of the pernicious effects of the Ring, and a consequence of Isildur's claiming the Ring as a weregild for Elendil and Anarion, though doing so betrayed all they had fought

for, and as an "*heirloom of the North Kingdom.*" (FR 2.i.252) Whatever the "true" story, this is the one Frodo knew and took so seriously that he believed that the Ring rightly belonged to Aragorn, the heir of Isildur. See further on pages 125–26.

10. *Seemed* and *felt* frequently describe Bilbo's, Frodo's, and Sam's perceptions of its weight and size: see FR 1.ii.47, 50, vii.132–33, 2.i.232, iv.311–12; TT 4.ii.630; RK 6.i.898. The same is true of Isildur (FR 2.ii.253). The Ring does not change size when Bombadil puts it on, but this might also reflect the powerlessness of the Ring over him (1.vii.133). Still, some changing of size would seem necessary for it to fit all hands. Before his second death and loss of the Ring at the end of the Second Age, Sauron had also been able to take different shapes and sizes. It follows that the Ring will have needed to possess this property, but it does not follow that the Ring is consciously choosing to change its size.

11. Note that in *The Hobbit*, Bilbo is *reaching* for the Ring, so he can escape from the goblins (135).

12. In what follows, I indicate with a (c) the uses of *hate* I consider colloquial hyperbole: FR 1.ii.55 (six times), 57 (twice), 59; vii.130; xi.189; 2.iv.307 (c twice); x.402 (c); TT 3.ii.426; iii.445, 458 (c); iv.473; vii.537 (twice), 539; viii.546, 547; ix.568 (Quickbeam); x.582, 584, 585, 586; 4.i.605 (c), 606 (c), 613 (twice); ii.633; iii.641 (twice); vi.686, 688; ix.721; RK 5.i.765 (twice); iv.809; v.832 (twice, Ghân-buri-Ghân); vi.842, 848; viii.858; 6.i.907; ii.918 (c), 923, 926; iii.936, 943; iv.948, 949; vi.980 (twice), 983 (twice); viii.1007, 1019 (twice), 1020. Quickbeam hates Saruman passionately, but his trees have suffered greatly at Saruman's hands.

13. At Weathertop, Strider calls Frodo's invocation of Elbereth "more deadly" to the Witch-king than his sword (FR 1.xii.198). Clearly he does not mean *deadly* literally. In the next sentence, he says the same of the Morgul knife, which does not kill its victim. If saying "Elbereth" alone were enough to drive off the Ringwraiths, they would hardly be so fearsome: they would be the Knights Who Say Ni. Elbereth must have responded to Frodo's invocation.

5. FROM RIVENDELL TO AMON HEN

1. Before the 2004 fiftieth anniversary edition, most texts of *The Lord of the Rings* did not italicize *I*, but Hammond and Scull note that this reading has the support of the manuscript at Marquette (RC 326). So, too, Christopher Tolkien: "In Frodo's question ... 'I' should be italicized" (*Treason* 266n34).

2. On Mount Doom, even what we might consider a glancing blow from the Eye, which is again unaware of his presence and attention, is enough to strike Frodo to the ground (RK 6.iii.942).

3. I thank Laura Lee Smith for her insight here, not least for the biblical quotations.

4. Bilbo, Frodo, Isildur, Déagol, and Sméagol all are fascinated by the beauty or fairness of the Ring (FR 1.ii.47, 53 [twice], 56, 60, 2.ii.253). While Sam gives no thought to its beauty, his temptation grows in part from the beauty he thinks he could create using it. Bombadil of course sees through its beauty (1.vii.133).

6. FROM THE EMYN MUIL TO THE DEAD MARSHES

1. In *TT* 3.iii.455–56, the only mention of Gollum in book 3, Merry and Pippin run a dangerous risk with Grishnákh, playing up to him and pretending they can help him find the Ring, which the orc clearly seems to know about. He also certainly knows about Gollum, which tends to confirm the indications in book 2 that Gollum at times cooperated with the orcs (*FR* 2.ii.254–55, vi.344, 349). At *TT* 4.iii.642, Gollum admits he had been in touch with orcs before he encountered Frodo and Sam.

2. Tolkien may well have known Stoker's description of Dracula, whom Jonathan Harker sees in a very similar moment "begin to crawl down the castle wall over that dreadful abyss, face down" (43). Harker likewise notes the moonlight and Dracula's inhuman ability to find handholds on the wall. Lisa Hopkins has also noted the similarity of Gollum and Dracula in these passages (286–87).

3. Amy Amendt-Radeuge avers that "we never pity the Ringwraiths; their demise comes as an intense relief" ("Better Off Dead"). Yet *never* is too long a word even for the Ringwraiths. Surely the words about the loneliness heard in the Black Riders' cries, which she also quotes, suggest that the narrator at least feels some quantum of pity. While I agree that we feel relief at their demise, even as a child reading this tale for the first time that loneliness stirred pity within me, just as the characterization of the Barrow-wight's song did.

4. See also *RK* 5.ii.780, where Aragorn, fresh from his contest of wills with Sauron, "sternly" rebukes Gimli but catches himself and returns to his kindlier manner. At 5.ix.869–70, he affects this lordly tone in jest.

5. See Tolkien's words on the Ring in *Letters* no. 131, p. 160: "The primary symbolism of the Ring, as the will to mere power, seeking to make itself objective by physical force and mechanism, and so also inevitably by lies."

6. Regrettably, Humphrey Carpenter edited the summary out when he published the letter to Waldman (*Letters* no. 131), but Hammond and Scull preserve it in their *Reader's Companion* (746). Note that Prospero dominates both Caliban and Ariel through the power of magic. In Letter no. 64, p. 77, Tolkien likens Sam's treatment of Gollum to Ariel's treatment of Caliban. Again regrettably, Carpenter breaks off the text here, leaving us to wonder whether Tolkien expanded further on the comparison. Nevertheless, in both these letters, written seven years apart, Tolkien sees Frodo as Prospero, with Sam and Gollum in his service, lesser in station if not in humanity. On Caliban and Gollum, see also Lisa Hopkins (281–93).

7. Given the use of OE *láf* in *Beowulf* to describe a sword left as an "heirloom" (ll. 453, 2612; also *yrfeláf*, 1906), Isildur's assertion that the Ring would become an "heirloom of the North Kingdom" probably indicates that he views it as a weapon (*FR* 2.ii.252). See also Faramir at *TT* 4.v.670 and 680 and Aragorn at *FR* 2.ii.268.

8. See, for example, Gollum looking over Sam's shoulder at Frodo as he sleeps (*TT* 4.iv.652), Frodo's "betrayal" of Gollum at Henneth Annûn (4.vi.686–92), and Gollum's moment on the Stairs (4.viii.714–15).

7. FROM THE BLACK GATE TO ITHILIEN

1. See *OED* "personality" 4b: "The quality or collection of qualities which makes a person a distinctive individual; the distinctive personal or individual character of a person, esp. of a marked or unusual kind"; and 4c "*Psychology* and *Sociology*. Personal individuality as a subject of psychological and sociological study." *Personality*, moreover, fits so well with the ways psychology both clinical and popular has taught us to view not only ourselves but our literary characters—and even both at once—that too facile an application of psychology or of a literary-psychological theory to Gollum here, diagnosing him into some category or another, could obscure rather than illuminate the text. On the various psychological analyses of Gollum, see Yvette Kisor (3100–212). Most recently, see John Rosegrant, who regards Gollum as an example of "abjection" (61–62).

2. Comparing the inner voices Sam later hears to Gollum's, Charles Keim notes that "it is this stable ego, this ability to arbitrate, that we would say *is* Sam," while Gollum is "suspended between his own contrary impulses" (298). Yet, as I will argue (on pages 143–47), Gollum and Sméagol each have a very strong *sense of self*, even though there is no unified and stable self.

3. See also Leslie Stratyner: "Tolkien's use of the riddle game itself foregrounds his intention for us to view his characters appositively. And it is here that we can see the nature of apposition itself with regard to character, because apposites are not opposites. Gollum is not Bilbo's opposite. He is not 'opposed to' or completely different from Bilbo. He is *apposite*, meaning we are supposed to see the two characters as side-by-side" (81). This article builds on Tom Shippey's solid observation that Tolkien "did not read *Beowulf* like a literary critic, but like a philologist. His insight tended to be drawn from tiny detail" ("*Beowulf*-poet" 13).

4. The phrase occurs eighteen times in *The Lord of the Rings*. Sam says it thirteen times (FR 1.ii.63, iii.75, iv.105, 2.i.238, ix.403 twice; TT 4.i.611, v.665, 680; RK 6.i.911, ii.918, 927, 929), Butterbur four times (FR 1.ix.154, 156, 1.x.166; RK 6.vii.991), and the Gaffer once (RK 6.viii.1014). It always signals deference to those of a higher status than the speaker, and in Sam's mouth it often introduces a difference of opinion he is aware he probably should not voice. Compare "with your leave" at FR 1.x.165, where Sam's outspokenness to Frodo makes Pippin, his social superior, uncomfortable, and at RK 6.ix.1025, where Sam asks Frodo's permission to name a child after him. For views of class within Tolkien, see Marjorie Burns (139–52); Jane Chance ("Subversive Fantasist" 153–68); and Tom Shippey ("Noblesse Oblige" 285–301).

5. TT 4.i.616; ii.624 ("Trust Sméagol now?"), 625, 628, 629, 634.

6. Unsurprisingly, the analysis of Gollum's speech patterns overlaps considerably with the analysis of his psychological condition. For discussion, see Yvette Kisor (3100–212). As she observes, Gollum's speech patterns and use of pronouns and other words to describe himself demonstrate how the Ring has destroyed his identity by severing him from himself and his community. On Gollum's speech patterns, see on pages 143–47.

7. In addition to the passages quoted in the text, see TT 4.i.618, 619, ii.625, 632, 633, iii.638, 642, 643.

8. Jane Chance (*Mythology* 88) and Gergely Nagy ("Lost" 61–62) thus lay too much stress on Frodo's first use of *Sméagol*.

9. The first I conversation takes place on 29 February and the last on 5 March. Note that all Shire months have thirty days (*RK* App. D 1103). Yvette Kisor likewise notes that "this period of relative psychological wholeness, indicated through his patterns of pronoun use, does not last long," but without exploring why this period may end when it does (3197).

10. Admittedly, "Come not between *The* Gollum and his fish" just doesn't have the same ring to it.

11. They meet on 29 February, reach the Black Gate on 5 March, and part in Shelob's lair on 12 March.

12. Besides Gollum's "once upon a time," he speaks of "wonderful tales" he heard and told as a child (*TT* 4.iii. 638, 641). These Sam answers with memories of tales the hobbits in the Shire knew, in particular the "Oliphaunt" (4.iii.646–47). This leads Frodo to imagine a fairy-tale ending: Gandalf, whom he thinks dead, breaks down the Black Gate at the head of a thousand oliphaunts, which he believes to be mythical (4.iii.647).

13. By contrast, we presently encounter a dream Sam has—Sam who had not dreamed at all in Bombadil's house (*TT* 4.vii.699). The dream is predictably unsettling and about home. Sam never forgets where he comes from.

8. FROM ITHILIEN TO CIRITH UNGOL

1. Jane Chance states that Denethor "sends his favorite son on a mission that he foresees will enable a steward to have true power, through the Ring" (*Mythology* 108). This suggests that Denethor knew exactly what "Isildur's Bane" was when he sent Boromir to seek the meaning of the dream and chose Boromir rather than Faramir because he thought Boromir would obtain the Ring and bring it to him—a dark interpretation, to be sure, but one that may well be right. For it makes sense of Boromir's phrasing at *FR* 2.ii.246, which clearly suggests he believed his father knew more than he would disclose. We don't use a phrase like "this only would he say" otherwise.

2. I have emphasized *is* here because that, I believe, is where the stress best falls given the context. Faramir has several times made remarks that suggest he has wondered if, but not actually believed, Isildur's Bane is in fact the One Ring. His choice of the word *heirloom* echoes Isildur's, his secretive, compound apotropaic euphemism about removing the Ring from Sauron's hand, and his dismissal of the possibility that Isildur's Bane refers to orc arrows—added to his reference to Gandalf and the archives—strongly suggests that Faramir, too, had read Isildur's account. Stunned, he learns his impossible guess was right (*TT* 4.v.669–71).

3. Jane Chance puts it correctly when she says, "The power of the king resides in his ability to heal, to knit together, to bring peace and fruitfulness to the community, to

return or renew that which has been torn or debilitated" (*Mythology* 123). Whatever Aragorn's inherited claim to the throne, he justifies it by his actions for its people.

4. Galadriel's contempt for the thought of compelling her guest to surrender the Ring to her (FR 2.vii.365) serves as commentary on Faramir's restraint here and his father's unseemly wish that he had seized the Ring (RK 5.iv.813). Thinking of the Ring as a gift won by force does not leave Denethor in the best company.

5. Given the discussion of Faramir and Aragorn above (on pages 156–57), Aragorn's reference to Minas Tirith as "Minas Anor ... my own city" is surely noteworthy (FR 2.ix.393). He says this as they approach the Argonath. It is at this the point Strider the Ranger becomes Aragorn son of Arathorn, the rightful king, in Frodo's eyes. The narrator will only call him Strider once more, at Amon Hen, where the epithet reflects the significant difference Sam recognizes between the length of Strider's stride and his own (2.x.405). To call him *Strider* here makes a point *Aragorn* would have missed.

6. Noetzel builds on Tolkien's comment that Bombadil's is "a natural pacifist view" (*Letters* no. 144, p. 179).

7. As we shall see, subsequently there will be no perception of external commands when the hand moves independently: RK 6.iii.935–36, 942–43; see also 6.i.904.

8. See also the words of Haldir, speaking of the battle between Galadriel and Sauron: "In this high place you may see the two powers that are opposed one to another; and ever they strive now in thought, but whereas the light perceives the very heart of the darkness, its own secret has not been discovered. Not yet" (FR 2.vi.352).

9. See RC 669–70; Thompson 13; C. Tolkien, *Sauron* 109, 112n2.

9. HOBBITS IN DARKNESS

1. Shippey on the complexity of evil in Middle-earth is fundamental, but the field is fertile (*Road* 140–50). See Christopher Garbowski (417–30) and Scull and Hammond (C&G 2.458–64). What we need, however, is book-length scrutiny of Tolkien's primary texts both synchronically and diachronically, so we may can understand the actual dynamics of evil in the Secondary World. We may then apply Primary World theories and theologies profitably.

2. As noted on page 172, Galadriel's particular gift to the Ring-bearer indicates her foresight, and she had also seen at least some of what Sam saw in her Mirror. The waters of her Mirror are the medium through which she sees across time and space, and the phial contains the light of Eärendil caught in those waters. That touching the Mirror might have caught Sauron's eye seems implicit in her warning to Frodo against touching the water. She may then be able to make contact through the Mirror, as through a palantír. The importance of water, as shown by her Ring, her mirror, and her phial, could point to a link with Ulmo, as Sam McBride points out (87). Further, in "Ósanwe-kenta" Tolkien writes that "distance in itself offers no impediment whatsoever to ósanwe," and that urgency on the part of the sender and receiver can strengthen the "transmission of thought" (*Nature* 209). The image of Galadriel Sam

sees in his mind recalls the *indemmar* or "mind-pictures" that "some extremity of need" could communicate (199). If so, it would be her voice speaking through Frodo and Sam when they invoke Eärendil and Elbereth. She did bid Frodo remember her and her mirror when giving them the phial. So Sam's cry to Galadriel may be spot on.

3. As Anna Vaninskaya remarks, "if the Christian aspect stands behind Sam's vision of hope in Mordor, 'heathen' despair (in close connection with suicide) reappears at crucial moments as well" (177). Vaninskaya's observations on despair and suicide focus on Denethor, noting that Denethor's suicide and Sam's glimpse of the star occur on the same day, but overlooking Sam's prior contemplation of taking his own life (176).

4. See, for Frodo on saving the Shire: FR 1.ii.62; RK 6.ix.1029; Gollum: TT 4.i.618, ii.632; iii.638, ix.724; Frodo on Boromir: 4v.665; Frodo on Gollum: x.714. See also Frodo to Gollum: 4.vi.687, 688, 690. In the last passage, Gollum weaves together quite a few elements: promises and flattery, fawning and pleading, and the invocation of the Ring through the wink of secret knowledge shared by Gollum and Frodo.

5. Unsurprisingly, the OED definition of *bow* in the sense of "submit" uses the words "bend the neck under a yoke ... hence ... submit" ("Bow, v.1").

6. See Gordon, "The Battle of Maldon," lines 312–13: "*Hige sceal þe heardra, heorte þe cenre, / mod sceal þe mare þe ure maegen lytlaþ.*"

7. Whether Tolkien's interpretation is correct is irrelevant to our concerns here. As Mary R. Bowman has written: "Even if his reading of the poem were universally rejected it would still be legitimate to regard it as informing his use of the poem in his fiction" (95).

8. For "leer," see FR 1.vi.121; TT 3.v.489, ix.566, 4.viii.703; "paw": TT 3.iii.455, ix.564, 4.i.618, ii.633, 634, iii.637, viii.714 (twice); and "treasure": FR 1.ii.40, iii.66, xii.208; 2.ii.243, 247; RK 5.ix.879, 6.i.912, 943.

9. Anna Smol highlights this difference thus: "Frodo's memories, unlike Sam's do not return to his group of friends, but to Bilbo and a youthful, innocent past that Frodo has already lost" (42). The text bears this out. Sam refers to his Gaffer (most often), but also to his uncle Andy, his grandfather, his little sister, Marigold, and of course to Tom, Jolly, Nibs, and Rosie Cotton (FR 2.vi.347; vii.361, 363, 366; 4.i.608, 611; ii.623; iii.637; iv.654; v.680; vii.700; 6.iii.934; vii.995; viii.1004, 1011). Frodo, too, mentions the Gaffer, but only in response to Sam's mentioning him first (TT 4.i. 608, 611; ii.624).

10. For "longed" or "longing," see 1.i.35, 40, ii.56, viii.147, x.170, xi.192, 195, xii.203; 2.ii.240, 270, vi.351, ix.382; 3.iii.791, iv.482; 5.v.831, vii.852, ix.873; 6.i.908, iii.936.

11. See also "He dude him seoluen bitweonen us & his feader þe þreatte us forte smiten ase moder þe is reowðful deð hire bitweonen hire child ant te wraðe sturne feader hwen he hit wule beaten" (187/17–20) ("He put himself between us and his Father who was threatening to smite us just as a mother who is merciful puts herself between her child and the wrath of a stern father when he wishes to beat him.")

12. Hood further remarks that "once Frodo undertakes to enforce this oath, he becomes a Dark Lord to Gollum, and Sam begins to perceive elements of the Dark Lord in him without quite understanding what he is seeing" (16).

13. See also the words of Anna Smol: "Moments before entering the Sammath Naur, Frodo says farewell to Sam, looking at him as if he were far away. In leaving Sam and entering the heart of Sauron's realm, Frodo chooses to claim the Ring" (55). It is as if in entering the heart of his realm, Frodo entered Sauron's very heart.

14. Tolkien considers "attempting to conquer Sauron with the Ring" an exceptionally bad idea, because it inevitably corrupts the conquerors (*Letters*, no. 66, p. 78). That Tolkien expressed this opinion in May 1944, while writing book 4, in which Frodo begins to use or to try to use the Ring to this end, falls into the category of "chance, if chance you call it." See also his comments to W. H. Auden on the rightness and wrongness of causes and how those on either side can do deeds morally at odds with their cause (no. 183, pp. 242–43).

15. See also Katharyn W. Crabbe's assessment: "The very proximity to the Ring that will allow him to save the world threatens to make of him the source of its destruction. That is, on the edges of the cracks of doom the Ring succeeds in making of Frodo a hobbit Sauron" (87).

16. According to the Tenth Article of Henry Tuberville's *Douay Catechism*, the one Tolkien would have known, God's "mercy is far above our malice." Mercy thus "negates and erases the effects of malice," as Matthew DeForrest has summed it up (228). In turn, this suggests that mercy such as Bilbo and Frodo showed Gollum might be expected to promote, but not achieve, the healing Gandalf hoped to see in Gollum. For human mercy is less than Divine Mercy in the same way that human pity is less than Divine Pity, and so not enough to heal the effects of the Ring's (and Sauron's) malice.

17. Jane Chance, building on Frodo's threat that he could successfully order Gollum to commit suicide, if he so chose (*TT* 4.iii.640), suggests that this is what happens: "At the end, Gollum so desires the Ring that he obeys when Frodo apparently commands him to do so" (*Mythology* 87). There is no evidence in the text, however, to make this apparent. Frodo no longer has the Ring when Gollum goes over the brink and had great difficulty controlling Gollum when he still possessed it. So, we may well doubt the force of so unlikely a command from Frodo who has just claimed the Ring for himself. Gergely Nagy, moreover, emphasizes that "Gollum's fall is clearly described to be accidental" and a command from Frodo "would severely impair the eucatastrophic or providential nature of this simple accident" ("Gollum" 247).

18. On this moment as an exemplification of this section of The Lord's Prayer, see Letter no. 181, p. 233, and another letter of the same period, unpublished but preserved in Shippey (*Road* 145n). We should also bear in mind that both of these letters reflect Tolkien's annoyance at a comment in the *Times Literary Supplement* review of *Return of the King* in November 1955 about the lack of mercy shown to Orcs.

10. FROM THE BLACK LAND TO THE UNDYING LANDS

1. *FR* 1.i.21, ii.40, iii.68, vii.144, 2.ii.248, 249, 264; iii.291; *TT* 3.vi.511, viii.597, xi.593 (twice), 594, 4.iv.656, v.669, vii.695, x.733, 741; *RK* 5.vi.842 (twice), viii.859, 6.i.912, iii.947, viii.1,001.

2. See John Garth ("Frodo" 41–56); Michael Livingston (9–22) and Andrew Krokstrom (131–43).

3. Her words in "The Passing of the Grey Company" are important, but indirectly reported (*RK* 5.ii.775). From her words there and in "The Tale of Aragorn and Arwen," it is clear that Tolkien quickly envisaged her as "all in" from the plighting of their troth onward. What that might have led to, given the active role Lúthien played and with the time to develop Arwen's role from, say, Rivendell on, is intriguing but not relevant here.

4. Commenting on the words *wigspeda gewiofu*, "weavings of victory," that is "victorious fortunes" (thus Tolkien), Friederich Klaeber noted that "as the context shows, the conception of the "weaving" of destiny . . . has become a mere figure of speech" (*Beowulf* 597). Tolkien tended to agree (*Beowulf T&C* 267). Fred Robinson rightly wonders "whether figures of speech are 'mere' when they occur in poetry" (46n63). As we have seen, it is a figure of speech Tolkien used more than once.

5. The widely found reading "hopes end" resulted from a printer's error for "hope's end" since corrected (see Hammond and Scull, *RC* 563).

6. In addition to the threat of informants found both in Mordor and the Shire, the driving of the Shirriffs along the road by Frodo and his companions recalls the orcs' driving of Frodo and Sam along the road in Mordor and of Merry and Pippin across Rohan (*RK* 6.ii.924–25, 929–31, vi.984, viii.1002–03; *TT* 3.iii.444–59).

7. In an earlier draft of this scene, Sam goes on to say precisely this: "But I'm glad I didn't know before. All the time in the bad places we've been in I've had the Shire in mind, and that's what I've rested on, if you take my meaning. I'd not have had a hope if I'd known all this" (*Sauron* 90).

8. Faramir twice uses this form of command, drawing a line that must not be crossed (*TT* 4.v.675, vi.691).

11. PITY AND POWER IN TIME

1. Note that in quoting W. P. Ker, Tolkien slightly misquoted his final phrase: "The Northern gods have an exultant extravagance in their warfare which makes them more like Titans than Olympians; only they are on the right side, though it is not the side that wins. The winning side is Chaos and Unreason; but the gods, who are defeated, think that defeat is not refutation" (57–58).

2. Tolkien, among others, believed there are problems with the text of *Beowulf* here. He considered lines 168–69 and 180–88 later interpolations (*Beowulf T&C*, pp. 169–86). Deleting these lines makes "Swylc wæs þeaw hyra / hæþenra hyht"—"Such was their custom, the hope of the heathens"—a more forceful poetic and judgement on the Danes (ll. 178–79).

Anna Vaninskaya sees Denethor as representative as of the hopelessness of heathens, rightly, but does not distinguish, as I have tried to do, between those like Denethor and those like Théoden, Éomer, and Éowyn (178–79). Denethor's "part," as Gandalf tells him, "is to go out to the battle of your City, where maybe death awaits you" (RK 5.vii.852). Even Éowyn, by contrast, though fey and hopeless, does not seek death through suicide and certainly does not acquiesce to defeat (5.iii.803). She goes to her death (as she thinks) as Beowulf goes to his.

3. See *Letters* no. 144, p. 178–79 (quoted above on page 84). The passage beginning "but if" clearly supports the idea that the "temptation" comes from within.

4. Thus, Brian Rosebury remarks of "The Children of Húrin" that Morgoth is hardly the "master-manipulator" of Túrin or the direct cause of the events in his life. Túrin "acts as he does because of the kind of person he is" (15). On Túrin and Oedipus, see Dimitra Fimi (43–56).

5. In the second section of his first lecture on *Macbeth*, Bradley is discussing Macbeth's Fate and the Witches. So "fatal" is quite literal, as the emphasis indicates. Given Tolkien's emotional engagement with *Macbeth* and his familiarity with Bradley's lectures (first published in 1904)—he checked them out of the Exeter College library in 1915 to help him study for his exams (Cilli 26)—Bradley's view of how Macbeth succumbs to evil, that is, from within, may well have influenced, for example, Tolkien's portrayal of Boromir, who had thought of being king long before he fantasized aloud about it to Frodo on Amon Hen (FR 2.ix.398; TT 4.v.670).

6. See Verlyn Flieger (*Question of Time* 191–93) and Hillman et al. ("Eldar" 135–36).

7. For discussion of the pagan and Christian coloring of *Beowulf*, see the introduction to *Klaeber's Beowulf* by Fulk, Bjork, and Niles (lxvii–xxv).

8. In *Beowulf* lines 2815–17 we hear Beowulf's last words: "Ealle wyrd forsweop / mine magas to metodsceafte, / eorlas on elne. Ic him æfter sceal." "Fate has swept away all / my kinsmen at their appointed time, / warriors in their strength. I must go after them." The juxtaposition of the fate of his kinsmen *at their time* with his need to follow them shows that he sees this as his time, just as it was not his time against either Grendel or his mother. On this rendering of "to metodsceafte," see W. S. Mackie (96).

9. The *Beowulf*-poet was not the only one to live in that moment of fusion. In the *Heliand*, the Old Saxon heroic retelling of the story of Christ, its poet more than once refers to pagan and Christian concepts in the same breath. See, for example, lines 127–28: "*sô habed im uurdgiscapu, / metod gimarcod endi math godes*": "So have the fates, the measurer, and the power of God marked out for him." James E. Cathey remarks: "That is, the authority of the pre-Christian concepts of those forces which preordain the course of one's life are equated here with the might of the single Christian God" (143–44).

10. Testi translates the French of Louis Capéran (592) that "the damnation of all pagans that have never heard of Jesus Christ has never been a Catholic doctrine" (131). Just so. Yet whether *any* pagans *might* be saved and what a pagan needed for salvation were enduring questions of more than metaphysical import. In the late seventh century, Redbad, king of the Frisians, refused baptism upon learning at the last moment that his ancestors, who had not been baptized, were damned. A northern king who lived in the time to which many, including Tolkien, have dated the composition of *Beowulf* preferred Hell with his ancestors. For Redbad, it was a world well lost. On Redbad, see now Nijdam and Knottnerus (90–91). On the "problem of paganism" through the

early eighteenth century, see John Marenbon. On the much-contested date of *Beowulf*'s composition, see Fulk, Bjork, and Niles (pp. clxii–clxxxiii).

11. Tom Shippey writes: "His characters are heathens, strictly speaking, and Tolkien, having pondered for so long on the *Beowulf*-poet's careful balances, was as aware of this fact as he was aware of the opposing images of open Christianity poised at many moments to take over his story" (*Road*, 202).

12. In a 1944 letter to his son Christopher, Tolkien criticized the Allies' efforts to win the war: "We started out [the war] with a great many Orcs on our side" (*Letters*, no. 66, p. 78).

13. Claudio Testi notes that the word *Providence* never occurs in *The Lord of the Rings* (117). Instead, we find *fate* or *doom*, which indicate a pagan rather than a Christian perspective.

14. Frye further says, "The encyclopaedic knowledge in such poems is regarded sacramentally, as a human analogy of divine knowledge" (57). By "encyclopaedic," he means "epic" rather than "episodic," and "such poems" refers to those produced by poets held to be "inspired."

15. See Amelia A. Rutledge's fine analysis of the dilemma faced by the Valar (and Tolkien) in coming to terms with what Justice means in Arda Marred (59–74).

16. Tolkien summarized *The Lord of the Rings* book by book in his 1951 letter to Milton Waldman of Collins, but Humphrey Carpenter omitted the summary from his edition of Tolkien's *Letters*, wrongfully as it preserves many intriguing details (no. 131, p. 160). Hammond and Scull provide the entire summary (*RC* 742–49).

17. In sending Gandalf back, Ilúvatar makes good the failure of the policy of his servants: "He was sent by a mere prudent plan of the angelic Valar or governors; but Authority had taken up this plan and enlarged it, at the moment of its failure" (*Letters* no. 156, p. 202). On the use of the passive in "I was sent back," see pages 253–54 with notes.

18. For the Kyrie, see the extensive discussion of Josef Jungmann, who dates its introduction into the Roman liturgy to the fifth century, though it was familiar far longer than that (333–46).

19. While Lewis and Tolkien were by no means in agreement everywhere, in chapter eleven of *Perelandra* we may see Lewis exploring a similar notion regarding Divine Mercy and Pity, beginning with "'My name also is Ransom,' said the Voice" (126). In *Letters* no. 154, p. 189, Tolkien makes clear that immortality and reincarnation for Elves (*not* Men) is likewise an exploration in a Secondary World of how God might have done things differently than he did in the Primary World. He thus assumes a different theology in the Secondary World than in the Primary.

20. Tolkien knew well where the paths of glory lead. See Janet Brennan Croft ("War" [2004] 127–47; "War" [2020] 461–72) and John Garth ("Great War" 287–313) for balanced and thoughtful assessments of Tolkien's feelings.

21. Fred Robinson writes: "The obliqueness with which the poet presents his characters' spiritual status, averring that they are pagans and yet presenting them in a way

that keeps their paganism in abeyance, is closely consonant with the studied laconism and indirection of the appositive style. It is through this style, I believe, that the poet creates a spiritual setting in which his audience can assess the men of old for what they were. He does not deny his characters' heathenism but uses the traditional diction and appositional effects to free the audience of the mind-numbing alarm which a graphic description of a pagan society would cause" (30).

22. Within *The Lord of the Rings*, characters mention the destruction of Númenor several times, always as if referring to a known tale. See FR 2.ii.242; TT 4.v.676; RK 5.ii.789, x.889, 6.v.962, App. A 1035–37, App. B 1084.

23. With the arrival of Eärendil in Tírion while all its people were absent at a festival, we may compare the earlier arrival of Melkor in Valimar at a similar moment. Their purposes of course could not have differed more. Eärendil came seeking pity and mercy while Melkor had come for revenge. The evils done and set in motion by Melkor that day required the Valar's direct intervention. As Simon Stacey says, Tolkien links the two moments explicitly, much as he does here, I would add, by linking the endings of the Second and Third Ages (94–95). For a perceptive account of the important links of the untold tale of the Last Alliance at the end of the Second Age to *The Lord of the Rings* at the end of the Third, see now Peter Grybauskas (25–49).

24. According to Plato's *Timaeus*, not only did the island of Atlantis "sink beneath the sea and vanish" (κατὰ τῆς θαλάττης δῦσα ἠφανίσθη), but the entire Athenian army, which had defeated an invasion from Atlantis, "sank beneath the earth" (ἔδυ κατὰ γῆς) (*Atlantis Story*, 25c–d). The fate of the Númenóreans thus combines that of the Atlanteans and the Athenians. Since both δῦσα (*dusa*) and ἔδυ (*edu*) are different forms of the verb δύω (*duo*), which means "sink" or, when applied to the sun, "set," it seems no coincidence that *dûn* means "west" in Sindarin, from the Primitive Elvish root √ndu, possessing much of the same range of meaning as δύω.

25. In his survey of many such legends (204–20), E. S. Hartland recounts the following story: "A body of the Emperor Karl the Great's warriors had become so puffed up by their own successes that at last they pointed their guns and cannon against heaven itself. Scarcely had they discharged their pieces when the whole host sank into the earth" (216). Given that the Númenóreans who attacked Valinor had artillery, the combination of similar details in Hartland, that is, a great king, a war on heaven, arrogance, cannon, and burial, suggests Tolkien may have known this particular tale (*Lost* 12, 15, 67).

26. Corey Olsen has correctly noted this in "Council of Elrond 56," episode 180 of *Exploring the Lord of the Rings* podcast, 30 March 2021, https://youtu.be/Dl_NxL4VvPQ?t=5050, starting at 1:24:10.

27. Although Freeman also mentions Hebrews 11.1, he does not connect the wording of Finrod's description of *amdir*, its implications for the meaning of *estel* with which Finrod is contrasting *amdir*, and the wording of the appositive phrase in Hebrews.

28. In *Letters* no. 43, p. 51 and no. 250, p. 337, Tolkien speaks of Faith as an act of will, both in terms of being faithful in marriage and religion. WJ 318–19 preserves a note written on a late typescript (ca. 1970) of a much earlier manuscript (1951): "*estel*, was used in Q[uenya] and S[indarin] for "hope"—sc. A temper of mind, steady, fixed

in purpose, and difficult to dissuade and unlikely to fall into despair or abandon its purpose." This definition is as fine a description of Aragorn's character as one could imagine. The name Estel suits him well.

29. William Lane writes: "A review of the linguistic evidence for the meaning of the term [ὑπόστασις] at the time Hebrews was written demonstrates that ὑπόστασις denoted tangible reality in contrast to mere appearance" (325, note b). In calling this a "common patristic interpretation" of Hebrews 11.1, he draws on the article of Michael A. Mathis and Lino Murillo (79–89). See also at 326, note e: "Syntactically, the second clause is in apposition to the first, with the result that ὑπόστασις, "reality," "realization," is strengthened by ἔλεγχος. This shows that ἔλεγχος has an obj[ective] rather than a subj[ective] sense: 'proof,' 'evidence,' 'demonstration.'"

30. For discussion of the "divine passive" in Tolkien, see Kusumita P. Pedersen (23–26). Pedersen plausibly suggests that Tolkien could have known of the usage from texts he may have used to study New Testament Greek but also concedes that he could easily have recognized on his own how the passive voice works in such instances. Knowledge of the "divine passive" as such is not necessary for recognition of what Gandalf and Elrond are communicating, especially since the text does not just use this device but draws attention to its doing so. Fleming Rutledge suggests that the divine passive's "allusion" to God "is easy to miss... because it is veiled under those passives" (63). I will agree that Frodo does not understand the allusion, but he is aware that Gandalf is making one. Despite a nudge and a wink from Gandalf, Frodo seems to lack the knowledge to get the allusion. Why Gandalf cannot speak more plainly is an intriguing question, whose answer may lie in allowance for the exercise of free will. In Arda there appears to be no prohibition against speaking the divine name, as there is in Judaism, and which forms the basis for the divine passive and other circumlocutions.

On the "divine passive" in the New Testament, see first Joachim Jeremias, who points out that Jesus uses it to speak apocalyptically of the actions of God not just in the end times, as was the norm, but also in the present (9–14). Elrond and Gandalf employ it of the present.

31. Gandalf's divine passive "I was sent back" represents the one of the few certain instances of direct divine intervention mentioned in *The Lord of the Rings*, since he had died and left the world entirely (*TT* 3.v.502). He was thus beyond the reach of the Valar; only Ilúvatar could have sent him back. The intervention of the One in Númenor is stated directly, but that is outside the tale proper (*RK* App. A I.i.1037). The two comments by Tolkien quoted above (pages 245–46) demonstrate that he saw Eru, not the Valar, as the agent who meant Bilbo and Frodo to have the Ring. This suggests that the same is true of the council of Elrond. With one extraordinary exception, Ilúvatar remains hidden, as do his servants, the Valar, and their messengers, the Istari. Yet, consider the recent intriguing efforts of Sam McBride to explore such interventions in the Third Age (47–141).

32. Note that "her people" here refers to the people of Gondor, that is, to Men, but in Elrond's phrase "Evenstar of her people," the reference is to Elves (*FR* 2.i.227; *RK*

6.v.972, App A I.v.1059). Sam McBride has it that "the direct description (light of her eyes quenched) and the figurative language (night with no stars) suggest a physiological transformation from Elf to Human" (207). Yet, according to App A I.v.1062, it was on the departure of Elrond over a century earlier that "Arwen became as a mortal woman, and yet it was not her lot to die" until Aragorn had. The words *as a mortal woman* pinpoint the moment and the extent of the change. In every other regard, she appeared the same. The description and language of which McBride speaks thus marks the moment she finally accepts the implications of her choice of Mortality—which she viewed as "long over"—but they do not mark a physiological change. This is in keeping with her nature and her understanding of it until now. See note 33 below.

33. Hammond and Scull report an unpublished Tolkien letter of 1963 in which he said of Arwen that "although she had become mortal, by nature she was still Elvish, with the long view of life held by that immortal race" (*RC* 701).

34. The OE noun *læn* means "loan, grant, gift," commonly of something given that will or may be recalled by the giver ("Læn, n."). The adjective *læne* thus describes something granted in this way, and as such "granted for a time only, not permanent, temporary, frail" ("Læne, adj."). The first quotation illustrating the use of *læne* in the entry here cited directly contrasts it with *éce* (*æce*), "eternal": "*Ac ic wolde witan hweðer hyt ðe þuhte be ðam ðe ðu hæfst hweðer hyt were ðe læene ðe æce.*" "But I wished to know whether what you have seemed to you to be temporary or eternal."

35. In Boethius' *The Consolation of Philosophy,* Lady Philosophy explains God's perspective on time: "Therefore, since every judgement takes up those things which come under it according to its own nature, and since God's state is everlasting and ever present, his knowledge also stands above every movement of time and abides in the simplicity of his own present; and encompassing the infinite spaces of past and future time in his simple perception, his knowledge observes them all as if they are happening now" (5.P6.58–64).

36. As noted above, Arwen's calling Aragorn by his Elven name as he dies plays on its meaning. At their final meeting, not long before her death, Gilraen also plays on *estel* as his name and as "hope" in her parting words: "Ónen i-Estel Edain, ú-chebin estel anim," which Tolkien renders "I gave Hope to the Dúnedain, I have kept no hope for myself" (*RK* App. A.I.v.1061).

37. According to Scull and Hammond's chronology, Tolkien may have begun "The Tale of Aragorn and Arwen" as early as September 1952 but will have made the final revisions to which Christopher Tolkien refers by March or April 1955, when *The Return of the King* was in proof (*C&G* 1.411, 476).

38. Nicholas Birns writes: "As in most of Tolkien's revision-during-composition process, the later an element appeared, the more serious it was" ("Grown" 82). Here, he builds on his earlier arguments ("Enigma" 113–26).

39. Gwindor's remarks to Finduilas about her hopes for the love of Túrin can also serve as commentary on Aegnor and Andreth (*S* 210). The differences in their lifespans make a match unfitting, unwise, and a thing "fate" will "suffer once or twice only, for some high cause of doom."

40. Christopher Tolkien quite reasonably dates the "Athrabeth" to 1959. Since, however, there is only one manuscript draft, which would be rather unusual for Tolkien, and since there are notes on "slips made from documents of the year 1955," Christopher Tolkien wisely allows that he may have been working on it for several years (*Morgoth* 303–04).

41. Thingol's regarding Túrin as his own child goes all the way back to "Of Turambar and the Foalókë" in *The Book of Lost Tales* (BL 2.77). In this context, one of Túrin's many names stands out: Adanedhel, or Man-Elf. His mother, Morwen, from whom Túrin got his looks was called Eledhwen, "Elfsheen," that is, "a woman of elfin beauty," from Old English *ælfsciene*, a word applied in Old English poems retelling parts of Bible to women who are strong and significant as well as beautiful. In "Genesis A" this word twice describes Sarah (Doane, ll. 1827, 2731). In "Judith" we find it used once of Judith (Cook, l. 14).

42. In his letters, Tolkien describes his legendarium variously as an "imaginary world," an "imaginary historical moment," an "imaginary time," an "imaginary mythical Age": *Letters* no. 124, p. 136; no. 131, p. 143 (twice); no. 142, p. 172; no. 144, p. 174 (twice); no. 153, p. 188, 189; no 163, p. 212, 215; no. 183, p. 239 (three times), 244; no. 190, p. 250 (three times); no. 211, p. 283; no 247, p. 333; no. 294, p. 375 (twice); no. 297, p. 385; no. 316, p. 405.

43. Yet we need not infer from the presence of this evil that creation itself is flawed. John William Houghton points out that "while the contrast [between the Primary World as Christians understand it and the Secondary World as Tolkien understood it] is a legitimate one, it does not seem to me that Morgoth's pollution reaches to the level of a flaw in Creation. The evil in Ëa, however primordial, still has a place in the pattern of Ilúvatar, while Augustine would say that God's assessment of the world as 'very good' includes evil—it is a verdict on the whole of the universe as unfolded in time, not merely on the state of affairs at the moment of Creation" ("Augustine" 182n10).

44. For his humility on this issue, see above on page 244. At *Morgoth* 354–56, Christopher Tolkien discusses a note of his father's on the "Athrabeth," which touches also on the question of telling of the Fall and "The Tale of Adanel." While the meaning of the note is somewhat vexed, Tolkien was uncomfortable addressing the subject: "Is it not right to make Andreth refuse to discuss any traditions or legends of the 'Fall'? Already it is (if inevitably) too like a parody of Christianity. Any legend of the Fall would make it completely so?" (354).

45. See Elizabeth Vandiver on the syncretism of the age: "Some poets invoked not just classical allusions but the Olympians, by name, and in a tone that would imply utter sincerity did we not know that the soldiers of 1914–1918 did not, in fact, worship the pagan gods" (206).

46. Halliwell writes in *Aristotle's* Poetics: "That the *Poetics* is the work of a philosopher, not just in the trivial biographical sense, but by the nature of its ideas, its methods, and its underlying values, ought to be, but in fact is not, a platitude. A major reason for this is the division within modern scholarship between specialized study of Aristotelian philosophy, which regards the *Poetics* as marginal to the system (when it regards it at all), and study of the *Poetics* by literary scholars who often show little interest in the

work's relation to its author's wider thought. The serious interpreter of the treatise will wish, so far as his competence allows, to resist this dichotomy" (2–3).

47. On Sophocles' *Oedipus Tyrannos* in the context of Athens at the time of the play's production in 430 BCE or soon thereafter, see Bernard Knox's *Oedipus at Thebes: Sophocles" Tragic Hero and His Time*.

48. On this earlier dating for "The Music of the Ainur," see John Garth ("Chronology" 89–105).

Works Cited

"Ælfen. n." *The Dictionary of Old English,* https://tapor.library.utoronto.ca/doe/?E01839. Accessed 15 January 2023.

Alford, C. Fred. "Greek Tragedy and Civilization: The Cultivation of Pity." *Political Research Quarterly,* vol. 46, no. 2, 1993, pp. 259–80. JSTOR, https://doi.org/10.2307/448886.

Amendt-Raduege, Amy. "Better Off Dead: The Lessons of the Ringwraiths." *Fastitocalon: Studies in Fantasticism Ancient to Modern,* vol. 1, no. 1, 2010, pp. 69–82.

———. *"The Sweet and the Bitter": Death and Dying in J. R. R. Tolkien's* The Lord of the Rings, Kent State University Press, 2018.

Aquinas, Thomas. *Summa Theologiae.* 5 vols. Biblioteca de Autores Cristianos, 1955–58.

Aristotle. *Poetics,* Edited and translated by Stephen Halliwell. Harvard University Press, 1955–58.

"Astrai, adj. & adv." *Middle English Compendium.* https://quod.lib.umich.edu/m/middle-english-dictionary/dictionary/MED2693. Accessed 12 May 2022.

Augustine. *The City of God against the Pagans, Books 8–11 [De Civitate Dei].* Translated by David S. Wiesen. 1968, Harvard University Press, 2007. Vol. 3 of *The City of God against the Pagans.*

Augustine and James H. Baxter. *Select Letters.* Rev. ed. 1953, Harvard University Press, 2006.

"Automatism, n." *OED Online,* Oxford University Press, https://www.oed.com/view/Entry/13469. Accessed 25 May 2022.

"Between, prep., adv., and n." *OED Online,* Oxford University Press, https://www.oed.com/view/Entry/18395. Accessed 11 May 2022.

Birns, Nicholas. "The Enigma of Radagast: Revision, Melodrama, and Depth." *Mythlore: A Journal of J. R. R. Tolkien, C. S. Lewis, Charles Williams, and Mythopoeic Literature,* vol. 26, no. 1, 2007, pp. 113–26.

———. "'You Have Grown Very Much': The Scouring of the Shire and the Novelistic Aspects of 'The Lord of the Rings.'" *Journal of the Fantastic in the Arts,* vol. 23, no. 1, 2012, pp. 82–101.

Birzer, Bradley J. *J. R. R. Tolkien's Sanctifying Myth: Understanding Middle-Earth.* Intercollegiate Studies Institute, 2003.

Boethius, Anicius Manlius Severinus. *De Consolatione Philosophiae Opuscula Theologica.* 2nd ed. Edited by Claudio Moreschini. K. G. Saur, 2005.

Bosworth, Joseph, and Thomas Northcote Toller, editors, *An Anglo-Saxon Dictionary Online,* Faculty of Arts, Charles University, 2014, https:/bosworth toller.com. Accessed 22 May 2023.

"Bow, v.1." *OED Online,* Oxford University Press. https://www.oed.com/view/Entry/22188. Accessed 11 May 2022.

Bowman, Mary R. "Refining the Gold: Tolkien, 'The Battle of Maldon,' and the Northern Theory of Courage." *Tolkien Studies,* vol. 7, no. 1, 2010, pp. 91–115.

Bradley, Andrew C. *Shakespearean Tragedy: Lectures on* Hamlet, Othello, King Lear, Macbeth. Penguin, 1991.

Brown, Sara. "The Importance of Home in the Middle-earth Legendarium." Forest-Hill, pp. 99–107.

Burns, Marjorie. "King and Hobbit: The Exalted and Lowly in Tolkien's Created Worlds." Hammond and Scull, *Blackwelder,* pp. 139–52.

Caldecott, Stratford. *The Power of the Ring: The Spiritual Vision Behind* The Lord of the Rings *and* The Hobbit. Crossroad, 2013.

Camacho, Pamina Fernández. "Cyclic Cataclysms, Semitic Stereotypes, and Religious Reforms: A Classicist's Númenor." Forest-Hill, pp. 191–206.

Capéran, Louis. *Le problème de salut des infidèles: Essai théologique.* 1912. Grande Séminaire, 1934.

Carpenter, Humphrey. *Tolkien: A Biography.* Houghton Mifflin, 1977.

Carr, Brian. "Pity and Compassion as Social Virtues." *Philosophy,* vol. 74, no. 289, 1999, pp. 411–29.

Cathey, James E., editor. *Hêliand: Text and Commentary.* 1st ed, West Virginia University Press, 2002.

Chance, Jane. The Lord of the Rings: *The Mythology of Power.* Rev. ed., University Press of Kentucky, 2001.

———. "Subversive Fantasist: Tolkien on Class Difference." Hammond and Scull, *Blackwelder,* pp. 153–68.

———, editor. *Tolkien and the Invention of Myth: A Reader.* University Press of Kentucky, 2010.

———. *Tolkien the Medievalist.* Taylor & Francis, 2008.

Chesterton, G. K. *The Coloured Lands: Fairy Stories, Comic Verse, and Fantastic Pictures.* 1938. Dover Publications, 2009.

Christensen, Bonniejean. "Gollum's Character Transformation in *The Hobbit.*" *A Tolkien Compass,* edited by Jared Lobdell, 2nd ed., Open Court, 2003, pp. 7–26.

Cilli, Oronzo, and T. A. Shippey. *Tolkien's Library: An Annotated Checklist.* Luna Press, 2019.

Cohen, Jeffrey Jerome. "Monster Culture (Seven Theses)." Cohen, pp. 3–25.

Cohen, Jeffrey Jerome, editor. *Monster Theory: Reading Culture.* University of Minnesota Press, 1996.
Cook, Albert S., editor. *Judith: An Old English Epic Fragment.* Heath, 1904.
Cook, Simon. *The Apprenticeship of J. R. R. Tolkien.* Kindle ed. Rounded Globe, 2018.
Crabbe, Katharyn W. *J. R. R. Tolkien.* Rev. and Expanded ed., Continuum, 1988.
Croft, Janet Brennan. "War." Lee, pp. 461–72.
———. *War and the Works of J. R. R. Tolkien.* Praeger, 2004.
Croft, Janet Brennan, editor. *Baptism of Fire: The Birth of the Modern British Fantastic in World War I.* Mythopoeic Press, 2015.
———. *Tolkien and Shakespeare: Essays on Shared Themes and Language.* McFarland, 2007.
Croft, Janet Brennan and Leslie Donovan, editors. *Perilous and Fair: Women in the Works and Life of J. R. R. Tolkien.* Mythopoeic Press, 2015
DeForrest, Matthew M. "Pity, Malice, and Agency in Tolkien's Subcreation." *Critical Insights:* The Lord of the Rings, edited by Robert C. Evans, Salem Press, 2022, pp. 227–40.
"Desolate, adj. and n." *OED Online,* Oxford University Press. https://www.oed.com/view/Entry/50916. Accessed 6 June 2022.
Dickerson, Matthew. *A Hobbit Journey: Discovering the Enchantment of J. R. R. Tolkien's Middle-earth.* 2003. Brazos Press, 2012.
Doane, A. N., editor. *Genesis A: A New Edition, Revised.* Arizona Center for Medieval and Renaissance Studies, 2013.
Drout, Michael D. C., and Hilary Wynne. "Tom Shippey's *J. R R. Tolkien: Author of the Century* and a Look Back at Tolkien Criticism since 1982." *Envoi,* vol. 9, no. 2, 2000, pp. 100–67.
Eaglestone, Robert, editor. *Reading* The Lord of the Rings: *New Writings on Tolkien's Classics.* Continuum, pp. 85–98.
Eden, Bradford Lee, editor. The Hobbit *and Tolkien's Mythology: Essays on Revisions and Influences.* McFarland, 2014, pp. 161–80.
Enright, Nancy. "Tolkien's Females and the Defining of Power." Croft and Donovan, pp. 118–35.
Fimi, Dimitra. "Wildman of the Woods: Inscribing Tragedy on the Landscape of Middle-Earth in *The Children of Húrin.*" *Tolkien: The Forest and the City.* edited by Helen Conrad-O'Briain and Gerard Hynes, Four Courts Press, 2013, pp. 43–56.
Flieger, Verlyn. *A Question of Time: J. R. R. Tolkien's Road to Faërie.* 1997. Kent State University Press, 2004.
———. *Splintered Light: Logos and Language in Tolkien's World.* 2nd ed., Kent State University Press, 2002.
———. "Tolkien's French Connection." *There Would Always Be a Fairy Tale: More Essays on Tolkien,* Kent State University Press, 2017, pp. 201–12.
Flieger, Verlyn and Carl F. Hostetter, editors. *Tolkien's Legendarium: Essays on the History of Middle-earth.* Greenwood, 2000.

Forrest-Hill, Lynn. *The Return of the Ring: proceedings of the Tolkien Society Conference 2012*, vol. 1. Luna, 2016.

Freeman, Austin M. "*Pietas* and the Fall of the City: A Neglected Virgilian Influence on Middle-Earth's Chief Virtue." Williams, pp. 131–64.

Frye, Northrop. *Anatomy of Criticism: Four Essays*, 1957. Princeton University Press, 2000.

Fulk, R. D., Robert E. Bjork, and John D. Niles. Introduction. Fulk, Bjork, and Niles, pp. xxiii–cxc.

———, editors. *Klaeber's Beowulf and the Fight at Finnsburg*. Fourth ed., University of Toronto Press, 2014.

"Fundamentally, adv." *OED Online*, Oxford University Press. https://www.oed.com/view/Entry/75500. Accessed 11 May 2022.

Garbowski, Christopher. "Evil." Lee, pp. 417–30.

Garth, John. "The Chronology of Creation: How J. R. R. Tolkien Misremembered the Beginnings of His Mythology." Ovenden and McIlwaine, pp. 89–105.

———. "Frodo and the Great War." Hammond and Scull, *Blackwelder*, pp. 41–56.

———. *Tolkien and the Great War: The Threshold of Middle-earth*. Houghton Mifflin, 2003.

Gill, Glen Robert. "Biblical Archetypes in The Lord of the Rings." Kerry and Miesel, pp. 69–78.

Gordon, Eric Valentine, editor. *The Battle of Maldon*. 1937. Appleton-Century Crofts, 1966.

Grybauskas, Peter. *A Sense of Tales Untold: Exploring the Edges of Tolkien's Literary Canvas*. The Kent State University Press, 2021.

Guite, Malcolm. *Lifting the Veil: Imagination and the Kingdom of God*. Square Halo Books, 2021.

Halink, Simon, editor. *Northern Myths, Modern Identities: The Nationalisation of Northern Mythologies since 1800*. Brill, 2019.

Hall, Alaric. *Elves in Anglo-Saxon England*. Boydell & Brewer, 2009.

Halliwell, Stephen. *Aristotle's Poetics*. University of Chicago Press, 1998.

———. *The Poetics of Aristotle: Translation and Commentary*. University of North Carolina Press, 1987.

Hammond, Wayne G., and Christina Scull. The Lord of the Rings: *A Reader's Companion*. 2005. HarperCollins, 2014.

———, editors. The Lord of the Rings, *1954–2004: Scholarship in Honor of Richard E. Blackwelder*. Marquette University Press, 2006.

Hartland, Edwin Sidney. *English Fairy and Other Folk Tales*. 1893. Singing Tree Press, 1968.

Hillman, Thomas. "A Long-Expected Parenthesis—Textual Clues to How Much of The Lord of the Rings Bilbo Wrote." *Alas, Not Me*, 19 May 2023, https://alasnotme.blogspot.com/2023/05/a-long-expected-parenthesis-textual.html.

———. "Not Where He Eats, but Where He Is Eaten: Bilbo's Bread and Butter Simile." *Tolkien Studies*, vol 16, 2019, p. 141.

———. "These Are Not the Elves You Are Looking For: 'Sir Orfeo,' *The Hobbit*, and the Reimagining of the Elves." *Tolkien Studies*, vol. 15, 2018, pp. 33–58.

Hillman, Thomas, et al. "Do Eldar Dream of Immortal Sheep? Dreams, Memory, and Enchantment at the End of the Third Age." *A Wilderness of Dragons: Essays in Honor of Verlyn Flieger*, edited by John D. Rateliff, Gabbro Head, 2018, pp. 114–40.

Holmes, John R. "'Like Heathen Kings': Religion as Palimpsest in Tolkien's Fiction." Kerry, *Ring and the Cross*, pp. 119–44.

Homer. *Homeri Opera*. 3. Odyssey 1–12. Edited by Thomas William Allen. 2nd ed. 1908. Oxford: Clarendon, 1917.

Hood, Gwenyth. "Sauron and Dracula." *Mythlore: A Journal of J. R. R. Tolkien, C. S. Lewis, Charles Williams, and Mythopoeic Literature*, vol. 14, no. 2, December 1987, pp. 11–17, 56.

Hopkins, Lisa. "Gollum and Caliban." Croft, *Tolkien and Shakespeare*, pp. 281–93.

Houghton, John William. "Augustine in the Cottage of Lost Play." Chance, *Tolkien the Medievalist*, pp. 171–82.

Houghton, John William et al., editors. *Tolkien in the New Century: Essays in Honor of Tom Shippey*. Kindle ed., McFarland, 2014.

Hutton, Ronald. "Can We Still Have a Pagan Tolkien: A Reply to Nils Ivar Agoy." Kerry, *Ring and the Cross*, pp. 90–105.

Jeremias, Joachim. *New Testament Theology: The Proclamation of Jesus*. Scribner's, 1971.

Joyce, James. *Dubliners*. 1914. Penguin, 1993.

Jungmann, Josef A. *The Mass of the Roman Rite: Its Origins and Development (Missarum sollemnia)*. Translated by Francis A. Brunner. 1962. Benziger Bros., 1975.

Kail, Josef., editor. *Twenty-six Political and Other Poems (includjng "Petty Job") from the Oxford mss. Digby 102 and Douce 322*. Early English Text Society, 1904.

Keim, Charles. "Of Two Minds: Gollum and Othello." Croft, *Tolkien and Shakespeare*, pp. 294–312.

Ker, W. P. *The Dark Ages*. 1904. Thomas Nelson, 1955.

Kerry, Paul E. "Introduction: A Historiography of Christian Approaches to Tolkien's *The Lord of the Rings*." Kerry, *Ring and the Cross*, pp. 17–53.

Kerry, Paul E., editor. *The Ring and the Cross: Christianity and* the Lord of the Rings, Fairleigh Dickinson University Press, 2013.

Kerry, Paul E. and Sandra Meisel, editors. *Light beyond All Shadow: Religious Experience in Tolkien's Work*. paperback ed, Fairleigh Dickinson University Press, 2011.

King James Version Personal Size Bible. Holman, 2021.

Kisor, Yvette. "'Poor Smeagol': Gollum as Exile in *The Lord of the Rings*." Houghton et al., locations 2989–3363.

Klaeber, Friederich, editor. *Beowulf and the Fight at Finnsburg: Edited with Introduction, Bibliography, Notes, Glossary, and Appendices*. Heath, 1922.

Klinger, Judith. "The Fallacies of Power: Frodo's Resistance to the Ring." Wells, pp. 355–69.

Konstan, David. *Pity Transformed*. Duckworth, 2004.

Knox, Bernard. *Oedipus at Thebes: Sophocles' Tragic Hero and his Time*. 1957. Yale University Press, 1998.

Krokstrom, Andrew. "Silent Wounds." Croft, *Baptism of Fire*, pp. 131–43.

Kullmann, Thomas. "Points of View." Kullman and Siepmann, pp. 89–127.

Kullmann, Thomas, and Dirk Siepmann, editors. *Tolkien as a Literary Artist: Exploring Rhetoric, Language and Style in* The Lord of the Rings. Palgrave Macmillan, 2021.

"Læn, n." Bosworth and Toller, https://bosworthtoller.com/20960. Accessed 22 May 2023.

"Læne, adj." Bosworth and Toller, https://bosworthtoller.com/20965. Accessed 22 May 2023.

Lane, William L., editor. *Hebrews 9–13*. Edited by David A. Hubbard et al. 1991. Nelson, 2008.

Le Guin, Ursula K. *The Language of the Night*. Edited by Susan Wood, Harper, 1991.

Lee, Stuart D., editor. *A Companion to J. R. R. Tolkien*. 2011. Wiley Blackwell, 2020.

Lewis, C. S. *Collected Letters of C. S. Lewis*, vol. 3: *Narnia, Cambridge and Joy, 1950–1963*. Edited by Walter Hooper. HarperOne, 2004.

———. *The Discarded Image: An Introduction to Medieval and Renaissance Literature*. Cambridge University Press, 1967.

———. "Obituary: Professor J. R. R. Tolkien, Creator of Hobbits and Inventor of a New Mythology." *Mallorn: The Journal of the Tolkien Society*, vol. 8, 1974, pp. 40–43.

———. *Perelandra*. 1943. Scribner, 2004.

———, editor. *Essays Presented to Charles Williams*. 1947. Eerdmans, 1981.

Livingston, Michael. "The Shell-Shocked Hobbit: The First World War and Tolkien's Trauma of the Ring." Croft, *Baptism of Fire*, pp. 9–22.

Mackie, W. S. "Notes upon the Text and Interpretation of 'Beowulf,' II." *The Modern Language Review*, vol. 36, no. 1, January 1941, p. 95. *JSTOR*, https://www.jstor.org/stable/3717264?origin=crossref.

Malpas, Simon. "Home." Eaglestone, pp. 85–98.

Marenbon, John. *Pagans and Philosophers: The Problem of Paganism from Augustine to Leibniz*. Princeton University Press, 2017.

Mathis, Michael A., and Lino Murillo. "Does 'Substantia' mean 'Realization' or 'Foundation' in Hebr. 11.1?" *Biblica*, vol. 3, no. 1, 1922, pp. 79–89.

McBride, Sam. *Tolkien's Cosmology: Divine Beings and Middle-earth*. Kent State University Press, 2020.

McIntosh, Jonathan S. *The Flame Imperishable: Tolkien, St. Thomas, and the Metaphysics of Faërie*. Angelico Press, 2017.

Miesel, Sandra. "Life-Giving Ladies: Women in the Writings of J. R. R. Tolkien." Kerry and Miesel, pp. 139–52.

Milbank, Alison. *Chesterton and Tolkien as Theologians: The Fantasy of the Real*. T & T Clark, 2009.

"Mischief, n." *OED Online*, Oxford University Press. https://www.oed.com/view/Entry/119293. Accessed 11 May 2022.

Murdoch, Iris. *Nuns and Soldiers*, edited by Karen Armstrong. Penguin, 2014.

Nagy, Gergely. "Gollum." *J. R. R. Tolkien Encyclopedia: Scholarship and Critical Assessment*, edited by Michael D. C. Drout, Routledge, Taylor & Francis Group, 2013, pp. 246–48.

———. "The 'Lost' Subject of Middle-earth: The Constitution of the Subject in the Figure of Gollum in The Lord of the Rings." *Tolkien Studies*, vol. 3, no. 1, 2006, pp. 57–79. *Project Muse*, https://muse.jhu.edu/article/197463.

———. "Saving the Myths: The Re-Creation of Mythology in Plato and Tolkien." Chance, *"Tolkien and the Invention of Myth,"* pp. 81–100.

Nijdam, Han, and Otto S. Knottnerus. "Redbad, the Once and Future King of the Frisians." Halink, pp. 87–114.

Noetzel, Justin T. "Beorn and Bombadil: Mythology, Place and Landscape in Middle-earth." Eden, pp. 161–80.

Olsen, Corey. *Exploring J. R. R. Tolkien's* The Hobbit. Houghton Mifflin, 2012.

———. "A Modest Proposition." *Exploring* The Lord of the Rings, episode 180, 30 March 2021, https://youtu.be/Dl_NxL4VvPQ?t=5050.

Ovenden, Richard, and Catherine McIlwaine, editors. *The Great Tales Never End: Essays in Memory of Christopher Tolkien*. Bodleian Library, 2022.

Pedersen, Kusumita. "The 'divine passive' in The Lord of the Rings." *Mallorn*, vol. 51, Spring, 2011, pp. 23–26.

"Personality, n. and adj." *OED Online*, Oxford University Press. https://www.oed.com/view/Entry/141486. Accessed 11 May 2022.

Plato. *Euthyphro, Apology of Socrates, and Crito*. Edited by John Burnet. 1924. Oxford University Press, 1977.

———. *Plato's Atlantis Story: Text, Translation and Commentary*. Edited and translated by Christopher Gill. Liverpool University Press, 2017.

"Purpose, v." *OED Online*, Oxford University Press. https://www.oed.com/view/Entry/154973. Accessed 12 May 2022.

Rateliff, John D. "'And All the Days of Her Life Are Forgotten': *The Lord of the Rings* as Mythic Prehistory." Hammond and Scull, *Blackwelder*, pp. 67–100.

Reckford, Kenneth. "'There and Back Again'—Odysseus and Bilbo Baggins." *Mythlore: A Journal of J. R. R. Tolkien, C. S. Lewis, Charles Williams, and Mythopoeic Literature*, vol. 14, no. 3, March 1988, pp. 5–9.

Resnick, Harry. "An Interview with Tolkien." *Niekas*, vol. 18, 1967, pp. 37–43.

Robinson, Fred C. *Beowulf and the Appositive Style*. University of Tennessee Press, 1987.

Rosebury, Brian. *Tolkien: A Cultural Phenomenon*. Palgrave Macmillan, 2003.

Rosegrant, John. *Tolkien, Enchantment, and Loss: Steps on the Developmental Journey*. Kent State University Press, 2022.

Rutledge, Amelia A. "'Justice Is Not Healing': J. R. R. Tolkien's Pauline Constructs in 'Finwë and Míriel.'" *Tolkien Studies*, vol. 9, no. 1, 2012, 59–74.

Rutledge, Fleming. *The Battle for Middle-earth: Tolkien's Divine Design in* The Lord of the Rings. William B. Eerdmans, 2003.

Scull, Christina, and Wayne G. Hammond. *The J. R. R. Tolkien Companion and Guide.* 2nd ed. 3 vols. HarperCollins, 2017.
Shakespeare, William. *The Complete Works.* 2nd ed. Edited by Stanley Wells et al. Oxford University Press, 2005.
———. *The Tragedy of Hamlet, Prince of Denmark. Complete Works,* pp. 681–718.
———. *The Tragedy of Macbeth. Complete Works,* pp. 969–93.
Shippey, Thomas A. "Noblesse Oblige: Images of Class in Tolkien." Shippey, *Roots and Branches,* pp. 285–302.
———. "Principles of Conversation in Beowulfian Speech." Sinclair, pp. 109–26.
———. *Roots and Branches: Selected Papers on Tolkien.* Walking Tree Publishers, 2007.
———. "Tolkien and the *Beowulf*-Poet." Shippey, *Roots and Branches,* pp. 1–18.
Shippey, Tom. *The Road to Middle-earth: How J. R. R. Tolkien Created a New Mythology.* Rev. and exp. ed. Houghton Mifflin, 2003.
———. *J. R. R. Tolkien: Author of the Century.* Houghton Mifflin, 2000.
Shrimpton, Paul, editor. *Inklings of Truth: Essays to Mark the Anniversaries of C. S. Lewis and J. R. R. Tolkien.* Grandpoint House, 2018.
Sinclair, John McHardy, et al. editors. *Techniques of Description: Spoken and Written Discourse: A Festschrift for Malcolm Coulthard.* Routledge, 1993, pp. 109–26.
Smol, Anna. "Frodo's Body: Liminality and Transformation in *The Lord of the Rings.*" Vaccaro, pp. 39–62.
Spacks, Patricia Meyer. "Power and Meaning in The Lord of the Rings." Zimbardo and Isaacs, pp. 52–67.
Stacey, Simon. "Tolkien's Tone and the Frequent Failure to Hear It." Shrimpton, pp. 75–97.
"Stern, adj., n.2, and adv." *OED Online,* Oxford University Press. https://www.oed.com/view/Entry/189993. Accessed 11 May 2022.
Stoker, Bram. *Dracula: Authoritative Text, Contexts, Reviews and Reactions, Dramatic and Film Variations, Criticism.* 2nd ed. Edited by John Edgar Browning and David J. Skal. Norton, 2021.
"*Strai,* n." *Middle English Compendium.* https://quod.lib.umich.edu/m/middle-english-dictionary/dictionary/MED43187. Accessed 12 May 2022.
Stratyner, Leslie. "Tolkien and Apposition." Houghton et al., *Tolkien in the New Century,* pp. 78–84.
Testi, Claudio Antonio. *Pagan Saints in Middle-earth.* Walking Tree Publishers, 2018.
Thomas, Paul Edmund. "Some of Tolkien's Narrators." Flieger and Hostetter, pp. 161–81.
Thompson, Kristin. "*The Hobbit* as a Part of *The Red Book of Westmarch.*" *Mythlore: A Journal of J. R. R. Tolkien, C. S. Lewis, Charles Williams, and Mythopoeic Literature,* vol. 15, no. 2, December 1988, pp. 11–16.
Tolkien, J. R. R., editor. *Ancrene Wisse: Edited from MS. Corpus Christi College Cambridge 402.* Oxford University Press, 1962.
Tolkien, J. R. R. *The Annotated Hobbit: The Hobbit; Or, There and Back Again.* Edited by Douglas A. Anderson, Houghton Mifflin, 2002.

———. *The Battle of Maldon together with The Homecoming of Beorhtnoth and "The Tradition of Versification in Old English."* Edited by Peter Grybauskas, HarperCollins, 2023.

———. *Beowulf: A Translation and Commentary: Together with Sellic Spell [and the Lay of Beowulf]*. Edited by Christopher Tolkien, Houghton Mifflin, 2014.

———. *Beowulf and the Critics*. Edited by Michael D. C. Drout, 2nd ed., ACMRS, 2011.

———. *The Book of Lost Tales, Part 1*, vol. 1 of *The History of Middle-earth*. Edited by Christopher Tolkien, Houghton Mifflin, 1984.

———. *The Book of Lost Tales, Part 2*, vol. 2 of *The History of Middle-earth*. Edited by Christopher Tolkien, Houghton Mifflin, 1984.

———. "The Chronology of The Lord of the Rings." *Tolkien Studies*, edited by William Cloud Hicklin, vol. 19, supplement, 2022, p. 155.

———. *The Fall of Arthur*. Edited by Christopher Tolkien, Houghton Mifflin, 2013.

———. "Fate and Free Will." Edited by Carl F. Hostetter, *Tolkien Studies*, vol. 9, 2009, pp. 183–88.

———. *The Hobbit; Or, There and Back Again*. Facsimile 1st ed. 1937. HarperCollins, 2016.

———. *The History of the Hobbit*. Edited by John Rateliff, HarperCollins, 2011.

———. *The History of Middle-earth*. Edited by Christopher Tolkien, 12 vols. Houghton Mifflin, 1984–96.

———. *The Lays of Beleriand*, vol. 3 of *The History of Middle-earth*. Edited by Christopher Tolkien, Houghton Mifflin, 1985.

———. *The Letters of J. R. R. Tolkien*. Edited by Humphrey Carpenter, with Christopher Tolkien, Houghton Mifflin, 1981.

———. *The Lord of the Rings*. 50th anniversary 1 vol. ed., Houghton Mifflin, 2005.

———. *The Lost Road and Other Writings: Language and Legend before* The Lord of the Rings, vol. 5 of *The History of Middle-earth*. Edited by Christopher Tolkien, Houghton Mifflin, 1987.

———. *The Monsters and the Critics and Other Essays*. Edited by Christopher Tolkien, HarperCollins, 2006.

———. *Morgoth's Ring: The Later Silmarillion, Part 1, the Legends of Aman*, vol. 10 of *The History of Middle-earth*. Edited by Christopher Tolkien, Houghton Mifflin, 1993.

———. *Narn i Chîn Húrin: The Tale of the Children of Húrin*. Edited by Christopher Tolkien, Houghton Mifflin, 2007.

———. *The Nature of Middle-earth: Late Writings on the Lands, Inhabitants, and Metaphysics of Middle-earth*. Edited by Carl F. Hostetter, Houghton Mifflin, 2021.

———. *The Peoples of Middle-earth*, vol. 12 of *The History of Middle-earth*. Edited by Christopher Tolkien, Houghton Mifflin, 1996.

———. *The Return of the Shadow*, vol. 6 of *The History of Middle-earth*. Edited by Christopher Tolkien, Houghton Mifflin, 1988.

———. *Sauron Defeated: The End of the Third Age*, vol. 9 of *The History of Middle-earth*. Edited by Christopher Tolkien, Houghton Mifflin, 1992.

———. *The Shaping of Middle-earth: The Quenta, the Ambarkanta, and the Annals, Together with the Earliest Silmarillion and the First Map*, vol. 4 of *The History of Middle-earth*. Edited by Christopher Tolkien, Houghton Mifflin, 1986.

———. *The Silmarillion*. 1977. Edited by Christopher Tolkien, 2nd ed., Houghton Mifflin, 2001.

———. *The Story of Kullervo*. Edited by Verlyn Flieger, HarperCollins, 2015.

———. *Tolkien on Fairy-Stories*. Edited by Verlyn Flieger and Douglas A. Anderson, 2008, HarperCollins, 2014.

———. *The Treason of Isengard*, vol. 7 of *The History of Middle-earth*. Edited by Christopher Tolkien, Houghton Mifflin, 1989.

———. *The War of the Jewels: The Later Silmarillion, Part Two, the Legends of Beleriand*, vol. 11 of *The History of Middle-earth*. Edited by Christopher Tolkien, Houghton Mifflin, 1994.

———. *The War of the Ring*, vol. 8 of *The History of Middle-earth*. Edited by Christopher Tolkien, Houghton Mifflin, 1990.

———. *Unfinished Tales of Númenor and Middle-earth*. Edited by Christopher Tolkien, Houghton Mifflin, 1980.

Tuberville, Henry. *The Douay Catechism of 1649*. https://archive.org/details/The1649DouayCatechismTubervilleHenryD.D.4515/page/n23/mode/2up.

"Upon, prep." *OED Online*, Oxford University Press. https://www.oed.com/view/Entry/220029. Accessed 11 May 2022.

Vaccaro, Christopher, editor. *The Body in Tolkien's Legendarium: Essays on Middle-earth Corporeality*. McFarland, 2013.

Vandiver, Elizabeth. *Stand in the Trench, Achilles: Classical Receptions in British Poetry of the Great War*. Oxford University Press, 2013.

Vaninskaya, Anna. *Fantasies of Time and Death: Dunsany, Eddison, Tolkien*. Palgrave Macmillan, 2020.

Waito, David. "The Shire Quest: The 'Scouring of the Shire' as the Narrative and Thematic Focus of *The Lord of the Rings*." *Mythlore: A Journal of J. R. R. Tolkien, C. S. Lewis, Charles Williams, and Mythopoeic Literature*, vol. 28, no. 3, April 2010, pp. 155–77.

Wawrykow, Joseph P. *The Westminster Handbook to Thomas Aquinas*. Westminster John Knox Press, 2005.

Wells, Sarah, editor. *The Ring Goes Ever On: Proceedings of the Tolkien 2005 Conference*, vol. 1, Tolkien Society, 2005.

Whittingham, Elizabeth A. *The Evolution of Tolkien's Mythology: A Study of The History of Middle-earth*. McFarland, 2008.

Williams, Charles. *Taliessin through Logres and the Region of the Summer Stars*. Apocryphile Press, 2016.

Williams, Hamish, editor. *Tolkien and the Classical World*. Walking Tree, 2021.

Wise, Dennis Wilson. "Harken Not to Wild Beasts: Between Rage and Eloquence in Saruman and Thrasymachus." *Journal of Tolkien Research*, vol. 3, no. 2, 2016, p. 37.

Zimbardo, Rose, and Neil D. Isaacs, editors. *Understanding* The Lord of the Rings: *The Best of Tolkien Criticism*. Houghton Mifflin, 2004.

Index

Aegnor, 259-60
Aeschylus, 74
Ainur, the, 45
Alford, C. Fred, 6
Allen & Unwin, 1, 3, 60-61
Amendt-Radeuge, Amy, 236, 243
Amon Hen, 96-111, 114, 119, 122, 124, 127, 130, 132, 140-41, 162, 173, 175-76, 179, 184, 192-93, 202
Amon Sûl, 102
Anarion, 19
Anborn, 153
Ancrene Wisse, 196
Anderson, Douglas A., 62, 73
Andreth, 259, 260
Anduin, 42, 122, 130, 188
Angband, 141
Annotated Hobbit, The (Anderson), 62
Annunciation, the, 34
Apology of Socrates (Plato), 2
Apprenticeship of J. R. R. Tolkien, The (Cook), 2
Aquinas, Thomas, 5, 244, 246
Aragorn, 17, 45, 61, 78, 81, 89, 118-21, 125, 140, 146, 154-56, 179, 196, 211, 215-19, 238, 247, 250-51, 253, 255; death, 254-57; and the Ring, 104-6, 157-58, 250, 253, 255-56, 258. *See also* Strider
Arda, 8, 235; end of the Third Age, 6; in the First Age, 21; Marred, 119, 216, 234, 243, 260-64; as Morgoth's Ring, 23, 110; Re-made/Healed, 261, 263; substance of, 21, 23
Argonath, 118
Aristotle, 72-73, 238, 264

Arnor, 256
Arkenstone, the, 58
Arwen, 45, 211, 216-19, 222, 232, 248; Choice of Lúthien and, 216-18, 255-58; gift to Frodo, 217, 254; pity of, 254-67
Augustine (Saint), 5-6, 52, 171
Aulë, 22
automatism, 143

Balrog, 123
Barad-dûr, 107, 184, 202
Barahir, 257
Barrow-wight, 21, 88, 90, 95, 127, 160, 162, 175
Battle of Maldon, The, 181-82
Battle of the Pelennor Fields, 233
Beleg, 22
Beowulf, 2, 4, 11, 74, 84, 214, 234, 236-37; Beowulf, 233, 236-39; *Beowulf*-poet, 3, 9, 11, 35, 181, 233-38, 240, 246, 264; Christianity in, 235-38, 240; Fróda, 31; Grendel, 234, 236-38; Hrothgar, 31, 236, 239; Ingeld, 31; Scyld, 236, 238; Unferth, 238; Yggdrasil, 233
"*Beowulf*: The Monsters and the Critics" (Tolkien), 3-4, 24, 31, 84, 233, 240, 257
Beregond, 211
Beren, 8, 57, 98, 165, 172, 177-78, 217, 239, 248, 255, 259-63
Bilbo, 50, 120-21, 131, 165-66, 212, 216, 232; age, appearance of, 25-27, 37-47, 216, 221, 230; departure, 38-39, 41, 76, 77, 93, 109; desire for rest, 38, 76, 222-23; eating habits, 64, 71; giving up the Ring, 27-31, 37, 41-44, 46-47, 51, 53-54, 61, 76-77, 81, 110, 126, 129,

Bilbo (cont.)
140, 187, 189, 256; lie, 16–36, 39, 41, 57–58, 60–62, 68, 86, 89; memoirs, 9, 18, 39, 68; mercy, 17, 70, 179; Mercy, 52; morality, 17; pity, 4–5, 7–8, 12, 17, 24, 34–57, 59, 62, 69–74, 78, 82, 87, 98, 104–5, 113, 115–16, 118, 120, 168, 178–80, 189, 195, 197, 203, 208, 226, 234–35, 239, 249, 253–54, 265; Pity, 6, 18, 43, 52, 205, 266; practical joke, 26–27, 29, 40, 93; Riddle Game, 30, 42, 64, 68, 70–71, 88, 116, 124, 174; and the Ring, 5–7, 12, 16–61, 63–64, 66–72, 76–80, 82–83, 86, 89, 91, 93–94, 98–99, 104, 110, 115, 127, 162, 172, 176, 191–92, 207, 211, 221, 228, 231, 234–35, 238, 245, 251, 254, 256; in Rivendell, 97–99, 117–18, 124, 130, 135, 139–40, 150, 158, 168, 186–87, 189, 194–95, 204, 219–21, 228, 230; similarities to Gollum, 64–65, 67, 73–74, 76, 112; social status as a hobbit, 32–33; sword, 62–63, 140, 178
Bill Ferny, 94
Birns, Nicholas, 258
Birzer, Bradley, 238
Black Gate, 136–49, 158–59, 176, 195, 204–5, 221, 239
Black Riders, 36, 39, 75, 78–83, 86, 88–95, 102, 123, 127, 162, 192, 196. *See also* Nazgûl; Ringwraiths
Boethius, 19, 171
Book of Lost Tales, Part 1, The (Tolkien): "The Music of the Ainur," 266; "Of Turambar and the Foalókë," 266
Boromir, 10, 101, 120–22, 136–37, 142–43, 158, 161, 172, 176, 179–80, 184, 192, 196, 208, 238, 251, 265–66; death, 140, 142, 154–55, 157; the Ring and, 19, 32, 36, 86, 102, 104–11, 115, 119, 132, 140, 142, 150, 156, 198, 214, 228, 231
Bradley, A. C., 235
Brandir, 21
Brandywine River, 76–77, 83, 92
Bree, 156, 157
Bretherton, Christopher, 1

Caldecott, Stratford, 34
Carr, Brian, 5–6
Celeborn, 100–101
Celebrían, 254
Celebrimbor, 202
Celegorm, 136
Cerin Amroth, 255
Chance, Jane, 35
Christensen, Bonniejean, 62
Círdan, 125, 207, 250
Cirith Ungol, 45, 117–18, 165, 169, 172, 180, 230, 251

City of God (Augustine), 5
Collins, 3, 4
Consolation of Philosophy (Boethius), 19
Cook, Simon J., 2, 11
Cracks of Doom, 10, 34, 45, 134, 139, 201, 243
Crickhollow, 85, 88
Crucifixion, the, 34
Curufin, 136

Dagor Dagorath, 263
Dark Tower, 199
"Dead, The" (Joyce), 136
Dead Marshes, 127, 130, 135, 144, 146, 232, 266
Dead Men of Dunharrow, 81, 158, 249
Déagol, 42–44, 47, 49–50, 59, 61, 64, 73, 87, 89, 109, 130, 132, 140, 148, 168, 174, 179, 204, 207–8, 228, 235
Denethor, 35, 115, 155–56, 160, 196, 198, 204, 220, 234, 238, 265
Doriath, 259
Dúnedain, 45–46, 125, 218
Dwarves, 22, 39, 57, 193, 264
dyscatastrophe, 120, 247, 248

Eagles, 22
Eärendil, 85, 151, 172, 176, 178, 217, 260
Ecclesiastes, 196
Elbereth, 92, 95, 177, 218
Eldar, 45, 46
Elendil, 248
Elendur, 125
Elrond, 25, 45, 57, 77, 96–100, 109, 122, 132, 176, 203, 207, 216, 219–20, 222, 245, 248; Council of, 61, 68, 87, 115, 120, 139, 229, 250–52
Elven King, 57, 58
Elves, 39, 83, 106, 120–21, 155, 161, 193, 216, 238–39, 244–45, 249; fading of, 219–20, 252–67; and the Rings of Power, 7, 20, 56, 235–36
Elwing, 260
Emyn Muil, 16, 18, 114, 126, 138–39, 147, 153, 176, 195–96, 198, 209
Enright, Nancy, 217
Ents, 22
Entwives, 83
Eöl, 22–23
Éomer, 154, 218, 233
Éowyn, 5, 56, 196, 211, 215, 218, 233, 257
Eressëa, 167
Eru, 34, 241, 248–49, 252, 260, 262; Will of, 119–20
eucatastrophe, 10, 73, 74, 120, 178, 209, 237–46, 248, 265

Faramir, 5, 35, 31, 101, 136–37, 140, 151–56, 158–59, 165, 195–96, 198, 211, 215, 218, 220, 247, 257; and the Ring, 36, 155, 157, 160
Farmer Cotton, 172
Farmer Maggot, 39, 161
Farnell, I. R., 72
Fellowship of the Ring, The (Tolkien), 66; "At the Sign of the Prancing Pony," 93–95; "The Breaking of the Fellowship," 109, 121; "The Flight to the Ford," 94; "A Long-expected Party," 18–19, 25–27, 30, 37, 39–42, 53, 56, 59, 61–62, 93–94, 98, 120–21, 187, 200, 223; "The Mirror of Galadriel," 20, 28, 75, 99, 106, 108; "The Shadow of the Past," 5, 7, 18–19, 32–33, 38–41, 49, 51–52, 56, 57–75, 121, 123–24, 152, 166, 196–97, 200, 211, 225–26, 234–35, 242–44; "Three Is Company," 80
Fields of Time, 236, 238, 241, 253
Findegil, 257
Fingolfin, 141
Finrod, 20, 251, 258–59, 261
Finwë, 243
Flieger, Verlyn, 73, 120, 134
Ford of Bruinen, 75, 95, 103, 125, 147, 163, 165, 222, 229–31
Freeman, Austin M., 252
Frodo, 11–16, 58, 71, 76, 132, 237, 247, 249, 261; at Amon Hen, 96–111, 114, 119, 122, 124, 127, 130, 132, 141, 162, 173, 175, 176, 192–93, 202; appearance of age in, 39–40; at Bag End, 6, 11, 20, 21, 23, 37–38, 46–47, 52, 68, 71, 75–76, 102, 106, 113–16, 123, 127, 130, 152, 154, 163, 166, 179, 186–87, 189, 208, 225–26, 253; as Bilbo's heir, 37–38, 61, 177; at the Black Gate, 136–49, 159, 176, 195, 204–5, 221, 239; burden of the Ring, 1–9, 31–32, 54–55, 76, 78, 83–89, 91, 98–99, 106, 115, 120–21, 123–29, 131, 138–39, 150, 152, 159, 161, 186–88, 193–95, 198–99, 201, 203, 210–11, 223–24, 227, 229, 232, 250–51, 253, 266; captivity, 189; concern for friends, 36, 39, 75, 78–83, 86, 88–90, 92, 105–6, 109–10, 115, 125, 191–95, 204, 221; at the Cracks of Doom, 34; death, appearance of, 177–78, 187, 198, 208; destruction of the Ring, 19, 53–54, 59, 71, 74, 76–77, 85, 101–2, 104, 119, 122, 124, 130, 148, 158–59, 168, 176, 179, 194, 198–99, 201–3, 206–7, 210, 212, 214, 221, 226, 229, 231, 250–51, 254; dreams and visions, 76–77, 85, 88, 97, 103–8, 119, 152, 155, 164–65, 167; effect of the Ring on, 25, 39, 49, 76–77, 80–83, 91, 96–98, 102, 104–5, 108–11, 115–16, 118–19, 122–25, 130–31, 134, 143, 149, 151, 158, 161–62, 168, 172, 179, 185–87, 192–95, 200, 203–6, 208–11, 214–15, 218–20, 222, 228, 230, 234, 256, 266; forgiving Gollum, 8, 168, 206–18, 220, 224, 242; forgiving Saruman, 8, 220, 225, 227–29, 242; in House of Elrond, 96–99, 229; identity and memory, 8, 10, 18, 77, 87, 90–91, 108, 119, 124, 130–31, 134, 139, 142, 149–50, 152, 163, 165, 173, 175–76, 186–89, 192–94, 200, 203, 205, 211–12, 215, 223–24, 232, 266; in Ithilien, 150–59, 161, 212–18; in Mordor, 91, 143, 186–205; at Mount Doom, 8, 16, 19, 31, 36, 149, 193, 195, 197, 205, 207–11, 220, 240, 242, 250; parents, 76–77; pity, 5, 8, 17–18, 24, 49–51, 53–56, 58–62, 71, 74, 104–6, 108, 112–20, 129, 134, 140–46, 152, 154, 158, 166–67, 196–97, 203–5, 208, 211, 224–25, 227, 234, 242–43, 253, 265–66; Pity and, 53, 205; possession and use of the Ring, 10, 16–19, 31–36, 42, 52, 75, 77, 79, 81–83, 85–87, 91–96, 98, 100–104, 109–10, 111, 115–16, 118, 121, 124, 135, 137, 139, 143, 150, 162–63, 172, 176, 180, 187, 190–92, 198–99, 201–4, 206–7, 211, 225, 229, 231, 235, 250–52, 265–66; as probable narrator, 9–10, 18, 32, 131, 167, 188, 191; receiving the Ring, 30–31, 37, 41, 47–48, 54, 58, 61–62, 70, 74, 80, 104, 129–30, 176–77, 204, 239; relinquishing the Ring, 53, 99, 102–3, 105, 109, 123, 126, 157, 200–201, 210; return to the Shire, 220–27, 232–32, 253, 258; in Rivendell, 75–111, 115–16, 118, 124, 130, 136–37, 139–41, 158, 168, 186–87, 189, 194–95, 204, 219, 229–30; in Shelob's lair, 132, 170–76, 187–88, 229; social status as a hobbit, 32–33; stature, 45, 55, 99–100; two, 31–35; using the Ring for domination, 53, 81, 99, 103, 116–17, 119, 123–25, 127, 131, 137–40, 142–43, 148, 150, 152–53, 158, 163, 182, 185, 195, 201, 205, 209, 211, 221, 231, 239–40, 250; wounds, 89–90, 95–98, 102, 106–7, 115, 122, 127, 161–63, 211–12, 222, 229–30
Frye, Northrop, 241

"Gaffer" Hamfast Gamgee, 25, 33, 78, 80, 90, 220
Galadriel, 10, 20, 40, 75, 86, 105, 122, 129, 132, 136–37, 154, 159, 182, 190, 206, 218–19, 226, 228, 255–56; laughter, 99–104; lembas, 194; mirror, 99, 103, 105, 107–8, 127, 175, 177, 197; Nenya, 100, 107, 126, 128, 219; phial/star-glass, 151, 163–64, 170–77, 187, 213, 217; refusal of the Ring, 19, 32, 36, 59, 99, 102–5, 109, 157, 161, 202, 253; revisions to character, 48–49, 125; tests, 28, 100–101, 103–5, 108; warning about the Ring, 44–45, 81, 99–103, 110, 119, 123–24, 139, 163–64, 182, 201, 211

Gandalf, 4–5, 31, 67, 120–22, 128, 131–32, 136–38, 147, 176, 219, 222, 224, 227, 236, 245, 250–51; at Bag End, 6, 20–21, 26–30, 38, 40–41, 43–44, 46–47, 50–52, 57, 61–62, 68, 71, 75, 81, 91, 106, 109–10, 113–16, 123, 127, 140, 152, 154, 166, 186, 187, 204, 208, 225–26, 253, 256; at the Council of Elrond, 87, 100; hope and, 6, 8, 17, 49–51, 55, 72, 78, 97–99, 129, 133, 151, 166, 209, 226, 243; in Ithilien, 212–14; Mercy, 7, 52, 62, 242; pity, 5–6, 8, 24, 35, 50–51, 53–56, 58–59, 61–62, 69, 71, 74, 83, 105, 108, 110, 114–15, 118, 134, 141, 150, 182, 196–97, 203, 208–9, 225, 234, 242–43, 253, 265, 267; Pity, 6–7, 52–53, 71, 242; prophecy, 18, 203; on the Ring, 19, 22–24, 35, 37, 40–41, 44–45, 47–48, 53, 59, 61, 67–70, 77–80, 83, 86, 88, 90, 97, 99–100, 109–10, 115–16, 119, 121, 123–27, 134, 156, 160, 179, 182, 192–93, 202, 204, 211, 214, 231, 235, 249, 256; at Rivendell, 76, 89, 92, 96–97, 100, 102, 115; refusal of the Ring, 6, 17–18, 32, 52–55, 59, 74, 76, 105, 123, 157, 200–202, 219–20, 250; stature, 54–55

Gildor, 76–77, 82, 89, 92, 97, 127, 161, 177, 229

Gil-galad, 19, 248

Gill, Glen Robert, 241

Gilraen, 258

Gimli, 17, 109, 122, 215, 218

Glóin, 61, 86

Goldberry, 24, 85, 87

Golden Wood, 154, 159–60, 236

Gollum, 4–5, 31, 62, 91, 108, 123–24, 131, 165, 228–29; birthday present, 9, 41–42, 47, 61, 67, 72, 88–89, 232; at the Black Gate, 136–49, 176, 195, 204–5, 221, 239; eating habits, 64; fear of Sauron, 120, 128–29, 133, 137, 148; forgiveness of, 8, 168, 206–18, 220, 224, 242; grandmother, 42–44, 47, 50, 59, 64, 209; healing, hope for, 6, 8, 17, 49–51, 55, 72, 78, 116, 119, 129, 132–33, 138, 150, 166–68, 209, 226, 230, 243; home, 64; in Ithilien, 150–59, 161; malice and deception of, 43, 50–52, 59, 67–68, 70–71, 89, 95, 110, 115, 120–21, 129, 132, 134–35, 140, 153, 174, 177, 179, 187, 197, 201, 203–6, 228; in Mordor, 116, 144, 146; on Mount Doom, 149, 202, 205, 207–11, 240; pity for, 7–8, 17–18, 24, 27, 35–36, 49–51, 53, 55, 56–59, 69–71, 73–74, 82, 87, 98, 105–6, 113–15, 118–19, 121, 140–46, 150, 152, 154, 158, 166–68, 186, 189, 194, 196–97, 204–5, 208, 211, 224, 226, 234–35, 242–43; portrayal of, 18, 44, 52–53, 56, 60, 68–69, 71, 112, 118, 120–21, 165–66; repentance, 22, 36, 45, 72, 166–67, 169, 232; Riddle Game, 30, 42, 64, 68, 70, 71, 88, 116, 124, 174; the Ring and, 9, 16, 19–21, 23, 25, 28–30, 36, 41–42, 44, 46–47, 49–50, 52, 54, 56, 58–59, 61, 66–67, 69–71, 77–79, 81, 86–87, 91, 104, 109–10, 116–17, 119, 121–31, 133, 135, 137–43, 147–50, 152–53, 162–63, 166–67, 174, 176, 179–80, 182, 185, 193, 195, 197, 201, 203, 209–10, 214, 221, 228, 231, 235–36, 239, 243–44, 250; in Shelob's lair, 132, 170–76, 179; similarities to Bilbo, 64–65, 67, 73–74, 76, 112; as Sméagol, 19–20, 24, 31, 42–44, 46–51, 53, 56, 59, 64, 73, 88, 89–109, 115, 116, 119, 124, 129, 130, 132–35, 139–40, 144–47, 149–50, 166, 168, 173–74, 176, 203–4, 207–9, 228, 235–36; stalking Frodo, 66, 102, 112–13, 122, 165–66; stature, 44–46, 126, 132; two voices of, 50, 78, 130–38, 140, 142–49, 174, 179, 201

"Gollum's Character Transformation in *The Hobbit*" (Christensen), 62

Gondolin, 260

Gondor, 137, 160–61, 211, 215, 256; Men of, 152, 218; Stewards of, 155, 233

Green Dragon, The, 39

Grima Wormtongue, 149, 219, 221, 226

Guite, Malcolm, 11

Haldir, 122, 175, 253

Hall of Fire, 186

Halliwell, Stephen, 264

Háma the Doorward, 149

Hammond, Wayne G., 9, 42, 61, 181, 213

Harry Goatleaf, 94

Hebrews, 252

Henneth Annûn, 152–53, 198

History of the Hobbit, The (Tolkien/Rateliff), 62

History of Middle-earth, The (Tolkien), 1; "Sauron Defeated," 199

Hobbit, The (Tolkien), 1, 25–26, 30, 34, 40, 42, 60, 79, 82, 106, 136, 222, 254; revisions to, 16–31, 25–26, 30, 57–74, 120, 147–48; "Riddles in the Dark," 16–17, 25, 37, 42, 47, 58, 60–73, 93, 134, 147–48, 179, 195; "An Unexpected Party," 25, 37–38

Homer, 66, 73, 222–23, 238

Hood, Gwenyth, 197

Hostetter, Carl F., 10, 245, 248

Houses of Healing, 155

Húrin, 21, 177, 235, 260

Hutton, Ronald, 34

Idril, 260

Ilúvatar, 22, 136, 247–48, 254, 258; Children of, 8, 45, 239, 253, 260; Gift of, 235; Third Theme of, 18, 68–69, 267; Will of, 119

Inklings, 25
Ioreth, 211–12
Isengard, 225
Isildur, 88–89, 104, 125, 155; death, 19, 250; the Ring and, 9, 19, 105, 125–26, 158, 176, 207–8, 248–51
Istari, 56
Ithilien, 143, 150–59, 212
Ivy Bush, The, 39

Jackson, Peter, 8, 35
Joyce, James, 136

Keepers of the Three, The, 125
Ker, W. P., 234
Khamûl, 79
King of the Dead, 107
Klinger, Judith, 199–201

Lane, William, 252
Last Homely House, The, 222
Lay of Leithian, The, 74
Legolas, 17, 81, 109, 121, 140, 158, 215, 257
LeGuin, Ursula K., 171
Lewis, C. S., 1, 4, 19, 25
Lobelia Baggins, 33
Lord of the Rings, The (Tolkien), 1, 79; Appendix B, 34; Christianity in, 1, 33–35, 55–56, 107, 234, 237, 238–42, 244–45, 264; dates used in, 34, 109; Death as a theme in, 2–4, 7, 10, 18, 244–45, 256, 258–59, 264–65, 267; evil in, 170–76; first draft of, 4–5, 7; first two chapters of, 18, 37, 60, 69, 120; ghosts in, 56, 123; Immortality as a theme in, 2–4, 7, 10, 18, 217, 244–45, 258, 264–65, 267; narrator, 9, 113; pity as a theme in, 4–7; Pity as a theme in, 6–7; Power realized in Art as a theme in, 4; Power realized in Domination as a theme in, 4, 8, 18, 264–65, 267; prologue, 60; revisions to, 71, 92; title page, 9
Lord of the Rings, The: A Reader's Companion (Scull & Hammond), 9
Lórien, 102, 122, 127, 154, 159–60, 175, 236. *See also* Lothlórien
Lost Road and Other Writings, The (Tolkien), "The Fall of Númenor," 248–49
Lothlórien, 48, 90, 108–9, 122, 126, 151, 154, 253, 255–56, 258, 261. *See also* Lórien
Lúthien, 8, 57, 98, 165, 177–78, 217, 239, 247–48, 259–62; Choice of, 216–18, 255–56, 258

Maedhros, 136
Maiar, 45

Mandos, 260
Manicheanism, 171
Manwë, 22, 243
McIntosh, Jonathan S., 34
Melian, 22
Melkor, 43, 69, 120, 136, 161, 247–48, 260, 262, 267. *See also* Morgoth
Men, Doom of, 14, 254, 257–59, 264
mercy, 52–53
Mercy, 7, 243–45, 249; definition of, 52–53
Merry Brandybuck, 22, 33, 58, 88–89, 94–95, 109, 117, 142, 179, 198, 208, 215, 224, 227, 231, 253, 257
Miesel, Sandra, 217
Milbank, Allison, 173
Milton, John, 246
Minas Anor, 159
Minas Ithil, 159
Minas Morgul, 159–62, 164, 171
Minas Tirith, 102, 140, 147, 216, 247, 254, 257
Miriel, 243
Mirkwood, 106, 120–21, 209
Misty Mountains, 16, 18, 72, 87, 165, 226
Mithrandir, 212
Mordor, 42, 50, 85, 91, 107–8, 116, 121–23, 127, 131, 136–37, 140–41, 143, 146, 165, 176, 179, 186–205, 207, 221, 223; road to, 11–15; Two Watchers at, 21
Morgoth, 21, 23, 48, 110, 141, 216, 260–61. *See also* Melkor
Morgoth's Ring (Tolkien), 4; "Athrabeth Finrod ah Andreth," 4, 258–59, 263; "Laws and Customs among the Eldar," 4, 242, 244; "Notes on Motives in *The Silmarillion*," 4; "The Tale of Adanel," 262
Morgul Vale, 123, 160, 163, 170, 172, 180–81, 186, 199
Moria, 66, 102, 122–23
Mount Doom, 7–8, 16, 19, 130, 134, 149, 184, 193, 195, 197, 199, 202, 205, 207–11, 220, 240, 242, 247, 250
Murdoch, Iris, 136
Murray, Gilbert, 72
Music of the Ainur, the (event), 8, 15, 22, 119

Nagy, Gergely, 143
Nature of Middle-earth, The (Tolkien/Hostetter), 10, 257
Nazgûl, 7, 102, 115, 144, 188. *See also* Ringwraiths
Necromancer, 57
Nienna, 48, 242–43, 267
Nienor, 177

Nimrodel, 160
Noetzel, Justin T., 160
Normandy Invasion, 265
Númenor, 73, 104, 106, 132, 207; downfall of, 245, 247–49, 256
Nuns and Soldiers (Murdoch), 136

Oathbreakers, 56
Odyssey, The (Homer), 66
Oedipus Tyrannos (Sophocles), 8–9, 72, 265
Old Forest, 127, 151
Old Man Willow, 83, 88, 102, 160, 175
On Fairy-stories (Tolkien), 3, 4, 10, 38, 90–91, 240
orcs, 17, 22, 95, 102, 117–18, 121, 125, 177–78, 180, 192
Orodruin, 184
Oxford University, 72

Pagan Saints in Middle-earth (Testi), 245
Parth Galen, 105
Paths of the Dead, 56, 158
Peter (Saint), 43
Pippin Took, 22, 33, 58, 80, 83, 88–89, 91, 95, 109, 117, 127, 142, 171, 179, 198, 208, 215, 224
pity, 12, 18, 48; definition of, 5, 6, 7, 52–53; failure of, 17–18; invitation to, 74; limits of, 185–205; necessity of, 36; paradox of, 52–56; or the Ring, 7–11; as a social virtue, 5–6
Pity, 11, 18, 48, 245, 249, 251, 253; definition of, 6, 7, 52–53; transcendent nature of, 6
Plato, 2, 220, 247
Poetics, The (Aristotle), 72–73
Prancing Pony, the, 75, 91–92, 94, 172
prohairesis, 72

Rateliff, John, 62, 65
Red Book of Westmarch, 9, 68, 182
Republic (Plato), 220
Return of the King (Tolkien), 258; Appendix A, "The Tale of Aragorn and Arwen," 45, 253–54, 256–59, 261–63; Appendix F, 31; "The Field of Cormallen," 210–11, 215–16; "The Grey Havens," 9–10, 167–68, 231; "Homeward Bound," 211, 222; "The Last Debate," 22–23; "Many Partings," 218–20, 222; "Mount Doom," 118, 187, 207–8, 210, 226;; "The Passing of the Grey Company," 218; "The Road Ever Goes On," 221–23; "The Scouring of the Shire," 224–25, 231; "The Steward and the King," 215; Third Theme, 18; "The Tower of Cirith Ungol," 118, 185–87
Ring, the One, 11, 234; addictive quality of, 35, 164; beauty of, 207; as burden, 1–9, 19, 31–32, 54–55, 76, 78, 83–89, 91, 98–99, 106, 115, 120–21, 123–29, 131, 138–39, 150, 152, 159, 161, 186–88, 193–95, 198–99, 201, 203, 210–11, 223–24, 227, 229, 232, 250–51, 253, 266; consciousness of, 21, 23–24, 121–22; corrupting power of, 17, 19, 23–25, 30, 32, 41, 52, 55–56, 60, 75, 102–3, 124, 132, 159, 182, 185, 220, 228; creation of, 8, 39, 89, 111, 207, 211, 250; delusions caused by, 19, 40–41, 147, 183–87, 199–200, 206, 212, 250–51; destruction of, 19, 22–23, 33–34, 42, 53–54, 59, 71, 76–77, 85, 101–2, 104, 119, 122, 124, 126–27, 130, 148, 158–59, 176, 179–80, 194, 198–99, 201–3, 206–7, 210, 212, 214, 221, 226, 228–29, 231, 234, 245, 250–51, 254; identity and, 8, 10, 18–20, 24, 31, 38, 42–44, 46–50, 53, 56, 59, 64, 74, 77, 87–91, 108–9, 115, 119, 123–24, 129–35, 139–40, 142, 144–47, 149–50, 152, 163, 165–66, 168, 173–76, 186–89, 192–94, 200, 203–5, 207–9, 211–12, 215, 223–24, 228, 232, 235–36, 266; immortality conveyed by, 7, 30, 38–41, 77, 90; inscription, 20; invisibility, 26–27, 31–32, 40, 43, 45–47, 69, 80–82, 86, 94–95, 118, 126, 130–31, 133, 156, 172, 177–80; lust for, 20, 47, 74, 77–78, 133, 135, 142, 144, 148, 174, 179; mortals and, 7, 19, 45, 48, 56, 124, 131, 211, 216, 256; nature of, 8–9, 21, 40, 94–95, 126, 157, 200–201; pity and, 6, 7–12, 55; as possession, 5–8, 10, 12, 16–19, 30–36, 42, 52, 56–61, 63–64, 66–83, 85–87, 89, 91–96, 98–104, 109–11, 115–16, 118, 121, 124, 127, 135, 137, 139, 143, 150, 162–63, 172, 176, 180, 187, 190–92, 198–99, 201–4, 206–7, 211, 221, 225, 228–29, 231, 234–35, 238, 245, 250–52, 254–56, 265–66; power of, 7, 9–10, 12, 16–18, 21–22, 25, 86, 91, 106–7, 122, 131, 239; power used for domination, 8, 21, 45, 53, 81, 91, 99, 116–17, 119, 123–25, 127, 131, 137–40, 142–43, 148–50, 152–53, 158, 163, 182, 185, 195, 201–2, 205, 209, 211, 221, 231, 239–40, 250; pull of, 19, 20, 27, 32, 35–36, 38, 41–43, 46, 54–55, 78, 83, 86–87, 102, 106, 110, 115, 122–23, 125, 129, 132, 134, 140, 142, 148, 15, 153, 156, 159–60, 167–68, 172, 175, 178, 183, 194, 198, 206, 214, 225, 231, 234; relinquishing/rejecting, 6, 17–19, 27–32, 35–37, 41–44, 46, 47, 51–55, 59, 61, 74, 76, 77, 81, 99, 102–5, 109–10, 123, 126, 129, 140, 157, 161, 187, 189, 200–202, 210, 219–20, 250, 253, 256; temptation of, 9, 16, 19, 32–33, 35, 75, 80–82, 88, 91–94, 97, 101–2, 109–10, 132, 202–3, 226; threat to the Shire, 33, 42, 74, 76–80, 128, 163, 189–90; transformation of,

16; treachery/deception of, 9, 35–36, 40–41, 47–52, 77, 86, 89, 129, 135, 163–64, 219–20, 240; understanding, 19; verse, 119, 216, 235; warnings about, 19, 22–24, 35, 37, 40–41, 44–45, 47–48, 53, 59, 61, 67–70, 77–81, 83, 86, 88, 90, 97, 99, 100–103, 110, 115–16, 119, 121, 123–24, 127, 134, 139, 156, 160, 163–64, 179, 182, 192–93, 201–2, 204, 211, 214, 231, 235, 249, 256

Ring-bearer(s), 79; character of, 18–19; power of the Ring on, 9, 16, 17, 19–21, 23–25, 29–30, 32, 35–36, 38–41, 44, 46–52, 56, 58–59, 61, 67–71, 75–77, 80–83, 86, 90–91, 93–94, 96–98, 102, 104, 107–9, 110–11, 115–19, 121–31, 133–35, 137–43, 147–53, 158, 161–63, 166–68, 172, 174, 176, 179–80, 182, 185–87, 192–95, 197, 200–201, 203–6, 208–11, 214–15, 218–22, 228, 230–31, 234–36, 239, 243–44, 250, 256, 266

Rings of Power, 92, 235–36, 256

Ringwraiths, 56, 76, 78, 83, 90–91, 93–98, 106, 115, 122, 127–28, 135, 138, 141, 144, 159, 161–62, 220, 236, 265. *See also* Nazgûl

Rivendell, 75–111, 115–18, 124, 130, 135–37, 139–41, 150, 158, 168, 186–87, 189, 194–95, 204, 219, 221, 228–30

Robinson, Fred, 246

Rohan, 136–37, 154, 251

Rohirrim, 218

Rory Brandybuck, 26

Rosie Cotton, 189

Sackville-Bagginses, 31–33, 47, 94, 172, 227

Sammath Naur, 16, 199, 201–2, 205–6, 231, 239

Samwise Gamgee, 10, 11, 50, 68, 80, 83, 89, 95, 98, 113, 114, 116–17, 122–23, 128, 130, 134–35, 145, 165–67, 169, 209, 231, 237, 247, 251, 258; at the Black Gate, 136–49, 195; dismissal of, 197–99; in Ithilien, 150–59, 161, 189, 212–19; in Mordor, 21, 32, 85, 91, 143, 186–205; at Mount Doom, 19, 31, 193, 195, 205, 207–11, 220, 240; as narrator, 9, 32, 131, 133, 167; pity, 5, 8, 36, 112, 167–68, 189, 194–95, 197, 203, 234; recitation of "Oliphaunt," 150, 165; return to the Shire, 220–27, 232; the Ring and, 19, 32, 59, 91, 103, 117–18, 133, 135, 139–40, 143, 157, 160, 175, 176–88, 191–92, 197, 199, 208, 214, 226; in Rivendell, 101–2, 107–8, 161; in Shelob's lair, 132, 170–76, 180–81; visions, 196–97; will, hardening of, 181–82

Saruman, 24, 86, 95, 125, 149, 176, 196, 214, 228; death, 7, 225–26, 229; Fall, 160, 220; malice of, 218–28; pity for, 8, 220, 225, 227–29, 242, 266; and the Shire, 223–27

Sauron, 33, 51, 55, 68, 74, 81, 100, 104, 106, 110–11, 115–16, 119–21, 136, 138–39, 143, 147–48, 158, 162–63, 171, 184–85, 197, 206, 219, 234, 245, 251, 255, 262, 265; downfall, 34, 110, 125, 215, 247–48, 249; Eye of, 36, 103, 105, 107–8, 121, 123–29, 131–32, 181, 188, 192, 194, 199, 202–3, 232; malice of, 20, 43, 48, 50, 95, 128, 227–28; pity and, 6; the Ring and, 6–8, 18, 20–23, 42, 71, 77, 91, 119, 126, 137, 145–46, 173, 181–82, 202, 207, 235, 239, 241, 266; Road, 231

Scull, Cristina, 9, 42, 61, 181, 213

Seat of Seeing, 106–7

Serkis, Andy, 35

Shakespeare, William, 73, 196, 235

Shaping of Middle-earth, The (Tolkien), "The Ainulindalë," 266

Sharkey, 225. *See also* Saruman

Shelob, 16, 132, 148, 170–76, 179–81, 187–88, 201, 229–30

Shippey, Tom, 11, 34–35, 149, 160–61, 171, 174, 200, 214, 241

Shire, the, 189–90, 216–18, 258; Bag End, 5–7, 11, 18–21, 23, 26–30, 32–33, 37–41, 43–44, 46–47, 49–52, 57–76, 81, 85, 91, 102, 106, 109–10, 113–16, 121, 123–24, 127, 130, 140, 152, 154, 163, 166, 179, 186–87, 189, 196–97, 200, 204, 208, 211, 225–26, 234–35, 242–44, 256; damage done to, 223–28, 231; return to, 220–27; saving, 224–29, 231, 253; threats to, 33, 42, 74, 76–80, 128, 163, 189–90, 192

silmaril, 151, 172, 217, 260

Silmarillion, The (Tolkien), 57, 79, 136; "The Ainulindalë," 69; "The Akallabêth," 45, 247; "Of Aulë and Yavanna," 22; publication of, 3–4

Smaug, 22, 57

Sméagol, 19–20, 24, 31, 42–44, 46–51, 53, 56, 59, 64, 73, 88–89, 109, 115–16, 119, 124, 129–30, 132, 133–35, 139–40, 144–47, 149–50, 166, 168, 173–74, 176, 203–4, 207–9, 228, 235–36. *See also* Gollum

Smol, Anna, 186

Sophocles, 265

Stone of Orthanc, 158

Story of Kullervo, The (Tolkien), 72–73

Strider, 89, 122, 156. *See also* Aragorn

Summa (Aquinas), 5–6

Tale of the Children of Húrin, the, 72–74, 178

Tempest, The (Shakespeare), 85

Testi, Cladio, 245

Thain's Book, 257

Théoden, 196, 198, 208, 233
Thingol, 57, 260
Thomas, Paul Edmund, 63
Thorin, 58, 189, 191
Timaeus (Plato), 73
Tol Eressëa, 22
Tolkien, Christopher, 1, 4, 93, 94, 113–14, 146, 199, 224, 258, 264–66
Tolkien, J. R. R., 1, 167, 209, 212; Christianity and, 10–11, 17, 34–35, 55–56, 70, 72, 196, 240–41, 244, 264; on evil and, 132, 170–76; language, use of, 44–45, 79–80, 90–91, 113–14, 131–32, 136, 138–39, 150–51, 181, 191, 231, 238–39, 251–52, 257–58; Letter 131, 3, 4, 22, 23, 119, 248; Letter 144, 84, 87; Letter 156, 45; Letter 181, 5, 131–32, 134–35, 166, 245–46, 248, 254; Letter 186, 259; Letter 200, 45; Letter 246, 5, 7, 45, 55, 166, 207, 218, 230, 232, 242; letter to readers (1956), 2–3; letter to readers (1958), 2–3; on Mercy, 5, 7, 242; on Moral Choice, 72; on myth, 24–25; at Oxford, 72–73; on pity, 6, 55; on Pity, 5, 242; Primary World and, 2–3, 171, 261–63, 265, 267; reading of Plato, 2; revision of works, 1, 4–5, 7, 16–31, 48–49, 57–74, 92, 94, 114, 125, 146–47, 213, 224, 231, 258, 267; on the Ring, 19–20, 23, 26; Secondary World of truths in, 2, 171, 241, 261–63; on Tom Bombadil, 83–84, 86
Tolkien on Fairy-stories (Flieger, Anderson), 73
Tom Bombadil, 75, 83–85, 88, 90, 92, 94–95, 127, 152, 155, 160–61, 167, 170–71, 173–75, 232, 257–58; questioning of Frodo, 85–87, 108, 124, 152, 176, 203; and the Ring, 36, 45–46, 84–87, 91, 156–57, 160, 175, 191, 234, 251
Tower of Cirith Ungol, 208, 220
Tower of the Moon, 159
Tower of Sorcery, 159
Tragedy, 72, 74, 178, 226; *anagnorisis*, 72; Drama and, 73; of the incarnate, 233–37; *metabole*, 72; *peripeteia*, 72; pity and, 73
Treebeard, 22, 84, 236
Tuor, 259–60
Túrin Turambar, 22, 73, 136, 177, 234–35, 260, 263; black sword of, 21–23

Two Towers, The (Tolkien): "The Choices of Master Samwise," 131, 179; "The Council of Elrond," 121; "The Forbidden Pool,"159; "Of Herbs and Stewed Rabbit," 198; "Many Meetings," 121, 185, 195, 204; "The Passage of the Marshes," 50, 115, 123, 131–32, 135, 138, 174, 201; "Shelob's Lair," 198; "The Stairs of Cirith Ungol," 174, 187, 198, 201, 209–10, 226; "The Taming of Sméagol," 7, 18, 60, 71–72, 109, 112, 125, 131, 145, 174, 226

Ulmo, 120, 259
Undying Lands, 45, 85, 249
Unfinished Tales of Númenor and Middle-Earth (Tolkien): "The Disaster of the Gladden Fields," 125–26; "The Hunt for the Ring," 79; "Of Tuor and His Coming to Gondolin," 4
Unwin, Stanley, 61

Valar, the, 45, 46, 161, 254, 260
Valinor, 161
Vaninskaya, Anna, 1, 233, 254–55, 261, 263
Varda, 136

Waito, David M., 229
Waldman, Milton, 3, 4, 119
War of the Last Alliance, The, 42
War of the Ring, The (Tolkien), 146–47
Weathertop, 75, 89, 91–95, 97, 103, 147, 161–62, 191–92, 229
White Rider, 107
Whittingham, Elizabeth A., 4
Williams, Charles, 158
Wise, Dennis Wilson, 219–20
Witch-King, 56, 79, 81, 92, 95, 123, 147, 159, 162–65, 176, 182, 188, 191, 193, 211, 215, 230, 233, 236, 257
Wood, Elijah, 35
Woodmen of Mirkwood, 121
World War II, 265–66

Yavanna, 22